Henry Chukwudi Okeke

The Spirituality of the Igbo People of Nigeria as an Example of Religious Modernization in a Global World

Studien zur systematischen Theologie und Ethik

gegründet (und herausgegeben bis Band 64) von

Prof. Dr. Eckhard Lessing (Universität Münster)
Prof. Dr. Peter Neuner (Universität München)
Prof. Dr. Dres. h. c. Dietrich Ritschl, D. D. (Universität Heidelberg) (†)

herausgegeben von

Prof. Dr. Michael Beintker (Universität Münster)
Prof. Dr. Reinhold Bernhardt (Universität Basel)
Prof. Dr. Ralf Miggelbrink (Universität Duisburg-Essen)
Prof. Dr. Peter Neuner (Universität München)
Prof. Dr. Bertram Stubenrauch (Universität München)

Band 69

LIT

Henry Chukwudi Okeke

The Spirituality of the Igbo People of Nigeria as an Example of Religious Modernization in a Global World

LIT

This book is printed on acid-free paper.

Bibliographic information published by the Deutsche Nationalbibliothek
The Deutsche Nationalbibliothek lists this publication in the Deutsche
Nationalbibliografie; detailed bibliographic data are available on the Internet at
http://dnb.d-nb.de.

ISBN 978-3-643-91109-4 (pb)
ISBN 978-3-643-96109-9 (PDF)
Zugl.: Duisburg-Essen, Univ., Diss., 2019

A catalogue record for this book is available from the British Library.

© LIT VERLAG GmbH & Co. KG Wien,
Zweigniederlassung Zürich 2019
Klosbachstr. 107
CH-8032 Zürich
Tel. +41 (0) 44-251 75 05
E-Mail: zuerich@lit-verlag.ch   http://www.lit-verlag.ch
Distribution:
In the UK: Global Book Marketing, e-mail: mo@centralbooks.com
In North America: Independent Publishers Group, e-mail: orders@ipgbook.com
In Germany: LIT Verlag Fresnostr. 2, D-48159 Münster
Tel. +49 (0) 2 51-620 32 22, Fax +49 (0) 2 51-922 60 99, e-mail: vertrieb@lit-verlag.de
e-books are available at www.litwebshop.de

DEDICATION

To Late Archbishop Stephen N. Ezeanya
Archbishop of Onitsha (1985-1995)

Towards more realization of peace, unity,
spiritual growth and development in Igboland.

CONTENTS

CHAPTER ONE

CHAPTER TWO

2. THE CONCEPT OF INDIVIDUAL AND COMMUNITY SPIRITUALITY: IGBO PERCEPTION

CHAPTER THREE

3. THE IMPACT OF WAR ON HUMAN SPIRITUALITY: EVIDENCE FROM NIGERIA-BIAFRA WAR

CHAPTER FOUR

4. THE EFFECTS OF THE NIGERIA-BIAFRA WAR ON THE IGBO 251

CHAPTER SEVEN

ACKNOWLEDGEMENTS

I owe my deepest gratitude to God Almighty who made it possible for me to compose this dissertation. It is obvious that without God's mercy and love, I would not have succeeded in writing this dissertation. To Him be the glory.

I would like to show my gratitude to my Local Ordinary, Most Rev. Dr. Valerian M. Okeke, the Archbishop of Onitsha and Metropolitan of Onitsha Ecclesiastical Province, for his fatherly support and encouragement. I thank also His Lordship, Most Rev. Dr. Denis C. Isizoh, the Auxiliary Bishop of Onitsha.

My unalloyed gratitude goes to my moderators: Prof. Dr. Ralf Miggelbrink and Prof. Dr. Detlev Dormeyer for their ideas and criticisms which helped a lot in making this dissertation to be what it is.

I am grateful to my brothers in the priesthood: Very Rev. Mgr. Basil Onwuasomba, Rev. Fr. Dr. Pius Ejiofor, Very Rev. Fr. Theophilus Odukwe, Rev. Fr. Dr. Robert Okongwu, Rev. Fr. Dr. Augustine Oburota, Pastor Wilhelm Ausel, Pfarrer Klemens Schneider, Rev. Fr. Zakarias Sago, Rev. Fr. Barrister Dr. Kenneth Oraegbunam, Rev. Fr. Dr. Cyril Udebunu, Rev. Fr. Daniel Chukwuleta, Rev. Fr. Dr. Linus Okika, Rev. Fr. Dr. Lotenna Olisaemeka, Rev. Fr. Dr. Celestine Umeh, Rev. Fr. Dr. Patrick Omutah, Rev. Fr. Dr. Charles Anene, Rev. Fr. Dr. Gregory Ekeh, Rev. Fr. Dr. Fidesbayo Kwazu, Rev. Frs. Anthony Obumse, Fabian Ekeh, Samuel Uzondu, Victor Ezeanya and Martin Eluke.

I am ever thankful to Prof. Dr. Christian Müller, Dr. Nnaemeka Udoh, Mr. & Mrs. J. Volbracht, Prof. Dr. Gerhard Hotze, my brother Chinedu Okeke, my sister Dr. Phina Okeke, Mr. Christopher Enusiahu, Mr. Damian Egbutu, Frau Toni Fridag, Frau Loy, Herrn Alfred Senkbeil, Diakon Klaus Siegemeyer, Andreas Mersmann, Frau Ute Albrecht, Herrn Otto Kamphues, Mr. & Mrs. J. Degener, Mr. & Mrs. Richard Huget, Mr. & Mrs. Georg Knebel, Mr. & Mrs. Abumchukwu Chukwujekwu, Mr. Ernest Onu and Mr. Kingsley Chimenta, for their love and generosity.

ABBREVIATIONS

1.1. MAGISTERIAL AND VATICAN DOCUMENTS

AG	Ad gentes
AT	Africae Terrarum
DH	Dignitatis Humanae
DV	Dei Verbum
EA	Ecclesia in Africa
EN	Evangelii Nuntiandi
ES	Ecclesia Suam
EV	Evangelium Vitae
GS	Gaudium et Spes
LG	Lumen Gentium
NA	Nostra Aetate
PP	Populorum Progressio
RH	Redemptoris Hominis
RMI	Redemptoris Missio
SRS	Sollicitudo Rei Socialis
TMA	Tertio Millennio Adveniente
UR	Unitatis Redintegratio

1.2. OTHER ABBREVIATIONS

ADC	Aide-de-camp
AG	Action Group
ATR	African Traditional Religion

BBC	British Broadcasting Corporation
CIA	Central Intelligence Agency
3Ds	Demobilization, Dismantling and Devitalization
EATWOT	Ecumenical Association of Third World Theologians
ed./eds.	Editor/Editors
et al. et alii	(and other persons)
FRCN	Federal Radio Corporation of Nigeria
GNPP	Great Nigerian People's Party
IMF	International Monetary Fund
IPOB	Indigenous People of Biafra
JAH	Journal of African History
MASSOB	Movement for the Actualization of the Sovereign State of Biafra
NAP	Nigerian Advance Party
NCNC	National Council of Nigeria Citizens
NDA	Niger Delta Avengers
NPC	Northern Peoples' Congress
NPN	National Party of Nigeria
NPP	Nigerian Peoples Party
NEPU	Northern Elements Progressive Union
NGOs	Non-Governmental Organizations
NJT	Nigerian Journal of Theology
OAU	Organization of African Unity
PRP	Peoples Redemption Party
RAP	Research and Production Unit
RRR	Reconciliation, Rehabilitation and Reconstruction
SECAM	Symposium of Episcopal Conferences of Africa and Madagascar

SEDOS	(Documentation and Research Service/Centre)
TNCs	Transnational Corporations
UN	United Nations
UNESCO	United Nations Educational, Scientific and Cultural Organization
UNO	United Nations Organization
Vat. II	Second Vatican Council
WCC	World Council of Churches

GENERAL INTRODUCTION

There has been the assumption that African beliefs (Igbo beliefs inclusive) were all borrowed from outside world; this includes even their belief in God. Mbiti states:

> All kinds of theories and explanations were put forward on how the different religious traits had reached African societies from the Middle East or Europe.[1]

A major concern in this work is to prove that in Igbo Traditional Religion the Igbo worship not only their individual gods (alusi) but also recognize the existence of the Supreme Being (God) and worship Him through their minor gods. In line with the above argument, we have two camps:

1. The Polytheistic camp: which holds that the idea of the Supreme Being (God) in Igbo Traditional Religion is a foreign missionary import. For them, the traditional religionists worship many gods (polytheism). The concept or idea of the Supreme Being is an imported idea.

2. The Monotheistic camp: this holds that the concept of the Supreme Being among the Igbo people is an indigenous concept. Although the Igbo traditionalists worship other minor gods, they recognize the existence of the Supreme Being and also worship Him.

One may notice a kind of dualism which we will later make effort to clarify. Our thesis is based on the combination of the two camps: Polytheistic and Monotheistic camps, which we may call "mono-polytheism". This concept holds that the idea of the Supreme Being (God) did not come to the Igbo traditionalists as a foreign concept. Although the Igbo traditionalists worship the Supreme Being (God) and believe in His existence, they see Him as being very far away from them and cannot be worshipped directly like the Christians do; rather they prefer to reach Him through the mediation of other gods (alusi). One of the proponents of polytheism in Igbo Traditional Religion, Nze argues that:

> There is no single instance where Igbo people perform sacrifices to or worship a single being of the Christian concept. Because the Igbos perform sacrifices as acts of appeasement or worship and because there exists no occasion when a Supreme Being of the Christian description is appeased or wor-

---

[1] Mbiti J.S., *African Religions and Philosophy*, USA., Anchor Books, Doubleday and Company, Inc., 1970, pp. 7 - 8.

shipped, it can be said that this being does not exist at all or exists but is not recognized; he is passive. Our fathers worshipped gods and not a God.[2]

From the Monotheistic camp, Nkeonye holds that:

Although the Igbo worship many spirits and gods, these are ranked in an ascending order of magnitude, and are of religious, social and cultural relevance. Most importantly, these lesser gods and spirits are subject and subordinate to Chi-ukwu the Supreme God. It is neither sufficient nor entirely correct to regard the Igbos as polytheists, without this essential qualification; essential because the Igbos do not put Chi-ukwu the Supreme God and their earth god – "Ajani" or the god of iron – "Idigwe", on the same pedestal. The domain of Chi-ukwu (the Great God) is radically differentiated from, and is higher than that of the lesser gods, and of man.[3]

Isichei's view brings out more clearly what the Igbo traditionalists believe and practice. She holds that:

The followers of traditional religion, generally speaking, did not seek converts. They tended to believe that the full truth about God cannot be known, and that each people have that version of religion which is most suited to its own culture and circumstances. West African religions (Igbo inclusive) tended to hold that the Supreme God is benevolent, but that He stays remote from the affairs of men. It is therefore believed that worshippers should give most of their devotion to many lesser spirits, who interfere constantly in daily life.[4]

We notice a kind of dualism in some of the commentators on Igbo traditional theology. This dualism comes from the Igbo world-view. For us to have a clear understanding of Igbo traditional theology we have to understand their world-view. The Igbo world-view is seen as a world in which the visible and the invisible forces, the living and the dead and unborn interact. In the process of their interactions, they shape and improve our living.

The Igbo people see reality in complementary duality of say nwoke na nwanyi (male and female), madu na mmuo (human being and spirit) and in general negative and positive. The traditional Igbo see objects and people, events and

---

[2] Chukwuemeka Nze., *"Pragmatism and Traditionalism in Concept of God in African Culture"*, in Uche, *Journal of Department of Philosophy, University of Nigeria, Nsukka,* Nigeria, 1981, p. 23, in Mbaegbu C., *Hermeneutics of God in Igbo Ontology,* Fab Educational Books, Awka, Nigeria, 2012, p. 17.

[3] Nkeonye Otakpor, *"Pragmatism and Traditionalism in the Concept of God in African Culture"*, *A reply to Dr. Nze, Uche, Journal of the Department of Philosophy, University of Nigeria, Nsukka,* Nigeria, 1982, p. 66, in Mbaegu C., *Hermeneutics of God in Igbo Ontology, op. cit.,* p. 18.

[4] Isichei E., *History of West Africa since 1800,* Macmillan Education Limited, London and Basingstoke, 1978, pp. 13 - 14.

situations as existing and functioning in duality. They recognize that things may change their nature.[5]

Chinua Achebe maintains that:

> Without an understanding of the nature of "Chi" in Igbo ontology, one could not begin to make sense of the Igbo world-view and yet no study of it exists that could even be called primary.[6]

For Achebe, many may visualize a person's "Chi" as his other identity in spirit land, his spirit being complementing his terrestrial human being "for nothing can stand alone, there must always be another thing standing beside it. (*Ife kwulu, ife akwudobe ya*)."[7]

There is a kind of dualism that comes into play in the understanding of "Chi" in Igbo ontology which we will later take time to study in detail. The Igbo world-view is the door that leads to the understanding of the Igbo as a people, the way they think, their culture, tradition, religion, etc. Nwala for example, defines Igbo world-view as:

> The complex of beliefs, habits, laws customs and tradition of the Igbo people. It includes the overall picture they have about reality, the universe, life and existence, their attitude to life and to things in general; what they do think of what life is, what things are worth striving to attain, what man's place is in the scheme of things; whether or not man has an immortal soul; whether or not life has a meaning and purpose, etc.[8]

A traditional Igbo man understands things through dualism. For example, if we have the idea of "good", therefore "bad" must be in existence. If there is an effect, therefore, there must be a cause, etc. The Igbo believe that these polarities for example: good – evil, spiritual – material, cause – effect, etc., do not exist in isolation, they interact. Hence, when we discuss whether the Igbo traditionalists practise monotheism or polytheism, this dualistic mind setting among the Igbo traditionalists will be an immense help to us in order to understand the concepts we are dealing with.

CHAPTER ONE: Chapter one of this work brings out the major beliefs and practices in Igbo traditional religion and studies them critically. It was the philosopher Heraclitus that concluded that nature is always in the process of change.

---

[5] Igbo P.C., *Elements of Igbo Culture and Tradition*, Good Mark Prints Inc., Onitsha, Nigeria, 2012, p. 27.

[6] Cf., youngafrikanpioneers.wordpress.com/2014/03/20/chi-in-igbo-cosmology, accessed 24.7.2017.

[7] Ibid.

[8] Nwala T.U., *Igbo Philosophy*, Niger Books and Publishing Company Ltd., Nigeria, 1985, p. 41.

"Like a river, nature flows ever onwards. Even the nature of the flow changes. We both step and do not step in the same rivers. We are and are not."[9] It is an obvious fact that both human beings and things in the world are involved in the process of change. All religions in the world are in the process of modernization and change. Igbo Traditional Religion is no exception. In this chapter we shall bring out those things that have undergone the process of change in Igbo Traditional Religion.

CHAPTER TWO: We shall notice this dualism we earlier talked about in this chapter; when we shall be discussing individual and community spirituality in Igbo Traditional Religion.

CHAPTER THREE: This x-rays the causes of Nigeria-Biafra war, the part played by the international bodies and the politics behind it.

CHAPTER FOUR: This chapter deals with the impact of the Nigerian civil war on the Igbo people. The Igbo believe that this war has dual impact on them. It has spiritual as well as material impact. Once again, we see this duality in play. We shall investigate the changes this war brought to Igbo spirituality, the material effects it had on the Igbo and how it has affected their traditional practice of monotheism and polytheism.

CHAPTER FIVE: It discusses modernity and Igbo Traditional Religion. It brings out some of the defining characteristics of modernity: - the good qualities of modernity, its shortcomings and the Church as a vehicle of civilization and development in Igboland.

CHAPTER SIX: This chapter investigates the possibility of bridging the gap between Christianity and Igbo Traditional Religion. It studies the possible avenues by which Christians and Igbo traditional religionists can live together and have better understanding of one another. It studies also the areas of agreement and disagreement between Christian theology and the ideologies of Igbo Traditional Religion.

CHAPTER SEVEN: General Conclusion.

---

[9] Cf., https://www.bing.com/search?q=Heraclitus+his+philosophy+on+change&form, accessed 27.7.2017.

CHAPTER ONE

1. THE IGBO UNDERSTANDING OF HUMAN PERSON AS A SPIRITUAL ENTITY

1.1. INTRODUCTION

This introductory chapter begins with a critical look at the Igbo people; who they are, their origin, their world-view and their spirituality. It gives a brief description of the objects of belief or main features of the Igbo Traditional Religion and how the various parts of the structure are interrelated. It examines in particular the past and the present practices in Igbo Traditional Religion.

In this chapter some of the controversial issues in Igbo Traditional Religion, for example "Chi", "Ancestor veneration", "reincarnation", "sacrifice", are critically examined. The aim of this chapter is to present, analyze, the past and the present practices in Igbo Traditional Religion, and bring out the changes that have taken place in it.

1.2. THE IGBO PEOPLE OF NIGERIA

The Igbo people are among the three largest ethnic groups in Nigeria. They belong to black race in Africa. They have their own native language called 'Igbo'. The word 'Igbo' or 'Ibo' has been used in the past and up till today to refer to this ethnic group of people who occupy mainly the South-East of Nigeria.

In some books for example: *The Nigerian Revolution and Biafran war* by **Madiebo Alexander**, *History of West Africa* by **Onwubiko K.B.C.**, *Among the Ibos of Nigeria* by **Basden G.T** and *Tribes of the Niger Delta* by **Talbot P. Amaury**, just to mention but a few, one would find out that 'Ibo' instead of 'Igbo' is used.[10] This was the mistake made by the European colonizers and Missionaries who could not pronounce the double but elided consonants or implosive 'gb'.

In current books like, *The Influence of Igbo Traditional Religion on the Socio-Political Character of the Igbo* by **Oguejiofor J.**, *African Religions and Philosophy* by **Mbiti J.S.**, *The Biafran War and the Igbo in Contemporary Nigerian Politics* by **Obiezuofu-Ezeigbo E.C.**, *Sacrifice in Igbo Traditional Religion* by **Arinze**

---

[10] Cf., Madiebo A., *The Nigerian Revolution and the Biafran War*, Fourth Dimension Publishing co., Ltd, Enugu, Nigeria, 1980.
Onwubiko K.B.C., *History of West Africa,* Africana Educational Publishers, Nigeria, in association with FEP International Private Limited, Singapore, 1973.
Basden G.T., *Among the Ibos of Nigeria,* Academy Press Ltd, Lagos, Nigeria, 1921.
Talbot P.A., *Tribes of the Niger Delta,* Seldon Press, London, 1932.

F.,[11] just to mention but a few, one would notice that the word 'Igbo' instead of 'Ibo' is used. The word `Igbo' was first made use of before it was mutilated as `Ibo' by European colonizers and missionaries. The original word, however, is Igbo. 'Egbo', 'Igbo', 'Ebo' and 'Ibo' are the various spelling found in some books referring to this ethnic group. The term Igbo is now generally accepted to designate three entities:

(1) The geographical territory,

(2) the cultural group (tribe) occupying this geographical territory,

(3) the language spoken by this ethnic group.[12]

Leonard tried to trace the origin of the Igbo people but arrived at the conclusion that "it is difficult today to attain to any reasonable result. The origin of the Igbo people is a maze within a maze".[13]

One discovers that "experts are not yet certain about the origin, and the meaning of the word 'Igbo'. It certainly did not originally refer to the whole Igbo tribe as we know it today, for before the arrival of Europeans over one hundred years ago, there was no common name for the whole tribe, but each town or village had its particular name often taken from an ancestor. Such derivations as these have been suggested: 'the people', 'man of the bush', and secondarily, 'slaves'. Until recently people applied the word 'Igbo' (earlier written as Ibo) primarily to the language and secondarily to Igbo speaking groups other than one's own".[14] Nevertheless, the Igbo certainly have their history. This history was in oral form until not long ago when some scholars started putting it in writing. Therefore, one can say that the written history does not date back to many centuries.

The Igbo people are seen almost in all parts of the world today. So, one begins to ponder actually the origin of this people. Many hypotheses have been given but they are mere speculations, without reliable archaeological and historical facts to back them up. We have so many speculative arguments and theories

---

[11] Oguejiofor J., *The Influence of Igbo Traditional Religion on the Socio-Political Character of the Igbo*, Fulladu Publishing Company, Nsukka, Nigeria, 1996. Mbiti J.S., *African Religions and Philosophy*, Anchor books, Doubleday and Company, USA., 1970. Obiezuofu-Ezeigbo C.E., *The Biafran War and the Igbo in Contemporary Nigerian Politics*; Pan Negro Continental Ltd., Lagos, Nigeria, 2007. Arinze F., *Sacrifice in Igbo Traditional Religion,* St. Stephen's Press, Inc., Onitsha, Nigeria, 2008.

[12] Echiegu A.O., *Sacral Igbo and its Rhetoric*, K. Rave, Ottmarsbocholt, Germany, 1984, vol.3, p. 7.

[13] Cf., Leonard A., *The Lower Niger and its Tribes,* London, 1906, p. 31, in Arinze F., Sacrifice in Igbo Traditional Religion, op. cit., p. 2.

[14] Arinze F., *Sacrifice in Igbo Traditional Religion,* op. cit., p. 1.

on the etymology, meaning of the word "Igbo" and the origin of the Igbo people. But we do not intend here to go into extensive discussion on this.

1.3. THE ETYMOLOGY AND MEANING OF THE WORD "IGBO"

We have two camps on the etymology and meaning of the word "Igbo"; namely the homeland hypothesis and none-homeland hypothesis. Under non-homeland hypothesis we have Meek who proposed that "the word 'Igbo' etymologically comes from Sudanic roots 'Bo' or 'Po' meaning people. This may also mean slaves, a title said to be conferred by the 'Igala'; (Igala is an ethnic group in Nigeria)."[15]

An example of homeland hypothesis is Yoruba hypothesis (Yoruba is one of the tribes in Nigeria). This hypothesis holds that "Igbo is a word indicative of bush. It is used to refer to the aboriginal inhabitants, the autochthons whom the Yoruba migrants displaced to take possession of the present Yorubaland, and who are known in Yoruba tradition as 'Igbo', 'bush', or forest of backward people".[16]

For the Igbo people, 'Igbo' in their language means early or ancient people. It means aboriginality. In Igbo language, "ndi gboo" refers to the ancestors, the aborigines and the ancient people.[17] Onwuejeogwu suggests that the word 'Igbo' means "the community of people".[18] Talbot, who worked many years in southern Nigeria discovered that, "to the Igbo of *Asaba, Ika* and *Sobo*, west of the river Niger, the term *Igbo* refers to those they called slaves."[19]

1.4. THE ORIGIN OF THE IGBO PEOPLE

The origin of the Igbo people is still enveloped in mystery. A number of hypotheses have been advanced in this regard, but they remain purely speculative as there is yet no substantial archaeological reinforcement of these hypotheses. There are two main hypotheses: The oriental and Igbo homeland hypotheses.

---

[15] Cf., Meek C.K., *Law and Authority in a Nigerian Tribe,* Oxford University Press, London, 1937, p. 2, in Nwala T.U., *Igbo Philosophy, (second edition),* Niger Books and Publishing Company Ltd, Nigeria, p., 29.

[16] Afigbo A. E., *Igbo Enwe Eze: Beyond Onwumechili, Okigwe,* Whytem Publishers, Nigeria, 2001, in Nwala, ibid.

[17] Cf., Nwala T. U., *Igbo Philosophy,* op. cit., p. 30.

[18] Onwuejeogwu M.A., "*Short history of the Odinani Museum, The Journal of Odinani-Museum, Nri, vol.1,* 1972, in Nwala T. U., op. cit., p. 30.

[19] Talbot P.A., The People of Southern Nigeria vol. II, Oxford University Press London, p. 404 in Onuwa U., *Studies in Igbo Traditional Religion*, Pacific Correspondence College and Press Ltd, Nigeria, 1990, p. 2.

1.4.1. ORIENTAL HYPOTHESIS

The oriental hypothesis argues that the Igbo people came from the Middle East. Some commentators had speculated that the Igbo people were either "one of the lost 'tribes' of Israel or Egypt and that for some inexplicable circumstances, they left the East and wandered across until they finally came to their present abode. The exponents of this theory found similarity of culture between that of the Igbo and some of the Eastern people. Circumcision, system and manner of naming children, sentence structure and similarity in some words, religion and ritual symbols, love of adventure and enterprise were used to explain derivation from the East".[20]

The oriental hypothesis has since 1940 been abandoned because of its ideological basis and lack of archaeological corroboration. This hypothesis is based on religious and linguistic affinities between the Igbo and some oriental cultures. It is also based on linguistic kinship and environmental argument. Olaudah Equiano, an Igbo ex-slave and a commentator on Igbo society, "links the Igbo with the Jews".[21] Basden asserts that "the investigator cannot help being struck with the similitude between them (the Igbo) and some of the ideas and practices of the Levitical Code".[22]

1.4.2. THE IGBO HOMELAND HYPOTHESIS

The Igbo homeland hypothesis, based on linguistic and environmental factors, suggests that the Igbo people originally came from the Guinean zone of the middle belt region further north of Nigeria and settled in the northern Igbo zone. From there they migrated southwards, until they settled into what is now considered Igbo heartland.[23] It is now generally accepted, relying on archaeological evidence, especially the result of archaeological work of Hartle that the "Igbo began to exist as a distinct cultural unit with a characteristic language, about six thousand years ago."[24]

1.5. THE ANTHROPOLOGICAL AND GEOGRAPHICAL DELIMITATION OF IGBOLAND

The Igbo people are those who have as their natural home the Igboland which is located in the southern part of Nigeria. The River Niger divides Igboland into

---

[20] Ofomata G.E.K., ed., *A Survey of the Igbo Nation,* Africana First Publishers Ltd, Onitsha Nigeria, 2002, p. 40.

[21] Edwards P., ed., *Equianos's Travels,* London, p. 12, in Ofomata G.E.K., ed., *A Survey of the Igbo Nation,* op. cit., p. 40.

[22] Basden G.T., *Among the Ibos of Nigeria,* op. cit., p. 39.

[23] Cf., Isichei E., *A History of the Igbo People*, Macmillan Press Ltd., London, 1976, pp. 3- 4.

[24] Hartle D.D., "*Archaeology in Eastern Nigeria*", Nigerian Magazine 93, 1967, pp. 134 - 143.

two unequal parts with the overwhelming part lying in what was formerly called Eastern Region and the other part in the Western Region. The Igbo are those who have been grouped into the **Kwa** linguistic stock but with variations of dialect. Their territorial divisions cover the whole area stretching from the coastlines of the Bight of Benin and continue to the outskirts of **Ibibio** and **Efik** territories in the east with its eastern boundary being formed by the Cross-River. On the Southern and Western sides, it stretches to the borders of **Ijaw**, **Jekri**, **Igado** and other Ethnic groups, and spreads across the Niger to the confines of Benin. Its utmost Northern limits reach the boundary between Southern and Northern Nigeria where the **Akpoto** and **Mushins** are the nearest neighbors.

In the new political dispensation, the Igbo people are found in 7 states of Nigeria. 5 out of these 7 states are purely Igbo, namely (Enugu, Imo, Anambra, Abia, Ebonyi). Igbo are found also in Rivers and Delta states of Nigeria. "In terms of longitude and latitude, Igboland is roughly circumscribed between 6° and 8 $^1/_2$ East Longitude and 4 $^1/_2$ ° and 7 $^1/_4$ North Latitude".[25]

It is, indeed, most appropriate to regard the Igbo people as among the true citizens of the world, not being barred by geography, climate, language or religion. The genius, courage and drive of her citizens are recognized and respected all over the world. "In 2005, the population of the Igbo people was estimated to be about 50 million."[26] Religious warriors, an aggressive commercial class and a highly intelligent clerical class populated the Igbo traditional society. The republican nature of Igbo society "encourages individualism, egalitarianism, achievement-oriented and adaptability. At the same time and paradoxically too, the communalistic character of their culture, makes them highly collectivistic, self-reliant and hospitable".[27]

1.6. IGBO WORLD-VIEW AND PHILOSOPHY OF LIFE

For us to understand Igbo spirituality, Igbo views on the human person, their culture, tradition and their philosophy of life, we have to look at their world-view, how they understand the world, how they see the world and how they interpret what they see around them. We often make use of or come across the phrase "world-view" in books. What does it actually mean? Onuoha defines it thus.

---

[25] Nwala T.U., *Igbo Philosophy,* op. cit., p. 22.
[26] Ibid.
[27] Ibid., p. 21.

It is a conceptualization of the universe providing a structured and unified picture of the cosmos and defining man's place and role in it. It comprises a set of values, concepts, and images which guide man's perception and interpretation of facts and events. It is a mental map of the universe.[28]

Man's innate ability as a rational being is greatly manifested in his ability to assign meaning to his activities, and to events and things independent of him. Meaninglessness is a concept completely foreign to the nature of man. In his day-to-day relations with the cosmos, he always strives, and often unconsciously, to have a base in the form of a unifying factor which is understood as "terminus a quo" (origin) and "terminus ad quem" (end). The result of this innate quest for explanation, for meaning in life, constitutes what is known as a world-view.[29]

The Igbo world-view can be resolved into three fundamental orders of existence: "Muo" – the spiritual order of the dead, "Madu" – the order of the living human beings and, "Ife" – the material order of things. When we understand these orders of existence in Igbo world-view, it helps us to understand the concept of "Madu" (human being) in Igbo ontology when we shall be discussing it. The Igbo world-view is seen as a world in which the visible and the invisible forces, the living, the dead, and unborn interact. In the process of their interactions, they shape and improve our living. The Igbo people see reality in complementary duality of say "nwoke na nwanyi" (male and female), "madu na mmuo" (human being and spirit) and in general negative and positive. The traditional Igbo see objects and people, events and situations as existing and functioning in duality. They recognize that things may change their nature.[30]

Igbo traditional world-view "includes the overall picture they have about reality, the universe, life and existence; their attitude to life and to things in general; what they do think of what life is, what things are worth striving to attain, what man's place is in the scheme of things; whether or not man has an immortal soul, whether or not life has a meaning and purpose etc. The Igbo world-view is enmeshed in the practical life of the people; in particular in their economic, political, social, artistic and religious life. It embraces the practical philosophies of life of the traditional Igbo as well as the theoretical expressions of that philosophy. In order words, we are referring to the fundamental princi-

---

[28] Onuoha E., *Four Contrasting World-views*, Empress Pub., Ltd., Enugu, 1987, in Mbaegbu, C. A., *Hermeneutics of God in Igbo Ontology*, Fab Educational Books, Awka, Nigeria, 2012, p. 103.
[29] Oguejiofor J.O., *The Influence of Igbo Traditional Religion on the Socio-Political Character of the Igbo, op. cit.*, p. 47.
[30] Igbo P.C., Elements *of Igbo Culture and Tradition*, Elites Publishers, Onitsha, Nigeria, 2012, p. 26.

ples and values that underlie their world outlook, as well as the way and manner they express them in their reasoning and language".[31] Igbo world-view is reflected in the philosophy, culture and religion of the Igbo.

1.7. IGBO TRADITIONAL RELIGION: ITS PREDOMINANT ELEMENTS AND ITS RELATIONSHIP WITH AFRICAN TRADITIONAL RELIGION

1.7.1. THE OBJECTS OF BELIEF IN IGBO TRADITIONAL RELIGION

The Igbo are a truly religious people of whom it can be said as it has been said of the Hindus, that they eat religiously, drink religiously, bathe religiously, dress religiously and sin religiously. Religion of these natives is their existence and their existence is their religion.[32]We have three major objects of belief in Igbo Traditional Religion. Namely:

(1) **The Supreme Being – God**, (2) **the Non-human Spirits**, (3) **and the Ancestors.**[33] By objects of belief we mean the formation of beliefs among the Igbo. The Igbo believe that God created the world; the non-human spirits assist God in the preservation of the world; while the ancestors are left with the role of aiding and shaping of things and events of the world. They are also capable of influencing the destinies and actions of mankind. According to Nwala:

> It is possible to discuss the philosophy of people or even the philosophy of an individual without reference to the religion of the people or the individual. For a people or an individual may have a philosophy without a religion. But no people and no person have a religion without a philosophy which underpins it.[34]

Religion can be defined objectively and subjectively. "Subjectively, religion is the consciousness of one's dependence on a transcendent Being and the tendency to worship Him. Objectively, religion is the body of truths, laws and rites by which man is subordinated to the transcendent Being."[35] Religion and philosophy relate to each other in their belief content. "Both involve certain basic beliefs, which not only generate actions and influence behavior, but provide

---

[31] Nwala T.U., Igbo *Philosophy,* op. cit., p. 41.

[32] Leonard M.A.G., *The Lower Niger and its Tribes*, London, Frank Cass and Co., Ltd, 1968, p. 429, in Nwala, T.U., *Igbo Philosophy*, op. cit., p. 165.

[33] Cf., *Arinze F., Sacrifice in Igbo Traditional Religion,* op. cit., p. 15, Nwala T.U., *Igbo Philosophy,* op. cit., p. 166.

[34] Nwala T.U., *Igbo Philosophy*, op. cit., p. 164.

[35] Arinze F., *Sacrifice in Igbo Traditional Religion*, op. cit., p. 14.

the basis for understanding those actions and behaviors. Philosophical and religious beliefs also influence individual and national character."[36]

The Igbo people do have their own religion that is original to them, that was not imported from outside Igboland and this is known as **Igbo Traditional Religion.** When we speak of Igbo Traditional Religion, we mean the indigenous religious beliefs and practices of the Igbo people. It is the religion which arose from the sustaining faith held by the forefathers of the Igbo. This religion is rooted basically in oral transmission. Its rituals, mode and canons are not written down on paper but in peoples' mind. This religion has no missionaries and does not have the intention of having any in future.

1.7.2. WIDESPREAD BELIEF IN A SUPREME GOD, UNIQUE AND TRANSCENDENT GOD

Ludwig questions: "How can the untutored African conceive God"?[37] What Ludwig failed to acknowledge at that time is the existence of intuitive knowledge, knowledge by intuition, knowledge acquired not through formal education, or learning. Schmidt disagrees with Ludwig position here. He maintains that:

> The belief in, and worship of one supreme deity is universal among all really primitive people – the high God is found among them all, not indeed everywhere in the same form or with the same vigor, but still everywhere prominently enough to make his dominant position indubitable. God is by no means a late development or traceable to Christian missionary in Africa.[38]

The concept of *Chukwu* (God) among the Igbo is that of a Being that has absolute powers, greater and powerful than other beings. "Among the Igbo people there is a distinct recognition of a Supreme Being – beneficent in character – who is above every other spirit, good or evil. He is believed to control all things in heaven and earth and dispenses rewards and punishments according to merit. Anything that occurs, for which no visible explanation is forthcoming, is attributed either to Him or to evil forces. But *Chukwu* (as He is called) is supreme, and at His service are many ministering spirits whose sole business it is to fulfill His commands."[39]

Many scholars of African Traditional Religion do agree that "there are three major objects of belief and worship in African Traditional Religion (Igbo Tradi-

---

[36] Nwala T. U., *Igbo Philosophy,* op. cit., p. 164.
[37] Parrinder E.G., *African Traditional Religion, 3rd, ed.*, Sheldon Press, London, 1974, p. 9.
[38] Schmidt, *African Ideas of God,* Edinburgh, 1966, p. 1.
[39] Basden G.T., *Among the Ibos of Nigeria*, Academy Press Ltd., Lagos, Nigeria, 1983, p. 215.

tional Religion inclusive) and they are: God, non-human spirits and the Ancestors."[40]

Some commentators have argued in the past that the Africans could not conceive God, like Emil Ludwig who questioned the ability of the 'untutored Africans' to conceive God. But it has been proved that the Africans, the Igbo people inclusive had the knowledge of God before the coming of the missionaries in Igboland. If they could not conceive Him or did not believe in His existence, how could they have prayed to Him or requested His help in times of danger. They even gave their children names which reflected the existence and the attributes of God. We shall give examples of these names later.

We must note that no person, persons or nation can claim to have a full knowledge of God. The Igbo say that God is "Ama-ama-amasi-amasi" (one known but never fully known). Therefore, all are striving to know God better in order to communicate with Him better.

The Sierra Leonean writer Harry Sawyerr, notes that there is a strong belief of God among the Igbo. He states thus: "one cannot but be impressed by the fact that among all the tribes which have been studied, there is always some reference to God as the center of the supreme authority which controls the world – *Chukwu*, (God) among the Igbo''.[41]

Some of the earliest missionaries to Africa did understand the fact that the traditional Africans (including the Igbo), whom they met on their arrival, had a preconceived knowledge of God. Naylor says that:

> It is a fact of tremendous significance that despite the centuries of the Pagan's blind groping after demonical spirits, despite the barbarities with which his daily life has abounded for generation upon generation, despite the 'abnormal folds of animalism' with which it is covered, the idea of God persists, and is capable of revival and enlargement.[42]

---

[40] Parrinder E.G., *African Traditional Religion*, 3rd edition, Sheldon Press, London, 1974, pp. 33-58.
Arinze F., *Sacrifice in Igbo Traditional Religion,* St. Stephen's Press, Onitsha, Nigeria, 2008, p. 15 Mbiti S.J., *African Religions and Philosophy,* Doubleday and Company, USA, 1967, pp. 75-118; Nwala T.U., *Igbo Philosophy, Niger Books and Publishing Company Ltd, Nigeria,* 2010, pp. 166-167.
[41] Sawyerr H.E, *God, Ancestor or Creator? Aspects of Traditional Belief in Ghana, Nigeria and Sierra-Leone*, Longman, London, 1970, p. 3.
[42] Naylor W., *Daybreak in the Dark Continent,* United Society Christian Endeavour, Chicago, USA, 1905, p. 89.

The Igbo man believes firmly in the existence of a Supreme Being. This Supreme Spirit has three chief names: "*Chukwu* (*Chi-ukwu,* the Great Spirit), *Chineke* (the Spirit that creates) and *Osebuluwa* (Lord who upholds the world)". But there are other names given to the Supreme Being (God) by the Igbo like:

Ama-ama-amasi-amasi	One known but never fully known
Chi di n'uwa	God of the world or universe
Chineke	Creator
Chukwu	Great Spirit
Chukwuokike	The one who creates
Eze bi n'igwe ogodo ya na-akpu n'ani	King who lives in the sky and his clothes touch and roll on the ground
Ezechitoke	The king that creates
Eze enu	King of heaven
Obasi bi n'igwe	God above
Obasi di n'enu	God above
Onye kelu enu kee ani	The one who created heaven and earth
Onye no n'enu	The one who is above
Onye okike	The one who creates
Osebuluwa	Lord who upholds the World.
Igwe ka ani	Heaven greater than earth.

Apart from these names given to God by the Igbo, there are names which reflect the existence and the attributes of God that the Igbo give to their Children. Names like:

Chukwuneke or *Chukwukelu*	God creates
Chukwunyelu	God gave
Chukwuma	God knows
Chukwumaijem	God knows my steps or my journey
Chukwuka	God is greater
Chukwunweike or *Ikechukwu*	Power is with God
Chukwu ka odinaka	it is all in God's hands
Ifeanyichukwu	Nothing is impossible with God
Chukwuemeka or *Olisemeka*	God has done much
Ekene dili Chukwu	thank God
Arinzechukwu	thanks to God, that is, were it not for God…
Ngozichukwu or simply *Ngozi*	God's blessing
Chukwulozie	may God think it rightly, that is, consider my unmerited suffering
Chukwumailo	God knows my enemies
Chukwuzoba	may God save/protect
Chukwuagbanarinam	may God not be far from me
Chukwujioke	God is the sharer
Chukwukadibia	God is greater than doctor
Chukwuebuka	God is Great
Chukwudi	God exists

The various names for God are descriptive of his character, and emphatic that He is a reality and not an imaginary being. The personal theophoric names arising out of personal contact with and experience of the gracious mercy of God likewise demonstrate his reality.

It is necessary to observe that these are traditional Igbo names and have not been coined by Christians. The Christian Church came to the Igbo people only in the second half of the nineteenth century, and these are names of grandparents who died long before the first Christians reached Igboland, and of children of Igbo traditional religionists still living. These Igbo names can be used as baptismal names in Christian Churches because they are not inimical to the gospel of Christ. In line with the oral nature of Igbo Traditional Religion, culture, cosmological myths, folk tales and songs, personal names, and particularly private and public prayers, found in all the areas of Igboland provide us with sure means of information on the Supreme Being.[43] The question many ask is: If the Igbo people can conceive God, what prevents them from worshipping Him directly without any intermediaries like the deities or the ancestors? For us to give a reasonable answer to this question, let us look into the etymology of the Name "Chukwu" (meaning God) from Igbo background.

1.7.2.1. THE ETYMOLOGY OF THE NAME "CHUKWU" (GOD) FROM IGBO BACKGROUND

The most common name in Igboland for the Supreme Being is "Chukwu". God has no proper name nor generic name. Arazu argues that:

> Chukwu (known by many in Igboland as the name for the Supreme Being) is rather the proper name for a prominent god in Igbo traditional religion. Chukwu was a proper name for one of the divine personalities in the Igbo pantheon. Before missionary indoctrination destroys all the evidence, we must insist that in the traditional religious set-up of the Igbo, Chukwu was one of the personalities who enjoyed the divine prerogative.[44]

Here Arazu argues against the name 'Chukwu' which many Igbo call God. But Arazu does not say that the Igbo do not believe in the Supreme Being. He agrees that they do believe in the Supreme Being – God, but the name 'Chukwu' was not used originally to refer to God. Contrary to Arazu's view here, Arinze states that "the Supreme Spirit has three chief names in Igbo Traditional Religion. They are: *Chukwu* (*Chi–ukwu,* the Great Spirit), *Chineke* (the Spirit that creates) and *Osebuluwa* (Lord who upholds the world). We observe here that the Supreme Being (God) is not called or invoked by one name – *Chukwu*".[45]

---

[43] Kalu O.U., *Igbo Traditional Religious System*, in Ofomata G.E.K. (ed.), *A Survey of the Igbo Nation,* op. cit., p. 354.
[44] Arazu R.C., Our *Religion – Past and Present*, Martin-King Press Awka, Nigeria, 2005, pp. 13 - 14.
[45] Arinze F., *Sacrifice in Igbo Traditional Religion,* op. cit. p. 15.

Arazu argues that the name 'Chukwu' came as a result of the influence of Christianity on Igbo Traditional Religion. He explains that:

> The founder of the Holy Ghost Fathers, Igbo Mission warned his nephew that: all those who go to Africa as missionaries must be thoroughly penetrated with the thought that the Dark Continent is a cursed land, almost entirely in the power of the devil.[46]

Arazu argues further that "this mentality among the missionaries explains why they chose one divinity from among the gods of Igbo traditional religion and wrote the rest of the gods off as diabolical."[47] The full etymology of the name "Chukwu" gives a better understanding of the idea or belief behind it. The name Chukwu comes from two Igbo words "Chi" and "ukwu" which implies the great "Chi" – the great spirit. We shall explain in detail what is meant by "Chi" later in this work. But suffice it to say here that "Chi" is the name for smaller gods or spirits. These spirits are regarded by some to be personal guardian spirits. We have a rule in Igbo linguistics called – "iwu ndakorita udaume".

In the word "Chukwu", two words "chi" and "ukwu" are married together to become "Chi-ukwu". When this is done, an umlauting occurs that is to say that the vowel "i" in the new word or name is dropped, so that the word is now left as – "Chukwu" – the Great Spirit, meaning in Igbo (God).[48]

God is called many names in Igboland depending on which area one comes from. Among these names some of them extol God as creator: "Onyeokike" (the one who creates), "Chukwuokike" (God the creator), "Onye kelu enu kee ani" (the one who created heaven and earth), "Ezechitaoke" (the king that creates), just to mention but a few. But one may ask from where the Igbo got the idea of these names, they call God. From where did the Igbo man derive these names, he gives the Supreme Being – God? The Igbo derived these names from God's attributes. For example, the Igbo call God "Onyeokike" (the person who creates), "Chineke" (the Spirit that creates). This is because it is clear to the Igbo that there is only one being that creates and that is the Supreme Being – God. They call this being that creates "Chukwu" (the Great Spir-

---

[46] Isichei E., *Seven Varieties of Ambiguity, Some Patterns of Igbo Response to Christian Missions,* reprinted from *'Journal of Religion in Africa'* vol. iii, Fasc 3, 1970, p. 210 in Arazu R.C., *Our Religion Past and Present*, op. cit., p. 109.

[47] Ibid., p. 109.

[48] Metuh I.E., *God and Man in African Religion,* Geoffrey Chapman, London, 1981, p. 24; African Religion in Western Conceptual Schemes, Pastoral Institute, Ibadan, Nigeria, 1985, p. 38; Ilogu E., *Christianity and Igbo Culture,* University Publishing Com. Onitsha, Nigeria, 1985, p. 34, in Oguejiofor J., *The Influence of Igbo Traditional Religion on the Socio-Political Character of the Igbo,* op. cit., p. 54.

it, the Great "Chi"), bearing in mind that among the divinities there is one that is the greatest.

The Igbo people did not acquire these attributes from any foreign religion. They already ascribed these attributes to God before the coming of the missionaries to Igboland. Nevertheless, what we have to note is "the fact that the Igbo people recognize God in their theophoric names and in their proverbs, it remains a curious matter that all generally agree that only in rare cases do the traditional Igbo offer sacrifices to God. It is generally agreed that the Igbo invoke *Chukwu* (God) in their traditional morning prayer, while invoking other divinities and ancestors."[49] This assertion brings up the earlier question posited in this work; which asks why the cult of "Chukwu" (God) is not popular in Igbo Traditional Religion like the cult of deities and the ancestors. For the Igbo traditional religionists, there is an atmosphere of mystery about "Chukwu" (God). The Igbo people: "are not sure how exactly to worship him. His awe and majesty perplex them. He is entirely transcendent. Hence, they think it more courteous and more within man's range to appeal to the spirits – (deities and the ancestors) to obtain requests from God. But the Igbo need no one to tell them that without God, not even the strongest 'alusi' (spirit) can do anything. The idea of God is too high and too vague to warrant elaborate cult and symbolic representations." [50]

It is also suggested that the Igbo do not have altars for *Chukwu* like they have for other spirits – deities and ancestors. "*Chukwu* (God) is so benevolent that there is no need to worry about him, and that he is invoked as a last resort. Another reason is that God is the ultimate recipient of all sacrifices to lesser divinities, and that the prayers and petitions addressed to them are all eventually directed to him."[51] There are no statues or images of God - *Chukwu* among the Igbo.

Sacrifices are generally made to the small gods and divinities, just because the people believe that these are not necessarily executives of the Supreme God but supernatural powers who stand between them and the Supreme God, the creator. These in their nature have powers over human beings and their affairs. Since these are generally believed to be just and strict, their opinions and punishments are always regarded as just and indiscriminate and therefore

---

[49] Talbot. P.A., *Tribes of the Niger Delta,* op. cit., p. 40, in Oguejiofor J., The *Influence of Igbo Traditional Religion on the Socio-Political Character of the Igbo,* op. cit., p. 53.
[50] Arinze F., *Sacrifice in Igbo Traditional Religion,* op. cit., pp. 18 - 19.
[51] Oguejiofor J., *The Influence of Igbo Traditional Religion on the Socio-Political Character of the Igbo,* op. cit., p. 53.

reflect the mind of the Supreme God, therefore, sacrifices are made directly to them and indirectly in some cases to the creator.

The Igbo belief in the existence of the Supreme Deity (God) is not a doctrine taken from another foreign religion. For example, the people of "Adazi-Nnukwu" in Anambra state Nigeria, call God "Eze-Enu" (the King of Heaven) who is so high that no human is considered competent to serve as His priest nor any place considered fit for His altar.[52]

The Igbo people do not have temples or shrines dedicated to the Supreme Being (God). This is due to the fact that He is not localized in the thought of the people. God is regarded as being everywhere. This means that to them, the Supreme Being (*Chukwu*) is great, so undimensional and so majestic that He cannot be confined within space and time.

1.7.3. THE CONCEPT OF "CHI" IN IGBO TRADITIONAL RELIGION

"Chi" as a concept in Igbo ontology has been one of the most controversial concepts in recent times. This is because of the different views, interpretations and meanings attributed to it by different researchers. In this section, the concept of "Chi" will be explored: the role of "Chi" in one's life, the origin of "Chi" and other facts concerning "Chi."

1.7.3.1. WHAT IS "CHI"

In Igbo ontology, there are several usages and meanings of "Chi". But for easy understanding of its usages and meanings, we have to group our discussions into two major parts. (1) "Chi" in reference to non-spiritual beings and

(2) "Chi" in reference to spiritual beings.[53]

1.7.3.2. "CHI" IN REFERENCE TO NON-SPIRITUAL BEING

This refers to *chi ofufo* – meaning (day breaking) and *chi ojiji,* (night fall), etc. The Igbo also talk of *mgbachi* (the hours between noon and night-fall). Our major concern here should be to x-ray the meaning of "Chi", its roles in man's life and how it affects the spirituality of the Igbo. We are not going to go into the philosophical or theological analysis of the meaning of and the role of "Chi" which so many scholars have done. Our focus would be: "Chi" in reference to spiritual beings and not "Chi" in reference to non-spiritual beings.

---

[52] Ogbukagu I.N.T., *Traditional Igbo Beliefs and Practices, (A study on the Culture and People of Adazi-Nnukwu),* Novelty Industrial Enterprises Ltd, Owerri, Nigeria, 1997, p. 264.
[53] Achebe C., youngafrikanpioneers.wordpress.com/2014/20/chi-in-igbo-cosmology, accessed 15.2.2016.

1.7.3.3. "CHI" IN REFERENCE TO SPIRITUAL BEINGS

Without an understanding of the nature of "Chi", one could not begin to make sense of the Igbo world-view and yet no study of it exists that would even be called preliminary. We may visualize a person's "Chi" as his other identity in spirit land.[54] "*Chi* is the essence of being, the inner person that guides man's activities in life."[55]

Most Igbo believe that each individual has a spirit, a genius or spiritual-double, his "Chi", which is given him at conception by "Chukwu" (God) and which accompanies this individual from the cradle to the grave. "Chi" is strictly personal, hence the Igbo saying: *Ofu nne na amu, ma ofu Chi adighi eji* (the same mother, yes, but not the same *Chi*). The ordinary Igbo man regards his "Chi" as "his guardian spirit on whose competency depends his personal prosperity."[56]

"Chi" is a personalized providence from God, a spark of divine being given by God to man. "Chi" is a person's spiritual counterpart. "Chi" is the protective spirit analogous to the Christian guardian angel.

> It is man's other transcendental self, differing from his life force since it is immortal. As a portion of God's divine nature deputizing for Him, "Chi" goes with man all through his life and reverts to God at a man's death.[57]

The Igbo believe that what someone's "Chi" does not approve would never happen to him. It is also with the approval of one's "Chi" that something happens to the person involved, either good or evil. When one meets accident on one's way, the Igbo say: "*obu ihe ya na chi ya kpebiri; obu otua ka chi ya siri dee ya*" (this is what he and his "Chi" decided – this is how his "Chi" destined it).

Parrinder interprets "Chi" as: "a guardian genius which overshadows or protects a man. This guardian genius gives good and bad fortune, like fate. It may offer advice in the low voice of conscience or if angered may be responsible, directly or indirectly, for an accident occurring to its ward."[58]

---

[54] Ibid.

[55] Quarcoopome T.N.O., *West African Traditional Religion,* African Universities Press, Ibadan Nigeria, 1987, p. 99.

[56] Arinze F., *Sacrifice in Igbo traditional religion*, op. cit., p. 28.

[57] Mbaegbu C., *Hermeneutics of God in Igbo Ontology,* Fab Educational Books, Awka, Nigeria, 2012, p. 170.

[58] Parrinder E.G., *African Traditional Religion, 3rd ed.,* op. cit., p. 136.

1.7.3.4. "CHI" AND MAN'S DESTINY

The Igbo attach another meaning to the concept of "Chi"; namely, destiny package. We are able to deduce this other meaning of "Chi" from Igbo proverbs. These include:

1. *Agbataghi ajo Chi n'uzo olu* (you cannot escape bad fortune by resourcefulness).

2. *Onye ajo Chi kpatalu nku ewu talu* (a goat eats the firewood of an unlucky man).

3. *Chi jiri onye ajo chi adighi efo-efo* (when night falls for an unlucky man it is endless).

4. *Chim kegbulum ekegbu* (I am ill-fated or unlucky).

5. *Chi ya keziri ya ekizi* (he is a lucky one).[59]

With the above assertions, does it mean that "Chi" has absolute power over man? This brings us to the problem of predestination or fatalism (which leaves man to the mercy of destiny). "This problem is mitigated by ascribing a measure of will power and initiative to man. One can influence one's "Chi" through 'brave' or good conduct and this knocks the horn out of fatalism or predestination in Igbo philosophy.[60] Power so complete, even in the hands of "Chi" is abhorrent to the Igbo imagination. Therefore, the makers of Igbo proverbs created avenues that would set a limit to "Chi's" exercise. Hence, the popular saying "onye kwe Chi ya ekwe" (if a man agrees, his Chi agrees). Therefore, the initiative, or some of it at least is returned to man.

We know that sometimes a man may put in his ultimate best or effort in something, for example, in his work or business yet he is not successful. The man plans to be successful but what happens to his "Chi" in this case? Quite simply the Igbo say of such a man: "Chi ya ekwero" (his "Chi" does not agree). This problem is still a puzzle for scholars of Igbo Traditional Religion.

One observes that some commentators of Igbo Traditional Religion have branded "Chi" as the agent of good and bad, good fortune and bad fortune, good luck or bad luck. "Chi" is bound up with the issues of man's destiny on earth; that is, destiny depends on how far this entity is in good state itself. "Chi" guards one's steps and brings prosperity, or else puts obstacles in one's paths. For example, a husband's double may make or mar the wife's fortune,

---

[59] Mbaegbu C., *Hermeneutics of God in Igbo Ontology*, op. cit., p. 176.
[60] Nwala T.U., *Igbo Philosophy,* op. cit., p. 62.

so a father's or a mother's and vice versa.[61] The above idea by Idowu is so complicated. If "Chi" is to be taken as one's guardian angel as many have said, the question one may ask is: From where did the Igbo people get the idea of guardian angel in the first place if not from Christianity; is guardian angel originally an Igbo concept? I do not buy the idea of Idowu that one's "Chi" does affect another person's "Chi". This leads us into the issue of fatalism which we may not like to discuss here.

Some ascribe the responsibility of decision taking to "Chi" alone and not to man. "The personal god 'Chi' brings a man all his good, sometimes bad fortune, as well as poverty and sickness. God puts one's destiny package or fate into parcels and one's lot depends upon what 'parcel' the personal god picks up. Consequently, every bad thing is attributed to the individual's personal god and in turn is blamed for his mistakes in life. At death, the sum-total of the choices made by the individual's god is sanctioned and ratified by God. The Igbo believe that these choices made by man's personal god are inscribed by God on both palms of the child at birth, hence, the Igbo say: *Obu Ihe akala aka mmadu nyere ya* (it is what has been destined and written on a man's palms)."[62] The Igbo belief system on "Chi" principle touches on all that make Igbo human person, what he/she is. Thus, all human successes or failures are alluded to him. *(Ebe onye dalu ka chi ya kwatulu ya)* say the Igbo, (where one has fallen, there one's "Chi" has struck one down.[63]

These assertions by Mbaegbu and Adibe also lead us to the problem of fatalism. If one's "Chi" is to be blamed for whatever goes wrong in one's life as asserted by Mbaegbu and Adibe above, then man has no moral responsibilities. Morality is then meaningless for man. All the mistakes which man makes should be attributed to his "Chi".

1.7.3.5. THE ORIGIN OF "CHI"

From the standpoint of Christianity, God created man and the angels including guardian angels. For the Igbo people, "Chi" is taken to be benevolent, protective and personal spirit; which means that "Chi" cannot be evil and does not come from evil. Obodoegwu Felix Ikedonu from Nnewi, Anambra State Nigeria, during my tour of various towns in Igboland in the course of my research was consulted and he stated that "Chi comes from God and returns to God when a

---

[61] Idowu B.E., *African Traditional Religion; A Definition*, SCM Press Ltd, Great Britain, 1973, p. 177.
[62] Mbaegbu C., Hermeneutics *of God in Igbo Ontology*, op. cit., p. 171.
[63] Adibe G., *Igbo Issues: Values, Chi, Akala Aka, Ikenga, Magic, Agwu and Manipulation of Divinities,* Mid-Field Pub. Ltd, Onitsha Nigeria, 2009, p. 66.

person dies."[64] Onunwa affirms this; he asserts: "whenever a man dies, his 'Chi' returns to *Chukwu* (God) to give account of his stewardship on earth. When a person reincarnates, he is given a different 'Chi' by *Chukwu* (God)".[65] We shall discuss reincarnation in Igbo ontology later in this work.

The question is: Who gives account of stewardship? Is it "Chi", that some claim to control man's destiny on earth or man himself? If one is not qualified to join the company of the Ancestors in the land of the spirits after one's death, who shoulders the responsibility? Who do we blame in this situation? Is it man's "Chi" or man himself? If it is man, then, it is illogical and meaningless. This is because part of man's affairs is controlled and manipulated by man's "Chi" which many commentators we have quoted in this work agree to. On the other hand, if it is man's "Chi", it means then, that man is totally free from his actions and does not have moral obligations. In both cases, there is a logical error.

> In some localities there is a rather hazy notion of Chi and some may in a vague way almost regard him as an emanation of Chukwu (God). Where however this is found, it is only a deviation and a local one at that.[66]

1.7.3.6. "CHI" AS SUPREME BEING

In 1973, Christopher Ezekwugo defended a doctoral thesis in theology with the title "Chi the true God in Igbo Religion".[67] As the title suggests, he does not reject the concept of one Supreme God in Igbo Traditional Religion. But he asserts that God in Igbo Traditional Religion is neither "Chukwu" nor "Chineke", but rather "Chi".' Ezekwugo is not the only person that holds this opinion. He was preceded by Talbot, who, writing in 1926, also asserted that the Igbo Supreme God is "Chi", and that such names as "Chukwu", "Chineke", "Chi n'uwa", "Chukwu oke abiama" are only variants of the original "Chi".[68]

Perhaps one may see some meaning in what Ezekwugo says when we evaluate some of the Igbo names. Examples of these names are:

- *Chikaodiri* (all decision-taking is left for God).

---

[64] Bodega Felix Ikedonu is from Nnewi town in Anambra State. Date of Interview: 22/9/2016. He was well over 65 years at the time of this interview.

[65] Onunwa U., Studies *in Igbo Traditional Religion,* Pacific Publishers, Nigeria, 1990, p. 101.

[66] Arinze F., *Sacrifice in Igbo Traditional Religion,* op. cit., p. 28.

[67] This thesis was published in 1987 and the same title by the pastoral Institute Kerala, India. Cf., Oguejiofor J., *The Influence of Igbo Traditional religion on the Socio-Political Character of the Igbo,* op. cit., p. 55.

[68] Ibid.

- *Chikadibia* (God takes over when the physician has reached his limits).

- *Chimaelu* (God knows everything).

- *Chiamaeze* (God is no respecter of persons).

- *Ibeabuchi* (people are not gods to their neighbors).

- *Onyekachi* (who is greater than God).

- *Maduabuchi* (human beings are not gods).

In these names, "Chi" can be interpreted as the Supreme Being. He alone is the giver of life. These personal names coined with "Chi" prove that "Chi" could mean the Supreme Being.

1.7.3.7. THE RELATIONSHIP BETWEEN "CHI" AND CHUKWU (GOD)

Some commentators are of the opinion that "Chukwu" (God) is one of the names that the Igbo give to the Supreme Being. Part of the relationship lies in the name itself. The names imply that we have different "Chi" – (different spirits). But this particular one is greater than all other "Chi". Achebe affirms this when he says:

> Chi-ukwu (or simply, Chukwu) means literally Great Chi. Thus, whatever Chi may be, it does seem to partake of the nature of the supreme God.[69]

The Igbo believe that from all indications, it is *Chukwu* that creates. "The active role of *Chi* (that is small *Chi*, so to say) includes interceding with God on behalf of the parents and in conjunction with God, fixes the (destiny package) – (*Akara aka*) of the child, its total achievements and failures and what the child will be, thus: Its sex (whether male or female), its term of life (whether long or short), its social and economic standing (whether noble or base, rich or poor), its occupation and trade (whether a farmer, a diviner, a herbalist, an artist) etc."[70]

It is the role of this protective spirit to intercede with God, fix with him the destiny of any human being or persons to be born into this life, namely, all that the human person will be and achieve during his earthly life: its sex, its span of life, its social and economic status, its profession in life.[71]

---

69 Achebe C., youngafrikanpioneers.wordpress.com/2014/20/chi-in-igbo-cosmology, accessed 19.3.2016.
70 Ezekwugo C.U.M., *Chi the True God in Igbo Religion*, Mar Mathews Press, Muvattupuzha, India, p. 142, in Mbaegbu C., Hermeneutics *of God in Igbo Ontology*, op. cit., p. 171.
71 Ibid., p. 169.

It is therefore a clear demonstration of lack of adequate knowledge or false conceptions of Igbo traditional thought and practice to suggest as some did that the Igbo have no other Supreme Being than their personal gods and that their fathers worshipped only gods and not God. It is evident that within the spirit-category of beings, we have one that occupies the highest position whose name is "Chukwu" - God. But because the Igbo man has no specific or generic name for God and indeed because God's principal name "Chi" is the generic name for all the deities in the spirit-category, the Igbo devices a means to avoid this ambiguity or the alternative nature of the term "Chi". One such device or alternative is to add a suffix "ukwu" (greatest) to the root word "Chi". "Hence, the name of the Ultimate Being in Igbo ontology is 'Chi-ukwu' (the Great Spirit). Where the suffix 'ukwu' (greatest) is the root added to the word 'Chi' (spirit) the meaning is immediately and correctly determined from the context in which it is used."[72] We should not confuse the role of "Chi" in Igbo Traditional Religion with that of God. We have to affirm here that "Chi" is taken by many Igbo as analogous to guardian angel. "Chi" is neither God nor greater than Him. Although the Igbo believe in the deities which we may in this work regard as minor gods, they do not regard these minor gods – deities, as having same power or attributes with **Chineke – God.**

1.7.3.8. ATTRIBUTES OF GOD (*CHUKWU*) FROM IGBO PERSPECTIVE

Attributes of God are those words or phrases ascribing traits, properties, qualities or characteristics to the Supreme Being. The importance of this study cannot be overemphasized. By studying these attributes, interpreting and analyzing them, it is expected among other things that "we come face to face with what the people really think God is, what they consider to be his nature and characteristics and what they believe to be his role and position to the world and the supersensible."[73]In discussing the attributes of God, we have to divide them into two categories. (a) The eternal and intrinsic attributes of God. (b) Moral attributes of God.

1.7.3.8.1. THE ETERNAL AND INTRINSIC ATTRIBUTES OF GOD

These attributes of God are difficult to grasp and express since they pertain more to the realm of the abstract than concrete thought forms. Broadly speaking, Igbo thought forms are more concrete than abstract. Under the eternal and intrinsic attributes of God according to Igbo perception, we have omni-

---

[72] Mbaegbu C., *Hermeneutics of God in Igbo Ontology,* op. cit., p. 192.
[73] Cf., Omosade J., & Adelumo P., *West African Traditional Religion* (Ibadan: Onibonoje Press and Book Industries (Nig), 1979, p. 46.

presence, omnipotence, omniscience, transcendence. Only the Supreme Being enjoys these intrinsic attributes and does not share them with any other being.

1.7.3.8.1.1. OMNIPRESENCE OF GOD

Omnipresence of God means that God is simultaneously everywhere. The concept of God's omnipresence is found in Igbo ontology. The Igbo acknowledge that "Chukwu" is present everywhere. He is not limited by space and time. The primary concept of God as the Greatest Spirit has influenced Igbo notion of God as omnipresent. For the Igbo, "Chukwu bu Muo" (God is Spirit). He is pictured as an active and creative spirit (Chi-na-eke). The Igbo conceive God as Spirit; consequently, they conceive Him as being everywhere not bound in space and time.

God's principal names, namely, "Chi-ukwu", "Chi-na-eke", "Eze-achi-te-oke", are conceived under the generic term Spirit, such is easily seen from his names why He is said to be everywhere simultaneously. The spirits transcend space and time; therefore, the Igbo attribute to God the quality of omnipresence. Some of the Igbo expressions which indicate the omnipresence of God include: "Onye na-ede n'Igbo na-ede n'olu" or simply "Odenigbo" which refers to God as a being whose fame has no boundaries. "Odenigbo" as attributed to God by the Igbo emphasizes His real presence in the whole universe. The traditional Igbo conception of the ubiquity of God tarries with the Christian concept of the omnipresence of God. The Book of Psalms in the Bible emphatically and in picturesque language demonstrates the concept of God's omnipresence. The Psalmist writes:

> Where shall I go to escape your spirit? Where shall I flee from your presence? If I scale the heavens you are there, if I lie flat in Sheol, there you are. If I speed away on the wings of the dawn, if I dwell beyond the ocean, even there your hand will be guiding me, your right hand holding me fast.[74]

The traditional Igbo belief is that God's omnipresence encircles the created order. He is the source of all things; giving them existence, sustenance and preservation. In the Igbo world-view, God is believed to be everywhere. He may be in the thunder, but He is not thunder; He may shoot foot like a waterfall but He is not waterfall. He may be associated with the sky, but He is not the sky. Edeh would say that "He is entirely different from everything and everyone else. God transcends all boundaries."[75] God sees comprehensively; He

---

[74] Cf. Psalm 139, verse 7 - 10, *The New Jerusalem Bible*, Standard edition, Darton, Longman & Todd Ltd.,1985, London.

[75] Edeh E.M.P., *Towards an Igbo Metaphysics,* Chicago: Loyola University Press, 1985, p. 133.

hears everything, nothing escapes His knowledge. He is therefore present eve-rywhere. The Igbo say: "Chukwu nozu ebe nile" (God is present every-where).

1.7.3.8.1.2. OMNIPOTENCE OF GOD

In traditional Igbo societies, God is considered to be omnipotent, that is, He is almighty. This is what Tempels means when he described God as the "Great Muntu - the great person, the great powerful life force … he is force itself which has force within itself."[76] The notion of God's omnipotent nature is re-flected in names which Igbo parents give to their children and more important-ly some of his praise-title names express his omnipotence. Such names include: *Ifeanyi Chukwu* (nothing is impossible with God), *Chukwuka* (God is almighty, God is not equaled in power), *Chukwunwike* or *Ikechukwu* (God is Power), *Chidiebere* (merciful God), *Onyedika Chukwu* (who is like God), *Chikadibia* (God takes over where the physician has reached his limit), *Ekejike* (power belongs to God). All these show that God is Almighty, that is, that God's power is all-embracing; even the impossible is possible with Him (*onweghi ihe nyiri ya omume*). He is *Olisebulu-uwa* (God, carrier of the world). Such a being carrying, supporting and hence providing for the world also implies the notion of om-nipotence. Discussing God's omnipotent nature, Ifesie remarks that:

> The Igbo epitomize His strength, fidelity and kindness when they call him Dike anakpo ofu ugbolo oza ugbolo asaa (the warrior, who when asked for help, answers seven times…) Chi n'emelu onye n'enweghi onye n'emelu ya… (The almighty God who does things for the helpless).[77]

The Igbo see "power" as being hierarchical, in which God is at the top as the omnipotent; beneath Him are the spirits and natural phenomena; and lower still are men who have comparatively little or no power at all.

1.7.3.8.1.3. OMNISCIENCE OF GOD

The Igbo people acknowledge another intrinsic attribute of God, namely, His omniscience, that is, God is considered among the Igbo to know all things. Nothing escapes His knowledge. Placide Tempels must have had the Igbo in mind when he reports about the Bantu in their Ontology. He describes God as "the Supreme Wise Man who knows all things."[78]

---

[76] Quoted by Janheinz Jahn Muntu., The *New African Culture*, New York, Grove Press Inc., 1961, p. 104, in Mbaegbu C.A., *Hermeneutics of God in Igbo Ontology,* op. cit., p. 21.
[77] Ifesie E., *Religion at the Grass Roots: Studies in Igbo Religion,* Enugu: Snaap Press (Nig) Ltd., 1989, p. 274, in Mbaegu C.A., *Hermeneutics of God in Igbo Ontology,* op. cit., p. 217.
[78] Temples P., *Bantu Philosophy,* Presence Africaine, Paris, 1959, p. 39.

Consequently, God is conceived to occupy the highest position of honor and respect because wisdom commands great respect in Igbo traditional society, as well as in today's Igbo modern and pragmatic society. To the Igbo, God does not only know and see everything; He is also conceived as being able to hear everything and these are metaphorical ways of explaining the concept of God as omniscient in a concrete way, easy for people to understand. Some literary conceptions of God like: "onye na-afu n'ife na-afu na nzuzo" (He who sees in day-light and in darkness) portray God in Igbo traditional setting as the omniscient from whom nothing is hidden; since nothing can escape His vision, hearing or knowledge. For the Igbo, "Chukwu" knows everything, observes everything and hears everything without limitations and without exceptions. The practice of divination and consultation of oracles in Igbo traditional life and practice point to their recognition of God as omniscient.

1.7.3.8.1.4. TRANSCENDENCE

For most of their life, African people place God in the transcendental plane, making it seem as if He is remote from their daily affairs. But they know that He is immanent, being manifested in natural objects and phenomena and they can turn to Him in acts of worship, at any place and any time. The distinction between these related attributes could be stated that, in theory God is transcendental but in practice He is immanent.[79] Therefore, the Igbo call God "ono nso elu aka" (One who is near but cannot be reached).

The Igbo believe that God is a transcendent being in the sense that He is located outside nature or outside His creation. This does not imply that communication with Him is impossible. The gods are supposed to be nearer to human beings and they are the immediate intermediaries in communication. When the Igbo talk of the transcendence of God, they also at same time refer to His immanence in the world. This may sound paradoxical, but we do accept the fact that the two attributes: "transcendence" and "immanence" are paradoxically complementary. God is "far" and men cannot reach Him, but God is also "near", that is, he comes close to man and men can communicate with Him. Thus, John Mbiti says that:

> The attribute of God's transcendence must be balanced with that of His immanence, since these two are paradoxically complementary. This means that He is so "far" (transcendental) that man cannot reach Him; yet, He is so "near" (immanent) that He comes close to men. Many foreign writers have gone

---

[79] Mbiti J.S., *African Religions and Philosophy,* op. cit., p. 43.

astray here, in emphasizing God's remoteness to the exclusion of His near-ness.[80]

In spite of God's transcendence, He is immanent so that men can and do in fact establish contact with Him. The concept of God's transcendence is summarized well in a "Bacongo" saying, that "He is made by no other; no one beyond Him is."[81] There cannot be, and there is no "beyond" God. He is the most abundant reality of being, lacking no completeness. He transcends all boundaries; He is omnipresent everywhere and at all times. He even defies human conception and description; He is simply "unexplainable". Ontologically, He is transcend-ent in that all things were made by Him, whereas He is self-existent. In status He is "beyond" spiritual beings, the spirits, men and natural objects and phe-nomena. In power and knowledge, He is supreme.

The notion of God's transcendence therefore suggests or offers an explanation why the Igbo traditionalists rarely offer direct worship to "Chukwu", their Greatest Spirit, but regularly prefer to go to Him through many intermediary gods. Again, there is that notion of mystery surrounding "Chukwu" in the sense that He is entirely transcendent. His awe and majesty frighten the Igbo tradi-tionalists; therefore, they do not know how to approach him. This explains why they prefer to approach Him through the gods.

Names and praise-titles given to God by the Igbo depict Igbo conception of God as a transcendent Being. Examples of such names are: "Chi-ukwu" (The Greatest Spirit), "Okaka" (The most Supreme Being), "Igwe ka ala" (He who is greater than all) etc. "His praise title in Igbo world-view also throws more light on His nature as a transcendent being namely, 'Amama Amasi Amasi' (known but never fully known)"[82] The attribute of God's transcendence implies His immaterial and incorporeal nature. The nature of God as Supreme Being – Spirit, is generally accepted by the Igbo. In speaking of God's immateriality, Mbiti says that in African traditional world-view:

> It is commonly believed that God is spirit, even if in thinking or talking about Him, African people may often use anthropomorphic images. As far as it is known, there are no images or physical representations of God by African people: this being one clear indication that they consider Him to be a Spiritual Being.[83]

---

[80] Ibid., p. 41.

[81] Cf., Claridge G.C., *Wild Bush Tribes of Tropical African,* London, 1922, p. 269, in Mbiti J.S., *African Religions and Philosophy,* op. cit., p. 423.

[82] Cf., Edeh E.M.P., *Towards an Igbo Metaphysics,* Chicago: Loyola Unity Press, 1985, p. 122,

[83] Mbiti J.S., *African Religions and Philosophy,* op. cit., p. 34.

The non-existence of image or physical representations of God among the Igbo is a clear indication that they conceive God to be a Spiritual Being. The name "Chukwu" (the Greatest Spirit) testifies to the above stated fact. The fact that He is spirit leads many Igbo to visualize Him as an invisible that cannot be given physical representation. In Igbo ontology, God is conceived as a spirit; therefore, the Igbo people believe that God cannot be comprehended. Hence, His incomprehensibility and mysteriousness stem from His attribute as a spirit.

The unique nature of God as incomprehensible yet comprehensible which is characteristic of Igbo traditional belief-systems is well rendered by Mbiti. He writes:

> It is a paradox that they know him, and yet they do not know Him; He is not a stranger to them, and yet they are estranged to him; He knows them, but they do not know Him. So, God confronts men as the mysterious and incomprehensible; as indescribable and beyond vocabulary.[84]

According to the principle of mutation, every positive change is a gradual trend to perfection. But God is perfect Himself. Therefore, He is unchangeable. Looking at the laws of nature, the Igbo see that they are always constant and unchangeable. From there, they concluded that God the creator of everything that exists is Himself immutable.

1.7.3.9. THE MORAL ATTRIBUTES OF GOD

The difference between eternal, intrinsic attributes of God and the moral attributes of God is that the eternal and intrinsic attributes, only the Supreme Being "Chukwu" enjoys them and no other being. But concerning the moral attributes of God, human beings and other beings can equally have a share in these attributes.

1.7.3.9.1. THE GOODNESS OF GOD

The majority of African people regard God as essentially good. For some, the goodness of God is seen in His averting calamities, supplying rain, providing fertility to people, cattle and fields.... "There are however, situations when calamities, misfortunes and suffering come upon families or individuals, for which there is no clear explanation. Some societies would then consider these to be brought about by God, generally through agents like spirits or magic workers, or as punishment for contravening certain customs or traditions. By

---

[84] Mbiti J.S., *Concepts of God in Africa,* op. cit., p. 20.

so doing, they do not consider God to be intrinsically 'evil' as such; that is simply a rational explanation of what may otherwise be hard to explain."[85]

The phenomenon of rare direct sacrifices to God in Igboland can only be explained by their notion that God is so good that He does not require any sacrifice or offerings. Some of the main reasons for sacrifices in Igboland are to ward off and avert the evil machinations of bad spirits. That the Igbo rarely sacrifice to God directly is indicative of the fact that He is good, that He does nobody any harm and that no one should be afraid of communicating with Him.

The Igbo regard the physical world as the hand-work of God; perfectly, structurally and beautifully designed by Him. "It is a beautiful world whose author is a good God. This explains why the Igbo do not attribute evil to God. Rather, all the evils existing in the world are the negation of the perfect cosmic order usually caused by the actions of men and the spirits especially the malevolent spirits. God created the world good but the children of men have spoilt it. For the Igbo, God is good and He is responsible for the beautiful world, a perfect world, a world that is not in itself evil per se."[86]

It is because of this double belief, namely, essential goodness of the world and the existence of evil in the world that the Igbo are always in search of an explanation to this, because that seems to disturb this ontological order. Thus, in Igbo world-view, the causes of continuous drought, long periods of famine, epidemic diseases, bad deaths, etc., must be ascertained by divination and appropriate cults performed to avert such evils.

We see also in some Igbo names the affirmation of the goodness of God by the Igbo people. Such names like "Chiamaka" - (God is good), "Chidimma" - (God is good). From the analysis we have given above, it is evidently clear that the Igbo believe and affirm with reasons the goodness of God to whom they also attribute the role of creation and providence for all creatures.

1.7.3.9.2. THE HOLINESS OF GOD

The concept of God's holiness is also indicated from the fact that many African people have strict rules in performing rituals directed to God. Sacrificial animals, for instance, have to be of one sacred colour, and priests or officiating elders must abstain from sexual intercourse and certain foods or activities

---

[85] Ibid.
[86] Mbaegbu C.A., *Hermeneutics of God in Igbo Ontology*, op. cit., p. 231.

before and after the ritual. These ritual formalities clearly show that people regard God as holy.[87]

When offering a direct sacrifice to the Supreme Being known as "Aja Eze Enu" (sacrifice to the king of heaven) found in some towns in Igboland, the priest must be a good man, free from any abomination and honorably married. In every ritual celebration in which the Igbo find themselves before the throne of God for one reason or the other, they always manifest that deep sense of His holiness. Even the shrines where they make their sacrifices and offerings are pervaded by a feeling of holiness. Silence pervades, sandals or foot-wares must be left outside the shrines. "In fact, the idea of the holiness of God in Igbo traditional life and practice is likened to the Judaic sense of the holiness of God. The Arc of the Covenant was for the Jews a symbol of Yahweh's presence in his essential nature and attributes. Its power was formidable. Hence, the second Book of Samuel (2 Samuel 6:6) reports that Uzzah was struck dead for touching the Arc of the Covenant which according to the priestly code, can only be approached by the Levites when and only when it had been veiled by the priest and carried with poles which were never taken off it."[88]

The Igbo notion of holiness of God is also demonstrated by the fact that persons, places, objects dedicated to God must be clean and pure. At least, they must possess certain degree of holiness in order to be acceptable before God. Fundamental to Igbo conceptions of God is their deep-rooted sense of the holiness and sacredness of God. *Onweghi onye di ka Chukwu, mobu nwe onye yiri ya* (none is like God, neither is there His like).

1.7.4. THE ONENESS OF GOD AND THE PLURALITY OF THE DEITIES (UNITY IN DIVERSITY)

The Igbo have the notion of the oneness of God. They conceive God as being "one", "true", supreme or ultimate Being whom other gods serve. The belief in the existence of minor deities raises the question whether the Igbo worship them and at the same time worship the Supreme Being? We have discussed this issue earlier in this work but we are going to throw more light on it in another chapter. Mbaegbu would say that:

> For the Igbo, God is one. The existence of intermediary gods should not be conceived in terms of polytheism but in terms of God having many facets which seem to reflect Him into a multiplicity of being, a plurality but He is one. And among the traditional Igbo, belief in one God is grasped from their attrib-

---

[87] Mbiti J.S., *African Religions and Philosophy*, op. cit., p. 49.
[88] Mbaegbu C.A., *Hermeneutics of God in Igbo Ontology*, op. cit., p. 238.

uting creation to no other being except One Supreme God. Hence, the name Chukwu kere (God creates) is common to the Igbo people.[89]

If Mbaegbu means by the above statement that in Igbo Traditional Religion the Igbo people practise only monotheism, I would disagree with him on this point. If he means that the Igbo do not practise polytheism at all in Igbo Traditional Religion, I stand also to disagree with him. From all indications and from the facts before us, which we have demonstrated earlier in this work, in Igbo Traditional Religion, the Igbo practise both monotheism and polytheism. In this work we used the term "mono-polytheism" to qualify this practise. In the next chapter, we shall clarify more what we mean by "mono-polytheism" and why we took this position.

"Chukwu" – the Supreme Being is conceived all over Igboland as being unique and one. But the local deities are many. Thus:

> Each village may have up to five or more local deities. These local deities have shrines where sacrifices and feasts are held. They also have priests who minister to them. Priests offer regular prayer, offerings, maintain their temples and shrines and receive and celebrate sacrifices in their honor.[90]

What interpretation can one give to "sacrifice," "prayers" and "offerings" given to the deities if not worship? Nwala holds thus:

> No matter what other writers may say, polytheism (if it means belief in several gods) is practiced in the traditional Igbo society. However, all the local deities are not of equal importance and influence.[91]

If Nwala accepts the fact that the Igbo traditional religionists practise polytheism, it can also imply that they worship many gods. If the Igbo people worship their minor gods, what it means in effect is that they equally worship the Supreme Being – "Chukwu". This is because the minor gods are seen as the intermediaries between the Supreme Being – "Chukwu", and man.

It is pertinent to say that the local deities can be disposed of by their worshippers, that is, by any village in Igboland which holds any deity as its local deity. That village can equally import another deity in replacement for the deity it has disposed of. But in the case of the Supreme Being "Chukwu", He remains one and the only Supreme Being whom all must adore and worship. The gods are capable of good and bad. They are both benevolent and malevolent. They avenge wrongs done against their people and protect whatever is entrusted to

---

[89] Ibid., p. 227.
[90] Nwala T.U., *Igbo Philosophy,* op. cit., p. 170.
[91] Ibid., p. 169.

their care. But "Chukwu"– the Supreme Being is conceived in Igbo Traditional Religion as ever benevolent and loving. "From the hierarchy of beings in Igbo ontology, God's place in ritual practices as the ultimate recipient of all prayers and petitions made to the gods, one is enlightened more on the Igbo concept of God as one and unique."[92]

1.7.5. THE WORKS OF GOD

1.7.5.1. "CHUKWU" AS THE CREATOR AND SUSTAINER OF THE WORLD

The Igbo people acknowledge creation as God's hand-work. The idea of God as the creator is not a foreign or borrowed concept in Igboland. The names *Chi-na-eke* and *Ezechi-te-oke* given to the Supreme Being by the Igbo people express God's creative activity. The word *Chineke* is a popular creative name attributed to God as the Creator of the universe. The name *Olisa* is familiar in Western Igboland and it means the same thing as *Chineke*.[93] The full authority of *Chukwu* is brought out by the Igbo in their proverb thus: "Chukwu ji Ji jide mma, onye O wanyere o rie" (God has both the yam and knife, only those for whom He slices a piece can eat).

God is conceived as both the creator and sustainer of the world. As supporter of the universe, He continues to provide and sustain it. This fundamental belief of the Igbo in God's providence and sustenance of the universe finds expression in one of the principal natures of God, namely, "Osebuluwa" (God, bearer of the world). God as the principle of continued existence and dependence of all creatures causes sunshine and rainfall to illumine and water the earth respectively. He also gives fertility to creatures and causes life to increase and multiply.[94] The Igbo traditional practices like prayer before the breaking of kola-nut, announcing decisions of a tribunal, administration of oaths, even prayers of protest, are particular instances when an Igbo man expresses his unflinching belief in God as the source of continued survival, dependence and existence of all creatures.

1.7.6. GOD (CHUKWU) AS KING

The Igbo regard "Chukwu" as "Ezeigwe" (king of heaven or king that inhabits the heavens). Some Igbo describe "Chukwu" as "Eze bi n'igwe ogodo ya na-akpu n'ala" (literally this means God the great king in the heavens who lets the hemline of his kingly apparel touch the earth). "Ogodu Ikpu n'ala" in this con-

---

[92] Mbaegbu C.A., *Hermeneutics of God in Igbo Ontology,* op. cit., p. 121.
[93] Uchechukwu Dine, G.G., *Traditional Leadership as sample of African Democracy among the Igbo of Nigeria: Christian Evaluation;* Snaap Press, Nig. Ltd, Enugu, Nigeria,2007, p. 16.
[94] Mbaegbu C.A., *Hermeneutics of God in Igbo Ontology,* op. cit., p. 240.

text is rich in significance. It is a symbolic expression which shows that Chukwu's heavenly kingship and splendor also extend to the earth. The word "Eze" implies ruler in the sense of complete control.

For the Igbo, "Chukwu" is a Supreme divine King and just ruler. He can delegate his power to agents of spirits and human beings. "Chukwu" is regarded as the source of leadership values such as service, justice, truth and peace. The Igbo believe strongly in the strict and just prosecution of cases among them. This is done before the constituted authority in the communities. The judgments of situations or cases can be influenced by certain human limitations. Only "Chukwu" poses as the ultimate just judge.

1.7.7. THE RIGHTEOUSNESS AND JUSTICE OF GOD

"Chukwu" (the greatest spirit), "Ani" (the earth goddess) and "Ndi-Ichie" (the ancestors) are regarded by the Igbo as the custodians of morality. The earth goddess, the ancestors and sometimes "Ama-dioha" (the thunder god) are believed to punish every breach of morality, especially the grave ones. But "Chukwu" is regarded as the ultimate source and arbiter in moral issues. This is because the Igbo acknowledge that justice and righteousness are moral attributes of God. For them, god is righteous and just. They believe that God is the impartial judge who dispenses and punishes evil and has no favorite. He rewards the good and punishes the evil ones. He is just and right always. He is the highest and the only true judge because He is by nature Omniscient.[95]

"Chukwu" is justice itself, and therefore He is the only absolute reliable just judge. "Chukwu" sees everything, knows everything, including "ihe di n'obi mmadu" (what is in the hearts of men and what is outside of them) and this is why He is called "Onye ikpe nkwumoto" (the just judge). Nobody can deceive Him or hide facts from Him. When the Igbo say "Chukwu ga-ekpe" (God will judge), they have made the highest appeal to the highest judge.

There are some known traditional Igbo phrases that express the justice and righteousness of God: "Chukwu ji ofo" (God is right). "Ofo" as a central symbol of authority symbolizing the link between God and man, the dead and the living, is a symbol of justice, righteousness and truth. Hence, "Chukwu ji ofo" is another way of saying that God is right, just and truthful.

The Igbo do say: "Chukwu nwe obo." When subjected to analysis and interpretation this means that God as a just and righteous being will mete out due judgment for the evil and good deeds respectively. He punishes the evil and

---

[95] Mbaegu C.A., *Hermeneutics of God in Igbo Ontology,* op. cit., p. 233.

vindicates the right of the oppressed. "Chukwu nwe ugwo", that is, only God is just in giving adequate reward based on merit. With the Igbo deep sense of justice and righteousness of God, it is customary among them to invoke the name of God when taking oaths and announcing the decisions reached by the assembly of the elders. These expressions are common in traditional Igbo life and they express their deep-rooted belief in the justice and righteousness of God.

God in Igbo belief is a dreadful and fearful God whose anger can be aroused by peoples' manner of life that is not in consonance with the Igbo traditional moral standards. God is invoked against the evil doers, like thieves, immoral persons, desecrators of the land, and so on. Though God punishes evil persons, He does not, according to the Igbo, kill anyone unjustly. Only evil doers suffer His destructive retribution. It must be noted that the fearful and dreaded aspects of the Supreme Being do not in any way contradict the Igbo notion of His goodness. He remains essentially good but at the same time greatly feared and dreaded. The dreaded nature of God as conceived by the Igbo however stems from the Igbo idea of the sacredness and holiness of God.[96]

1.8. SPIRITS – DEITIES AND ANCESTORS IN IGBO TRADITIONAL RELIGION

1.8.1. BELIEF IN DEITIES

Some are of the opinion that the earlier descriptions and studies of African religions, Igbo Traditional Religion inclusive, left the people with terms which were inadequate, derogatory so to say and also prejudicial in describing African Traditional Religion (Igbo Traditional Religion). One of such terms is "animism".

Animism is a word derived from the Latin word "anima" meaning – breath, breath of life, and hence carries with it the idea of the soul or spirit. This term "animism" was first used by Tylor, an English anthropologist. He thought that the so-called "primitive people" imagined the animals to be capable of leaving their bodies and entering other men, animals or things, and continuing to live after death. Pursuing the theory further, Tylor, went on to say that such "primitive" men considered every object to have its own soul, thus giving rise to countless spirits in the universe.[97]

---

[96] Mbaegbu C.A., *Hermeneutics of God in Igbo Ontology,* op, cit., p. 237.
[97] Mbiti J.S., *African Religions and Philosophy*, op. cit., p. 9.

This term "animism" was widely used in describing traditional religions of Africa which later developed into another term "polytheism" used also in describing African religion (Igbo religion). Nwala argues that:

> No matter what other writers may say, polytheism if it means belief in several gods is practiced in the traditional Igbo society. However, all the local deities are not of equal importance and influence. In every village or town, there is a major deity with whom the destiny of the village or town is associated. Such a deity is the most influential and occupies a central position in the life, culture and activities of the town.[98]

The belief in Spirits and ancestors as the Igbo do have, does not rule out their belief in the Supreme Being - God. Oxford Advanced Learner's Dictionary 6th edition defines Polytheism as: "the belief that there is more than one god".[99]

Here, we talk of polytheism in comparison with monotheism. In this sense, the Igbo people believe in one Supreme God (Chukwu), but also worship the deities and venerate the ancestors. They do not regard the deities and the ancestors as having the same power or being in the same level with God, the Supreme Being. Therefore, one can rightly say that the Igbo people do not practise only polytheism but also monotheism.

1.8.1.1. THE ROLES OF THE DEITIES IN THE LIVES OF THE IGBO PEOPLE

In this work "alusi," "deities" and "gods" are used interchangeably. They mean one and the same thing in the religious thinking of the Igbo people. They cannot be separated without the danger of imposing foreign ideas on the Igbo Traditional Religion.

Apart from dependence on the deities by the Igbo traditionalists for their major needs such as fertility, security and necessities of life, the cult of deities in Igbo Traditional Religion exercises control over the daily affairs of the Igbo and ensures that there is a moral order especially obedience to the taboos and prescriptions usually associated with each particular deity.

Every major and mysterious happening or misfortune such as famine, disaster, death, sickness, drought, flood, etc. is attributed to the action of one deity or the other, as a retribution for an offence committed by some person(s) in the community. The gods (deities) are capable of good and bad. They are both benevolent and malevolent. "They avenge wrongs done against their people

---

[98] Nwala T.U., *Igbo philosophy, op. cit.,* 169.
[99] Cf. Oxford Advanced Learner's Dictionary of Current English, A.S Hornby, edited by Sally Wehmeier, Oxford University Press, N.Y, USA.

and protect whatever is entrusted to their care".[100] The deities are called "alusi" in Igbo Traditional Religion. There are two categories of "alusi" (deities), namely major and minor deities.

1.8.1.2. MAJOR DEITIES

These are non-human, non-personal spirits who were originally spirits and have never been human beings. They may be rightly referred to as "nnukwu alusi" (major deities) as opposed to "obele Alusi" (minor deities). The most important ones include: "Anyanwu" (the sun god), "Igwe" (the sky god), "Amadioha" (the thunder god) and "Ala" (the earth goddess).[101] These major deities are popular in Igboland.

1.8.1.3. MINOR DEITIES

These are gods whose activities are localized to villages, groups or families.

> They are gods believed to inhabit certain localities or natural features situated within the boundaries of the land owned by a community or group. Their abode may be a stream (water deities), a forest (forest deities), a cave (cave deities) or a grotto. Such gods become somewhat village or clan protectors, defending the interest of his servitors. It avenges itself of those who kill its servitors or rob them of their possessions when on an official journey.[102]

Examples of these local deities include: "Haba" in "Agulu". This deity is more popular in "Agulu" than in any other town. There is "Omaliko" in "Abatete" and so forth. Each village may have many minor deities. These local deities or gods have their local shrines where sacrifices and prayers are held. They have also individual priests who minister to these deities. The functions of these priests are to offer regular prayers, offerings to the deities when needed and to maintain the shrines of the deities. They also receive or offer sacrifices in honor of the deities. It is important to note here that "Chukwu" (God) is said to be the ultimate receiver of the prayers, or sacrifices being offered to these gods or deities. These deities are seen by the Igbo as the messengers of "Chukwu" (God). A good example to demonstrate that the Igbo worship the deities is the Long Juju of "Arochukwu". (Arochukwu is a town in Igboland).[103]

---

[100] Nwala T.U., *Igbo Philosophy,* op. cit., 170.

[101] Mbaegbu C.A., *Hermeneutics of God in Igbo Ontology,* op. cit., 181.

[102] Ezekwugo C.U.M., *Chi the true God in Igbo Religion*, Mar Mathews Press, Muvattupuzha, India, op. cit., p. 142, in Mbaegbu C.A., *Hermeneutics of God in Igbo Ontology,* op. cit., p. 179.

[103] The Long Juju was the notorious "Aro's" oracle placed at Arochukwu. It was the Igbo's greatest oracle whose shrine later became the court of appeal throughout Igboland. To it, the most serious internal and inter-group strifes were often referred at that time. This made the "Aro" very important in Igboland, an importance which was based on the universal respect of the

1.8.1.4. ORIGIN OF "ALUSI" (DEITIES)

There is a lot of controversies as regards the origin of deities. In some places they are called "alusi". Some people regard "alusi" (deities) as natural forces, while others regard them as man-made. Arazu quotes:

> But it is men who establish these deities in every town. Whatever the men select, they establish it to be their spirit. In every town, something is established and whatever is established, becomes the Alusi of that people. Whatever a people establish becomes Alusi for them.[104]

Mgbobukwa affirms this by asserting that:

> It should be noted that no alusi exists before any community that has it. It is the community that needs alusi that takes the necessary steps to get one.[105]

From the investigations made on this, one could discover that in some towns in Igboland some deities were established by their worshippers.[106] There is

---

people of Eastern Nigeria for the Long Juju, which some interpreted as "Chukwu" – the Igbo name for the Supreme Deity. The Long Juju resided in a lonely cave situated in the heart of "Aro" land. The control over the deity gave the "Aro" people a large measure of respect among the other people of the land. They became mediators between the people and the Long Juju. And the "Aro" territory soon became trading centre tainted with religious sanctions. It was they who could travel in the land without any molestation of being held to ransom. All other people from the rest of Igboland had the problem of travelling alone.

Since the shrine of the Long Juju was located on the main trading routes to the Delta region, the "Aro" rulers found the deity (the Long Juju) a convenient instrument for the maintenance of the community's discipline. Cf., *Isichei E., History of Western Africa since 1800,* op. cit., p. 103.

[104] Arazu R.C., Ezenwadeyi of Ihembosi, in Oguejiofor, The Influence of Igbo Traditional Religion on the Socio-Political Character of the Igbo, op. cit. p. 65.

[105] Mgbobukwa J., *Alusi, Osu and Ohu in Igbo Religion and Social Life,* Fulladu Publication Company, Nsukka, Nigeria, 1996, p. 11.

[106] What is rather shocking is that virtually all the powerful *alusi* in every community in Igboland today were sealed by the violent death of some innocent human beings. Below is an account of the two main ways by which most *alusi* in Igboland were instituted. An innocent boy and a virgin girl of about five years each are kidnapped and kept in a hidden hut, generally known as *ulo nkpa.* They are kept for two years. This is constructed with an underground and tower projecting to the surface. It is completely sealed up with little openings in the tower for light and air. When these kids are brought in, if as expected, they begin to cry, they are taken underground. Most of these kids were said to cry for two to three months before resigning to fate – expecting nothing but the worst.

After about two years, it is time for the ritual. A known *dibia* (traditional priest) is invited from some distant town to preside over the ritual for the community. The leaders of thought select the site for the *alusi.* A grave big enough to contain the two kids is dug. They are brought in, facing each other. They are tied together and lowered to the grave – the boy on the ground and the girl on top. Having been lowered to the grave alive, ash is mixed with water, and with that, the children are covered. The *dibia* then performs his ritual, placing the talisman (*ogwu*) on top of the moistened ash with which the kids are covered. He immediately stipulates the very things

another way through which an "alusi" can come into existence. Like the Greeks who deified their heroes at death, certain Igbo communities establish alusi (deities) at the death of some great men in the communities.

The Igbo Traditional Religion holds that the deities stand in a unique relationship with God – "Chukwu". Hence, it may not be proper to regard the deities as the agents of the devil and therefore, the rivals of God. "Igbo Traditional Religion teaches that the divinities are the children of God. One cannot say that they were created because one never hears of the creation of the divinities. In African (Igbo) Traditional Religion, it will be correct to say that the divinities were brought into being, or that they came into being in the nature of things with regard to the divine ordering of the universe."[107] Many Igbo tend to believe that "Chukwu", (God) brought "alusi" (deities) into existence so that they might be His messengers in carrying out, each in his own office the functions connected with the theocratic governance of the earth. Ezeanya asserts that:

> The Supreme God occupies an altogether unique place in the religious life of the African…. It is to Him alone that creation is attributed. He is the maker of all things, visible and invisible… all other things owe their origin to Him. It was He who made the minor divinities through whom He governs the universe. Though direct cult to Him is scarce in many parts of Africa, He nevertheless remains the Supreme Power that governs the world and sustains things in existence.[108]

---

that would, on a regular basis, be used as sacrifice to the *alusi*. The grave is then covered. In some places, halved ball-shaped mud of up to two feet is erected on top of it. In other places, the spot is roofed, seeds are planted around it, among which could be *ogilisi* and *abosi*. According to Nze Anika of Enugu-Ukwu this was how many of the notable deities in some areas of Igbo land came to be. Even though it is the community that owns the *alusi,* as soon as it starts being effective, the community becomes inferior to it. It is the function of the chief priest to offer sacrifices to the *alusi*. If, however, there is need to know the mind of the *alusi*, the services of a diviner are called for.

The second account is that a young man is either bought or kidnapped. A narrow but deep pit is dug where the shrine is expected to be sited. This young man has his legs tied to a piece of wood. He is then lowered alive into the pit with his head projecting into it and his legs on the surface. He continues to hang there until he is dead. As soon as this violent death has taken place, the *dibia* (the priests) performs his ritual and the place is covered up. As usual, certain objects are placed to mark it. According to Nwankwo C., of *Arondizuogu*, that was the way many of the deities in some parts of Imo and Abia states were made. Cf., Mgbobukwa J., *Alusi, Osu and Ohu in Igbo Religion and Social Life*, op. cit., pp. 11 and 12.

[107] Idowu, B., *African Traditional Religion: A Definition*, p. 169, in Quarcoopome T.N.O., *West African Traditional Religion*, op. cit., p. 70.

[108] Ezeanya S.N., *"Spirit, God and Spirit World"*, *Biblical Revelation and African Beliefs*, in Kwesi Dickson and Paul Ellingweorth (eds.), New York, Mary-Knoll; Orbis Books, 1969, p. 30 - 46, in

The Igbo believe in the power of "alusi" and their ability to help or harm man. Nevertheless, their primary purpose is to procure benefits to man, either individually or as a community. It is very clear to the Igbo that the "alusi" (deities) do not function in isolation from God, (Chukwu). "They came into being to fulfil specific functions and through them people relate to God. They are, thus, intermediaries and immediate objects of worship."[109] Using the words of Idowu, "the deities are means to an end", as "half-way houses" to God Himself who is an ever-present, immanent reality in African traditional belief.[110]

Some non-Igbo commentators refer to the reverence and honour given to the divinities by the Igbo traditional religionists as idolatry. "Far from being the objects of idolatry, the divinities or traditional gods are in a father/son relationship with God; this is the belief Igbo traditionalists have. The deities have derived powers and are functionaries in the theocratic governance of the world."[111]

1.8.2. THE CULT OF THE ANCESTORS IN IGBO TRADITIONAL RELIGION

Apart from belief in the Supreme Being (Chukwu) and the Deities, belief in the Ancestors forms one of the pillars of belief in Igbo Traditional Religion.

1.8.2.1. WHO ARE THE ANCESTORS?

The ancestors are the forefathers of the Igbo communities, who have lived their lives well here on earth and are now in the spirit land, where they are welcomed. "They are not wandering restless ghosts".[112] They are called "ndi mbu na ndi egede" (the first and the second people; that is those of antiquity).

The ancestors, those who are really treated as *Ndichie* (titled men), were married and had children. The cult of ancestors includes a person's dead father, dead great-grand-father and so on. It includes mainly male parents, since female parents are seldom so revered.[113]

The ancestors are the souls of the departed heroes and heroines of the Igbo. Belief in the ancestors is based on the general notion that life continues after death and that communion and communications are possible between those

---

Nwoga D.I., *The Supreme God as Stranger in Igbo Religious Thought,* Ekwereazu, Hawk Press, 1984, p. 69.
[109] Opoku K.S*., West African Traditional Religion*, Kucena Damian Ltd, 1978, Awka, Nigeria, p. 73.
[110] Idowu B.E., *African Traditional Religion, A Definition*, op. cit., p. 173.
[111] Quarcoopome, T.N.O., *West African Traditional Religion,* op. cit., p. 70.
[112] Arinze F., *Sacrifice in Igbo Traditional Religion,* op. cit., p. 34.
[113] Nwala T.U., *Igbo Philosophy,* op. cit., p. 171.

who are alive here on earth and the deceased. The ancestors are believed to have power to influence the affairs of the living for better or for worse.

Generally, the Igbo people believe that, after death, the departed ones enter into a spiritual state of existence. The dead are believed to have the capability of being everywhere, at any time. Although they are dead, nevertheless they are living, but are in another kind of existence. It is germane to say that the ancestors are never worshipped by the Igbo rather:

> The ancestors are always revered and held esteem. In fact, after God who is the final authority in all matters, the one who is pre-eminent in all things, the ancestors come next in importance. All other spiritual beings may be spoken ill of or even ridiculed on occasion, but God and the ancestors are always held in awe.[114]

1.8.2.2. WHAT QUALIFIES ONE TO BE AN ANCESTOR?

Those who belong to the noble cult of the ancestors are those who have fulfilled the conditions required for this noble status. This means that not every dead person may qualify to be revered as an ancestor. The ancestral cult includes mainly the dead male parents, since female parents are seldom so revered.

A person's condition in this world and the manner of his death determine his entry into the ranks of the revered group of ancestors who form the back-bone of Igbo societies. Therefore, to become an ancestor one must have lived a life worthy of emulation, an exemplary life. One must also have lived to a ripe old age and had children. A person who dies childless is not acknowledged as an ancestor. He is believed not to have fulfilled the purpose for which he was created. "To become an ancestor, one must also have died a good death; one's death must not have been due to accident, suicide, or any form of violence. One's death must also not have be caused by such unclean diseases as lunacy, dropsy, leprosy and epilepsy."[115]

Ikenga-Metuh affirms the above assertions. He states:

> Death by suicide, accident, leprosy, dropsy, small-pox, epilepsy etc. are regarded as bad deaths. Victims of such deaths are not given the full funeral rites, and consequently cannot become ancestors.[116]

---

[114] Opoku K.A., *West African Traditional Religion,* op. cit., p. 36.
[115] Exceptions may be made in cases of heroic deaths in defense of one's community or society, but if it is found that one died while running away from battle or retreating ignominiously from the enemy, then one is obliterated from historical memory. Cf., Opoku K.A., ibid., p. 36.
[116] Metuh-Ikenga, E., *God and Man in African Religion;* Geoffrey Chapman, 1981, p. 85.

Other conditions that qualify one to be admitted into the cult of the ancestors are: "The individual must be successful, and his success is shown in his having a wife and children, especially male child and enough material possession. These conditions must be accompanied by a befitting burial. It is with this burial ceremony that the dead is received in the land of the spirits by his ancestors".[117]

On the other hand, there are conditions that disqualify one from gaining admittance into the company of the ancestors. The opposite of the conditions that qualify one disqualify one and in addition to the following: Those who died leaving nothing on earth (*enwe nta enwe imo*), those who died young, and those who for certain reasons were not given befitting burial. They are excluded from the company of the ancestors. These people are banished to a certain non-descript limbo, like the situation between the dead and the living *(ama ndi mmuo na mmadu)*. Such people do not reincarnate. But the persons accepted into the land of the spirits merit reincarnation and live out another cycle of life. We shall later discuss reincarnation in this work.

It appears also that there are those who although they are not strictly qualified in the way described above may be admitted into the spirit world of the deceased. This is because they were good and their days on earth are done, even though they may be young and childless.[118] For example, a young man who died a heroic death; who died for the cause of promoting or defending the interest of the community or the life of any of its members also joins the ancestral cult. This may be likened to the notion of martyrdom in Christianity.

1.8.2.3. WHY ARE THE ANCESTORS SO REVERED AND HONOURED BY THE IGBO?

Old age is highly respected by the Igbo. In Igbo culture, the ancestors are highly respected and venerated because they have gone through this path of life which we are now passing through. They are living in two worlds, world of the living and world of the spirits. Therefore, they know more than the living. The Igbo believe also that the ancestors are closer to God than the living. If we are to make an analogy here, the ancestors are revered and honored the way the Christians honour their saints. The Igbo sometimes ask their ancestors to inter-

---

[117] Oguejiofor J., *The Influence of Igbo Traditional Religion on the Socio-Political Character of the Igbo*, op. cit., p. 80.

[118] In certain areas of Igboland, belief in the continued existence and influence of this category of deceased person is symbolized in "Mmuo" (spirit), which are various manifestations of the fact that those who have passed into the spirit world of the departed members of the community are still a part of the social structure. Cf., Idowu B.E., *African Traditional Religion, a Definition*, op. cit., p. 187.

cede for them before God just like the way the Christians do pray to the saints to intercede for them before God.

The dead do not sever their links with their kinsmen but continue to be members of their individual families and keep on fulfilling their obligations in their families. "The relationship between the dead and the living is symbiotic as each group has a part for mutual benefit. The dead still show a keen interest in the affairs of the living and the living in turn have a duty towards the dead. The African family (Igbo family), therefore, has a supernatural dimension to it, for it is made of the living and the dead, both of whom have specific roles to play in the maintenance of the family and the society in general".[119] The roles of the ancestors are succinctly described thus:

> They return to their human families from time to time and share meals with them, however, symbolically. They know and have interest in what is going on in their families.... They are guardians of family affairs, traditions, ethics and activities. Offence in these matters is ultimately an offence against the forefathers who, in that capacity act as invisible police of the families and communities.[120]

The ancestors are invoked in prayers. Before starting to eat or drink, the devout Igbo traditionalist throws out a portion of his food or drink to his ancestors. The Igbo recognize always the presence of the ancestors in family gatherings. It is believed that the ancestors join their various families in their festivities. In return, the ancestors are expected to work hard for the benefit of the living. Possessed now of more spiritual powers, they are the closest link that man has with the spirit world.

1.8.2.4. THE BELIEF IN, AND THE VENERATION OF THE ANCESTORS, THE INTERPRETATIONS GIVEN TO IT AND WHAT IT PORTRAYS ABOUT THE IGBO PEOPLE

The belief in, and the veneration of the ancestors indicate a strong convention of the Igbo in the continuation of life after death. It also indicates that the Igbo believe that the dead continue to live and remain members of their families, clans and societies. Thus, human relationships cannot be broken, for not even death can cut off relations with one's relatives. They also show that obligation in Igbo society is unending, for it continues after death through time. The dead are expected to protect and guard the living, and as it is believed that death increases one's powers, the dead are able to offer more help or assistance.

---

[119] Opoko K.A., *West African Traditional Religion,* op. cit., p. 37.
[120] Cf., Mbiti J.S., *African Religions and Philosophy,* op. cit., p. 178, Arinze F., *Sacrifice in Igbo Traditional Religion,* op. cit., p. 35, Opoku K. A., *West African Traditional Religion,* op. cit., p. 37.

It is generally believed in Igboland that a living father or a living mother, by virtue of his fatherhood or motherhood, is endowed with the power to bless or curse an offspring effectively. That is why every passage of life and every undertaking by the offspring requires parental blessing. It is believed that parental dissatisfaction or displeasure may upset an undertaking or cause it to fail. It is no wonder, then, that it is believed that such power in a father or a mother who has passed into the ancestral world has become infinitely enhanced and continues to be actively effective accordingly.[121]

The ancestral beliefs also give concrete expression to the Igbo idea of community. For the Igbo, to be a human being is to belong to a community and to do so is to participate in the rituals, ceremonies and other activities of the community. The ancestors form the supernatural part of the human community in the world. Hence, this unseen part of the community is never left out in any communal activity and their participation is always sought. However, those who had bad deaths and those who, for various reasons, are not regarded as members of the revered group of ancestors are outside the communities. "The Igbo believe that their ancestors are deeply concerned by what happens in their families."[122] The belief also bears clear evidence of the firm acceptance of the return of the dead. Reincarnation is therefore an accepted fact.

The ancestral beliefs act as a form of social control by which the conduct of individuals is regulated. The constant reminder of the good deeds of the ancestors acts as a spur to good conduct on the part of the living. The belief that the ancestors would punish anyone who goes contrary to the morals and ethical customs of the society also acts as a motivation for good conduct. Ancestral beliefs, therefore, represent a powerful source of moral sanction, for they affirm the values upon which society is based.

1.8.2.5. IS IT PROPER TO USE THE TERM "ANCESTOR-WORSHIP" IN REFERRING TO THE CULT OF THE ANCESTORS IN IGBO TRADITIONAL RELIGION?

Oxford Advanced Learner's Dictionary, 6th Edition defines the term "worship" as: "the practice of showing respect for God or a god, by saying prayers, singing with others, etc."[123]This definition is a literal one and does not reflect well

---

[121] Idowu B.E., *African Traditional Religion, a Definition,* op. cit., p. 185.

[122] Everything that concerns the family, its health and fertility are of interest to the ancestors, since they are its elders and will also seek rebirth into the same family. The family land is their property, and they must be consulted when land is let out to other people. Cf., Parrinder E.G., *African Traditional Religion, 3rd* ed., op. cit., p. 59.

[123] Oxford Advanced Learner's Dictionary 6th ed., op. cit.

what we mean here. The word "worship" can have more than one meaning. For example, one can say: This woman worships her husband. This means that she has an extraordinary respect for her husband. In the case of a human being we can use the word respect but the proper word one should use in reference to God is worship. Although we respect God as the creator of all that exists, He deserves more than respect. Adoration is another word that fits into the meaning of what we have in mind here.

Do the Igbo worship their ancestors? Some people have made use of this term "ancestor-worship" without fully understanding the meaning of the term. An aspect of the cult of the ancestors which has attracted many comments is the attention paid to them, as well as the attitude towards them. The charge is that these things constitute worship. "To some extent this claim is justified for undoubtedly there are elements in the relationship and attitude of the Igbo towards their ancestors that look like real worship. These are the offering of prayers and sacrifices."[124]

I observe that the problem lies in the misinterpretation of the actions of the Igbo people by foreigners who regarded the veneration given to the ancestors as "idol worship" (*ife arusi*). This is because they did not understand the mindset of the Igbo and their cosmology. "At the individual level there are prayers that accompany libation and offering made to the ancestors. People ask for fertility (children), food, life, prosperity, peace and so on and so forth. From the Christian point of view this sense of dependence on the ancestors is worship in so far as the ancestors are looked upon as the source of life." [125]

This interpretation is wrong because the Igbo never regard their ancestors as the source of life. They regard God as the source of life – the creator of everything that exists (*Chineke*). It must be noted that in the traditional cosmology, the ancestors dispense things on behalf of God. They are the immediate representatives and intermediaries of God, and so to the living, they are some sort of big brothers. Nwala states that:

> By the divinity of the ancestors, we mean the reverence and adoration shown to them on account of their supposed supernatural powers. Indeed, in Igbo traditional society, ancestors and dead parents are revered and worshipped[126]

In another place, Nwala contradicted himself by positing:

---

[124] Quarcoopome T.N.O., *West African Traditional Religion*, op. cit., p. 131.
[125] Ibid., pp. 131 - 132.
[126] Nwala T.U., *Igbo Philosophy,* op. cit., p. 171.

> The ancestors act as intermediaries between their living children and the deities. They help to protect their living descendants, intervene on their behalf to ensure that no harm is done to them. In times of difficulties or sickness, you hear an Igbo man calling on his dead father and saying nna anyi ekwela – (our fathers do not allow this to happen).[127]

One begins to wonder what Nwala actually means here by these two words: "worship" and "intermediaries". If the ancestors are actually worshipped, they should not act as intermediaries between the living and the deities. Idowu clarifies this issue by stating that "those who set up the cult of ancestors inside Churches are careful not to use the term 'worship' they choose 'veneration' instead."[128]

The use of the wrong term in describing the cult of the ancestors can be misleading, especially to foreign investigators. It is wrong to say that the Igbo worship their ancestors. "The cult of ancestors does not represent entirely nor replace religion in Igbo Traditional Religion."[129] Although offerings, prayers and petitions may be offered to the ancestors that does not mean that they are being worshipped. Offerings, prayer and petition signify here veneration and not worship. The cult of the ancestors in Igbo Traditional Religion could be analogous to the cult of the saints in Christianity. People strive to live a good life in order to qualify for such an exalted status.

The ancestors are not worshipped in the way the Igbo worship God. They are not the final authority in all matters, nor are they given the same attributes as the creator. They are, however, revered, honoured and respected, not as gods but as spirits and elders and predecessors, who have trodden the path we are now treading. They are regarded as spirits who are not creator. This then is the spirit in which the Igbo regard their ancestors who form part and parcel of their society and whose continuous involvement in the activities of the Igbo people demonstrates in no uncertain terms, the indissoluble union which exists between the living and the dead.

In Igboland, different families erect or build shrines for their ancestors. The shrines are called "Ihu-Ndi-Ichie". During festivals in honour of the ancestors, fowls are killed in large numbers on the shrine of the ancestors. Normally, these shrines are built in front of the house. It is the responsibility of the oldest

---

[127] Ibid., p. 172.
[128] Cf., Idowu B.E., *African Traditional Religion, a Definition,* op. cit., p. 180.
[129] Onwubiko O., *Wisdom Lectures on African Thought and Culture,* Totan Publishers, Owerri, Nigeria, 1988, p. 55.

surviving members of various families to supervise the shrines and offer sacrifices to the ancestors when necessary.

Below is a typical Igbo traditional morning prayer (from the North-Western Igboland). In this prayer the worship of God, deities and the veneration of the ancestors are reflected.

Chineke (Ezechitoke)	-	Creator - God
Ekene.	-	greetings.
Ani,	-	land (deity)
Ekene.	-	greetings.
Igwe,	-	Sky deity
Ekene.	-	greetings.
Taa nu oji.	-	Take kola-nut, all.
Ogbuefi nna m,	-	Ogbuefi, my father,[130]
Ononenyi	-	"Onenenyi",[131]
Taa nu oji.	-	take kola-nut all.
Onu kwulu njo,	-	The mouth that speaks evil,
Gbaghalu.	-	forgive.
Mmefie adi,	-	If there be no offence,
mgbaghalu ama adi.	-	there will be no forgiveness.
Anyi na ayo ndu na nka,	-	We ask for life and old age,
na mbosi oma,	-	and for a good day.
Tata bu Eke,	-	Today which is *Eke* day,
nye anyi olili na onunu,	-	give us eating and drinking,
nye anyi omumu,	-	give us children,
di ji na di ede.	-	and rich harvest.

---

[130] "Ogbuefi" is a name of an ancestor.
[131] "Ononenyi" refers to an ancestor.

Okafor be'm,	-	May my son, Okafor,
ka o muta nwa nwoke,	-	beget a son,
kpata ago,	-	and get money.
Ka ndi be ya fekwaa ya,	-	May his children serve him,
ka o si fe m.	-	as he has served me.
Ka ndi na ekwulu m mma,	-	Both those who speak good of me,
ka ndi na ekwulu m njo,	-	and those who speak evil of me,
ife onye n'elolu madu,	-	as a person plans for others,
ka Chineke n'elolu ya.	-	so God plans for him.
Onye si Okafor be m	-	If anyone says my son, Okafor
amutana nwa,	-	shall beget no child,
nwa nke ya amutana	-	let his own son get none.
Onye si ani be m pue ata	-	Whoever says my compound grow spear grass
nke be ya pue elo	-	let his own grow fungus.
Obialu egbum, gbue onwe ya!	-	Let he who comes to kill me kill himself!
Ochu okuko nwe ada	-	The chaser of the fowl has the falling.
Onye m na emejoro	-	A person whom I have not offended,
O na eme m,	-	and he continues to offend me,
nya adinalu ya mma!	-	let it not fare well with him!
Onye si m nwua,	-	If anyone tells me to die
nya bulu Okuko uzo nakpue ula	–	Let him go to bed before the fowls!
Egbe belu, ugbo belu,	-	Let the kite perch, let the eagle perch,
nke si ibe ya ebena,	-	whichever says that the other must not perch,
nku kwaa ya!	-	let its wings break![132]

---

[132] Echiegu A.O., *Igbo and its Rhetoric, vol. 3,* op. cit., pp. 42 - 43.

1.9. THE CONCEPT OF MADU (HUMAN BEING) IN IGBO ONTOLOGY

"Madu" (human being) is one of the categories of Igbo ontology. The physical world of the Igbo is the domain of "Madu" (human beings) and "Ihe" – things. The nature of man in Igbo Traditional Religion is that he is both physical and spiritual being. The physical determines his ancestry and right of inheritance whilst the spiritual part links him with God. The spiritual part, the soul, is immortal and is connected with the destiny of man. Human being as a generic term includes both men and women in their differing qualitative characteristics. These are within the category of "Madu" (human beings).

In Igbo ontology, man is said to be endowed with a dual nature, namely body and soul. The implication is that man as man is capable of higher metaphysical operations. He has rational knowledge and understanding characteristics which brute, inanimate and animate realities popularly classified as "Ihe" (things) do not possess. Body and spirit meet in the human self or person and in concrete human life. Neither the body nor the spirit can be present alone. The essence of living self or person is that he is made up of body and spirit. Only in this way, he is a living human person who belongs to the category – "Madu" (human being).[133]

We have to note that the two principles that make up "Madu" (human being), namely matter and spirit must be conceived as complementary unit. They are not to be conceived as working in isolation from one another. "Madu" (human being) "refers to both the living and those about to be born."[134]

In traditional Igbo thought, man is conceived as both spirit and non-spirit. Man possesses two main parts "muo" (spirit) and "ahu" (body). The Igbo people believe that man is one of God's creatures. Etymologically, the Igbo word for human being (Madu) comes from two Igbo words – "Mma" which means "beauty" and "Ndu" which means "life". Therefore, the Igbo understand man (human being) as the beauty of life, "mma-ndu" in short form – "Madu", which means also the beauty of creation or the apex of creation. According to Okolo, human beings assume an enviable position in Igbo ontology. He says that man:

> Rightly claims a central and strategic position in the hierarchy of beings since the interactions and intercommunications between the visible created order and the invisible world of God, spirits, ancestors are only possible through him. He is therefore the ontological mean between beings existing above and below him. In this respect, man (human beings) in the African (Igbo) world-

---

133 Mbaegbu C.A., *Hermeneutics of God in Igbo Ontology, op.* cit., p. 139.
134 Nwala T.U., *Igbo Philosophy,* op. cit., p. 57.

view is the center of creation with intimate and personal relationships with beings above and below him.[135]

Man, in Igbo Traditional Religion is seen as a synthesis of all that is good in creation. Christians refer to human being as steward of creation, created by God in His own image and likeness. Man is superior to other created beings. Likewise, the Igbo believe in this idea of the superiority of man to other created beings. However, in Igbo Traditional Religion, we have categories of "Madu" (human being).

1.9.1. THE IGBO ONTOLOGICAL HIERARCHY OF "MADU" (HUMAN BEING)

Mbaegbu makes a distinction between ontological definition and qualitative characteristics of "Madu" (human being). He holds that:

> Ontologically, all men are rational beings and by this ontological definition all men are ontologically equal. On the other hand, qualitatively, that is, in terms of possession of certain qualities and powers for which human beings are accorded greater respect, honor and even dignity than the rest of human beings, all men by this qualitative characteristic are not equal. With these two distinctions, we recognize that the essence of human being is rationality. This is what makes man what he is. This is shared by all human beings and it makes all human beings ontologically equal. And so, we lay down the hierarchical order of all categories of human beings basing it on character, talents, functions, roles power, status, primogeniture (order of birth) and usefulness to the community.[136]

Nwala does not distinguish between ontological and qualitative characteristics of "madu" (human being) as Mbaegbu did. Therefore, for Nwala:

> All human beings are not ontologically equal. Some possess certain attributes, power and influences which far surpass others. These earn them greater respect, honor and even fear.[137]

I tend to disagree with Nwala here. If all men are not ontologically equal, it means that they were not created equal. This leads us into the problem of discrimination among human beings which we may not like to discuss here. "The traditional Igbo world, is a world in which many forces abound. The man who understands these forces and who can manipulate them as to influence the actions of the orders of beings, can also influence the lives and affairs of

---

[135] Okolo C.B., *Problems of African Philosophy and other Essays,* Enugu, Nigeria, Cecta, Nig. Ltd., 1993, pp. 23-24 in Mbaegbu C.A., *Hermeneutics of God in Igbo Ontology*, op. cit., p. 131.
[136] Mbaegbu C. A., *Hermeneutics of God in Igbo Ontology*, op. cit., p. 132.
[137] Nwala T.U., *Igbo Philosophy,* op. cit., p. 64.

his fellow human beings. Hence, such a man is held in respect and awe."[138]For example, "Ndi eze muo" (the traditional priests), "the Dibia Afa" (diviners) and "Ndi dibia Ogwu" (medicine men) are regarded as being on the top of the ladder in the ontological hierarchy. These are followed by "Ndi Okenye" (Elders), "Ndi Ogaranya" (the wealthy titled men), "Ndi Efu" (Ordinary men), "Ndi Ogbenye" (the poor men).[139] These are followed by "Umunwanyi or Ndi-iyom" (women) and "Di nalota uwa" (The unborn or those about to be born). These follow sequentially in the ontological order of hierarchy.[140]

1.9.2. LIFE (*NDU*) AS THE ULTIMATE GOOD AND GOAL OF MAN IN IGBO ONTOLOGY

The Igbo generally see life as a continuous process, as a process which does not come to an end. We shall explain this further when we discuss "reincarnation" in Igbo Traditional Religion. Nwala defines "life" (*Ndu*) from Igbo point of view as "a dynamic quality, reflecting material, social, moral and spiritual essence."[141] Igbo people cherish life. The Igbo say: "Ndu bu isi" (Life is supreme). "Ndu ka aku" (Life is greater than wealth). "Obu onye di ndu na acho ihe oga eme" (It is the one who is alive that looks for something to do). "Obu onye di ndu nwere nchekwube" (It is the person that is alive that has hope). This belief in the supremacy of life to other things is reflected or seen in all that the Igbo man does. It is reflected in his religion, in his security consciousness, in his social life even in the philosophy and culture of the Igbo. This is reflected also in Igbo idioms and proverbs. "For the Christians, the most general value or the highest good is union with God, for classical philosophers, it is wisdom. But for the Igbo traditionalists, it is Ndu (life)."[142]

Life has many dimensions. One can talk of the individual, communal, private, social, material, moral and spiritual life. When one talks about individual dimension of life, one refers not only to one's physical life, but this has to do with one's family, child or children, most especially male child, in the case of a man. When one does not have a child and dies in this condition, the Igbo believe that this person has not fulfilled the purpose for which he was created. It is an insult and a curse to say to someone in Igboland "onu ama gi chie." This

---

[138] Ibid., p. 64.
[139] The Igbo word "Ogbenye" (the Poor) is etymologically a combination of two words "Ogbe" which means "community" and "nye" which means "to give" or to "cater for". Hence, "Ogbenye" (the poor), in Igbo traditional setting and understanding means, a person who cannot cater for himself, who cannot feed or cloth himself etc., not because he is not bodily fit to do so. But because he is financially incapacitated. So, the "Ogbe" (the community) caters for him.
[140] Ibid., pp. 64-65.
[141] Ibid., p. 199.
[142] Ibid., p. 197.

literally means: "may your lineage ceases to exist." Or to say to a village or town "ka obodo unu chie" (let your village ceases to exist).

Therefore, the moral and spiritual dimensions of an individual's life (ndu), is measured in terms of how well and effective he fulfills his role as a man, according to his age and status in life. Generally, a man is said to be alive (o di ndu), if he has a family, capable of taking care of his family, can have children, (able to put his wife in the family way), has a visible barn if he is a farmer and physically active in doing that for which he is known. Such a man is said to be alive (*o di ndu*), or that he is a man, (*o bu nwoke*).[143]

We have to note here that the Igbo people detest individualism. The Igbo say: "ofu osisi adighi eme ofia." (One tree does not make a forest). Therefore, the life of the group, however, is regarded as of prior importance to the life of an individual. This is mainly because the individual is part of the group and his survival depends on conditions which only the group can guarantee. Hence, the Igbo say "Umunna bu ike" (kinsmen are strength).

1.9.3. "NDU OMA", "EZIGBO NDU" (GOOD LIFE) FROM IGBO RELIGIOUS/CULTURAL BACKGROUND

The Igbo people evaluate life not only from the spiritual point of view or moral, but also from the material point of view. The material and moral conditions of a person determine whether he has good life or not. If a person is able to fulfill his moral obligations as well as material obligations, then, he has a good life.

1.9.4. MATERIAL OBLIGATIONS

When a man has material means for his sustenance and that of his family and can do what other men do, both physically and financially, then he is said to have good life. When a man fails in these areas, the goodness of his life is in question. However, a man is blameworthy in this way if he is lazy, unambitious, does not strive to better his lot. If the failure is not his fault, then, he deserves sympathy. His kinsmen will ask the elders of the land to seek the help of diviners to find out the cause and how to overcome it. Meanwhile, he would deserve all the support he needed, the welfare support of modern decent societies, from his kinsmen.

The Igbo abhor suffering. "Suffering is not a positive value in Igbo traditional ethics. The Igbo people strive to possess the basic material necessities of life as well as to attain a good measure of social well-being. This does not amount to

---

[143] Ibid., p. 199.

pleasure-loving or hedonism."[144] On the other hand "individual achievements must have social significance."[145] Hence, the benefits of one's achievement must be enjoyed by his kinsmen. That is to say, one's individual achievements must have communal significance. This is all the more reasonable since the wealth of any person in such an extended family system must have been created through communal labour.

1.9.5. MORAL OBLIGATIONS

Moral obligation is summarized in the Igbo proverb that says: "onye ya na chi ya di na mma, ugbo ya na eme ofuma". Literally translated as (when a man is at peace with the gods and his ancestors, his harvest will be always rich).

To be at peace with the gods and the ancestors, entails living an upright life, fulfilling one's religious obligations, respecting and observing the social values as enjoined by the community and as enshrined in "Omenala" (tradition).[146]

1.10. "OGWU" (CHARMS, AMULET AND TALISMAN) IN IGBO TRADITIONAL RELIGION

Discussion on charms (amulets and talisman) cannot be omitted in this work. This is because in Igbo Traditional Religion, charms play a great role in the lives of the people. "Ogwu" is the general name in Igbo for charms, which includes amulet and talisman. Le Roy, defines "Ogwu" (charm) as:

> An object which, by some mysterious, immanent and unconscious power, is believed to preserve the bearer from evil, diseases, bullets or motor accidents, or to make one succeed in trade, in love affair, in fishing, in catching thieves, in passing examinations, etc.[147]

No understanding of the Igbo world-view is complete without understanding their conception of "ogwu" (charm). "Ogwu" may be interpreted as force, vital energy or mystical power. It is usually linked with medical, magical and witchcraft activities. All the various manifestations and forms of energy or force discovered by modern science, such as physical, chemical, electrical, thermodynamics, field of energy, remote control, pharmaceutical, psychological, etc.,

---

144 Nwala T.U., *Igbo Philosophy,* op. cit., p. 201.

145 Adibe G., *Igbo Issues: Values, Chi, Akala Aka, Ikenga, Magic, Agwu and Manipulation of divinities,* op. cit., p. 11.

146 *Omenani,* literally translated, means that which obtains in the land or community, according to the custom and social traditions of the community. That which obtains in the community means also that which is natural in the traditional Igbo world. Cf., Nwala T. U., *Igbo Philosophy,* op. cit., p. 77.

147 Le Roy A., *La Religion des Primitifs,* Paris, 1909, p, 272, in *Arinze F., Sacrifice in Igbo Traditional Religion,* op. cit., p. 38.

which are beyond the empirical knowledge of the traditional Igbo are treated as mystical manifestations of the activities of spiritual forces as well as "Ogwu".[148]

The early European missionaries who were first to visit Igboland were seen then as "spirits". The Igbo say "beeke bu agbara"- which means literally, that "the white man is a spirit." The European was regarded this way by the Igbo because of his seemingly superior ability to manipulate the forces of the universe. Hence, he does what an ordinary person cannot do. Therefore, he is not ordinary human being like others. Chinua Achebe captures this situation well in his famous novel "Things Fall Apart".[149]

For the purpose of this study, I would like to make distinction between, on the one hand, "Ogwu" in reference to charms for healing, prevention, protection that can enhance achievement and, on the other hand, "Ogwu" in reference to witchcraft, (black magic) and as instrument of aggression. It is pertinent that we make distinctions between these two polarities.

1.10.1. CHARM AS SOMETHING POSITIVE (AMULET AND TALISMAN)

Some charms are used for healing, protection, prevention or simply to enhance achievement. They are not used as an instrument of destruction. When an Igbo man finds it difficult to explain certain events, he may ascribe it to the power of "ogwu" (charms). For example, in the case of the early missionaries in Igboland who defiled "evil forest" (hitherto regarded as the den of powerful spirits) and went on to build their Church there, yet they incurred no harm. They did not die and their members were not affected in anyway. Many Igbo believed then that the missionaries possessed a very powerful "ogwu" (charms) with which they protected themselves from the danger of the "evil spirits".

---

148 Nwala T.U., *Igbo Philosophy,* op. cit., p. 87.

149 Every clan and village in "Igboland" had its "evil forest". In it were buried all those who died of evil diseases, like leprosy and smallpox. It was also the dumping ground for the potent fetishes of great medicine men when they died. An "evil forest" was, therefore, alive with sinister forces and powers of darkness. It was such a forest that the rulers of *Mbanta* gave to the missionaries. They did not really want them in their clan, and so they made them the offer which nobody in his right senses would accept. And to their greatest amazement the missionaries thanked them and burst into song. Everybody in *Mbanta* expected that the missionaries will die once they enter the evil forest. They did enter it. But what happened? The first day passed and the second and third and fourth, and none of them died. Everyone was puzzled. And then it became known that the white man's fetish (charms) had unbelievable power. It was said that he wore glasses on his eyes so that he could see and talk to evil spirits. Cf., Achebe C., *Things Fall Apart*, Pearson Education Limited England and Wales, 2008, pp. 119 -120.

The early natives who acquired the western habits, education and powers were believed to have acquired the white man's "ogwu" or mystical powers.[150] Therefore, one can rightly conclude that the concept of "ogwu" in Igbo traditional setting is used to explain events and happenings that appear strange and mysterious to the Igbo mind. On the contrary, if a man is unable to do the things which he normally does, failed in his pursuit, endeavours or has a technical hitch on man's way of being successful, some Igbo may attribute that to the power of charms by the enemies. Hence, in order not to be affected by these dangers planted by the so-called enemies of progress, some Igbo protect themselves with talisman and amulet (charms). How effective these things are, is not our concern here.

Arinze outlines some elements that indicate the religiosity of "ogwu". "They are generally prepared by *dibia* or diviners who may also be, and in many cases, are priests. In their preparation, sometimes sacrifices are made." [151]

"Ogwu" is also used as curative measure for treatment of various human ailments and for countering the effect of another dangerous "ogwu" or poison. "Ogwu" is a general name for medicines which are used for treatment of various illnesses. The name applies also to talisman and amulet used for protecting oneself. The name "Ogwu" also applies to black magic used as instrument of aggression.

1.10.2. "OGWU" (CHARMS) AS INSTRUMENT OF AGGRESSION

This is where magic belongs. Evil magic involves the belief in and practice of tapping and using this power to do harm to human beings or to their property. Here we find sorcery at work, in addition to other related practices.[152]

1.10.3. THE CONTENT OF CHARMS

A typical "ogwu" preparation may contain a combination of several things such as herbs, roots, leaves (burnt, boiled, or just cut into bits and put into wine or water), animal blood, feathers, chalk, egg, lizard, chicken and goat parts or the part of any other animal, bones, sand, water, wine, oil, fresh palm leaf, "ogirisi" plant, pieces of cloth, even human parts such as hairs, nail, clippings, salt,

---

[150] It was for this reason that several legends grew around Dr. Nnamdi Azikiwe's public activities and achievements. For example, the story about the assassination attempt on him was believed to have actually occurred with shorts fired at him but it is said that he escaped by the powers of *Ogwu*. The achievements of the Igbo leaders including Okpara, Ironsi, Ojukwu were attributed to the power of *Ogwu*. Cf., Nwala T.U., *Igbo Philosophy*, op. cit., p. 88.

[151] Arinze F., *Sacrifice in Igbo Traditional Religion*, op. cit., p. 40.

[152] Mbiti J.S., *African Religions and Philosophy*, op. cit., p. 260.

etc. The particular combination of these depends on the type of medicine and the recommendations of "dibia" (native doctor) or the medicine man producing the concoction or preparation.[153]

How do the traditional religionists regard these "ogwu"? They are certainly not regarded as personal nor as representing spirits or "umu alusi" (idols). "Ogwu" are not "nkwu" (images). They are "medicines", useful things charged with powers which man can exploit. Judging from the way many people act and excluding the aggressive charms which people call "ajo ogwu" (bad medicine), one is inclined to say that they are regarded as deriving their power from God, at least in some cases or from the Spirits.

1.11. PRIESTHOOD IN IGBO TRADITIONAL RELIGION

In Igbo Traditional Religion, we have the cult of the priesthood. The priest is directly involved in the activities that have to do with worship in Igbo Traditional Religion. The priesthood is a highly elevated and respected office in Igbo Traditional Religion. This office is open for both men and women. Mbiti defines priest in African Traditional Religion (this also applies to Igbo Traditional Religion) as:

> A religious servant associated with temples, who performs religious duties whether in temples, shrines, sacred groves or elsewhere.[154]

The priest is the chief intermediary that stands between God, divinity, ancestors and men. The duties of the priest in Igbo Traditional Religion are chiefly religious, but since Africans do not dissociate religion from other departments of life, the priest has or may have other functions. He is the spiritual and ritual pastor of the community or nation. It is he who officiates at sacrifices, offerings and ceremonies relating to his knowledge. Just as the King is the political symbol of authority, so the priest is the religious symbol of God's presence among His people. In answering the call to the priesthood in Igbo Traditional Religion, one has to receive some training. In certain areas in Igboland, the office of the priesthood is hereditary.

We have categories of priests in Igbo Traditional Religion. They are: "Diabia-afa" - diviner (one who inquires with the divinities/deities/spirits). "Diabia aja" – "priest" (one who mediates between man and the divinities and offers sacrifices to the divinities and asks for favours from the deities on behalf of humans). "Diabia oje n'muo" (mystic). "Diabia mgborogwu na mkpaahihia" (herbalist, medicine man). Nevertheless, the vocation to the priesthood in Igbo

---

[153] Nwala T.U., *Igbo Philosophy,* op. cit., p. 89.
[154] Mbiti J.S., *African Religions and Philosophy,* op. cit., p. 245.

Traditional Religion must be authenticated by the deity that calls the person to be his priest or her priest. Normally, this comes through some signs. Sometimes, this comes through extra-ordinary manifestations which are not common to human experience.

There is always a training that the person called to serve any deity must undergo. The candidate has to learn the ways of the deity he or she will minister to. The candidates for the priesthood in Igbo Traditional Religion learn while in training not only the ways of the deities they will minister to but also the customs, traditions and history of the society which they are going to serve. "Priests are therefore repositories of communal knowledge and traditions".[155] The priest does not work independently of the community he or she is serving. The main function of the priest is to mediate between men, the divinities, the ancestors and to receive favours on behalf of men.

They do not exert their influence by virtue of their own personal gifts which they demonstrate through wonder-working. They enjoy considerable authority because they are able through their training and experience, to explain the causes of events in human life which lie beyond common-sense explanations – explanations which people look for when misfortunes occur. [156]

They are custodians of culture and traditions of the land and also, as spiritual leaders, are expected to be of a high standard of moral behavior. It is highly believed by the Igbo that the refusal to obey the call to the cult of the priesthood in Igbo Traditional Religion could result to misfortune for the recalcitrant candidate. The functions of the priest in Igbo Traditional Religion are not restricted to religious matters alone for almost every aspect of human life is a concern of the priest.

1.12. THE CONCEPT OF EVIL/SIN IN IGBO TRADITIONAL SETTING

1.12.1. METAPHYSICAL EVIL

The word "metaphysical" used in qualifying evil here indicates that the deed or the action cannot be attributed empirically, logically and directly to the actions of human beings. However, the Igbo believe that they are indirectly the result of man's action. The persons that indicate that such evil exists in the society are diviners or seers. The examples of metaphysical evil include: Natural disasters such as fire outbreak, flood, earth-quakes, deformities, accidents and premature deaths, just to mention but a few. "They are evils attributed to hu-

---

[155] Ibid., p. 246.
[156] Opoku A.K., *West African Traditional Religion*, op. cit., p. 75.

man beings by inference, because of the traditional belief in retributive judgment. According to the traditional belief, nothing happens for nothing. All actions are willed by either man or spirits".[157]

When any of the above-mentioned calamities happens, the Igbo see it as abomination. They call it "nso-ala". They believe that "nso-ala" (abomination) occurs when a person or persons have disturbed the cosmic order through actions of errors of omission or commission. This attracts cosmic penalty or sanctions by the deities and the ancestors. "Nso-ala" can be defined as a grave act against the natural law (against the morals and norms) of a community. The culprit may be a human agent or an animal. Some example of "nso-ala" (abomination) are incest, stealing yam tuber, (for human); a hen hatching only a single egg, (for animals).

Most often the angers of the deities and ancestors are visible through mysterious manifestations that are very unusual to the people. For example, people may see strange objects they do not normally see. Igbo people believe that these are signs that the gods and the ancestors are angry. Therefore, the communities or persons involved must seek the face of the gods and the ancestors. In most cases, the offender has to appease the gods and the ancestors by making sacrifices. This type of sacrifice is called propitiatory sacrifice. This would not ordinarily be called moral evils, but for the traditional mind they are because individuals are ultimately held responsible for their occurrence.[158]

Another aspect of metaphysical evil involves going against the customs of the community. The traditional mind does not make distinction between laws and morals. In the traditional Igbo setting, the legal is the moral and the moral is the same as the legal. The breaking of taboos is an example of metaphysical evil.[159] This includes the killing of sacred animals. For example, in Idemili local government area in Anambra state, Nigeria, it was forbidding to kill pythons.

1.12.2. MORAL EVIL

Moral evil applies to something that is highly condemnable because it is bad, offensive, against the basic social and religious values and code of the community. We mentioned earlier that the Igbo traditional setting makes no distinction between the moral norms and the legal or the civil code of conduct.

Awolalu and Dopamu assert that sin in Igbo traditional setting is:

---

[157] Nwala T.U., *Igbo Philosophy,* op. cit., p. 202.
[158] Ibid.
[159] Taboos in Igbo traditional setting are regarded as being same as the criminal code in civilized societies. Cf., Nwala T.U., *Igbo Philosophy*, op. cit., p. 202.

> Doing that which is contrary to the will and directions of deities. It includes any immoral behavior, ritual mistakes, any offence against God or man, breach of covenant, breaking of taboos and doing anything regarded as abominable and polluting to disregard God, the divinities and ancestral spirits is to commit sin. Likewise, to disregard the norms and taboos of the society is to commit sin.[160]

Sin is an offence against a community and its customs, for one that commits sin brings supernatural beings into action in the affairs of men. The man who commits sin places himself and others in danger by doing something, which brings the spirits into negative action in men's affairs.

Anyanwu holds that:

> Any act that goes contrary to moral values, set down by God, by the divinities and the ancestors is regarded as sin. Such acts like theft, murder, suicide, breaking of the taboos, adultery, falsehood and fraud are regarded as vices.[161]

Idowu sees sin as "that which produces evil as its consequences".[162] From the explanation of Metaphysical and Moral evil, we can assert that sin according to Igbo traditional belief includes both metaphysical and moral evil. "The Igbo make no distinction between the metaphysical and moral evil. Both are taken to be willed either directly or indirectly by man. Even when they are being set into play by the purposeful actions of the ancestors or gods, they are regarded as reactions arising from the prior actions of human beings".[163]

From the above definition of sin, one may assume that moral evil in Igbo Traditional Religion is the consequence of metaphysical evil. The problem we have here, as already said, is that the Igbo people do not have any mental picture of the distinction between metaphysical and moral evils. One of the outstanding characteristics of Igbo traditional morality is the indispensable role of sanctions. These sanctions face any defaulter of the moral code. These sanctions include ostracism, propitiatory sacrifices, just to mention but a few. These sanctions have to be obeyed in order to assuage the feelings of the person wronged as well as the anger of the deities and gods who are the guardians of the system.

---

[160] Awolalu J.O., & Dopoamu P.A., *West African Traditional Religion,* Ibadan, Nigeria, 1978, P. 214, in Anyanwu H.O., *Religion and Societal Development: Contemporary Nigeria Perspectives,* edited by Okwueze M., Merit International Publications, Lagos, Nigeria, 2004, p. 277.
[161] Anyanwu H.O., *Religion and Societal Development: Contemporary Nigeria Perspectives,* op. cit., p. 277.
[162] Idowu E.B., *African Traditional Religion, A Definition,* op. cit., p. 103, in *Anyanwu H.O.,* op. cit., p. 277.
[163] Nwala T.U., *Igbo Philosophy,* op. cit., p. 203.

Reconciliation, purification and sacrifice are essential parts of Igbo Traditional Religion. We have vertical and horizontal reconciliations. Vertical reconciliation involves the actions of the offender or offenders to appease the angers of God, divinities and the ancestors. Sometimes, this involves sacrifices. Horizontal reconciliation involves reconciliation with the person or persons one has offended or wounded by one's evil act. For example, in the case of theft, or adultery, this involves double effects. The offender has offended God, the divinities and the ancestors and has to appease them; the person has also offended the owner of the article stolen or the husband of the woman in the case of adultery. In the case of theft, restitution is required which has to be proportional to the thing stolen. In the case of adultery, the mode of reconciliation differs from place to place in Igboland.

RECONCILIATION DIAGRAM

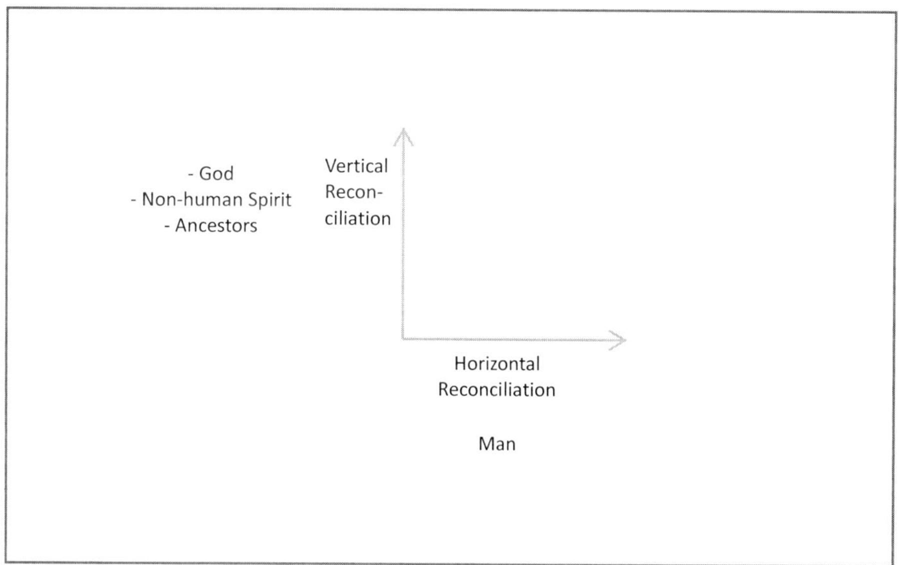

ILLUSTRATIONS

The act of confession is very necessary in the process of ritual reconciliation. The culprit usually does this. The emphasis on confession buttresses the Igbo concept of the word. To the Igbo, there is power in the word and the word creates, heals and kills. The acknowledgement of the evil act and its subsequent confession can warrant forgiveness of the evil committed. "A confession does not imply sorrow for the offenses committed or ... a form of satisfaction for some action against a deity. For the Igbo confession is a necessary form of liberation".[164]

Confession in Igbo Traditional Religion is a necessary form of liberation. The value of confession consists of relieving nervous strains, tension and other forms of hysteria and most importantly freeing the conscience of the offender. The central thing involved in the process of ritual reconciliation is the ritual meal. During the ritual meal, both parties (the angered and the culprit) share the drinks and meals together (oriko) showing reunion.

1.12.3. RECONCILIATION THROUGH SACRIFICIAL MEAL

Quarrel or misunderstanding is something often experienced among human beings who live in a committee, village or in families. When quarrels come up in Igbo traditional community and reconciliation is sought for, the Igbo have process by which true reconciliation can be established. When two parties or persons involved in a dispute are reconciled, there ought to be sacrificial meal which they have to partake from. The idea of union between the participants in the sacrificial banquet raised the question whether two enemies can take part in the same sacrificial meal, and what power this act has over a true reconciliation between them.

When husband and wife have fallen out with each other, separated and reconciled, the practice is to offer a sacrifice of reconciliation to the ancestors and some family spirits. This rite is called "aja nligha" or "igba oriko". The couple eat the offerings from the same plate. Henceforth, they can resume their normal life together. Failure to offer this sacrifice, say the traditional religionists, is to endanger the life of the husband.[165]

In the past, sacrifices of reconciliation after inter-town wars, were offered by the erstwhile belligerent towns. Some Igbo used to offer a slave for this and then there was no question of a meal. But some towns sacrifice two sheep at the boundary of the two towns that have fought a war. Representatives of both towns partook of the meal prepared with sheep meat and reconciliation was done.

There is also a rite to reconcile two or more enemies. It is called "ita oji ani" (eating of the earth kola-nut). Related to this, but somewhat different, is the

---

[164] Ogu C. *"Traditional Ritual Reconciliation pointer to Sacramental Reconciliation,"* Lucerna vol. 5. No. 1, p. 15, in Okwueze M.I. (ed.), *Religion and Social Development,* op. cit., p. 284
[165] Cf., Arinze F., *Sacrifice in Igbo Traditional Religion,* op. cit., p. 200.

ceremony of "igba ndu", (covenant) which is performed among people who suspect poisoning from someone in their midst. "Igba ndu" (covenant) however, does not seem to be a sacrifice at all but rather a mutual promise or an oath.[166]

In normal daily life, two confirmed enemies, for example, those who wish each other's death or grave injury, would not eat in the same sacrifice. In a community sacrifice, the priest asks the spirit to remove all evil men from their midst. He also prays: "Egbe belu ugo belu, nke si ibe ya ebena nku kapu ya" (let the kite perch and let the eagle perch, whichever says that the other must not perch let its wings break). All present respond: "ofo"! (Perfectly so)! Hence, if an evil man thus responds and also eats of the sacrifice, he has sworn against himself and is liable to suffer or even die. Therefore, he prefers not to eat, and indeed not to attend the sacrifice at all, if possible, for it is the normal thing for all present to participate fully, except those forbidden by special laws or customs. Be that as it may, it also happens that two enemies postpone their mutual enmity only for the days of a big religious festival. After the celebrations, their hatred regains its full swing. In that case, they might participate in the same sacrificial meal, but not from the same dish.

Therefore, participation in the same sacrificial meal does not, by that very fact alone, reconcile two enemies. It does so, however, when this is the precise intention of the sacrifice. When it is not, then the two enemies would normally prefer not to participate in the same sacrifice.[167]

1.12.4. MORAL CODES, ETHICAL NORMS AND CONDUCTS IN IGBO TRADITIONAL SOCIETY

As we have affirmed earlier, Igbo Traditional Religion is originally African. Before the advent of Christianity to Igboland, the Igbo had already the sense of morality. They had already moral standards guiding them in the society. This means that these moral standards did not come from the western civilization.

One presumes that once there is religion, then morality or moral codes are bound to exist. "Though attempts have been made to separate morality from religion, one cannot deny the influence of religion on social and moral behaviour. The Igbo Traditional Religion sees morality as the fruit of religion. Social and moral patterns of behaviour are reflections of this belief."[168]

---

166 Ibid.
167 Ibid., pp. 201 - 202.
168 Quarcoopome T.N., *West African Traditional Religion,* op. cit., p. 159.

For example, the Igbo man knows that murder is a serious crime. It is "nso ala" (an abomination). He did not learn it from the western culture or religion. He acquired it from nature. The traditional emphasis on good character shows that, contrary to some ideologies, God and good life are closely connected.

The 'dos' and 'don'ts' of the society come under ethics and taboos and these are religious, social, political and economic in content. On the whole, the taboos are stabilizing factors as they emphasize the role of religion in maintaining law and order in the society. It is clear to the Igbo mind that what it holds as moral standards do not go contrary to God's commandments. West Africans (as well as the Igbo) strongly believe that:

> Moral values are not invented by human beings but are the offspring of religion. This is so because God has put his laws into man and it is this which is referred to as conscience. Thus, man is expected to use this conscience to behave in a morally good way in order to avoid the 'wrath' of God.[169]

The word "moral" comes from the Latin word "moralis" which means morals or manners. It also means custom. Custom implies usages, practices, standards of norms and codes, which are common to certain groups, or classes of people and which regulate the group's action in both religious and social obligations.[170] Morality is also "defined as a specific form of social consciousness, of awareness of your relatedness to others without which societal life would be impossible".[171] Among the Igbo people, traditional morality, which is in line with the above definition, could be understood in the form of "Omenani" (tradition and custom).

"Omeani" is the totality of laws of the land, customs and tradition, a complex of beliefs and practices, which every Igbo man inculcates as a guiding philosophy and code of behaviour. All the taboos, totems and prohibitions hedged around "Omenala" are designed to ensure that the natural order is not violated and that a proper relationship among spirits, between spirits and men, among men, between men and the lower beings, between husband and wife, child and parent among kinsmen are maintained.[172]

---

[169] Ibid., p. 163.

[170] Cf., Shorter A., *African Christian Theology: Adaptation or Incarnation?* Geoffrey Chapman, London, 1975, p. 113, in Okwueze M.I. (ed.), *Religion and Societal Development: Contemporary Nigeria Perspective,* Merit International Publications, Lagos, Nigeria, 2004, p. 242.

[171] Okwueze M.I. (ed.), *Religion and Social Development: Contemporary Nigeria Perspective*, op. cit., p. 242.

[172] Nwala T.U., *Igbo Philosophy*, op. cit., pp. 76-77.

In Igbo traditional society, the various structures which ensure the evolvement and maintenance of morals and values, such as the family, the peer group also called the age grade, the village, the clan and the community are obtained in every Igbo community. "The highest principle within "Omenala", which underscores the behavior and actions of all beings, is "Ofo" (Justice), symbolized in "Ofo stick" held by the elders, priests and the initiated. The holders of "Ofo" are the guardians of "Omenala" and all its codes, which protect this cosmic, natural and social balance."[173]

1.13. "OFO" IN IGBO TRADITIONAL RELIGION

There is always in man a religious instinct, which inspires him to seek the divine. Religious instincts are also noticed among the Igbo people. They desire like others to communicate directly with God, ancestors, and other divinities. In order to mediate and satisfy their desires, they create some visible religious objects to serve as medium of communication with the gods, spirits, ancestors and divinities. "Ofo" is among these visible religious objects.[174]

1.13.1. WHAT IS "OFO"?

The term "Ofo" is the name proper to two related objects in Igboland. In an immediate sense, it stands for a particular plant, species, which grows in the Igbo area and in a derived sense, it also represents the twig from the wood of the tree. However, both the plant and its sticks are referred to as "Ofo". "Ofo" is one among the several cultic symbols, which the traditional Igbo people employ in performing religious, political, ethical and social functions. It is a symbol of authority, honesty and righteousness. In Igbo Traditional Religion, "Ofo" is a medium of communication through which the Igbo people relate to the supreme God, their personal gods, the ancestors and the spirits.[175]

"Ofo" is the central symbol of Igbo religion. In addition to being a staff of authority, "it is an emblem symbolizing the link between "Chukwu" (God) and man, the dead and the living, the living and unborn. The "Ofo" also symbolizes justice, righteousness and truth".[176]

---

[173] Ibid., p. 77.

[174] Cf., Ofo – functional role in Igboland, uniprojectsearch.com, Published, June, 22, 2015, accessed 7.1.2016.

[175] Ofo – functional role in Igboland, uniprojectsearch.com, Published, June, 22, 2015, accessed 7.1.2016.

[176] Okafor F.U., *Igbo Philosophy of Law,* Fourth Dimension Publisher, Enugu, Nigeria, 1992, p. 29.

1.13.2. THE WRONG NOTION OR INTERPRETATION GIVEN TO "OFO".

The non-Igbo who could not understand what "Ofo" is and what it stands for, give it wrong interpretation and meaning. For example, the early western missionaries in Igboland regarded "Ofo" as idol or charm. On the contrary, for the Igbo people, "Ofo" is neither a charm nor an idol but a sacred symbol that serves as medium of communication between the Igbo people, the Supreme Being, non-human spirits and the ancestors.

1.13.3. SOURCE OF "OFO"

What is the source of "Ofo"? What is it made-up of? Ejizu states that "Ofo" comes from a tree known as "Detarium Elastica". The "Ofo" tree is believed to be one of the most respected and dignified trees among the Igbo. This is evident in the way the tree and its surroundings are cared for.[177]

"Ofo" has a material symbol made up of either a carved stick of about four to six inches long, thick at one end; or it could be made up of a bundle of "Ofo" sticks. It is made from a special tree called "osisi ofo". It is usually black owning to constant rubbing of blood and feather from fowls and other animals sacrificed onto it.

We have to note that "osisi ofo" (*ofo* stick) has to be consecrated before it symbolizes what it stands for. "Ofo" has spiritual, social, political and cultural significance. From material point of view, it is made up of a special wood called "Osisi Ofo" but from the spiritual point of view, the Igbo believe that after its consecration, it undergoes metaphysical transformation. Hence, it has some spiritual powers.

1.13.4. THE SPIRITUAL SIGNIFICANCE OF "OFO"

1.13.4.1. "OFO" A SYMBOL OF UNITY

"Ofo" tree is believed to be a mystical tree specially designed by providence for its role. When the carved branch or bundle of it is prepared as "Ofo" symbol, it is consecrated and becomes the central family cult, which unites the living and the dead.[178] The custodian of "Ofo" is usually the first male child of the family or community called "Okpara" (first male child) or the oldest man in the community. "Ofo" is seen as a symbol of spiritual authority, given by the deities and the ancestral spirits to the custodian of "Ofo". The custodian of "Ofo" has authority, rights and privileges which the people have to respect.

---

[177] Cf., Ejizu C.I, *Ofo, Igbo Ritual Symbol,* Fourth Dimension Publishers, Enugu, Nigeria, 1986, p. 123, in uniprojectsearch.com, published, June 22, 2015; accessed 7.1.2016.
[178] Ibid.

Whatever the holder of "Ofo" binds, condemns or approves is believed to be what the gods and ancestors bind, disapprove or approve. "Ofo" is said to be symbolic representation of "Ala" (the earth goddess as well as the Ancestors). "Ofo" is so much dreaded. This is because the Igbo believe that anybody that goes contrary to the principles of "Ofo" would be punished by the gods with the death penalty or be ostracized. This therefore, strengthens the bond of unity among the family or community members.

1.13.4.2. "OFO": A SYMBOL OF MORAL AND SPIRITUAL AUTHORITY

The custodian of "Ofo" has great spiritual and moral authorities given to him by the gods and the ancestors. We have to note here that the custodian of "Ofo" has to be honest, transparent, impartial and upright; otherwise he is visited with death, infirmity, or any other curse.[179]

The custodian of "Ofo" is the moral as well as the spiritual head of the family or community as the case may be. He is also the political head and holds the landed assets of the family in trust and has to ensure that each member receives his due share. As the spiritual head, he also performs sacrifices involving members of his family or other kinsmen. The "Ofo" controls the conscience of every member of the community. Because it works purely on equitable basis, its keeper must be above suspicion, corruption and mistake. Equity flows from "Ofo" (God of justice). Thus, both the keeper and users of "Ofo" principles must be above suspicion, corruption and wrong-doing.[180]

1.13.4.3. "OFO": A SYMBOL THAT DEPICTS POLITICAL AND LEGAL AUTHORITY

The custodian of "Ofo" is not only seen as a moral or spiritual leader, but also a political leader. "Ofo" acts as an invincible legal seal for every decision of the clan, community or family. Its presence in the community, village or family meeting gives legitimacy to the meetings as well as its proceedings.

1.13.4.4. "OFO": A STATUS SYMBOL

"Ofo" is also a status symbol because its holders are marked out from the rest of the community and usually accorded deep respect with corresponding privileges. Only the upright people respected for their moral and social distinction can hold the title of "Eze Ofo" or "Nze isi Ofo".[181]

---

[179] Nwala T.U., *Igbo Philosophy,* op. cit., p. 85.
[180] Ukaegbu F.N., *The Igbos: The African Root of Nations,* Heinemann Education Books (Nigeria) Plc, Ibadan, Nigeria, 2005, p. 28.
[181] Ibid.

1.13.4.5. "OFO": AN INSTRUMENT OF RECONCILIATION AND REUNION

"Ofo" is used as a judicial instrument. When a misunderstanding exists and people need reconciliation or are searching for the truth of the matter, "Ofo" may be brought in. Once "Ofo" is brought in, the people involved must say the truth. The Igbo believe that when one fails to say the truth and decides to tell lies in the presence of "Ofo", which is the symbol of justice and truth, the penalty may be grievous.

1.13.4.6. "OFO": THE SYMBOL OF TRUTH AND JUSTICE

"Ofo" is the symbol for truth and justice in Igbo Traditional Religion. "Ofo" is the defender of the innocent and the weak. The weak can be protected by this principle only if he is innocent.

1.14. SACRIFICE IN IGBO TRADITIONAL RELIGION

Sacrifice in Igbo Traditional Religion is a very important aspect of Igbo Traditional Religion. But we are not going to discuss this in detail. We are going to touch the areas that are relevant to this work. Sacrifice is the life-wire of Igbo Traditional Religion. Ofomata calls it "the summit of Igbo traditional religion".[182] The word "sacrifice" can be used in two ways, having different meanings: sacrifice can mean in a general sense "some renunciation for a motive". One can say "I am sacrificing my time for your own good". This means that this person is forfeiting his/her time for the good of the other.

The word "sacrifice" can also be used to refer to a religious act. Ritual sacrifice has its place only in religious public worship. So, the sense in which we use the word "sacrifice" here is in reference to religious worship. Quarcoopome defines sacrifice as: Means of contact or communion between man and God. It is man's best means of establishing and maintaining cordial and intimate relation between himself and his object of worship.[183]

"Sacrifice is an offering to God by a priest of a sensible thing through its immolation, in acknowledgement of His supreme dominion and man's subjection."[184] Arinze distinguishes between internal and external sacrifices. He states:

---

[182] Ofomata G.E.K. (ed.), A *Survey of the Igbo Nation*, op. cit., p. 359.
[183] Quarcoopome T.N.O., *West African Traditional Religion,* op. cit., p. 89.
[184] Arinze F., *Sacrifice in Igbo Traditional Religion*, op. cit., p. 63.

Internal sacrifice is the internal offering of ourselves to God who is our creator, preserver, and final end. External sacrifice is the external manifestation of this interior act when "something is done" to things being offered to God.[185]

One can rightly say that the external sacrifice is the external manifestation of the interior disposition. "Internal sacrifice is the soul of exterior sacrifice and is absolutely required for its moral worth. Without internal sacrifice, the external rite would degenerate into formalism, which is the enemy of true religion".[186]

Mbiti makes a distinction between sacrifice and offering. He holds that "sacrifices refer to cases where animal life is destroyed in order to present the animal, in part or in whole, to God, supernatural beings, spirits or living-dead. Offerings refer to the remaining cases which do not involve the killing of an animal, being chiefly the presentation of food stuffs and other items."[187]

In many parts of the Igboland, animate as well as inanimate objects are part of their daily life experience in the worship of their gods. The Igbo say "ife onye lili ka o nyelu muo o na-efe" (what a man eats he also gives to the spirits he worships). In Igbo traditional setting, some sacrifices basically belong to the divinities or the ancestors. But sometimes the worshippers may partake in the sacrifice being offered by eating some portions of the thing offered, if what is being sacrificed is edible.

In sharing the victim with the divine being, fellowship is strengthened and communion established. As an expression of this, bits of every item sacrificed are placed on or before the shrine as a token and the rest consumed by the worshippers. In certain cases, however, the whole of the sacrificial victim is given up to the divine being, usually on the advice of an oracle. The victim is burnt, exposed or buried.[188]

1.14.1. THE AIMS OF SACRIFICE IN IGBO TRADITIONAL RELIGION

The Igbo always acknowledge the fact that they receive many benefits and blessings from the Supreme Being (Chukwu), the deities and the Ancestors. Therefore, it is right and just that they have to thank God for these blessings and benefits. "The Igbo man also recognizes that he is not master of the world. There are superior powers, invisible spirits, the ancestors, and there are also human spirits of wicked deceased people".[189]

---

[185] Ibid., p. 60.
[186] Ibid., p. 59.
[187] Mbiti J.S., *African Religions and Philosophy,* op. cit., p. 76.
[188] Quarcoopome T.N.O., *West African Traditional Religion,* op. cit., p. 89.
[189] Arinze F., *Sacrifice in Igbo Traditional Religion,* op. cit., p. 77.

When a man offends the divinities and the ancestors by doing what is wrong, going against the ethical norms of the land, he must then as an obligation not only for himself but for the sake of the entire community to which he belongs, seek the face of the gods and the ancestors who are the custodians of the laws of the land. Sacrifice is made not only when one has offended the divinities and the ancestors. It can also be made when one seeks the help of the gods and the ancestors in certain matters or just simply to honour them. Sacrifice is also made when one wants to thank the divinities and the ancestors for many blessings received from them. The Igbo also make sacrifice in order to chase away the evil spirits and be protected against their attacks.

Arinze summarizes the aims (ends) of sacrifice in Igbo Traditional Religion as follows. He groups them under these headings: (a) Expiation (b) Sacrifice to ward off molestation from unknown evil spirits (c) Petition and (d) Thanksgiving.[190]

1.14.2. EXPIATION/PURIFICATION

The Igbo believe that sin/abomination (alu) defiles a man and attracts the anger of the gods and the ancestors. This is not only on the offender but also on his entire family and sometimes on the whole community to which the offender belongs. Therefore, the offender needs expiation and purification. When this is not done, the culprit bears the pinch of the anger of the divinities and the ancestors. Hence, in order to appease the divinities and the ancestors, expiatory sacrifice or purification ought to be made. Expiatory sacrifice can be categorized into two major parts. (1) Sacrifice to remove abomination (Ikpu alu) and (2) sacrifice for minor offences.[191]

1.14.3. SACRIFICE TO REMOVE (EXPIATE) ABOMINATION

Under this, we have crimes which the Igbo take seriously because they offend "Ani", the earth goddess.[192] Such moral crimes include, incest, stealing of yams and sheep, bestiality, wilful abortion, suicide by hanging and so forth.

---

[190] Ibid., p. 64.

[191] Arinze F., *Sacrifice in Igbo Traditional Religion*, op. cit., p. 65.

[192] For the Igbo the earth goddess tends to be closer to human beings than all other deities. She ranks second after the Supreme Being and is usually regarded as the "queen of the underworld" the owner of men and custodian of public morality in conjunction with the ancestors. The earth goddess is solely concerned with matters affecting the community and, as the guardian of public morality, she prohibits anti-social behaviors. Cf., Anyanwu H.O., *Sin, Reconciliation and development in Igboland, in Religion and Societal Development: Contemporary Nigerian Perspectives*, edited by Okwueze M., op. cit., p. 277.

The second level of abomination could be seen as acts which are not directly willed by man but are considered abnormal or unnatural. Some examples of these acts are: giving birth to twins,[193] a person dying without anyone to attend to him (ikpu iru), abnormal presentation in the birth of a baby (iji okpa puta uwa), a child cutting the upper teeth first (iwa eze-enu).

Certain actions from the animals are also seen as abomination and require expiatory sacrifice. This is to appease the angers of the gods and the ancestors against the community in which this abomination took place. Examples of such acts are: If a fowl lays only one egg or if a goat brings forth its young without anyone to attend to it (ewu imu n'ogbuli). In all these cases, whether the abominable action is performed by a human being or animal, they are seen as actions that defile the culprit and the land. Therefore, expiatory sacrifice ought to be made.

> The Igbo believe firmly that if such abominations are not atoned for, be they ever so secretly committed, the penalty is sure to descend on the culprit's head or on his relations and descendants. If the culprit in a major offence is known, he is cut off from social communication, he is ostracized from the market, and if he dies, he is not given full burial rites. Therefore, to hide one's crime or to refuse to sacrifice is to lead a dangerous life, to take a risk. Once, however, he offers the necessary sacrifice, the erstwhile wrong-doer is regarded as cleansed and any ensuing death is giving another interpretation.[194]

When an offender dies after he has performed the necessary sacrifices, he ought to have done, this should not be attributed to the previous abomination committed. The Igbo call expiatory sacrifice "ikpu alu or ikpocha ife" (removing an abomination or cleansing). This type of sacrifice is not performed by every priest. "It requires priests that come from *Nri* town."[195]

---

[193] Giving birth to twins before the coming of the Europeans in Igboland was seen as an abomination; for the Igbo, this is not a human act. Only animals do give birth to more than one. Cf., Arinze F., *Sacrifice in Igbo Traditional Religion,* op. cit. p. 65. But this mentality is no longer there today. We shall discuss this in full when we treat the changes in the spirituality of the Igbo and what brought about the changes.

[194] Arinze F., *Sacrifice in Igbo Traditional Religion*, op. cit., p. 67.

[195] "Nri" is a town in Igboland. "Nri" people are taken by the Igbo as the progenitors of Igbo race. "Nri" is the center of Igbo priesthood and "Nri" priests have undisputed power and priority throughout Igboland. The importance of "Nri" priests in the life of the ordinary Igbo traditional religionist is that "Nri" priests are the proper people to perform expiatory sacrifices necessary for the removal of an abomination (ikpu alu). This type of sacrifice is not done by the "eze alusi" (priest of a particular spirit) nor by the family priest. Hence, the Igbo see in "Nri" a center of priesthood in Igbo Traditional Religion with very wide influence, and in "Nri" priesthood we have a priesthood which is above the family priesthood and the priest of a particular spirit. "Nri" priests have, besides other religious and quasi-political powers, the power to offer expiatory

1.14.4. EXPIATORY SACRIFICE FOR MINOR CRIMES

This kind of sacrifice is meant for minor crimes or offences which are not generally regarded as abomination (alu). The crimes associated with this type of sacrifice differ from place to place in Igboland. For example, in some places in Igboland, people are forbidden to fish in a particular river. This is because the Igbo believe that the water-spirits that inhabit that river forbid that. Hence, anybody that fishes in that river has committed a crime against the spirits of that river and ought to make expiatory sacrifice to the spirits in order to appease them. Sometimes the priest of the offended spirits says in what form the sacrifice is to be performed. We have to note here also that some-times the diviner prescribes a sacrifice for unknown sins. The community has to obey the instructions of the diviner. Expiatory sacrifice can further be categorized into two. They are: Individual and public. Individual is the type we have discussed above. Public expiatory sacrifices in Igboland normally undertake special liturgical celebration of "scapegoat."[196] A town or a village could heap all its sins on a goat or cow (which serves as scapegoat or cow) and then offers it to the spirits. This is done through prescribed ritual activities. The advice of the diviner is indispensable before such moves. Some of these animals were first earmarked and left to wander in liberty. Others were tied and thrown into the forest.

On some occasions, the victim is tied to the top of a pole and set up in an open place chosen by the priest. This is usually done after a family or town has suffered from sickness or misfortune thought to be caused by evil spirits. The sacrifice is made so that the tormentor should accept it and leave the inhabitants in peace.

1.14.5. HUMAN SACRIFICE

This is another example of public expiatory sacrifices. Probably, there is no part of West Africa in which human sacrifice has not been customary at some period. This practice was eradicated by the influence of Christianity, modern civilization and the power of good governance. Among the Igbo people, the custom was widespread.[197] In the past, human beings were used to remove the ills of the multitude in a few places in Igboland. Why should the Igbo people use

---

sacrifices to remove abominations. Cf., Arinze F., *Sacrifice in Igbo Traditional Religion,* op. cit., pp. 143 -145.

[196] "Scapegoat" means victim that must bear the sins of the whole community; one that carries the burden of others; one that has to suffer and die in order that the sins of others, the sins of the entire community are cleansed and unforeseen dangers averted. The victim may be a goat, a cow or a human being in the case of human sacrifice. Cf., Arinze F., *Sacrifice in Igbo Traditional Religion,* op. cit., pp. 173 - 174.

[197] Basden G.T., *Among the Ibos of Nigeria,* op. cit., p. 230.

human beings as victims for sacrifice? Does it not go contrary to the belief of the Igbo which holds that life is of primary value and has to be cherished and protected?

The Igbo performed human sacrifice because they believed that it was the highest form of sacrifice and therefore the most potent. This sacrifice is made as an appeasement to the divinities in order that the society might be saved from some serious calamity such as floods, plagues, famine, drought and so forth. This type of sacrifice is no longer made in Igboland. It is no longer done as a result of the influence of foreign religions like Christianity with its doctrine of the atonement that the death of Christ had become the once and for all human sacrifice.[198] If human beings in Igbo Traditional Religion could be offered to the deities as the highest sacrifice one could offer, then it implies that the Igbo traditional religionists worship these deities to whom human beings were offered to. Here polytheism in Igbo Traditional Religion is port-rayed.

When is human sacrifice performed? This is not a frequent sacrifice. This type of sacrifice was performed when certain calamities were foreseen to befall a town; and recourse must be had to such measures as would lead to the removal of this evil. The "dibia" (priest) alone could discern the root cause of the calamity and indicate the remedy. "In many cases, resort was first had to the sacrifice of animals. It was only when all other forms of sacrifice failed that the Igbo traditionalists were finally driven back upon human beings as their last hope."[199] It is very important to note here that when this extreme form of sacrifice was needed the victim was never a fellow townsman. He was always a slave purchased especially for the purpose, or captive of war.[200]

Human beings were also sacrificed in connection with kings and chiefs. During the accession of a new king or chief, a human being was sacrificed as a protec-

---

[198] Cf., Quarcoopome T.N.O., *West African Traditional Religion,* op. cit., p. 91.

[199] Cf., Basden G.T., *Among the Ibos of Nigeria,* op. cit., p. 231.

[200] In Igboland, when a man kills a fellow-townsman either advertently or inadvertently, this is taken to be a crime against the earth goddess (abomination). It is more grievous when it is a murder, which means that the act was done advertently. This act is followed immediately with adequate sanctions. One of the sanctions is that the culprit has to leave his hometown and flee to his mother's kinsmen. This is called "igba oso ochu." The offender has to be in exile for a number of years, as stated by the sanction. When the time for the exile is over, he may then come back to his home- town. Chinua Achebe, in his famous novel: "Things Fall Apart" explains this well. When Okonkwo accidently killed a young man from his kindred, the only course open to Okonkwo was to flee from the clan. It was a crime against the earth goddess to kill a Kinsman and the man who committed it must flee from the land. The crime was of two kinds, male and female. Okonkwo had committed the female, because it had been inadvertent. He could return to the clan after seven years. Cf., Achebe C., *Things Fall Apart*, op. cit., p. 99.

tive measure to ensure a long period of reign. "Human beings were further ritually killed at the funerals of kings, chiefs and other royalties as attendants in the hereafter. At the foundation of a new town or village, human beings were also sacrificed."[201]

In the real sense of it, this is not sacrifice. The only instance where human sacrifice is taken traditionally as a sacrifice is in the instance of "scapegoat". In the sacrifice of human-scapegoat, the idea of substitution is very obvious. The chosen victim dies in place of the community and takes away its sins. But we have to affirm strongly that this type of sacrifice was performed long ago before the coming of Christianity to Igboland and it is no longer done today.

1.14.6. SACRIFICE TO DISPEL THE EVIL ACTIONS AND DISTURBANCES FROM UNIDENTIFIED MALIGNANT SPIRITS

The Igbo people strongly believe that every action in life has a cause. The concept of cause and effect is always at the back of the mind of the Igbo man. For the average Igbo man, "there is no smoke without fire". Every action has an effect. As we have said earlier, when the Igbo fail to explain any event or action, they attribute it to the invisible powers/forces. For example, when a person is sick and the sickness has defied all possible efforts for its cure, some Igbo may attribute it to the actions of the invisible spirits/forces. Normally the person who says which powers are into play in this type of situation is the fortune-teller. It is the fortune-teller that informs the person that is molested that he/she is being troubled by the evil spirits. These malignant spirits do not have shrines in Igboland. They are unknown. Their names are not known. The Igbo believe that they have no domain. They move about molesting, harming and frustrating people in their efforts to be successful in life. Nothing good comes from them. They always bring bad news. "Here it is enough to say that these are spirits that are regarded as entirely evil. They molest both guilty and innocent persons indiscriminately".[202] Normally, the only remedy to come out of this situation of molestation by the wicked spirits is to make sacrifice to them. The fortune-teller usually prescribes how the person affected would carry out the sacrifice. "Such sacrifices are offered without love; the victims are most ugly and disreputable".[203]

In this type of sacrifice, the victim for the sacrifice is never shared with the spirits. This means that the people dare not partake of the victim being sacrificed. It is therefore either buried or treated with oil and exposed. The "wrath"

---

[201] Cf., Quarcoopome T.N.O., *West African Traditional Religion*, op. cit., p. 90.
[202] Arinze F., *Sacrifice in Igbo Traditional Religion,* op. cit., p. 71.
[203] Ibid.

is believed to have been withdrawn. The purpose of this type of sacrifice is clear. The aim is that the molesting evil spirits should accept the sacrifice being offered and the danger of the person being molested is averted. After making this type of sacrifice, the Igbo strongly believe that the evil spirits will not harm or continue to molest the person who has offered the sacrifice.

This kind of sacrifice is performed also when there is definite knowledge of an impending disaster. An example is the prediction that some unnamed trouble or danger may be entering or passing through the community. When a village or town is already infested by a plague or any other adversity, such a sacrifice may prevent the calamity from spreading. An individual may also offer this type of sacrifice after an impending disaster had been revealed to him.

1.14.7. FOR PETITION

Sacrifice of petition is very common in Igboland. The Igbo people generally love achievement. Although no person dislikes achievement, the love for achievement and progress manifests always in the life of the Igbo. "The Igbo desire for achievement is somehow singular, given that the Igbo people give deference to achievement not linked to inherited positions." [204]

The character of being achievement-oriented manifests always in the spiritual life of the Igbo. The Igbo man wants always to succeed in whatever he does. Therefore, the Igbo are ready to offer something in order that their prayers are heard. They believe that God, the spirits or the ancestors hardly refuse this type of sacrifice when they are offered in good faith and properly made. Let us look at what the Igbo man generally requests for, while making this type of sacrifice to God, spirits or the ancestors.

Life is the ultimate good and goal of the Igbo traditionalists. Hence, prayer for longevity and good health are placed first in order of preference. They even manifest this in the type of names they give to their children. Such names include: "Ndubuisi", "Nduka" (life is supreme, life is greater than wealth), etc.

The Igbo do not discuss death, they do not speak about it. "Onwudiwe", "Onwudinjo" (death is wicked, death is bad) says the Igbo man. The value of life by the Igbo is also seen in the way they greet their traditional kings. They normally say: "Eze i ga adi ndu rue mgbe ebighi ebi" (my lord may you live forever). The Igbo man knows of course that he will one day die. But he esteems life and offers sacrifice for good health, for the recovery of the sick, to stop

---

[204] Odumegwu Ojukwu E., *"because I am involved"*, Spectrum Books, Ibadan, Nigeria, 1989, p. 95.

epidemics, for the preservation of travelers, for life in general and against death, especially where it is rather frequent or where it gets at young people.[205]

It is most important for the couple to have children after marriage. Although the Igbo know that children come ultimately from God, they also go to the spirits to ask for offspring with the conviction that they are following the proper procedure. A woman goes to the priest of the spirits of "omumu" (fertility) and presents her offerings. Prayers at such sacrifices always start with a mention of God's name, then the spirit in question, other spirits and the ancestors. The priest could pray thus: *Amutalu mmadu maya muta ibe ya. Bikonu, neenu* (names of those to be prayed for) *... na ayo nwa. Nyenu ya umu ofu ofu uno eju* (A person is born, and he has to beget others. Please, behold ... she is begging for a child. Give her children, one by one, till the house is full). It is to be noted that the prayer is for *ofu ofu* (one by one) because the Igbo did not want twins. Besides the spirits, the ancestors are also to be "fed". If they are neglected, they will "deny" the couple children.[206]

If a woman is pregnant, sacrifice is also offered so that the woman will have safe delivery. The sacrifice is performed by the oldest man in the community. The man - "Okpala" (first born in the family) is believed to be the nearest person to the ancestors, and hence their representative. When the Igbo are preparing for special ceremonies like "Ozo" title, coronation of a king, etc., they make sacrifices in order to obtain the protection of the higher powers and also to ask for protection throughout the period of the ceremony. For building of a new house, sacrifice is made. Quarcoopome calls it foundation sacrifice. He asserts:

> This type of sacrifice is usually done at the laying of the foundation of a house, village or town. It is a combination of propitiatory and preventive sacrifices. The purpose is to appease the spirits of the earth in order that all may be well with that which is being founded. It is also meant to prevent evil from entering the place.[207]

The Igbo people make sacrifices at the inauguration of a new market, for blessing on a long journey, for success in examinations, just to mention but a few.

---

[205] Arinze F., *Sacrifice in Igbo Traditional Religion,* op. cit., p. 74.
[206] Ibid., p. 75.
[207] Quarcoopome T.N.O., *West African Traditional Religion,* op. cit., p. 92.

1.14.8. VOTIVE OFFERING

This type of sacrifice is made in fulfilment of vows or promises, while supplicating for help from God through the divinities and the ancestors. Failure to perform this sacrifice for benefits received is counted as breaking faith and the offender is usually punished by the divine beings in the form of sickness or even death.[208]

1.14.9. SUBSTITUTIONARY SACRIFICE

This sacrifice has its basis in the African belief that there are wandering spirits (born-to-die spirits) who may enter the wombs of pregnant women. When the babies are born and it is verified that they are possessed by these spirits, then care is taken to keep them alive by a substitutionary sacrifice. This helps in preventing such children from dying. This sacrifice is performed usually when the children are seriously ill. We shall later explain this more when we discuss "Ogbanje" (rebirth). Substitutionary sacrifice is also performed when a person is believed to be under the "wrath" of a divinity or some evil spirits which could end in the death of the individual. A sheep is offered as a substitute for the victim. The sacrifice is treated like a corpse and buried with full funeral rites as if it was the suppliant.[209]

1.14.10. FUNERAL SACRIFICE

At funeral ceremony, sacrifices are made to the ancestors, asking them to receive the spirit of the deceased into their company; asking them also to overlook the misdeeds of the deceased person. This sacrifice indicates that the living and the deceased had good relationship. With this sacrifice, the Igbo believe that the good relationship that existed between the living and the deceased, when the deceased was alive, will still continue now that the deceased is in the spirit world.

The Igbo do not offer a real sacrifice to the deceased until the final funeral rites have been performed and the deceased is numbered among the ancestors. Only then does the person receive his symbol (*okpesi*) and his share of sacrifices and libations.[210]

1.14.11. THANKSGIVING SACRIFICE

The Igbo man always shows gratitude for every gift he receives. He manifests his thankfulness and joy for what he has received from God, the spirits or the

---

208 Ibid., p. 91.
209 Ibid., p. 92.
210 Arinze F., *Sacrifice in Igbo Traditional Religion,* op. cit., p. 79.

ancestors by act of sacrifice. The ancestors are regarded as nearest to man and most interested in the family well-being of their loved ones. In Igboland, the ancestors are called the living dead. Although they are no longer physically seen, they are believed to be always around spiritually. They have interest of their families and loved ones at heart. Example of this type of sacrifice is the sacrifice performed after child-delivery. The couple offers a sacrifice of thanksgiving to the spirit "Omumu", (goddess) to whom the woman had made a special request for a child.

1.14.12. SACRIFICE FOR THE FIRST FRUITS

This is performed every year, when the first fruits of the farm are being harvested. A sacrifice is performed after the first harvest of the new yam. Yam is taken to be the king of all farm products. Before the new yam is eaten every year, the Igbo make sacrifice to yam spirit. This is a thanksgiving sacrifice. The ceremony for the eating of the new yam is called "Iwa ji" (which means the cutting of the new yam). The very idea behind this sacrifice is that the Igbo believe that the first crops ought to be offered to the spirits. Then, people are free to harvest for themselves.

One may ask how one knows that the spirits have accepted sacrifice made to them? In public joyful sacrifices, there are special signs that depict that the spirits have accepted the offering. The appearance of vultures at the scene of sacrifice to scramble for the special offerings lying before the symbols of the spirits, is regarded as a very good omen. Hence, the proverb: "Achuba aja afuro udene, amalu na ife melu be ndi mmuo" (if no vultures appear during sacrifice, it means that something is wrong in the spirit land).

It is also a good sign when children flock to take the offered food from the symbol of the ancestors (*iseli nni n'okpesi*), or when some animals sacred to the spirit hover around the scene of sacrifice.

1.14.13. SACRIFICE AS INSTRUMENT OF AGGRESSION

This type of sacrifice is made when one seeks for the help of the spirits and ancestors to avenge on one's behalf against someone who has offended him or has stolen his property. It is a common scene in Igbo environment to see symbols of one alusi (spirit) or another special object being placed on trees, fruits valuable farm products, etc. These are placed by the owners of these products, invoking spirits to do harm to the person who tampers with their property. This is called "ido iyi". The spirit in question is invoked to take vengeance on thieves who tamper with such property under their special protection. In the strict sense this is not sacrifice. Generally, on the one hand, the Igbo perform sacrifice to expiate for offences or evil committed, to prevent the actions of the wicked spirits and, on the other hand, to show their subjection to the divinities and the ancestors.

Why should one make sacrifices at all? From Igbo back-ground, "sacrifices are offered, not from any desire to give, but because of the fear that unless one does so, that one's life and interests will be blighted".[211] Basden strongly emphasizes that "the Igbo never offers sacrifice until forced to do so by adversity; except at such times there is an utter neglect of sacrifice."[212]

This means that the Igbo do not make sacrifice for the sake of it. Sacrifices are made in order to win the favour and goodwill of the gods and divinities. They are, so to say, means of attracting the attention of the gods and powers who threaten and limit individual freedom and self-realization. "Some sacrifices lack love and sincerity, therefore, sincere repentance would also be lacking in them. This is because the whole sacrifice is made out of fear of death and punishment. On the other hand, the Supreme God who rarely punishes, and has no particular place of worship requires from the people no particular sacrificial rites or items but appears very liberal and loving."[213] Thus, many praises and intimate prayers are given to God. God has no particular place of worship, and while prayers and offerings could be made to Him everywhere, give one the impression that the people believe that He is always close at hand. At this point, one can rightly ask: Who are the ultimate receivers of Igbo traditional sacrifice? What are the objects of Igbo traditional sacrifice?

1.14.14. THE OBJECTS OF IGBO TRADITIONAL SACRIFICE

As we have stated earlier, there are three major objects of belief in Igbo Traditional Religion. (1) The Supreme Being (2) the non-human spirits and (3) the Ancestors. Sacrifices are not categorized as being same; therefore, their objects cannot be same. The nature of the object of belief determines the nature of sacrifice being offered. This is because, as it is said, whatever is received, is received according to the nature and manner of the one receiving it.

The objects of Igbo traditional sacrifice can be categorized into three groups. (1) God (always good), (2) Spirits with shrines (good, just, severe, never altogether bad or evil), (3) Ancestors (good, just, exacting; never altogether bad or evil). The fourth group comprises the unknown "ekwensu" or non-human spirits (always evil) and disgruntled ex-corporate human spirit called "Akalogeli"

---

[211] Basden G.T., *Among the Ibos of Nigeria,* op. cit., p. 223.
[212] Ibid., p. 225.
[213] Odoemene N.A., *The Fundamentals of African Traditional Religion* (A key to African development) Snaap Press, Enugu, Nigeria, 1988, pp. 48 - 49.

(always evil).[214] Joyful sacrifices are for expiation of sin, petition, thanksgiving and homage and they are made to God, the known spirits or the ancestors. The joyless sacrifice is offered to the unknown evil spirits "akalo-geli."

1.14.15. SACRIFICE OFFERED DIRECTLY TO GOD (*CHUKWU*) WITHOUT ANY INTERMEDIARIES

As we have noted earlier, the cult of "Chukwu" (God) is not popular like the cult of the spirits and the ancestors in Igbo Traditional Religion. We have also stated the reasons for this. But one discovers also that "Chukwu" has no temple, no priests and no feast days. Therefore, some conclude that there is no direct sacrifice to "Chukwu" (God).

Many people, even the Igbo, at first sight may say or think that there is no traditional Igbo direct sacrifice to God. Some would not even give this idea a second thought, and the reason is that they understand sacrifice as "aja"- which means a joyless sacrifice always offered to evil spirits to keep them away. But close investigation has revealed that there is the "aja eze enu" (sacrifice to the kind of heaven). This sacrifice is found in many towns in Igboland. This type of sacrifice is interpreted as a sacrifice only meant for God.

1.14.16. THE REASONS WHY SACRIFICE TO GOD IS NOT FREQUENT AND POPULAR IN IGBO TRADITIONAL RELIGION

In Igbo Traditional Religion, there are many reasons why sacrifices are not frequently offered directly to God. One of the obvious reasons is that God is always good. God is seen in Igbo Traditional Religion as a perfect being. But the spirits are not always good as one may expect. We should know that all deities are spirits, but all spirits are not deities. The Igbo always make a distinction between good spirits and bad spirits. The Igbo man believes that God harms nobody, but the bad spirits can. God is absolutely good. Some spirits are always evil and easily get angry when they are neglected. No normal Igbo man would like to have problems with these bad spirits. So, people offer sacrifice to them to appease them and to avert their anger and punishment.

The Igbo traditional religionists then argue that God is perfect and does not need sacrifice. He has everything. What can man then give Him in sacrifice? Man can neither add nor subtract from His honour and glory. So, the Igbo man in his practical way of reasoning arrived at the practical conclusion that it was

---

[214] Arinze F., *Sacrifice in Igbo Traditional Religion*, op. cit., p. 90.

futile offering sacrifice or any external worship to God who is the fount of all things.[215]

"Chukwu" is regarded as so majestic and awful that man does not know how to approach him. The traditional religionists fear God and they consider themselves unworthy to approach Him either to thank or beg Him of some-thing. Therefore, they go through intermediaries - spirits and other divinities (who are believed to be great and influential before God). That is why they owe so much thanks to the particular spirits and the ancestors. The mention of God's name so often during a sacrifice is to call His attention towards the mediators and to awaken His sympathy so that He will grant the prayers of the people through the intermediaries – the gods and the ancestors. However, the strongest argument of the Igbo man for not sacrificing frequently to "Chukwu" is tradition (*Omenani*). The Igbo often say: so, did our forefathers, so it ought to be done as they handed on to us.[216]

1.15. "OSU" AS VICTIM OF SACRIFICE IN IGBO TRADITIONAL RELIGION

The issue of "Osu" is one of the most controversial issues in Igbo Traditional Religion before and after the advent of Christianity to Igboland even up till date. This is one of the key issues in Igbo Traditional Religion that Christianity found it difficult to impact a change or abolish. Of all the elements one may find in Igbo Traditional Religion, the "Osu" has been the most misunderstood. The social stratification the "Osu" still suffer in some Igbo communities even in recent times testifies to this fact. This has continued because of the tyranny of ancient beliefs and ideologies on the minds of those communities and individuals that took part in this act. This depicts a legacy of traditional religious beliefs and a reflection of inherited ancestral religious attitudes.

In some areas of Igboland, people claim that "Osu" is no longer in existence. Some suggest that the influence of Christianity in Igboland has changed a lot in Igbo Traditional Religion. But a careful study shows that this still exists in some areas of Igboland. What is "Osu"? Who is an "Osu"? How does one become an "Osu"? "Osu" in Igbo Traditional Religion means "consecrated one", "a living sacrifice". In popular language, "Osu" is an out-cast. Arinze defines "Osu" as:

---

[215] Unegbu M., *"Ibos and Christianity" in Missionary Annals*, Feb., 1954, p. 12 in *Arinze F., Sacrifice in Igbo Traditional Religion,* op. cit., p. 105.
[216] Arinze F., *Sacrifice in Igbo Traditional Religion,* op. cit., pp. 105 -106.

> A person who is specially consecrated to a spirit that has a shrine. He is symbolically immolated and is then left to live on as a "child or slave" of his alusi (deity).[217]

Today, once the name, "Osu", is mentioned in any Igbo community, it bears a specific connotation and designates a particular group of people, who have been stigmatized from time immemorial as social outcasts, to the point of dehumanization. No one can say clearly how the "Osu" system came to have its present connotation. But as available evidence shows, the "Osu" system has its roots in the practice of human sacrifice in Igboland.

The "Osu" were used as victims for sacrifice to deities by a community or a group of people or families. Occasionally, circumstances arose in which human sacrifices were believed to restore harmony, and so they were resorted to, to pacify an enraged deity to save the community, a group or a family.[218]

Some of the gods in Igboland demanded human sacrifices during their festivals to remove the abominations committed in the communities within the past year. This was seen as imperative if the deities were to continue their believed task of protecting the community during the coming year. Since such sacrifices aimed at general security, each living individual in the community, no matter his age, contributed to the general purse and this was called "utu-aja". The money collected was used to procure the victim. Explicitly and implicitly, by this payment, everyone was involved in the sacrifice, during which a human being was immolated or renounced as a living victim – carrying the iniquity of the people. He then personified the rage of the gods. His presence reminded the people of the rage of the gods and the calamity that caused his being sacrificed.

1.15.1. THE NAME "OSU" AND ITS ROOT

In some parts of Igboland, people answer names such as "Osuagwu," "Nwagwu", "Njoku", "Nwaigwe", "Osuchukwu", "Nwosu", "Nwamuo", "Osuji" and so forth. These people bearing these names maintain their social stand as "di ala" (free born) in their respective communities. But one may ask the significance of the prefix "osu", in these names, and in what contexts they are used.

From the names enumerated above, one can say that they are associated with some deities or spirits in Igboland. Most of these names are given to children supposed to have been born under the tutelary influence of these deities or

---

217 Arinze F., *Sacrifice in Igbo Traditional Religion*, op. cit., p. 105.
218 Onwubiko O.A., *Facing the Osu Issue in the African Synod (A personal Response)*, Snaap Press Ltd., Enugu, Nigeria, 1993, pp. 24 - 25.

spirits. "Osuigwe", for instance, suggests the name of a person born after his parents had gone to "Igwekala umunneoha" (a deity) to perform the rites of getting children (*Iyo Nwa).* Also, is the name "Osuagwu" associated with the performance of the rites of "Agwu-Isi" and it is given to a child born after this rite.

So, the name "Osu" means, one connected with the deity or the divine in a special way, as opposed to the ordinary man, born under natural and normal circumstances of his "Chi". So, the people who bear these names mentioned above may not be actually "Osu". How does one become an "Osu"? "Osu" is categorized into voluntary and involuntary "Osu". Under voluntary Osu we have self-dedicated "Osu". And under involuntary "Osu", we have inherited Osu and Osu by infection or contact.

1.15.2. VOLUNTARY "OSU"

In this case one willingly declares oneself an "Osu". Naturally, one does not under normal circumstances opt to become an "Osu". Hence, certain conditions may compel one to declare oneself an "Osu". People do not just as soon as they are born become "Osu", except those who inherited the stigma from their parents. However, factors such as victimization and frustration, poverty, debt and laziness could compel one to opt to become an "Osu".[219]

---

[219] Victimization and frustration: In those days in Igboland superiority of wealth and strength were demonstrably recognized and those who were not blessed with wealth and strength suffered humiliation on account of being poor and uninfluential. For example, a wealthy or strong man could take by force the property belonging to his wretched neighbour or sell off the property and the children of a poor "diala" (freeborn) without help coming from any quarters. If the poor continues to be maltreated up to the extent of usurping his rights and that of his children, such a helpless "diala" would opt for refuge, he could embrace and surrender himself to a deity for protection that had been too remote from him.

Poverty and Indebtedness: Where and when poverty led a free-born to borrowing with interests accumulating to an amount that would be very difficult for him to repay and the "diala" became so seriously indebted that he was confronted and threatened by the lender with an "alusi" the freeborn tried to "settle his debt" by embracing a deity to scare away the lender, who would automatically cease to approach his "debtor" for his money. This was because of the Igbo belief that the lender was bound to attract the wrath of the deity if he or she compelled the debtor to pay who has embraced a particular deity.

For example, out of Ignorance, children who at moon light plays or during hide-and-seek games, inadvertently kill domestic animal owned by a deity, were subjected to pay back by making very serious, expensive and elaborate offerings to atone for their carelessness and "sins" to such deities. This is in spite of the established fact that the offender is a juvenile and, therefore, below the age of proper reasoning. Depending on situation and circumstances, the deity in question could refuse the first set of offerings of probably a cow, goat and food as being inadequate and instead prefer a human being. Once a human being or human skull was the demand, the

1.15.3. INVOLUNTARY DEDICATION

In this case, one was forced by the people to be dedicated as an "Osu" not because of the circumstances in which one found oneself as we have already explained. But because one was forced to do so. In most cases, the victim has committed an act which was forbidden in the community and the alusi (deity) that was offended requested that a human being should be dedicated to him.

1.15.4. DEDICATION BY GENERAL CONSENSUS OF THE COMMUNITY

In some cases, notorious criminals were generally agreed by the community to be dedicated to a deity, in order to make sure that they do not bring shame to their families and the society. When this is done, the victim becomes an "Osu".

A fortune-teller or diviner could also inform a clan, village or community that their deity had requested that a human being be dedicated to it so that it might ward-off an imminent calamity that would befall them. Once people were told this, they in keeping and in obedience to the laws of their traditional religion, decided on how to get someone that ought to be sacrificed to the gods in order to appease them. For this to happen, there must be a consensus.

---

kindred, clan, village or entire community on whom that collective demand was made, usually decided to offer the offender (the person who killed the deity's domestic animals). In this circumstance, age was not considered, but the ultimate wish of the deity must be carried out. In the same way when an "Osu" was accidentally killed, the deity that owned such an "Osu" requested that such an offender be dedicated to him or her as an atonement for the heinous offence committed.

Through ignorance also, a free-born could become an "Osu" by walking across the out-stretched legs of an "Osu" while he or she was sitting down. By the same token, if a nursing mother had left her child to run down the farm or stream very quickly for fire-wood or water, and in her absence the child started crying, any nursing mother of the "Osu" class around who ventures to nurse the baby whose true mother had gone to the farm or stream automatically renders the baby an "Osu" if her generous act to the baby was known to other free-born within the vicinity. Thus, the baby grows up to find himself against his wish an "Osu", the fact that the parents were freeborn notwithstanding. This is what "Osu" by infection/contact means.

Laziness: The lazy ones in the society were always conscious that they were ready commodities to slave dealers. Once they suspected that they might be sold into slavery they could run into or take refuge with the deity. Once this was done, they could not be sold again and nothing would be done to them by either their parents or the entire town even when they had, prior to their surrender to the deity, made away with people's belongings, no matter their market values. Hunger added fuel to the propagation of the system. In those days, the powers of the gods, goddesses and shrines could not be under-rated, and as such, the weaklings, who could not face the vagaries of their time, took refuge in them — believing they would be protected and fed properly. Such refugees were then branded "Osu". Cf., Okeke R., The *"Osu" concept in Igboland*, Dona prints, Enugu, Nigeria, 1986, pp. 29 -30.

An individual could be asked to dedicate himself on behalf of his family so that things, especially their harvests and businesses would boom.[220]

It is pertinent to say that when a normal person marries an "Osu", the person may not become an "Osu" automatically but his children and children's children become "Osu" by heredity. In social life, the position of the ndi "Osu" (dedicated persons, outcasts) was not an enviable one. "They are regarded as the lowest in the social ladder, and even more despicable than slaves. They could inter-marry only among themselves and were excluded from many social gatherings. And when a person becomes an "Osu" all his descendants became *ipso facto* ndi Osu."[221]

1.15.5. THE CEREMONY OF DEDICATION OF A PERSON AS AN "OSU"

The ceremony of dedication of a person who voluntarily offers himself to be given to a deity (*alusi*) as an "Osu" is not same as the one the community presents to be offered. The trend is that the person who offers himself does so to his own advantage while the community offers a person not to the person's advantage but to the advantage of the community. The end point, however, is that in both cases, the individuals concerned are the property of the "alusi" (deity) to whom they are sacrificed.

On the day of dedication, the person who voluntarily opts to be dedicated is taken to the shrine before which he stands. The priest begins his incantation thus: *Anyone who injures you or sheds your blood, may the gods take revenge on your behalf. If you go to war, may you be assisted by the gods*! After these words have been uttered, some portion of the ear is cut off. It is usually the left ear. The mark is also usually in a "V" shape. The cut-out portion of the ear is placed in the shrine. However, if the person is a woman, the ear is not cut off. An opening is made in one of the hands and blood is taken from there and the shrine smeared with it. The person is then given a cup of wine to drink, a kola-nut, and phallic chalk to chew. All these are the property of the "alusi" which he gives to the person in appreciation for the blood received and a mark of ownership on the person. The priest then picks up his "ofo", striking it religiously on the head of the victim. He finally says, "you are an Osu". The person is then informed that whenever the deity makes a demand of him, he or any of his children could be used to oblige the deity.[222]

---

[220] Okeke R., *The "Osu" Concept in Igboland*, op. cit., p. 35.
[221] Arinze F., *Sacrifice in Igbo Traditional Religion*, op. cit., p. 354.
[222] Mgbobukwa J., *Alusi, Osu and Ohu in Igbo Religion and Social Life,* Fulladu Publishing Company, Nsukka, Nigeria, 1996, pp. 17 - 18.

Another version of the dedication of an "Osu" states that the ceremony of dedication is called "igo mmadu osu" (consecrating a person an Osu). At Awka, Nigeria, for instance, it is a solemn religious ceremony. On the appointed day, all the "Ozo" men (titled men) and all the people gather at the shrine. The priest of the deity takes up his "Ofo" and dedicates the victim thus:

> Our father please, receive with a good heart this gift we offer you today; may trouble and sickness depart from us, our wives and children. May this "Osu" bear all these ills instead of us. Then all the people present respond heartily: Ise! O bu ife anyi yolu. (Yes, that is what we ask for). Then the victim is held strongly, one ear is cut off him, and his blood is sprinkled on the special part of the shrine containing the symbol of the Spirit. This is the symbolic immola-tion. Henceforth he is an "Osu", a living sacrifice.[223]

From the accounts given above of the dedication of a person to a deity, through which that person becomes an "Osu", one perceives that, to think of misfortune is to think of "Osu"; to think of ill is to think of "Osu"; to think of death is to think of "Osu". All these are expected to be the lot of an "Osu" and never of a free-born. Hence, everybody tries to distance himself as much as possible from an "Osu".[224]

1.15.6. THE ROLE OF "OSU" IN IGBO TRADITIONAL RELIGION

"Osu" has a unique role in Igbo Traditional Religion. "Osu" themselves in some communities in Igboland are priests of cults and are in most places subordinate to the chief priests".[225] "Osu" runs errands for the chief priest in deity's shrine. "Osu" can also become a chief priest. This occurs under certain circumstances.

Although an "Osu" may occupy the position of the chief priest, a sacred position, he is always seen by the people as a priest without power and prestige. Therefore, he does not command any respect nor is he being admired by the society. In some communities in Igboland, because of the restricted movements of the "Osu", they normally live together. Sometimes, unconsciously, they act as "watch dogs" keeping watch over the property of the free-born.

It was strongly believed in Igbo Traditional Religion that the "charms" prepared by the "Osu" were very powerful and effective. These charms were believed to be very powerful and difficult to defile because of the fact that the "Osu" do not neutralize any charm known to have been prepared by a fellow "Osu". Unfortunately, the free-born traditional doctors found it difficult to neutralize

---

[223] Arinze F., *Sacrifice in Igbo Traditional Religion*, op. cit., pp. 177 - 178.
[224] Mgbobukwa J., *Alusi, Osu and Ohu in Igbo Religion and Social Life*, op. cit., p. 19.
[225] Okeke R., The *"Osu" Concept in Igboland,* op. cit., p. 42.

the charms of the "Osu" for the simple reasons that before such could be done, the makers of such charms must give their blessing by teaching the free-born the method to adopt if they should neutralize the potency of the charm.[226] The charms prepared by the "Osu" were used during inter-tribal wars and they were found very effective.

1.15.7. THE IMMUNITY ENJOYED BY THE "OSU" IN IGBOLAND

It may sound contradictory to say that the "Osu" enjoyed little rights and privileges but had almost one hundred percent immunity from the laws of the land. One of the privileges that the "Osu" enjoyed was that they often go free even when they had committed capital offences because nobody was willing to prosecute them. The fear is that the prosecutor might incur the wrath of the deity which owns the "Osu". Be that as it may, one is constrained to agree with this observation because of the fact that an "Osu" could commit an offence no matter the gravity and go free. It simply means that he has an immunity which he enjoys as a privilege, no more, no less.

 It is on record that the "Osu" was not threatened for paying tax or community development levies; not because they were not well-off to pay but because they were neither asked to pay nor disturbed for failure to do so, since there was nobody that dared make such demand.[227] It is this immunity that the "Osu" enjoyed that gave them the courage sometimes to tamper with peoples' property and go free.

1.15.8. THE OSTRACISM WHICH FACED THE "OSU" IN IGBO SOCIAL WORLD

Of all the descriptions of an "Osu" and his situation, Achebe in his book "Things Fall Apart," most clearly describes what "Osu" is. He says that "Osu" was:

> A person dedicated to a god, a thing set apart – a taboo forever and his children after him. He could neither marry nor be married by the freeborn. He was in fact an outcast, living in a special area of the village, close to the great shrine. Wherever he went he carried with him the mark of his forbidden caste, tangled and dirty hair. A razor was a taboo to him. An "Osu" could not attend an assembly of the freeborn, and they in turn, could not shelter under his roof. He could not take the four titles of the clan, and when he died, he was buried by kind in the evil forest. [228]

"Osu" was renounced as a sacrificed person; and sacrifice as we know, involves a transposition of an object, animal or person, from the secular to the 'sacred'

---

226 Ibid., p. 43.
227 Ibid., pp. 55 - 56.
228 Achebe C., *Things Fall Apart,* op. cit., p. 143.

state. This transposition works a psychological change of attitude in the person who offers, contributes, provides for or performs the actual ceremony. In the case of an "Osu", this change of attitude determines and affects his future relationship with those who sacrificed him. This is why, when the life of an "Osu" was spared, he was still considered dead in all aspects of social life, so much so that anyone interacting with him, was believed to incur a ritual impurity which bears a consequent social contamination. In this belief then, he could not intermingle with the 'living', and thus could not attend the assembly of free-born.

Another belief that counts for the dehumanizing attitude towards the "Osu" is the fact that they belong to no common ancestral lineage and have no symbols of a common real and known ancestor, namely, "ndi-ichie", and "ofo", and as such, they are believed to have no morality and no after life. This is why they were thrown into the evil forest and no formal funeral ceremony organized for them. They were not "diala" of the community among whom they find them-selves. Since they cannot go back to their original homes in this life, it was further believed that they could not also trace their ancestors in the spirit world, and as such, they could not reincarnate.

It was believed that people could not trade safely with them; their very presence was abhorred. Myths were invented to mystify their condition. It was put forward that yams, bought from them, when planted, would cause the yams of the "diala" (free-born) not to yield abundantly. They were believed to be rich and extremely beautiful as a special mark from their owner - god.

Since the "Osu" were people from different and unrelated places, there were no traces of consanguinity and affinity between them; so, they could marry in the exogamous institution of marriage in Igboland. In due course, they increased and multiplied and gradually developed into a social group, sharing common values, interests and attitudes among themselves. It is the lack of proper understanding of their system of marriage that has made some to equate the "Osu" with the "untouchables" of the Indian caste system. The "Osu" is not chosen by the deity but rather conditioned to stay with or choose the deity as a last resort. He does not fall into any of the hierarchies of those who own the deity. He has no sacred function to perform, except the servile work he did and at times they can go on errands for the priest of the deity, especially as messengers of the deity, to someone sued before the court of the deity, and in this capacity, they could collect debts.

As the "Osu" gradually developed into little communities, they became a state within a state and organized themselves. Their increasing number worsened the social distortion which the slave trade had created. They took advantage of the repulsive attitude the people had towards them to claim lands, beyond those assigned to them originally; they started working themselves up for emancipation. The normal question which a non-Igbo person may ask is: Why are the "Osu" treated this way; were they not regarded as human beings? "The central point of Igbo world-view is that it is anthropocentric. The Igbo, like many other African communities place man (madu) at the center of their universe."[229] One may ask: Were the "Osu" not included in the category of human beings (madu)? Or were they less human according to the Igbo traditional mind? Mgbobukwa asserts:

> For the Igbo, this man who is at the center of the universe is the free-born. Those regarded as "Osu" are of course not there with them. The free-born does not in some cases after all regard "Osu" as a human being.[230]

The situation of the "Osu" was indescribable. The only way one can describe it in modern terminology is by using the word "apartheid." Apartheid policy is the only modern terminology that can describe a little what the situation of the "Osu" looked like. Dureke, in trying to give the world the mental picture of what the "Osu" went through states: "Umuosu" (descendants of or children of Osu) (or the Osu themselves) were sequestrated from society and as such suffered total ostracism. They could not sleep under the same roof with the so-called freeborn citizens – "diala" sons and owners of the land. They neither ate from the same pots nor drank with the same cups with the citizens. Marriage between the two groups was a taboo eternally. Children were forbidden to see the corpse of an "Osu". An "Osu" could not be a chief or a leader of any village…. If the corpse of an "Osu" was to be carried through the village of a "diala", palm fronds were placed everywhere to warn the people that evil was in the air and a bad event was to happen. "If an 'Osu' had sexual intercourse with a 'diala' woman, the offending woman was to be dragged to the 'Osu' to marry for free. Under no circumstances would a 'diala' run into the compound of an 'Osu' even if it was raining or he was being chased with a gun or machete. If one did so, one automatically becomes an Osu".[231]

1.16. "OHU" (SLAVERY) PRACTICE IN IGBO TRADITIONAL RELIGION

Slavery as an institution has existed in most ancient societies. Slave was an indispensable element of a household, especially of the rich. The first house-

---

[229] Oguejiofor J., *"The Spirit of the Igbo of Nigeria"*, Piestes Africaines, p. 62, in Mgbobukwa J., *Alusi, Osu and Ohu in Igbo Religion and Social Life,* op. cit., p. 32.
[230] Ibid., p. 32.
[231] Dureke C., Sunday Times Newspaper, Lagos, June, 13, 1985, p. 5 in Okeke R., *The "Osu" Concept in Igboland,* op. cit., p. 64.

hold, for Aristotle, is an association formed by men with women and slaves. He further advanced this view and affirmed that Hesiod was right to say: "Get first a house and a wife and an ox to draw the plough."[232]

The ox, Aristotle explained, was a poor man's slave. This brings to mind the fact that slavery in ancient times was the foundation of industry and a potent instrument in the expansion of wealth. Slavery (Ohu) has been practised in different forms in the past in Igboland and in many parts of the world. It is also today practised in different forms in some parts of the world. We are not going to discuss the practice of slavery in detail. But we are going to discuss only the aspect that touches Igbo Traditional Religion. In Igbo traditional setting, "Ohu" (slave) is a person bought by another, bought with money or has been exchanged for another valuable article.

In some cases, "Ohu" may be a person that was captured as a prisoner of war. In both cases, "Ohu" is subjected to the control of his master – the person that bought him/her. The life of "Ohu" is in the hands of his/her master. The owner of the slave may take his/her life anytime he wants. He may decide to sell him/her to another interested buyer. An "Ohu" is therefore "a person bought with money, expected in addition to render services to his master at whose discretion it is also to use the person so bought for some other purposes for which he so wishes".[233]

This is actually what an "Ohu" stood for in Igbo traditional context. In a general sense and in common language, an "Ohu" is taken to be a domestic slave to his master. This points to the fact that the "Ohu" has no personal rights as the case may be; his/her rights as a human being are subjected to the rights of his master. This has many implications. One of the implications is that anyone who offends a slave has offended the master of that slave. When we were discussing "Osu" in Igbo Traditional Religion, we said that whoever offends an "Osu" has offended the "alusi" (deity) that owns that "Osu". "Osu" is a person dedicated to an alusi (deity). In the same analogy, a slave is a person subjected in obligation and service to another person. The difference between "Osu" and "Ohu" is that "Ohu" "requires no sacrifices or dedication of human beings to fellow beings or deities. Rather, it is practicable and possible with the influence of money."[234]

---

[232] Aristotle, *The Politics, Bk 1, chap. 2,* in Onwubiko O.A., *Facing the Osu Issue in the African Synod, op.* cit., p. 18.
[233] Okeke R., The *"Osu" Concept in Igboland,* op. cit., p. 78.
[234] Ibid., p. 77.

As "Osu" is considered unclean, "Ohu" is also considered unclean. The difference is that an "Ohu" is less unclean than "Osu". Just as "Osu" is said to be consecrated to "alusi", the "Ohu" could well be said to be consecrated to their masters by virtue of the price paid on their heads. There are so many ways through which one can become an "Ohu". We have voluntary and involuntary ways by which one becomes an "Ohu". The voluntary method can be with the unfortunate role played by laziness, and to some extent, the political machinations of the aristocrats of early Igbo society. The involuntary ways are seen in the war situation, kidnapping, poverty and strong belief in Igbo Traditional Religion.

In Igboland, distinction must be made between the slaves owned by the deities – the "Osu", and the man-owned slaves – the "Ohu". It is the existence of the "Osu" and "Ohu" that accounts for the institution of domestic slavery, which the slave traders capitalized upon in their bid to depopulate Africa in the transsaharan and transatlantic slave traffic. The origin of slavery in Igboland is dual–religious and economic. We know that human sacrifice was, until quite recently, practised in Igboland and the victims were either war captives, kidnapped people, children who had some abnormalities at birth and the never-do-wells.[235]

The groups just mentioned could be bought and owned by men for domestic purposes and they become a sort of status symbol for their masters. "Ohu" is a person who is alienated from his real home by one of the reasons we have mentioned above. His only disability is that he is owned and he is not a free man. He cannot go when he wants unless he is redeemed. He enjoys the company of the people and is not stratified and discriminated against in the society, except in participation in certain religious matters like being the priest of a deity. But this does not prevent people from acknowledging his "di ala" (free-born) status as distinct from the "Osu" status. The "Ohu" lives in the same home with his master. He works with and for him and in due course earns some money to redeem himself if he is hard-working. He could be absorbed into the family of his master through marriage, in which case, it was forbidden, to mention facts of his origin.

In Igboland, a slave (Ohu) could save money of his own, carry on business and have his own slaves. There are some historical evidences to show that some "Ohu" rose to positions of honour and importance in their master's home in Igboland and eventually became men of great influence. The case of Jaja of

---

[235] Isichei E., *History of West Africa since 1800,* op. cit., p. 47, in *Onwubiko O. A., Wisdom Lectures on African Thought and Culture,* op. cit., p. 19.

Opobo is a good example. He was an "Nkwerre" man born in "Amaigbo" and sold for cutting the upper teeth first (*ipu eze enu)* which was a taboo.

1.16.1. LAZINESS AS ONE OF THE FACTORS THAT LEAD TO SLAVERY

In the pre-colonial era and shortly after that, when parents noticed that their children were very lazy and would become unproductive in future, sold them into slavery. The money realized from that was used in training other children who were believed would be more productive and useful in life to their parents. The lazy children in some cases, as soon as they suspected that they could be sold by their parents into slavery, took refuge in either a shrine or in the house of any of the wealthy men around, thereby rendering themselves voluntarily "Osu/Ohu". This is not done with the aim of securing a loan but to be freely fed and above all be protected. Okeke emphatically asserts that:

> Parents especially fathers also sold any of their children that they feel would bring shame to the name and reputation of their family in keeping with the saying 'that good name is better than silver and gold' – *ezigbo afa ka ego*.[236]

1.16.2. INTER-TRIBAL WAR CAPTIVES

In those early days throughout Igboland, any war captive, before he was told, normally regarded himself as a slave of the traditional ruler of the side that captured him or a "cult-slave", "Osu/Ohu alusi".

1.16.3. VICTIMS OF MARGINALIZATION AND KIDNAPPING

During the period when slavery was being practised in Igboland, the children of the marginalized parents were either taken away from them forcefully or being kidnapped by the rich. They were sold into slavery by the wealthy ones. "The prevalence of this rather pathetic development then forced the poor who is left now without any option, to find a way of seeking for protection where he could be tolerated and accepted. A refuge found under or during this period is not voluntary refuge as it normally turned the poor among the free born to domestic enslavement in the hands of the wealthy men. When this happens, their rights and privileges were not only measured but with some tyrannous masters, withdrawn completely."[237]

1.16.4. RELIGIOUS FAITH

This is the area where the issue of slavery touches directly Igbo Traditional Religion. "In some communities in Eastern part of Nigeria, people because of

---

[236] Okeke R., *The "Osu" Concept in Igboland*, op. cit., p. 81.
[237] Ibid., p. 82.

their faith in Igbo Traditional Religion, do not injure fellow human beings to the extent that blood is visibly seen flowing out from their body. This was because such acts were viewed as being serious and in some extreme cases as abominable. For this therefore, it was a rule that whoever does this should either be killed or sold."[238] Therefore, some who found themselves in this situation opted to be slaves (Ohu) to some powerful men in order to be protected and be saved from being killed or sold out to a foreigner.

It is pertinent to state here that the Igbo Traditional Religion welcomed in the past the practice of "Ohu". An "Ohu" could be dedicated to an "alusi" (deity). When this is done the "Ohu" becomes an "Osu". Human sacrifices were carried out in the past in many parts of Igboland with "Ohu" as a victim of the sacrifice. When an "alusi" (deity) demanded human sacrifice, the community involved in many occasions used "Ohu" for the sacrifice. In many cases "Ohu" became a victim of human sacrifice. We have to state categorically here, that this form of slavery stated in this work is no longer practised in Igboland and in Igbo Traditional Religion.

1.17. THE SECRET SOCIETIES IN IGBO TRADITIONAL SETTING

When we speak of secret societies in Igbo traditional setting, we do not necessarily mean secret cult in modern terminology. They are more of social clubs than secret cult. But one cannot use the term "social" for these societies, because we have always certain things that are secret about them.

We have many categories of secret societies in Igbo traditional society. But one common thing about these secret societies is that their membership is only open to males. These secret societies are so rooted in Igbo Traditional Religion and culture that Christianity finds it difficult to disorganize or Christianize. Up till today, we have disagreements that exist between these societies and Christians in some areas of Igboland. The most common of these secret societies is masquerade society known in some areas of Igboland as "Mmanwu" or "Mmuo".

Membership of a masquerade society is usually open to all the young men of fifteen and above. Full initiation into the society entails periods of tutelage for the new entrants. New members were often under oath not to reveal the secrets of a masquerade's society to non-members.[239] Why is it that these groups are associated with the term "secret"?

---

[238] Ibid.
[239] Ofomata G.E.K. (ed.), *A Survey of the Igbo Nation,* op. cit., p. 238.

One thing we have to know about the African world (Igbo inclusive) is that it is primarily a religious one in which any social organization or activity is given strong "religious" interpretation and meaning. Since religion permeates the outlook and understanding of the universe in African (Igbo) cosmology, there is nothing that is entirely beyond its scope. The societies that may be called "secret" in African (Igbo) world can be understood through the people's concept of "power", success and their use of the influence of the "peer group".[240]

To give a definition of "secret society" according to Igbo mind-setting that will be acceptable and understandable globally is difficult. Members of some of these secret societies which we describe as "secret" do not accept that the organizations are "secret". They know that what they do is not left unprotected from unnecessary intervention of non-members; yet they insist that anybody who is interested is free to apply for membership and if he is qualified, will be initiated into the cult. Wedgewood, has attempted a definition which is both comprehensive and illuminating. She defines secret society in Igbo setting as:

> A voluntary association whose members, by virtue of their membership possessed some knowledge of which non-members are ignorant of. The nature of the knowledge varies from one such association to another. It may comprise magical or religious ritual or spells, some sacred objects, the identity of the members, the ostensible functions of the society or indeed the very existence of family life.[241]

Although we said earlier that membership in secret societies in Igboland is optional, sometimes conditions may force someone to seek for membership.[242]

---

[240] Onunwa U., *Studies in Igbo Traditional Religion*, Pacific Publishers, a division of Pacific Correspondence College and Press Ltd., Obosi, Nigeria, 1990, p. 16.

[241] Wedgewood C., *The Nature and Function of Secret Societies*, Occeania, vol. 1, 1930, p. 132 in Onunwa U., op. cit., p. 17.

[242] For example, in some areas of Igboland, a person who is not a member of the masquerade cult is usually told by his age grades to stay indoors (with women) when the members of the society play outside in the street. If he comes out, he will be mercilessly flogged and disgraced. Similarly, a young man feels disgraced and embarrassed in Igboland when his mates in one masquerade society or another tell him and other women to stay off the road on the day the masquerades are performing. On the day the masquerades test their skills, a ceremony during which they try their skills and dangerous charms on their fellow "maskers" and other members of the society. The general public and particularly non-members of the society are seriously warned to keep off the roads and stay indoors. Those who walk along the streets that day are adjudged "strong and powerful". On such a day, members of the "secret society" demonstrate their ability to endure pains when flogged with strong canes by their fellows. Those who shy away are disgraced whenever the community assemble. Men who hide away (with little children and women) are considered immature, weak, and would find it difficult to speak up in public whenever

1.18. THE TRADITIONAL NOTION OF DEATH AND FUNERAL CEREMONIES IN IGBO ONTOLOGY AND COSMOLOGY

It would be an omission not to discuss the traditional notion of death and funeral ceremonies in Igboland in this work. This is because this has been one of the areas where we have differences between Igbo Traditional Religion and other religions. Some of these differences are partly due to customs and traditions obtained in some areas of Igboland and partly due to the religious beliefs of the Igbo traditionalists.

1.18.1. THE NOTION OF DEATH AND HEREAFTER IN IGBO TRADITIONAL RELIGION

The Igbo traditionalists see death as not the end of life; rather it is regarded as a transformation from this life to the yonder world with the possibility of reincarnation. The spirit of the dead person lives in the spirit world where he enjoys the company of "Ndi Ichie" (the ancestors). He is therefore an intercessor for his family and kinsmen.[243] In agreement with the above assertion, Opoku states thus:

> Death is a transition from this present earthly life to another life in the land of the spirits. It is a journey which man must make in order to reach the life beyond and continue to live as an ancestor. As death is not the end of man, it does not sever his connections with his family. On the contrary, death extends the family relationships into infinity.[244]

Although death is not the end of life, the Igbo generally dread it. This fear of death is reflected in the names the Igbo give to their children such as "Onwudinjo" (death is bad!), "Onwudiwe" (death is wicked!), "Onwuemelie" (death has defeated), "Onwubiko" (death please!), "Onwuchekwa" (death wait!). "Onwuatuegwu" (death is fearless), just to mention but a few. However, the Igbo see death as unavoidable end.

Death is conceived of as a departure and not a complete annihilation of a person. The spirit of the dead moves on to join the company of the departed, and the only major change is the decay of the physical body, but the spiritual

---

the community assembles to take decisions on certain matters. They are called all sorts of derogatory names. Such men are not considered "gallant" enough to fight in defense of their community in the days of inter and intra-village wars and as such should not be accorded the sort of respect due to "men of power and strength." Cf., Onunwa U., *Studies in Igbo Traditional Religion,* op. cit., p. 19.

[243] Cf., Nwala T.U., *Igbo Philosophy,* op. cit., p. 63.

[244] Opoku K.A., *West African Traditional Religion*, op. cit., p. 133.

moves on to another state of existence.[245] Death in Igbo Traditional Religion, therefore, is regarded as a transition from one state of existence to another. It is a passage from this earthly existence to another world. In view of this, great care is taken in burying the dead. There are elaborate funeral rites and ceremonies which reinforce the belief that death is only a transition and therefore there is life after death.

1.18.2. FUNERAL CEREMONY AND ITS SIGNIFICANCE TO THE IGBO TRADITIONAL RELIGIONISTS

Many Igbo traditional religionists believe that sometimes deaths are caused by some forces, deities or some other agencies. Hence, when someone dies, the cause of his death has to be ascertained. If there are problems which the deceased had before his death, which were not settled, that must be resolved before the funeral ceremonies take place. Such issues like debts owned by the deceased; atoning for any crimes the deceased may have committed; performing any unfulfilled rites to the dead parents, ancestors and the gods of the community; such things that ritually could have delinked the deceased from cultural and social groups like the age grade, associations and cults to which the deceased belonged while he was alive, etc. These issues must be settled before the funeral ceremonies take place. It is strongly believed that if this is not done and the funeral ceremony is not performed, the deceased will not rest in peace until all cases are settled and a befitting funeral ceremony performed.

Not all funerals take the same form. We have variations in funeral celebrations. Certain things come into consideration in determining the type of funeral ceremony that ought to be accorded to a deceased person. These are to be taken into consideration: How the deceased passed away, the type of illness he suffered before his death, his status in life, just to mention but a few. These conditions determine the type of funeral that should be accorded to the deceased. The funerals of kings are marked differently from those of ordinary folk. It is pertinent to note that the funeral ceremonies were not accorded to every deceased person in Igboland. With regard to this, Basden states thus:

> For a free-born man the best possible arrangements must be made – there must be no half-measures, and no stinginess on the part of the family. In the case of chief or rich person, the highest honors will be rendered and no expense spared to give their relative a worthy send-off. On the other hand, the bodies of lepers, and such as those from noxious diseases, and those whose death cannot be accounted for satisfactorily, are disposed of hurriedly. Lepers

---

[245] Mbiti J.S., *African Religions and Philosophy,* op. cit., p. 205.

and those who die of smallpox are not buried. They are simply thrown out into "ajo ofia" (evil forest).[246]

But this is no longer the practice today. We shall explain this more when we
discuss the changes in Igbo Traditional Religion. The Igbo believe that a deceased person whose funeral ceremony is not performed and who is qualified
to be in the company of the ancestors may not enjoy the company of the ancestors until the funeral ceremonies are performed. In affirmation of the above
assertions, Opoku states thus:

> Funerals are great social occasions in West Africa (Igboland inclusive). They
> generally involve the whole communities who gather together at these events
> to perform appropriate rites which help to strengthen the bond between the
> living and the dead. There is also a wide-spread belief in Africa that, unless the
> proper rites and ceremonies are performed, the spirit of the dead person may
> not be able to join the ancestral spirits. Thus, great satisfaction is derived from
> the performance of these funeral rites.[247]

In Igboland, it is not only seen as corporal work of mercy to bury the dead but
also an obligation. "It is the responsibility of the living to perform the funeral
rites of the dead properly and thereafter offer them sacrifice, food and drink
which constitute acts of remembrance and reverence. The dead, on their part,
begin to play a larger and more important role in human society in general and
in the life of their families in particular because of their increased powers.
Their role is to protect, direct, intervene and guide their families, and also
serve as elders of the family."[248]

1.19. THE CONCEPT OF REINCARNATION IN IGBO ESCHATOLOGY

1.19.1. REINCARNATION: ETYMOLOGY AND MEANING.

The noun "reincarnation" comes from the Latin roots **re,** meaning again, and
incarnare, meaning to take flesh. The word "reincarnation" does not have to
be a literal rebirth. However, the term can be used to mean a more figurative
reinvention or rebirth. If you believe in reincarnation, you believe that after
death a person's soul is reborn in another body. Certain religions hold this belief as a central tenet, including Hinduism and Buddhism.[249] In West African
traditional religion (Igbo Traditional Religion inclusive), reincarnation is con-

---

246 Basden G.T., *Among the Ibos of Nigeria,* op. cit., p. 114.
247 Opoku K.A., *West African Traditional Religion,* op. cit., p. 135.
248 Ibid., p. 133.
249 Cf., Vocabulary.com Dictionary.

ceived as the birth of the ancestor into the family and of certain category of persons into the world.

The Igbo believe strongly that man is a composite being of body and soul. They believe that the body may die and decay but the soul is immortal. Therefore, "the belief in reincarnation is based on the immortality of the soul".[250] The belief in the immortality of the soul is evident in the cult of the ancestors. The Igbo refer to their ancestors as the living dead. Although they are dead and cannot be seen physically, they still live on in spirit and are believed to be always around their loved ones.

Igbo belief in the survival of the human person after death in reincarnation in the ancestors, suggests their belief and concept of life after death. The eschatological view of the Bible does not therefore seem to tally with Igbo concept of after-life.[251] There are two forms of reincarnation, namely: - "igbanje" (repeat) for children and "ino uwa" (return to the world) for older people. The Igbo Traditional Religion holds that:

> For *igbanje*, not only are people believed to have been born again of the same or another mother, but also children who die young are believed to have 'decided' beforehand in their group when they would die, especially if they do not like the family. These children are called *ogbanje* (repeaters).[252]

With regard to "ino uwa", only the good progenitors are believed to reincarnate. Here is a practical reason how and why this is so: When a parent wishes to find out which of the good progenitors has returned, he goes to a fortuneteller and names all the ancestors. The fortune teller chooses from the list the name of the returned one. And as the parent only names the ancestors and pays the fortune-teller for his trouble, a bad progenitor never returns. Achebe in his famous novel "Things Fall Apart", describes *Ogbanje* illness and how it could be cured.[253]

---

[250] Opoku K.A., *West African Traditional Religion,* op. cit., p. 108.

[251] Onunwa U., *Studies in Igbo Traditional Religion,* op. cit., p. 96.

[252] Arinze F., *Sacrifice in Igbo Traditional Religion*, op. cit., p. 32.

[253] Ekwefi the wife of Okonkwo had suffered a good deal in her life. She had borne ten children and nine of them had died in infancy, usually before the age of three. As she buried one child after another her sorrow gave way to despair and then to grim resignation.
After the death of Ekwefi's second child, Okonkwo had gone to a medicine-man, who was a diviner of the "Afa" Oracle, to inquire what was amiss. This man told him that the child was an" Ogbanje", one of those wicked children who, when they died, entered their mothers' wombs again.
When Ezinma was born, everybody knew she was an "Ogbanje". Ekwefi believed deep inside her that Ezinma had come to stay. And this faith had been strengthened when a year or so ago a

1.19.2. REASONS FOR REINCARNATION

Are there other reasons why people reincarnate, except for one single purpose: to keep on living? Quarcoopome explains it thus:

> A person may reincarnate in order that an uncompleted destiny may be completed. This happens when a person dies prematurely in battle, accident or any other calamity and for this reason he was unable to complete his destiny. The person is then reborn to complete his destiny. In this case certain tasks to be performed, certain lessons to be learned and certain experiences to be undergone had all been unceremoniously terminated and that has to be completed.[254]

It is also believed that those who have lived unholy lives on earth are sent back to make amends.

1.19.3. THE GROUNDS OF BELIEF IN REINCARNATION ACCORDING TO IGBO TRADITIONAL MIND

Do we have reasons why an ordinary Igbo man should believe in reincarnation? How can he prove that reincarnation occurs? "The Igbo belief in reincarnation is complex. Any attempt to explain it on the basis of logical consistency is baseless and fruitless. For instance, ancestors are believed to have "come back" through reincarnation, yet offerings are made to them on their altars. It is therefore naive to look for empirical scientific and convincing reasons for the African (Igbo) belief in reincarnation."[255]

The belief in reincarnation is generally accepted by the Igbo traditional religionists but details of its understanding and application vary from place to place. Some of the reasons given by the elders from the different areas do not sound convincing. They also do not cut across all the culture areas of Igboland. However, three of the reasons stand out clearly. "The first is the idea of birth marks. Evidences have been given to the belief in the resemblance of a reincarnated baby with identical marks of the ancestors who died several years back. Scientifically this evidence has been dismissed with the genetic law of dominance and recession."[256]

---

medicine-man had dug up Ezinma's "iyi-uwa" - (bond with the world of Ogbanje). It was then that everyone knew that Ezinma would live because her bond with the world of "Ogbanje" had been broken. With the digging out of Ezinwa's "iyi-uwa" (the bond with the world of Ogbanje), she was automatically cured of "Ogbanje" illness. Cf., Achebe C., *Things Fall Apart*, op. cit., pp. 61 - 68.

[254] Quarcoopome T.N.O., *West African Traditional Religion*, op. cit., p. 102.

[255] Wilson I., *Reincarnation*, in Onunwa U., *Studies in Igbo Traditional Religion*, op. cit., p. 98.

[256] Onunwa U., *Studies in Igbo Traditional Religion*, op. cit., p. 98.

Another fact that points to the reality of the concept of reincarnation are the names given to children believed to be reincarnated ancestors. Different parts of Igboland have people who bear names like Nna-nna (father's father) or Nne-nna (father's mother) indicating that the bearer is believed to be the late father of his own father who had reincarnated. In the same way, the bearer of the second name is the "mother" of the father of the child.

People have given reports and evidences of babies who lost weight and disturbed their parents with persistent crying because the diviner could not give the correct names and identities of the ancestors who reincarnated in those babies. The problem is resolved soon after the correct names are given by the same or another diviner. [257]

These explanations given above are not enough to prove the reality of reincarnation in Igbo traditional setting. We may accept the concept of reincarnation on the basis of belief and not on empirical or scientific evidence.

We have to emphasize that several factors could militate against the chances of an ancestor reincarnating. Human factors are prominent in inhibiting an ancestor from reincarnating. This involves moral as well as ethical factors. For example, if a man was immoral, wicked and perhaps did not lead a transparently honest life while on earth, it is believed that such a person would not join the cult of ancestors in the spirit world. Those who were excluded and excommunicated from joining the council of elders in the spirit world are not "canonized" by the living. Thus:

> The living relatives can restrict a known wicked immoral man from 're-entering' the lineage. This is done through the services of a powerful 'medicine man' who used charms to bind the dead man in the spirit world. It is only those who had been recognized as ancestors that are believed and allowed to reincarnate.[258]

1.19.4. JUDGMENT, HEAVEN AND HELL IN IGBO ESCHATOLOGY

The Igbo have their own concept of judgment after death. It is different from the Christian concept of judgment after death. They believe that "in the hereafter judgment takes place. It is the general belief that the soul appears before God for judgment and the judgment is determined by one's conduct while on earth."[259]

---

[257] Quarcoopome T.N.O., *West African Traditional Religion,* op. cit., *p. 99.*
[258] Ibid., pp. 102 - 103.
[259] Ibid., p. 127.

For the Igbo people, the performance of appropriate funeral rites for a deceased is absolutely necessary for his admission into the spirit land. A person who for whatever reason is not given the final rites cannot get to the spiritual land. He remains on earth as a wandering spirit and haunts the living. At the completion of the funeral rites, the spirit of the deceased enters the ancestral shrine and can henceforth be venerated. Meanwhile, his spirit goes before "Chukwu" (God) for an interview. What are actually said during this interview are unclear. However, the Igbo believe that it is in the nature of a judgment. This is borne out by numerous sayings which imply that God will judge each person after death and mete out punishment or give reward. For example, a person who is wronged but cannot get a redress, may say, "you will see, God is not asleep". Other sayings, like "God will Judge", "justice is in the spirit land", certainly refer to this intervention by God to demand an account of one's life in this world. After this interview, God decides whether one reincarnates at once or remains for some time in the spirit land.[260]

> The deceased is permitted according to the wishes he expresses, either to remain forever in the land of the spirits or to return once more to the world.[261]

For Leonard, it is the deceased spirit that decides whether he would reincarnate or not. But contrary to this view, which we shall later examine, some hold that the decision lays entirely on God. One of the desires of every Igbo man at death is to reach the spirit world and enjoy the fellowship of the ancestors. Damnation and punishment mean total exclusion from clan life in the spirit world.

The ancestral joy of one who had lived well here on earth, had been considered fit to be in the company of the ancestors in the spirit world and being venerated as one of the ancestors, is a graphic expression of heaven according to Igbo Traditional Religion. Excommunication and exclusion from the company of the ancestors is regarded as a graphic expression of hell. Those souls who are in this state do not reincarnate.[262] Thus, the right to decide whether a spirit should reincarnate or not rests with and depends entirely on the Creator.

We have another aspect of reincarnation, which is called partial reincarnation or transmigration of the soul.[263] The conviction of the Igbo on the actual pro-

---

[260] Metuh-Ikenga E., *God and Man in African Religion,* op. cit., p. 260.

[261] Leonard A., *Lower Niger and its Tribes* (ed.), 1968 p. 186, in Metuh-Ikenag, E., *God and Man in African Religion*, op. cit., p. 260.

[262] Cf., Onunwa U., *Studies in Igbo Traditional Religion*, op. cit., p. 97.

[263] A dead person may decide to resume or continue life in another area far away from his former one. He settles down in his new environment by beginning life all over again. He may marry and get children, build houses, start business and carry on a new but normal existence until he

cess and form by which man reincarnates varies. One version of the concept of reincarnation holds that man reincarnates with his former body and all its characteristics, of height, strength and complexion. Another version holds that at death, human bodies decay. The soul, which is immortal enters into another body and reincarnates. "In all cases of reincarnation, it is the immortal soul that decides after the death and decay of the body to come back into this world by entering a womb."[264] The stand of Quarcoopome on this issue is not logically sound. He holds: the soul decides whether to reincarnate or not. The soul did not create itself. It returns to its creator when it separates from the body after death, even if it is going to enter another body for reincarnation according to the Igbo traditional mind.

1.19.5. ARGUMENTS LEVELLED AGAINST THE CONCEPT OF REINCARNATION

There are many arguments levelled against the concept of reincarnation. It is pertinent that we look into some of these arguments. If man reincarnates by the process of the soul taking up a new body not its former body, is this reincarnation according to the mind of the Igbo traditionalist? If the soul does not take up its former body and all its characteristics, height, strength, complexion, just to mention but a few, how do we prove that reincarnation has taken place?

When we were discussing the grounds of belief in reincarnation according to the Igbo traditional mind, we mentioned the idea of birthmarks. We stated that evidence has been given to the belief in the resemblance of a reincarnated baby with identical marks of the ancestors who died several years back. If the soul were to take up a new body and not the former body, then the idea of birthmarks is ruled out.

The Igbo believe that it is only the ancestors who can reincarnate and come back to their former families. This means that when one is not an ancestor, one cannot reincarnate. The Igbo venerate their ancestors. But how can one venerate a reincarnated ancestor who is no longer enjoying the company of the ancestors in the spirit world?

The general belief in reincarnation must be balanced against the practice of ancestral veneration. The ancestors are believed to be watching over their living relatives, guarding them and ensuring their general success in this life. At

---

either dies or moves to another place because his where about has been discovered by people who knew him in his former life. Cf., Quarcoopome T.N.O., *West African Traditional Religion,* op. cit., pp. 102 - 103.

[264] Ibid., p. 103.

the same time, they are thought to be reborn into their respective families and some are said to reincarnate several times. The difficulty here is whether an ancestor being venerated had not already reincarnated in another member of the family. Tempels tries to clear the logical incoherence that we notice in the reincarnation of the ancestors thus:

> This belief in the reincarnation of some ancestors seems at first sight to cancel all forms of veneration of ancestors. But it does not for the Igbo, or for Africans for that matter. It seems that only a part of the ancestor's spirit is believed born again. It is explicable by the philosophy of forces: the ancestor does not create the child. Africans do not hold that, for they know that God does this. It is not strictly the ancestral spirit that is reborn, but the child is supposed to come under his particular influence and to receive part of his vitality and qualities. Thus, the ancestral name is renewed in the family and the clan has an added advantage.[265]

Even with the above explanation given by Tempels, the concept of reincarnation in Igbo Traditional Religion still has a logical lacuna. If an ancestor reincarnates and does not do well morally in his next life, what happens then? Will he still enjoy the company of the ancestors after death? What happens to his soul? These and many more questions preoccupy the mind as regards this issue.

When we were discussing the reasons for reincarnation, we stated that a person may reincarnate in order to complete his destiny which he could not complete in his first life due to his sudden death. We also assert that those who are qualified to enjoy the company of the ancestors are those who died natural death, who did not suffer terminal illnesses before they died, who did not die of accident, were given befitting funeral, must have married and begotten a child or children, male child inclusive and have lived a good moral life. Based on these assertions, therefore, a person who died of accident and has not completed his obligation in life is not qualified to reincarnate because he is not qualified to be in the company of the ancestors.

The precise time the ancestral spirit enters the new child is uncertain. Beliefs found among some people suggest that it is at the time of conception, while others think that it is at the quickening or even at death. Apparently, all would agree that this happens in the womb before the child is born. The Igbo believe that God at conception creates a new individual spirit who eventually is born as a human being. Sometime before his actual birth, this spirit goes before God

---

[265] Tempels P., *La Philosophie Bantoue,* Paris, 1949, pp. 74-76, in Arinze F., *Sacrifice in Igbo Traditional Religion,* op. cit., p. 33.

and is allotted his destiny (*Chi*) and an ancestral guarding who then, as it were, imprints on this formless figure some of his own physical and character traits. Hence, the reincarnating ancestor is called "onye noro ya uwa" (the reincarnated personality). This shows that at least some Africans are aware that it is not the individuality of the ancestor that is reborn but his personality.

Since the doctrine of the extended self is a strong feature of African beliefs, this personality is thought of as the real self of the ancestor. So, the child may be given the same name as that of the supposed reborn ancestor, or simply given names as that of the supposed reborn ancestor, or simply given names which indicate who is reborn.[266] Hence, it is pertinent to say that reincarnation in Igbo ontology should be taken at the level of faith and not at the level of logic, reason or science.

1.19.6. THE PRESUPPOSED VALUES DERIVED FROM THE BELIEF IN REINCARNATION IN IGBO TRADITIONAL RELIGION

Many have levelled constructive criticisms against the belief in reincarnation. The question we should ask is: Has the belief in reincarnation helped in any way in building and observing the moral standard in Igbo traditional setting? "The concept of reincarnation has become a tool in the hands of the Igbo traditional philosophers and veritable religious specialists to explain many difficult and otherwise inexplicable questions of life."[267]The belief gives some psychological relief and solace to men and women who lost their parents and their loved ones early in life. Reincarnation makes meaningful the Igbo belief in life after death. Death is not the end of life. There is another life after death; and for the Igbo traditional religionists, the most practical way to make it meaningful is the belief in reincarnation.

The concept has for long served as a means of social and moral checks within the traditional society. The theory had therefore helped to minimize the rate of quarrels within the kin-group. Besides, it has given a strong family or lineage identity to people and assured them of their common destiny, mutual responsibility to one another as those who share common ancestors and pedigree. It has, therefore, helped to give validity to the Igbo belief in life after death and lineage identity. Denial of the chance to reincarnate and exclusion from the communion with the ancestors in the spirit world are ways the Igbo people explain the intriguing questions of hell and heaven.

---

[266] Parrinder, E.G., *African Traditional Religion,* 3rd ed., op. cit., p. 138, *Metuh-Ikenga E., God and Man in African Religion,* op. cit., p. 256.
[267] Onunwa U., *Studies in Igbo Traditional Religion*, op. cit., p. 103.

The Igbo through the belief in reincarnation struggle to build a traditionally clean, just and moral society. Man's excesses and rebellious tendencies had been held in check to a considerable extent in diverse subtle ways through the belief in reincarnation. The belief has been shown as another means by which the Igbo people express some fundamental truths about life after death, eternity, human destiny, heaven and hell, cult of the ancestors and the essence of moral life. The Igbo try to fight "DEATH", their greatest enemy, through this idea. It is an idea carefully designed to console one who is bereaved of a dear one. The belief in reincarnation comforts the dying persons who think that their status is not sufficiently raised in the life that is coming to an end. They hope therefore in the life to come that their status will be better.

1.20. WHAT HAS CHANGED WITH THE COURSE OF TIME IN IGBO TRADITIONAL RELIGION

1.20.1. INTRODUCTION

It is an obvious fact that a lot has changed in Igbo Traditional Religion. These changes may have come due to the influence of Christianity and foreign cultures and traditions. "Igbo atomistic organization and their openness to change has ensured many degrees of variations in almost every aspect of their religion and person."[268] These changes are not only seen in the spirituality of the Igbo but also in other aspects of their life. These reflect in their culture, mentality, politics, social life, just to mention but a few. Oguejiofor affirms this new development in Igbo Traditional Religion. He states:

> It is also important to note that much change has taken place in the sphere of Igbo Traditional Religion and hence Igbo character and cultural heritage. There has been the enormous influence of colonialism and the introduction of Igboland into a wider area known today as Nigeria. All these have led to a new way of life. There has been the influence of Western culture and Western technology which offered explanations for which the Igbo earlier sought the help of their deities.[269]

It is unrealistic and unintellectual to use today's yardstick to measure yesterday's events. A lot has happened in the past in Igbo Traditional Religion which one can call today 'atrocities', for example ritual killings, killing of twins, "Osu" cast system, just to mention but a few. Some of these 'atrocities' were committed based on one logic or the other inherent at that time which no longer applies. "Such mentality and belief like: The gods were the protectors of men;

---

[268] Oguejiofor J., The *Influence of Igbo Traditional Religion on the Socio-Political Character of the Igbo,* op. cit., p. 92.
[269] Ibid.

the gods had been offended therefore the gods should be pacified or propitiated. The evils were well-intentioned."[270]

From my investigations and findings, I discovered that some of the things which the Igbo people did in the past, which one can categorize as "atrocities" were done not that they wanted it that way. But they did it that way because it was enshrined in their religion and customs. They did those things which today can be tagged "atrocities" not because they appealed to reason. Some of these deeds were carried out under constraint. They were not done willingly. For example, no mother on earth would like her twins to be killed.

In those days the strongest argument of the Igbo man for doing certain things was: "the tradition (*omenani*) says so. The Igbo often say: so, did our forefathers, so it ought to be done as they handed onto us".[271] We have to note that these changes we notice today in Igbo Traditional Religion were able to take place because of the nature of the Igbo people. The Igbo are known to be docile in their character. They are ready to welcome change where it is necessary. It is observed that the Igbo receptivity to missions is not explained by anything distinctive in mission work among them, instead it is related to certain general features of Igbo culture. Oguejiofor affirms that:

> More than any other external factor, it is the combination of Igbo openness and receptivity to change, their adaptability, egalitarianism, devotion to hard work, concern for individual achievements just to mention but a few that explains the undeniable momentous success of Christian evangelism among them.[272]

Paradoxically, of all Nigerian people, the Igbo have probably changed the least while changing the most. While many of the formal elements of the social, religious, economic and political structures, such as lineage, family groups, age grades, and secret societies have been modified through culture contact, many of the basic patterns of social behaviour, such as the emphasis on alternative choices and goals, achievement and competition, and lack of strong autocratic authority have survived and are a part of the newly developing culture. Basic patterns of social behaviour, of interpersonal relationships, have changed a little, though new symbols of success replace old ones and new goals appear.

---

[270] Agbo C., *Culture and Arts in Pre-colonial Igbo Society*: in *Nigerian People and Cultures*, Eze-Uzomaka P. (ed.), *Nigerian Peoples and Cultures ed.*, Parakletos Immunnis Drive, Nigeria, 2016, p. 1.
[271] Arinze F., *Sacrifice in Igbo Traditional Religion,* op. cit., p. 106.
[272] Oguejiofor J., *The Influence of Igbo Traditional Religion on the Socio-Political Character of the Igbo,* op. cit., p. 93.

There are four major things which act as propelling forces for a shift from the old ways to new ideologies and beliefs in Igbo Traditional Religion. The four major things are: 1. Enlightenment, 2. development of science and technology in Igboland, 3. advent of Christianity to Igboland, 4. cross-fertilization of cultures and inculturation. Change does not occur without a cause. These four things mentioned above have acted as the propelling forces towards these changes we notice in Igbo Traditional Religion.

During pre-colonial era, when human sacrifice was being practised, when twins were being killed, when "Osu" were dedicated, the Igbo people were not as enlightened as they are today. They were not as educated as they are today. Science and technology had not been developed in Igboland as they are today. Some of their beliefs and actions were naive and irrational, for example, the killing of twins, human sacrifice and "Osu" cast system. However, we have to note that it is not everything that the Igbo people did in the past in the name of religion that can be tagged today as irrational. They have so many good things in their religion.

We have to emphasize here that Christianity would have had difficulties in penetrating the hinterland if the pre-colonial Igbo did not believe in "Chukwu", the Supreme God. Likewise, they would not have believed in the angels if they did not have the idea of "Chi", personal gods. Without their veneration of their ancestors, Christians of Igbo extraction would have found it difficult to believe in the cult of saints. All these are corollaries. One thing should be made clear here, the pre-colonial Igbo was monotheistic and at same time polytheistic. This idea of mono-polytheism has not changed with time.[273] We are not going to treat all the changes that have taken place in Igbo Traditional Religion in this chapter. The ones we have to handle here are the ones that concern this chapter.

1.20.2. CHRISTIANITY AND THE EMANCIPATION OF THE "OSU" IN IGBOLAND

As we have mentioned earlier, "Osu" were those dedicated to "alusi" (deities). There were several ways by which one could become an "Osu". We have already treated all that. The question is: Do the Igbo up till today practise "Osu" cast system in Igbo Traditional Religion? Arinze informs us that:

> Today no new "Osu" is being dedicated but many traditional religionists and some half-hearted Christians still observe these practices towards the descendants of the "ndi Osu", and still hesitate or refuse outright to have any

---

[273] Agbo C.O., *Culture and Arts in pre-colonial Igbo society*, in Eze-Uzomaka P. (ed.), *Nigerian Peoples and Cultures,* op. cit., pp. 18-19.

marital connections with them. It is hoped that with the spread of Christianity the "Osu" system and its practices will die.[274]

Reports of early Christian activities in 1863 in Igboland show that most of the foundation members of the Christian village "were converts who were slaves purchased by the missionaries or others who suffered from social disabilities, lepers, widows and a variety of others formed the hard core of the early Church congregation."[275]Christianity came with the message of universal brotherhood, equality, justice and love. The work of evangelization at that time was directed towards mental liberation, and for this, education was necessary to combat ignorance. Physical liberation was also emphasized and this was liberation from sickness and the breaking of the social barriers in Igboland. Thus, for the "Osu" in particular, Christianity was a religion of liberation (salvation). The Church preached the message of freedom and the "Osu" who had been suffering from societal dejection, for centuries, welcomed this message. Achebe asserts that:

> These outcasts or "Osu" seeing that the new religion welcomed twins and such abominations thought that it was possible that they would also be received. And so, one Sunday two of them went into the Church. There was an immediate stir; but so great was the work the religion had done among the converts that they did not immediately leave the church when the outcasts came. Those who found themselves nearest to them merely moved to another seat. It was a miracle.[276]

It is important to note, in the light of this quotation, that the same belief which effected the killing of twins was and still is the same belief that operates in the "Osu" system. While the "Osu" was used to cleanse an abomination committed by someone else through which people who incurred god's rage were safe, twins were killed because they were believed to have committed abomination in their former lives to cause the rage of the gods.

From this, one can see that right from the incipient stage of Christianity in Igboland, the Christian religion relentlessly directed its salvific energy towards the eradication of the obnoxious "Osu" practice. This was so successful that not long:

> Christian teachings of the love of one's neighbors began to undermine the worst forms of social oppression. Missionaries observed in Asaba, in 1870s

---

[274] Arinze F., *Sacrifice in Igbo Traditional Religion*, op. cit., p. 180.

[275] Ekechi F.K., *Missionary Rivalry and Enterprise in Igboland*, London, 1972, p. 12 in Onwubiko O. A., *Facing the Osu Issue in the African Synod, (A Personal Response)*, Snaap press Ltd., Enugu, Nigeria, 1993, p. 35.

[276] Achebe C., *Things Fall Apart*, op. cit., p. 142.

that titled men were turning against human sacrifices, which was supported mainly by a powerful interest group, dibia.[277]

The moves to accommodate the "Osu" was not an easy one; the eradication of the system in the society meant cutting across the roots of Traditional Religion itself. Yet the Christian missionaries were determined to save these souls, a task which was not without immediate adverse consequences on the evangelization of the Igbo. Realistically speaking:

> The early content of the congregation in fact militated against missionary work, for most people in society would not associate freely with these so-called social outcasts.[278]

This showed the depth of Christianization at the time, but as the missionaries were to see to their happiness and triumph within the first generation, there was a marked change of attitude. The free-born no longer consider it below their dignity to worship in the same place with the despised slaves. They have been gradually learning that in the sight of God, there is no difference – that all are alike – sinners, and that all need one thing which is very important – the salvation of their immortal souls.[279]

Though the free-born who became Christians looked more favourably towards the "Osu" as their brothers and sisters in faith, yet the attacks of the traditional religionists, in areas where the "Osu" system was an essential organ for promoting the cult of the deities, were constant. It became clear then that:

> While some people, however, were prepared to accommodate the new religion and the social changes that came with it, others were determined to maintain or to restore the purity of Igbo traditional life and religion. A movement towards this end was initiated in 1864. There were emissaries of one *Odosoruelu* (restorer of primitive style) in such towns as Obosi, Nkwere, Nsube, Ogbunike, and Ogidi.[280]

Such moves were obstacles which did not in the least make the missionaries relent in their efforts till today.

1.20.3. THE GOVERNMENT AND THE "OSU" SYSTEM

The "Osu" cast system was said to have been abolished in Igboland by then Eastern House of Assembly in 1956. The abolition based its stand/decision on

---

[277] Isichei E., *History of West Africa since 1800,* op. cit., p. 47.

[278] Ekechi F. K., *Missionary Rivalry and Enterprise in Igboland,* London, 1972, p. 12, in Onwubuiko O.A., *Facing the Osu Issue in the African Synod, (a personal response),* op. cit. p. 36.

[279] Ibid.

[280] Ibid., p. 37.

Section 20(1) of the then Constitution of the Federal Republic of Nigeria. This Section states that: "no person shall be held in slavery or servitude". Subsection (1) of section 23, provides that "every person shall be entitled to respect for his private and family life, his home and his correspondence."[281]

The then Eastern House of Assembly in 1956 passed a resolution abolishing "Osu" practices throughout Igboland. The law became effective from 10th day of May, 1956, as published in the Laws of Eastern Nigeria, 1963, Volume One. The Law states:

> Notwithstanding any custom or usage, each and every person who on the date of the commencement of this Law who is "Osu" shall from and after such date cease to be "Osu" and shall be free and discharged from any consequences thereof, and the children thereafter to be born to any such person and the offspring of such person shall not be "Osu", and the "Osu" system is hereby utterly and forever abolished and declared unlawful.[282]

The colonial administrators did not discriminate in their governmental and organizational systems, and so offered a protective front to the new awareness given to the "Osu" by the Christian religion. In heading public offices, the "Osu" were favoured and there were instances where some of the warrant chiefs were among this group. This gave them the opportunity to organize themselves into villages like the other villages, and in some cases, they took genealogical names – 'Ume'…prefixing a name of one of the ancestors of one of them, and from then they began to have the feeling of a common descent.

The official banning of the "Osu" system in Eastern Region in 1956 was a definitive stand of the colonial government on an issue it had hitherto handled with tacit caution. In fact, a Law was passed by the government prohibiting the use of the word "Osu" or "Ohu" to describe any member of this class. Speaking on the Second Reading of the abolition of the "Osu" system Bill, Dr. Azikiwe noted the aims of the Bill and said:

> …this Bill seeks to do three things: To abolish the "Osu" system and its allied practices including "Osu" and "Ohu" system, to prescribe punishment for their continued practice and to remove certain social disabilities caused by the enforcement of the "Osu" and its allied system.[283]

With this Law on their side, the "Osu" began to take titles in some Igbo communities. It has earlier been mentioned that they formed themselves into au-

---

281 Okeke R., The "Osu" Concept in Igboland, op. cit., pp. 112 -113.
282 Ibid., p. 113.
283 Nzimiro I., Studies in Ibo Political Systems, London, 1972, p. 27, in Onwubiko O.A., Facing the Osu issue in the African Synod, (A personal Response) op. cit., p. 38.

tonomous villages and kindred; so, they could perform the rites of "ozo ulo" on the kindred level, and the "diala" (free born) could not forbid them from performing the "ozo ama", on the town level. When they took titles, they were careful to take honorific names which would suggest that their ancestors were taking titles. Thus, "ozo" names such as "Durunaamuze" or "Okpalannanyere-ugo" were taken by them.

As a whole, they stopped carrying out any duties or functions connected with any customs that traditionally either perpetuated the practice or the concept of the system. They refused paying the customary allegiance which they were ought to pay to those who originally dedicated them or their ancestors to the cults of the deities. For instance, during festivals, they no longer went for the ritual renewal of their dedication whether they were Christians or not (it could be understood if Christians among them cut off traditional religious festivals, but what of the non-Christians among them?). They could sue the freeborn if they directly or indirectly tried to claim this right. It must be mentioned here that in the course of this research we came to know of many cases in this regard in the High Courts. [284]

One discovers that traditionally, "Osu" has no social right and by extension no legal right. In fact, "Osu" was neither sued nor was found worthy to sue anyone. His one and only arbiter is the "alusi" (deity) and his saviour in most communities is the fear which people have for "alusi", the fear of revenge which they believe is sure to come if the "alusi" is offended through his attendant.

1.20.4. THE IGBO ELITES AND THE "OSU" SYSTEM

The new and emergent Igbo men, on account of their education and Christianization, began early enough to act against the "Osu" system. Some of them married the "Osu" women (but it was a few and rare); as a matter of fact, many Igbo Christians through their education showed that they were mentally emancipated enough as not to be influenced and controlled by the traditional religious beliefs that scared the Igbo man away from the "Osu".

Recent and constant exposition of the ill of the system through the mass media has shown a progressive effort by the Igbo elite to reform opinions on this subject. Iwe, emphasizing the role Christianity plays in purifying Igbo culture and tradition, states:

---

[284] Onwubiko O.A., *Facing the Osu in the African Synod, (A Personal Response),* op. cit., p. 38.

As a Christian, I am prompted to single out there the 'Osu' system and practice for special condemnation and castigation. Ours is a God-fearing-worshipping society. It is becoming increasingly Christian in its value and religious orientations. According to the Christian and civilized vision and concept of human life, the 'Osu' system – or any other such caste system – stands condemned for it is the most iniquitous and unjustifiable form of social discrimination. It is the most mischievous and pernicious heritage devised and bequeathed to us by our elders through fear and ignorance. Now that we are of age, we must publicly and privately reject it by word and deed as absolutely unworthy of our age and religion. In the Christian eye, there is no 'Osu' and there can be no 'Osu'. All are 'Nwa-Afor' (Freeborn) and fundamentally equal in dignity and rights as human beings. To view it otherwise is to be objectively unchristian, mentally immature and morally underdeveloped and a hopeless prisoner of tradition. [285]

1.20.5. THE SELF DEFENCE MECHANISM ADOPTED BY THE "OSU"

In addition to the new forces that quickened the emancipation of the "Osu", the "Osu" themselves launched a self-defence mechanism against the "diala". First, they organized themselves into villages. Though their villages were numbered among the villages now in the towns, in reality, they did not become villages of towns. The "Osu" soon knew that their villages in many Igbo towns were still "Osu" villages and that this did more prominently set them apart. So, their war of self-defence included encroachment on the "diala" pieces of land and, when they could, with litigations and government support, lived on them. As such they could settle and live in the other villages in the towns. "Their other strategy was the use of their women and sexual intercourse to "enroll" some "dialas" into their fold. In fact, the situation was such that their attack was directed to individuals known to be too fanatical over traditional religious matters that promoted the "Osu" system and therefore impede the emancipation of the "Osu" in their communities."[286]

In some places, it was gathered that the "Osu" spinsters organized themselves to "make" their real opponents "Osu". These ladies would dress attractively and go to the market to price the articles sold by these men far below normal prices. These men, as usual, would be infuriated not only by the approach of the "Osu" near their stalls, but also by their meagre offer. They would turn around to drive the "Osu" ladies away from their stalls. But the "Osu" ladies in a dejected but composed manner, would retort: *Ekperima uchichi si na egwu na ata aru na efife*, and this means, (a night rogue says that a goat bites during

---

[285] Iwe N.S.S., *Christianity and Culture in Africa, Onitsha*, Nigeria, University press, p. 21 in Onwubiko O.A., *Facing the Osu issue in the African Synod, (A Personal Response)*, op. cit., p. 39.
[286] Ibid., p. 40.

day light). Then she would continue, *you are now pretending as if you dare not talk to me as if I am not a human being. When it is night, you will no longer care about what you say I am and, then, there will be no more difference. We will all be real human being, provided you get your satisfaction from one of us. Let me see you cross our side again and I will ask you what you are looking for.*

At this, people around would normally be startled to hear that the individual in question used to consort with "Osu" ladies. No one bothered whether it was true or false. The news would spread, and within a question of days, Mr-so-and-so would thenceforth be discriminated against, with his whole household, as "Osu". Two or three such cases would happen during one market day. As this kept on happening at intervals, those who were made "Osu" in this manner were scattered within the whole town and so they were no more living apart in a specific area in those places. We must admit that there are still some die-hard prisoners of tradition who are doing the much they can to frustrate all attempts to eradicate this obnoxious practice. There are very few places in Igboland where "Osu" cast system is still in practice. From my investigations and findings, the influence of Christianity on Igbo Traditional Religion has affected the "Osu" cast system in Igboland.

Most communities in Igboland have approached the eradication of the "Osu" system in a practical traditional religious way and have reclaimed the "Osu" from the gods. In "Idemili" Local Government Area, and in "Nnobi" in particular, the "Osu" system was abolished ritually on December 30, 1971. On this date, sacrifices were made to the deities, and three cows were used to appease them. After this, those who were "Osu" began to take titles. In "Ogidi", a town in Anambra state of Nigeria, in 1972, the "Osu" system was also abolished. One of those 'redeemed' took a title and became the head of "Ozo" society and "Ndichie" in "Ogidi". His son took to marriage the daughter of a prominent "Ogidi" family.[287]

Following the example of the "Nnobi" and "Ogidi" communities, in October 1972, the "Umuoji" and "Awka-Etiti", both also in "Idemili" Local Government Area, abolished the "Osu" system in their areas. The heathens are more practical in their approach to issues of this nature. As soon as they have their conscience satisfied through sacrifices, they turn their back to the past.[288]

---

[287] Ikemefuna C., *The Osu cast System, A Rejoinder, art. in the Renaissance*, Enugu, Nigeria, Tuesday, April 22nd, 1975, p. 10, in Onwubiko O. A., *Facing the Osu Issue in the African Synod (A Personal Response)*, op. cit., p. 42.
[288] Onwubiko O.A., *Facing the Osu Issue in the African Synod (A Personal Response)*, op. cit., p. 42.

One can say with certainty that no new "Osu" are being dedicated. The descendants of the "Osu" are Christians. So, now that both Christian and traditional religious forces have joined to fight the system, that it will soon be forgotten is obvious. Those who were "Osu" in the past participate today like others, freely in normal village activities, meetings and other events. Even when a person who was an "Osu" dies, today he is accorded a befitting burial.

1.20.6. "OGWU" (CHARMS, AMULET AND TALISMAN) IN IGBO TRADITIONAL RELIGION

Igbo traditional medicine has been developed to be very useful to healthcare in Igboland. It is today an alternative healthcare to orthodox medicine. But "Ogwu" (charms) as an instrument of aggression is always seen by the Igbo as evil even up till the present day. The use of charms for protection and for aggression are no longer strong as it used to be in pre-colonial days. This belief has changed. For example, the use of "Ogwu" as a means of protection is practised by very few people today. "During the precolonial days, people used 'ogwu' as antidote to ward off the malignant 'ogwu' of other people. It could also be used to neutralize the powers of spirits generally and especially the power of evil or malignant spirits; to protect oneself against dangers such as epidemic, drowning, bullets-attack or even machete-cut."[289]

During the Nigeria-Biafra war, most Igbo soldiers who fought on Biafra side sought the use of protective "Ogwu" in one form or the other. It was also said that other soldiers of non-Igbo origin who fought on the federal side, also used their own "ogwu."[290] This particular mentality and belief about the effectiveness and power of charms, amulets and talisman in the context explained above have today changed. This change was brought about by Christianity, education and enlightenment. Very few people today believe in "Ogwu" (charms). Geoffrey I.O. Anyanwu, in my interview with him, states: "The making and keeping of charms among the Igbo have been very much suppressed in the light of modern advancements."[291]

1.20.7. PRIESTHOOD IN IGBO TRADITIONAL RELIGION

There are very few people in recent times who have accepted the vocation to the priesthood in Igbo Traditional Religion. It is not seen today as an exalted position as it was during the pre-colonial days. Arinze explains that:

---

[289] Nwala T.U., *Igbo Philosophy,* op. cit., p. 89.

[290] Ibid.

[291] Anyanwu Geoffrery, I.O., is a traditional rule in Ahiara, Ahiazu- Mbaise L.G.A., Imo state, Nigeria. He was 71 years old at the time of this interview. This interview was done on 10th January 2017.

> Many people do not like to be priest in Igbo traditional religion today. Those who are priests today in Igbo traditional religion, accept the office when it falls to them because they dare not refuse. The modern traditional religionist young man especially, cannot stand to see his companions making fat purses at Onitsha, Enugu and Aba, while he remains in the village dirtying his hands with dusty statues and symbols of the spirit and shrieking fowls and waiting for worshippers who either never arrive, or are becoming fewer and fewer as days pass by.[292]

At the infant stage of Catholicism in Igboland, the Igbo people pigheadedly opposed any of their sons to be ordained priest in the Catholic Church. For them, since the Catholic priests do not marry and have no children, their status goes against the Igbo traditional ideology and belief over terrestrial and eschatological success. As we have stated earlier in this work, any Igbo man who failed to marry or was unfortunate not to have children, more importantly male child, was regarded as not being successful in life. "It is regarded as an abomination not to have male issues. This is the rationale for the hue and cry raised when an Igbo young man or woman wants to embrace the catholic priesthood or religious life by which they become celibates. This also explains why an otherwise good Christian gives up his religious practice to marry a second wife should his wedded wife not bear him a son."[293] All those who were childless or did not have male child and died in this state were not ranked among the ancestors in Igboland. There is a big change today in this mentality and ideology: Oguejiofor explains that:

> For quite a long time, the Igbo People resisted the aspect of Christianity, especially in the Catholic Church where it entails a loss of progeny. In more recent times, this resistance has gradually given way. Catholic seminaries are full of candidates for the priesthood; a good number of priests are ordained each year throughout Igboland.[294]

1.20.8. SACRIFICE IN IGBO TRADITIONAL RELIGION

1.20.8.1. HUMAN SACRIFICE

Undoubtedly, human sacrifice has come under strong criticism since colonial times as a violation of the fundamental right to life and therefore outmoded. Its past and present use for selfish ends by those in search of quick success in

---

[292] Arinze F., *Sacrifice in Igbo Traditional Religion,* op. cit., p. 142.

[293] Onyewuenyi I.C., *Igbo (African) Philosophy*, in Ofomata G.E.K. (ed.), *A Survey of the Igbo Nation,* op. cit., p. 419.

[294] Oguejiofor J., *The Influence of Igbo Traditional Religion on the socio-political character of the Igbo,* op. cit., p. 95.

life is condemnable. "The desire to offer the most valuable led to human sacrifice. The belief that the world of the dead is a faithful representation of the world we live encouraged the sacrifice of slaves at funerals, to provide for a retinue of aids and bodyguards for the dead man."[295]

It is gratifying that all things considered, the incidence of human sacrifice is reducing considerably. This is the result of the advent of modern civilization with its emphasis on the value of human life. It is also the result of the influence of foreign religions like Christianity with its doctrine of the atonement that the death of Christ had become the once and for all human sacrifice.[296] Arinze emphasizes that:

> As already noted, people were killed at funerals of only very important people. Among the Igbo however, far fewer people died as a result of this practice when compared with the alarming number of the unfortunate men put to death at funerals of Ashanti Kings. Such practices are now a thing of the past.[297]

Moreover, the Nigerian constitution and human right laws do not permit human sacrifice in any form. Human sacrifice is no longer performed in Igbo Traditional Religion in any form.

1.20.9. THE KILLING OF TWINS

Igbo traditional morality like other traditional systems accommodated much that was barbarous and cruel such as human sacrifice, killing of twins, slavery etc.[298] All these barbarous acts, so to say, cited above are no longer performed today in Igbo Traditional Religion. The question one may ask is: What was the moral justification for the killing of twins in Igboland in the pre-colonial days?

The seriousness with which the Igbo of the olden days held their religion led them into various acts of oppression, injustice and inhuman traditions. For instance, twin births were regarded as of the animal world and when seen in human it becomes an abomination, "alu". The babies were deserted in an evil forest, and their mother exorcized.[299] In the pre-colonial period, twins were regarded as evil, taboo (alu). It was not a human act to give birth to twins in those days. For the Igbo then, only animals give birth to more than one. When a human being gives birth to two or more it was an abomination, a bad omen.

---

295 Igbo P.C; *Elements of Igbo Culture and Tradition,* Elites Publishers, Onitsha, Nigeria, 2012, p. 175.

296 Quarcoopome T.N.O., *West African Traditional Religion,* op. cit., pp. 90 - 91.

297 Arinze F., *Sacrifice in Igbo Traditional Religion,* op. cit., p. 173.

298 Nwala T.U., *Igbo Philosophy,* op. cit., p. 221.

299 Igbo P.C., *Elements of Igbo Culture and Tradition,* op. cit., p. 175.

Therefore, the babies were evil. This was the moral ground for which the twins were killed in pre-colonial era.

Twins are seen today as a blessing and not a curse in Igboland. The killing of twins has stopped. Today twins are celebrated in Igboland. "This barbaric act was stopped through the help of Mary Mitchell Slessor (1848-1915) from Scotland who came to Igboland as a missionary".[300] Twins are seen today as normal babies. Ignorance was the major factor that contributed to the killing of twins in the past in Igboland. With the advent of Christianity, with more understanding of science and medicine and how nature functions, the Igbo have come to realize that twins are blessings from God and not a bad omen or a curse. Many families in Igboland have twins and they are living happily today.

1.20.10. BELIEF IN REINCARNATION/*OGBANJE* IN IGBO ESCHATOLOGY

The concept of reincarnation/*Ogbanje* in Igbo Traditional Religion have undergone serious criticisms based on the fact that it cannot be scientifically explained. The belief in "Ogbanje" has received a serious attack by the development of genetic engineering. With the discovery of sickle cell anemia, the mystery behind infant mortality in pre-colonial era was unfolded. Many Igbo have come to understand that this has to do with body mechanism. Therefore, it has nothing to do with Igbo belief in "alusi", gods or the ancestors as the case may be. Those who still believe in "Ogbanje" or reincarnation in general are few in Igboland. Onunwa holds that the idea of reincarnation/*Ogbanje* should be viewed from the point of view of belief and not science:

> It is naive as well as preposterous for one to demand clearly set, intellectual and logical explanation to which falls within the realms of faith and dogma. A purely theological issue that fits into the straitline jacket of intellectualism and rationalism, runs the risk of losing its moral and spiritual flavor.[301]

I disagree with Onunwa here. We should know that where reason stops, faith comes in. Belief or faith should not go against common sense and reason. God does not prevent us from using our discretion. God gave human beings the gift of common sense. To put my stand more clearly, let us take the example of the killing of twins or human sacrifice. Before the advent of Christianity to Igboland, killing of twins or human sacrifice was not seen as evil; rather it was seen as keeping the commands of the gods and the ancestors. But fundamentally, these acts were against human reason, then and now. They have no moral basis at all. The reasoning of the Igbo traditional religionists then was over-

---

[300] Cf., ask.naiji.com/who-stopped-the-killing-of-twins-in-nigeria-123387.html, accessed 2.2. 2017.

[301] Onunwa U., *Studies in Igbo Traditional Religion*, op. cit., p. 107.

shadowed by this naive belief that the will of the gods must be obeyed and "omenani" (tradition) must be kept. But with the development of science and the help of enlightenment through education in Igboland, these acts were truly seen in the mirror of morals and reason as barbaric and therefore should not be kept.

1.20.11. "ALUSI" (DEITIES)

From my encounter with people, I have noticed that the belief in "alusi" (deities) is diminishing like a fire going off. Many traditionalists have abandoned their "alusi".[302] Today, many towns have abandoned their deities. Many deities and their shrines are no longer in existence. They have been destroyed or abandoned because for some they are no longer active; they are powerless and negative-oriented.

1.20.12. LIMITED POWERS OF THE GODS AND THE ANCESTORS

Although the Igbo traditionalists have strong faith and belief in their gods and the ancestors, these gods must be effective and active in order to sustain their survival and well-being, otherwise they are discarded. The twin principles of justice and innocence place a limitation on the powers of the gods and even ancestors. And when a deity contravenes it, he is regarded as wicked. The Igbo are known to destroy an ineffective and malevolent deity or cult. When a deity proves very destructive or weak, it is sent back (in a ceremony), to the town or village known to be its traditional home, and its shrine in the former place is

---

[302] Arinze gives this narration: It happens on rare occasions that the worshipper acts in a strange and irreligious way. He scolds the spirits, or more often the ancestors, rather severely. He calls them deceivers who give no recompense for his many victims.

A friend told me how his father was once angry with his ancestors because his sacrifices to them were fruitless. He rebuked the images representing the ancestors, whipped them, and refused sacrificing to them any longer. He lost hope in them. Some of the images were no longer preserved but despised. Today people are neglecting several of their deities because petitions are receiving no answers.

Here is still more peculiar incident as narrated by another: "About twenty-five years ago a very unusual incident took place at "Umuabi" in "Udi" division. A certain deity was in the habit of asking an elderly man through the priest (dibia) for fowls, goats, and so on, for sacrifice. When the man became tired of offering sacrifice to this deity, he thought about what to do. He remembered that he was one of those who in his youth brought the deity from a nearby town. So, he took a decision. He was a hunter, and a crack shot at that. He loaded his gun with very powerful bullets. He went straight to the deity. When he reached there, he started to justify his act in the characteristic traditional religionist manner. He said: This deity, since you came, you have ever made demands on me, never giving me. I helped to carry you to this town. So, if you be older than I, kill. If not, I kill you". He shot the deity into pieces. People boycotted him and said he would die within one month. He lived more than fifteen years after. The deity has become "powerless" ever since. Cf., Arinze F., *Sacrifice in Igbo Traditional Religion*, op. cit., pp.186 - 187.

destroyed. The Igbo are known to "threaten an ancestor with hunger" if the ancestor no more fulfills his protective role for the family.[303]

1.20.13. DEATH AND BURIAL

The Igbo traditional religionists believe that "all deaths are caused by some forces, deity or some other agency".[304] In pre-colonial era, certain deaths were seen as abomination. For example, "deaths from leprosy (*ekpe nta*), smallpox (*kitikpa*), hernia of the stomach (*ito afo*), dropsy or hernia of the testicles (*ida ibi*) were attributed to abnormality. They were apportioned to have been caused by vengeance of gods; visitation of false oaths. Victims of such bad deaths were wrapped in their sleeping mats and cast into the evil forest."[305] They were not buried and their funeral ceremonies were not performed. Belongings of the victims that died in the above stated situations were tabooed and, in like manner, thrown away into the evil forest. Circumstances surrounding a person's death determine whether he has died well or not.

Some terminal illnesses were seen in the past as punishment from the gods. Sacrifices were performed to seek the forgiveness of the gods. Fatal accidents were seen as bad omen. It was seen as punishment from the gods. People who committed suicide were not buried by their Kinsmen. They were buried by the foreigners.[306] The "Nri" priests were called to carry out the burial rites. All these have changed today. Dead bodies are no longer thrown into the evil forest. In many places in Igboland, those who committed suicide are buried by their kinsmen and their funeral ceremonies performed.

With the aid of medical science, the mentality of the Igbo traditionalists has changed as regards these issues. Medical conditions are no longer left in the hands of the diviners alone to manage or to determine what should be done. With the advancement of medical science, many Igbo traditional religionists have realized that illness is a normal thing that can happen to anybody. The diviners are not left today to explain all medical conditions and to suggest solutions as they did in the past. Igbo traditional religionists today go to hospitals and seek for the help of modern medical science for treatment.

---

[303] Nwala T.U., *Igbo Philosophy,* op. cit., p. 82.
[304] Ibid., p. 63.
[305] Igbo P.C., *Elements of Igbo Culture and Tradition,* op. cit., p. 128.
[306] It is against the custom, an abomination for a man to take his own life. It is an offence against the Earth, and a man who commits it will not be buried by his clansmen. His body is evil, and only strangers may touch it. That was the situation of Okonkwo in Things Fall Part. Cf., Achebe C., *Things Fall Part,* op. cit., p. 165.

1.20.14. FUNERAL CEREMONIES

In many places in Igboland, funeral ceremonies have been extravagantly celebrated. This continues up till today. When a person dies, what preoccupies the minds of the bereaved is not only that their loved one has left them but also the burial cost that are involved. How expensive a burial ceremony will be, depends on how rich the deceased was and how rich the family of the deceased is. This issue of extravagant spending for burial ceremonies has been a problem in Igboland in recent times. It is even worse when the deceased was poor and his or her family is also poor. Some people go to the extent of borrowing money for the burial ceremonies in order to give their departed brother or sister a befitting burial. In their own mentality, some think that by organizing expensive funerals for their deceased brother or sister, that it manifests how much they loved that person. To make the matter worse, sometimes after the burial ceremonies, some families cannot pay back the money they borrowed for the funeral ceremonies because their purses are empty.

In some areas of Igboland, we still experience this elaborate preparation for burial ceremonies and this implies extravagant spending. In many cases, food and drinks are served during the burial ceremonies. This whole idea of elaborate preparation for the burial ceremonies by the Igbo traditional religionists has influenced some of the Christians in Igboland.

However, it is pertinent to note that elaborate preparation and extravagant spending for funeral ceremonies have been curtailed. For example, in the Archdiocese of Onitsha, Nigeria, to which these towns in Igboland belong: namely "Onitsha", "Nkpor", "Nnobi", "Awka-Etiti", just to mention but a few, the Catholic Church in Onitsha Archdiocese has made a law that the burial preparation should not exceed two months starting from the day the deceased passed on, to the day of the burial. This is to avoid the temptation of elaborate preparation and expenditure.

When the family of the deceased goes against this law, the Catholic Church in Onitsha, will not give the deceased a full Christian burial. The Christians may go for the burial if they wish but the priest will not bury the deceased. This has helped a lot to reduce the elaborate preparation and extravagant spending for burial ceremonies in many parts of Igboland. The Igbo traditional religionists have learnt from this action of the Church in Onitsha and are minimizing elaborate and extensive preparations for funeral ceremonies. Many towns in Igboland have curtailed this extravagant spending and elaborate preparations for burial ceremonies. This has reduced the burden of the people whenever they are bereaved.

1.20.15. METAPHYSICAL EVIL

As we have explained earlier, these evils are attributed to human beings by inference because of the traditional belief in retributive judgment. Nothing happens for nothing, according to the traditional belief, all actions are willed by either man or the spirits. Examples of these evils are: "deformities at birth, accidents, premature deaths, floods, drowning and earthquakes, just to mention but a few."[307]

The notion of metaphysical evil has changed with the course of time in Igbo Traditional Religion. What the Igbo in the past could not understand was attributed to mystical forces. The Igbo believed that the gods had all explanations for what the human mind could not understand. So, the reasons for natural catastrophes like the ones mentioned above were not understood by the Igbo. The Igbo saw them in the past as evils sent by the gods to punish the persons or communities that have offended the gods and the ancestors.

Through enlightenment from education and science, the traditional mind understands them better today as natural disasters. The reasons for their occurrence are better explained by science rather than the interpretations given by the diviners.

1.20.16. BREAKING OF TABOOS

Before the advent of Christianity to Igboland, there were certain acts that were regarded as taboos. Examples of these taboos were: killing of sacred animals, women climbing trees and a child having upper teeth first before the lower ones, just to mention but a few. These were seen as abomination. "All those serious offences that are grossly out of tune with general practices are punishable by the community. In addition, cleansing sacrifices are needed to completely absolve the criminal in the eyes of men, the ancestors and gods".[308]

Some of these things mentioned above are no longer seen as taboos today. For example, the python is regarded in Idemili Local Government Area, Anambra State, Nigeria, as a sacred animal. In the past, when one wilfully or accidentally kills a python, the person must bury the animal like a human being and perform its burial ceremony. Many believed then that if this was not done, the gods would pour their anger on the offender and the community to which the offender belonged. Mbiti throws more light on this issue. He asserts:

---

[307] Nwala T.U., *Igbo Philosophy*, op. cit., p. 202.
[308] Ibid., p. 203.

Clans are normally totemic, that is, each has an animal or part of it, a plant, a stone or mineral, which is regarded as its totem. Members of a particular clan observe special care in treating or handling their totem, so that for example, they would not kill or eat it. The totem is the visible symbol of unity, of kinship, of belongingness, of togetherness and common affinity.[309]

But today this norm is not as serious as it was before the advent of Christianity to Igboland.

1.20.17. THE INFLUENCE OF CHRISTIANITY

The greatest influence on Igbo Traditional Religion and consequently, on Igbo cultural heritage has, however, been the spread of Christianity in Igboland. We have earlier remarked that the success of Christian evangelization in Igboland must, by all computations, stand among the most spectacular in the entire history of Christendom. But the most conservative estimate must put the percentage of Igbo Christians at somewhere between 80 and 90 percent. There are certainly areas that are much more influenced than others. There are towns where we have tens of thousands of inhabitants who are Christians and only five or ten traditional religionists.[310] Ikenga-Metuh asserts that:

> As long as Igbo traditional religion does not reform itself sufficiently to meet modern needs and developments, it will continue to be dwindling minority, and its total extinction will only be a matter of time.[311]

It is pertinent to say that the nature of the Igbo people, their characteristics, their traits such as egalitarian individualism, hard work, competitiveness and the quest for achievement, encouraged by the introduction of education have rendered enormous help in the modernization we see today in Igbo Traditional Religion.

The persistence of these traits we find among the Igbo also indicates the persistence of the religious convictions underlying them. Many of the external structures of Igbo Traditional Religion have been strongly founded. But in spite of this, in many areas of Igboland, the deities have conspicuously been abandoned, and their shrines and groves allowed to decay.[312]

---

[309] Mbiti J.S., *African Religions and Philosophy,* op. cit., p. 137.

[310] Oguejiofor J., *The Influence of Igbo Traditional Religion on the Socio-Political Character of the Igbo,* op. cit., p. 92.

[311] Metuh E.I., *God and Man in African Religion,* London, Geoffrey Chapmann, 1981, p. 177, in Oguejiofor J., *The Influence of Igbo Traditional Religion on the Socio-Political Character of the Igbo,* op. cit., p. 93.

[312] Oguejiofor J., *The Influence of Igbo Traditional Religion on the Socio-Political Character of the Igbo,* op. cit., p. 94.

CHAPTER TWO

2. THE CONCEPT OF INDIVIDUAL AND COMMUNITY SPIRITUALITY: IGBO PERCEPTION

2.1. INTRODUCTION

One of the characteristics of the Igbo people which remained resistant to eroding foreign influence is the sense of community and kinship. In Igboland, community is placed first before the individual. Without the community the individual has no meaning. It is the community that gives the individual its identity. In Igbo traditional setting, the individual does not and cannot exist alone except corporately. The Igbo say: *ofu osisi adighi eme ofia* (one tree cannot make a forest). Therefore, "the individual owes his existence to other people, including those of past generations and his contemporaries. He is simply part of the whole. The community must therefore make, create, or produce the individual; for the individual depends on the corporate group. Physical birth is not enough: the child must go through rites of incorporation so that it becomes fully integrated into the entire society. These rites continue throughout the physical life of the person, during which the individual passes from one stage of corporate existence to another. The final stage is reached when he dies and even then, he is ritually incorporated into the wider family of both the dead and the living".[313]

The individual is only identified when he belongs to the community. Outside the community, the individual has no identity. Even when the individual is living abroad, outside his home town, he ought to identify himself with his kinsmen there and also at home. The individual becomes conscious of his own being, his own duties, his privileges and responsibilities towards himself and towards other people only when he belongs to the community. Outside the community he would not be able to achieve these.

The life of the individual is viewed as being pigeonholed into the life of the community, so that, he is carried along by the community in whatever the community does. "When the individual suffers, he does not suffer alone but with the corporate group; when he rejoices, he rejoices not alone but with his kinsmen, his neighbours and his relatives whether dead or living. When he gets married, he is not alone, neither does the wife 'belong' to him alone. So also,

---

[313] Mbiti J.S., *African Religions and Philosophy,* op. cit., p. 141.

the children belong to the corporate body of kinsmen."[314] The interwoven relationship between the individual and the community can be summarized thus:

> Whatever happens to the individual happens to the whole group, and whatever happens to the whole group happens to the individual. The individual can only say: 'I am,' because we are; and since we are, therefore I am.[315]

Explaining this further let us cite some examples in support of the above given statements. When we look at the majority of the ceremonies performed in Igboland, the members of the kindred are always involved. For example, one cannot perform traditional wedding ceremony without involving his or her kindred. It is even unthinkable of performing funeral ceremonies without the knowledge of the kindred of the deceased. The members of the kindred normally participate in the preparation of the funeral ceremonies and play major role during the burial ceremony.

When one wants to marry in Igbo traditional setting, one does not make decision alone whom to marry without consulting his father or mother. When one's parents have passed on, one should express this spirit of brotherhood and community consciousness by consulting his relations. One has to do all these because in Igboland, marriage is contracted between the kinsmen of the man involved and the kinsmen of the woman to be married. "For the Igbo, as for many Africans, to exist is to live in the group, to see things with the group, to do things with the group. Life is not an individual venture, each one for himself".[316]

The Igbo are very conscious of social effects of sin. This is because when an individual in the community offends the gods, in many cases the anger of the gods extends to the whole community. Thus, everybody in the community ought to be the custodian of the norms, tradition, dos and don'ts of the community. So, one sees individual spirituality being pigeonholed in the community spirituality. What affects the individual affects the community and what affects the community affects the individual. Total individualism is abhorred in Igboland.

When a child is born into a community, the community rejoices and takes part in the naming ceremony. When the person dies, the community fully participates in the burial ceremony. The life of a member of the community is interwoven with those of the others through the common blood which they share

---

314 Ibid.
315 Ibid.
316 Arinze F., *Sacrifice in Igbo Traditional Religion*, op. cit., p. 6.

and through the web of economic and social interdependence which practical-ly exists in the community. Consequently, the being of the community is larger than and prior to that of any of its individual members, since the being of the community as a whole is identical with the being of the total personality of the ancestors.[317] The unity that exists between the individual and the community is reflected in all aspects of the life of the Igbo. It is seen in their religion, in their economic activities, politics and social life, just to mention but a few.

The community is so concerned about crimes and moral offences because the ultimate powers that punish these wrongs – the ancestors and the spirits (es-pecially the Earth deity) – can assign collective punishment to the entire com-munity for the wrongs committed by individual members. Hence, it is said: *otu mkpisi aka ruta manu, ozuo oha onu* (when one finger touches oil, it soils the rest of the fingers). Individual wrongs may, therefore, hinder the attainment of the ideals which the community cherishes.[318]

In the area of morality, it is not only a communally enjoined system of individ-ual responsibilities; the community as a whole is held responsible for the con-duct of each individual member. A community can be made to suffer because of the bad conduct of anyone of its members; therefore, it is the responsibility of the whole community to control the conduct of its members. In this chapter, our aim is to x-ray the relationship that exists between the individual and the community and how this relationship affects the individual spirituality as well as the community spirituality of the Igbo.

2.2. FAMILY STRUCTURE: EXTENDED FAMILY, KINSHIP AND SOLIDARITY - (UMUNNA BU IKE)

2.2.1. THE FAMILY SYSTEM ACCORDING TO IGBO TRADITIONAL IDEOLOGY

The Igbo have great respect and love for marriage and the family. Family ties are strong. "Marriage is not just the affair of a young man and his fiancée, but a long process between both families, entailing the marriage dowry payments by the fiancé, a religious ceremony and sacrifice, and the celebration of the marriage itself."[319]

From the traditional point of view, marriage is a social rather than an individu-al affair. It is a social contract in which the lineages of the contracting parties

---

[317] Nwala T.U., *Igbo Philosophy*, op. cit., p. 61.
[318] Ibid., p. 204.
[319] Jorden J., *Bishop Shanahan of Nigeria*, Dublin, 1948, p. 222, in Arinze F., *Sacrifice in Igbo Traditional Religion,* op. cit., p. 4.

are greatly interested.[320] The Igbo say: *ofu onye adighi anu nwanyi n'ala Igbo.* (Marriage is not an affair that concerns only the couple, it extends to the kindred of both parties).

The Igbo have special love for children. The average family in Igboland, during the pre-colonial era, had between 6 to 9 children. Today many families have up to 6 to 7 children and some less. A family without children has little or no meaning for the Igbo.[321] This means that a family that has no child has not yet fulfilled the purpose for which it was instituted. For the Igbo, the family has a much wider circle of members than the word suggests in Europe and America. In traditional society, the family includes children, parents, grandparents, uncles, aunts, brothers and sisters who may have their own children, and other immediate relatives.

When we were discussing the cult of the ancestors in Igbo traditional religion, we said that the ancestors are still part of the members of their respective families irrespective of the fact that they are dead. It is observed that "people give offerings of food and libation to the living-dead because they are still part of the family. The food and libation offered, are tokens of the fellowship, communion, remembrance, respect and hospitality, being extended to those who are the immediate pillars or roots of the family."[322] The living-dead solidify and mystically bind together the whole family.

When we were discussing the concept of "Madu" (human being) in Igbo ontology in chapter one, we stated that "Madu" (human being) refers to both the living and those about to be born. "African (Igbo) concept of the family also includes the unborn members who are still in the loins of the living. They are the buds of hope and expectation, and each family makes sure that its own existence is not extinguished. The family provides for its continuation and prepares for the coming of those not yet born. For that reason, African (Igbo) parents are anxious to see that their children find husbands and wives; otherwise failure to do so means in effect the death of the unborn and diminishing of the family as a whole."[323]

Each family in Igboland makes effort to have a home. We must note here that there is a difference between a house and a home. In Igbo life setting, a house without a home is not an ideal one. A house as well as a home (*Ezinauno*) is what every Igbo man wants. A home means having a good wife and well-

---

[320] Quarcoopome T.N.O., *West African Traditional Religion*, op. cit., p. 12.

[321] Arinze F., *Sacrifice in Igbo Traditional Religion*, op. cit., p. 4.

[322] Mbiti J.S., *African Religions and Philosophy*, op. cit., p. 139.

[323] Ibid., p. 139 - 140.

behaved children. A home (*Ezinauno*) without a child or children is not complete according to Igbo traditional standard.

2.2.2. EXTENDED FAMILY SYSTEM

The Igbo people conceive the family not just in its nuclear form but also as an extended circle of relations. Hence, the Igbo word "nwanne" (brother or sister) refers to brother/sister born by the same parents and to other relatives (including uncles, aunts, cousins, nephews, nieces, kindred and town and fellow countrymen, and country women) in a generic sense.

Essential to Igbo extended family system is the practice of every child regarding all the parents in the village as father/mother and every parent taking all children in the village as his or her sons and daughters.[324] Those who see themselves as "nwanne" (brothers and sisters) feel obliged to help one another, especially the vulnerable: The hungry, the sick, the disabled, and the bereaved of the family. Pope John Paul II makes this remark about the Igbo families in general both Christians and non-Christians: He said:

> Your families have many positive and praise-worthy values, based on your family traditions. You have strong family ties. Children are regarded as a blessing and are desired as the crown of marriage. The extended family system provides a loving human environment for the care of orphans, the old and the poor.[325]

One of the benefits of the Igbo extended family system is that a person discovers his/her personality in group relationships. This touches on both the freedom and the responsibility of the individual in the community.

2.2.3. KINSHIP

The Igbo society places strong emphasis on lineage kinship system. They respect close relational ties. The deep sense of kinship with all it implies has been one of the strongest forces in Igbo traditional life. Kinship is reckoned through blood and betrothal (engagement and marriage). It is kinship which controls social relationships between people in a given community. It governs marital customs and regulations and determines the behaviour of one individual to-

---

[324] The Igbo consider every child to be everybody's son or daughter (*nwa bu nwa ora*) the responsibility of educating a child on core values, morals, mannerisms is considered a cooperate responsibility in such a way that any parent who neglects such a duty is regarded as being irresponsible. Similarly, any misbehaving child could easily be corrected/reprimanded by any adult present irrespective who the child may be.

[325] Burke R., and Prunty P., (eds.), *Pope John Paul II in Nigeria, Feb., 12th - 17th 1982, Homilies and Addresses*, Port Harcourt, Nigeria, Marian Books Centre Publications, 1982, p. 8.

wards another. Indeed, this sense of kinship binds together the entire life of the "tribe".

Almost all the concepts connected with human relationship can be understood and interpreted through the kinship system. This governs largely the behaviour, thinking and the whole life of the individual in the society of which he is a member. The kinship system is like a vast network stretching laterally (horizontally) in every direction, to embrace everybody in any given local group. This means that each individual is a brother or sister, father or mother, grandmother or grandfather, or cousin, or brother-in-law, uncle or aunt, or something else, to everybody else. That means that everybody is related to everybody else, and there are many kinship terms to express the precise kind of relationship pertaining two individuals.

When two strangers meet in a village, one of the first duties is to sort out how they may be related to each other and having discovered how the kinship system applies to them, they behave to each other according to the accepted behaviour set down by the society. If they discover, for example, that they are "brothers", then they will treat each other as equals, or as an older and younger brother. If they are "uncle" and "nephew", then the "nephew" may be expected to give much respect to the "uncle" where this type of relationship is required by the society. It is possible also that from that moment on, the individuals concerned will refer to each other by the kinship term of, for instance, "brother", "nephew", uncle", "mother", with or without using their proper names.[326] The kinship in Igboland shows how interwoven the Igbo society is. It is pertinent to note that: "the kinship system also extends vertically to include the departed and those yet to be born."[327] It is part of traditional education for children in many African (Igbo) societies, to learn the genealogies of their descent. The genealogy gives a sense of depth, historical belongingness, a feeling of deep rootedness and a sense of sacred obligation extend the genealogical line. Genealogical ties also serve social purposes, particularly in establishing relationships between individuals. By citing one's genealogical line, it is possible to see how that person is linked to other individuals in a given group. It is also on genealogical basis that organizational divisions have evolved among different people, demarcating the larger society into clans, families, households and finally individuals.

In Igbo communities, the smallest or basic socio-political unit is the ***"umunna"***. It is made up of a number of extended families or family groups (***ngwulu or***

---

[326] Mbiti J.S., *African Religions and Philosophy,* op. cit., p. 136.
[327] Ibid., p. 137.

ama). The large families are in turn made up of a number of nuclear families. A group of "*Umunna*" forms a village section (*ogbe)* or village itself. An aggregate of villages will in turn constitute a **town** or what is called an **autonomous community**. The above terms are illustrated with a diagram in the next page. The diagram shows how interwoven the family structure in Igboland is; how intimately connected the towns, villages, individual families and persons are. This diagram will help us to understand better why we say that the spirituality of the individual is pigeonholed in the spirituality of the community. Just like a fish cannot survive without water, the Igbo strongly believe that the individual cannot survive without the community to which he or she belongs.

The females, who hail from the same "*umunna*" are referred to as the "*umuada*" (the daughters of the family). These "*umuada*" can also settle disputes among their brothers only when invited. They also counsel or discipline any erring wife of their brothers. All women who are married in same "*umunna*" to different men from same "*umunna*" (kindred) are called "*ndi iyom di*". In different families, we have "*okpala*" and "*ada*" (the first son and the first daughter). These have important roles in the family. The "*okpala*" of different families are the visible successors of the families.

The most important person in the *umunna* is the *Okpala*. But he has limited political powers. He exercises control with other elders of the lineage as a kind of *primus inter pares* in matters relating to the *umunna*. Between the *umunna* and other patrilineages, he acts as a representative of his own *umunna*. He does not normally interfere in the internal affairs of the different families making up the *umunna,* except in cases where he is called to use his personal influence in the settlement of disputes.

Belonging to a village is based on family ties or genealogical streamlines, as members trace their genes through the paternal ties. The kindred are called the "*umunna*" which means children of a common ancestor (father). This group consists of all the male of different family compounds in a certain village. This group serves as the police of its members.

What is generally obtainable, is the division of each community into villages. Villages are in turn divided into smaller sections. The levels and number of subsections are constituted in line with the male children of the aboriginal ancestors.

2.2.4. THE IGBO FAMILY STRUCTURE

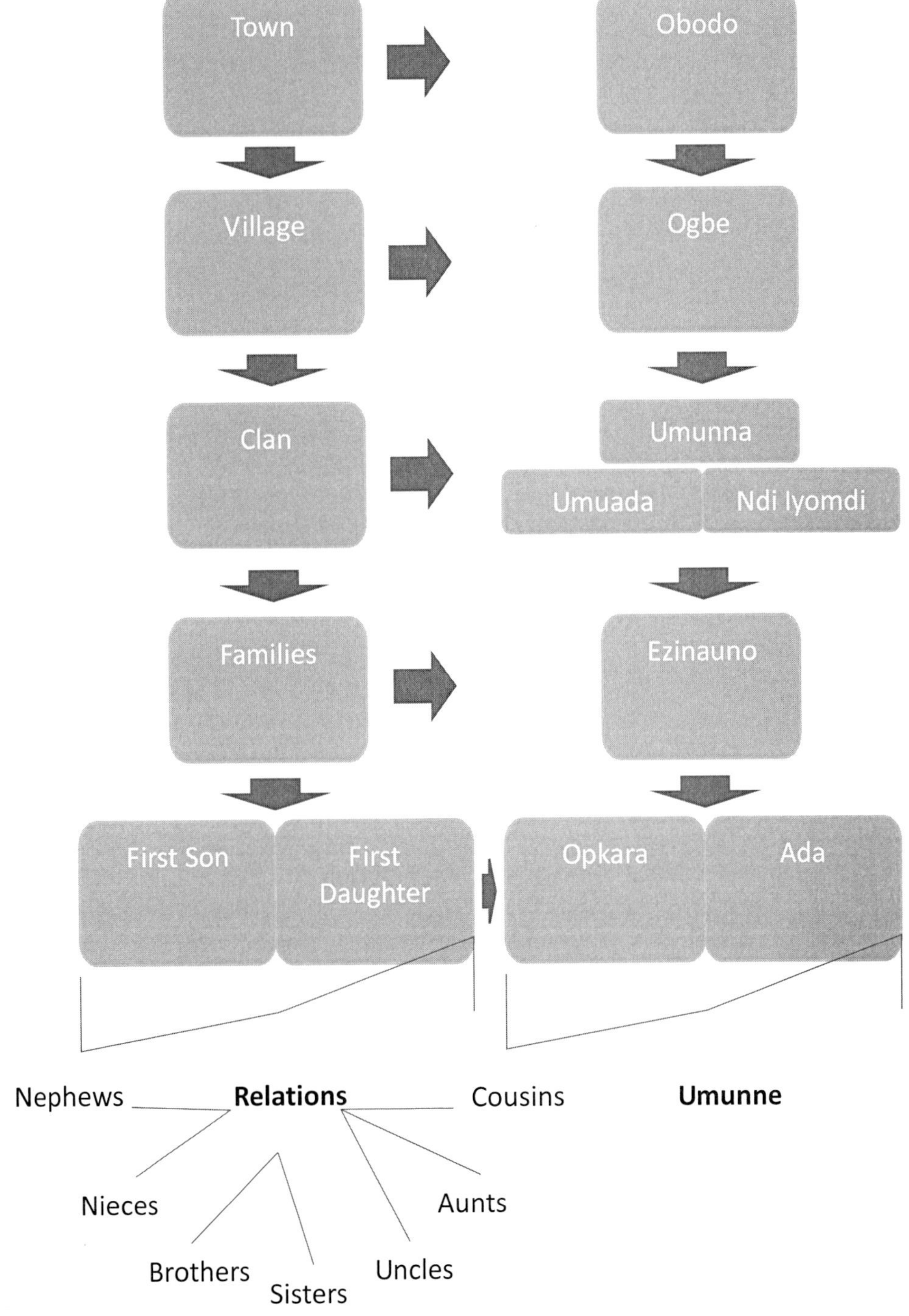

2.3. IGBO CULTURAL VALUES PIGEONHOLED IN THE COMMUNITY IMAGE AND SPIRITUALITY

2.3.1. IGBO SENSE OF SACREDNESS OF LIFE

The Igbo generally do not like violence and do not support it in any form. In Igboland, shedding of blood is abhorred. Life is sacred. Killing is only permitted when death sentence is passed on someone by the community or during wars. Thus:

> People who were killed were those whose continued existence was a threat to the life of others and to the peace of the community. In such cases, the principle that it is better for one man to die than for all the community to perish, applied.[328]

War, be it tribal or inter-tribal, is not encouraged. "War was only taken to as a last resort that is when all formal and normal courses of action to search for peace had failed".[329] We shall discuss this in details when we treat Nigeria-Biafra war.

The killing of another human being especially a fellow villager or a known person whether accidentally or intentionally is forbidden in Igboland. To kill a fellow kinsman other than an enemy under any circumstance is an abomination against God and the earth goddess because life is a prerogative of God; when and how to terminate it should be determined only by Him. When a man consciously killed another person, his fellow kinsman, the consequences for this action were grave. There are two conflicting opinions as regards this. Onwubiko states that the consequence was death penalty for the murderer. The community (the king, his advisers and the elders of the community) carried out the death sentence.[330]

But according to Anyanwu, the consequence and the corresponding reconciliation rite is such that "the murderer is expected to terminate his own life by hanging himself. There is no provision for public or secret execution of a murderer in most parts of Igboland. The most accepted way involves the death of the murderer by hanging himself."[331]

Anyanwu also affirms that suicide is the taking of one's life by oneself and is considered as an abomination in Igboland and regarded as bad death (*onwu*

---

[328] Onwubiko O.A., *Wisdom Lectures on African Thought and Culture*, op. cit., p. 29.

[329] Ibid.

[330] Ibid.

[331] Anyanwu H.O., *Religion and Societal Development: Contemporary Nigeria Perspective*, op. cit., p. 281.

ojoo). The reconciliation rite for this commences with the dumping of corpse into "ajoo ofia" (evil forest).[332] This idea of sanctity of life makes it an abomination for anyone, under any circumstances to take his own life. Suicide was never permitted. Punishment for it was such that the person was not buried since his corpse was also believed to be abominable to mother earth.[333]

In chapter one of this work, we stated that suicide is a taboo in Igboland. Anybody that commits this act has offended the earth goddess. If this is so, sentencing one to death by suicide as a punishment or reparation for committing murder is naive. This will put us into a vicious circle. I consider the submission of Onwubiko on this issue as being what was practised in many parts of Igboland. This is because one cannot condemn oneself. One cannot pass death penalty on oneself and carry it out. We have to state that before any capital punishment is given or carried out, the elders of the community have to pass judgment on the case. When death sentence was passed on a murderer, "after the murderer had been executed, his family would have to perform sacrifices and rites to remove the stain of evil and ward off the anger of the gods."[334] Life in its totality is regarded as being sacred. This sacredness of life applies to both the born and the unborn. "Unborn Children are protected and abortion is tabooed. Sources of life are sacred. Trees and animals believed to facilitate reincarnation are also sacred."[335]

The sacredness associated with life goes to explain the rigidity with which the Igbo treat and regard sexual intercourse and the sex organs. In fact, sex taboos and the demand for virginity before marriage stem from the fact that the Igbo believe that "the blood of virginity is the symbol that life has been preserved, that the spring of life has not already been flowing wastefully, and that both the girl and her relatives have preserved the sanctity of human reproduction."[336]

2.3.2. IGBO SENSE OF RELIGION

In traditional Igbo societies, there are no atheists. This is because religion in the indigenous African (Igbo) culture was not an independent institution. It was an integral and inseparable part of the entire culture. Mbiti describing how the African (Igbo) is intrinsically attached to his religion states:

---

[332] Anyanwu H.O., *Wisdom Lectures on African Thought and Culture*, op. cit., p. 29.

[333] Onwubuike O.A., *Wisdom Lectures on African Thought and Culture,* op. cit., p. 30.

[334] Amadi E., *Ethics in Nigeria culture*, Ibadan, Heinemann, 1982, p. 58, in Onwubiko O.A., *Wisdom Lectures on African Thought and Culture*, op. cit., p .29.

[335] Onwubiko O.A., *Wisdom Lectures on African Thought and Culture,* op. cit., p. 29.

[336] Mbiti J.S., *African Religions and Philosophy*, op. cit., p. 141, in Onwubiko O.A., *Wisdom Lectures, on African Thought and Culture*, op. cit., p. 30.

> Traditional religions permeate all the departments of life, there is no formal distinction between the sacred and the secular, between the religious and non-religious, between the spiritual and the material areas of life. Wherever the African (Igbo) is, there is his religion: he carries it to the fields where he is sowing seeds or harvesting a new crop; he takes it with him to party or to attend a funeral ceremony... religion accompanies the individual from long before his birth to long after his physical death.[337]

We cannot talk of Igbo people without talking of their religion. Religion is the strongest element in traditional background and exerts probably the greatest influence upon the thinking and living of the people concerned.

Major religions of the world like Christianity, Buddhism and Islam have their creeds. But "in Igbo traditional religion there are no creeds to be recited; instead, the creeds are written in the heart of the individual, and each one is himself a living creed of his own religion. Where the individual is, there is his religion, for he is a religious being."[338] One peculiar thing about the Igbo Traditional Religion is that morality is not separated from religion. Idowu observes that "with the Yoruba people of Nigeria, morality is certainly the fruit of religion. They do not make any attempt to separate the two; and it is impossible for them to do so without disastrous consequences".[339]

This Yoruba practice is also true about the Igbo. In Igbo traditional setting, morality and religion are interwoven. One cannot separate religion from morality. It is difficult to talk of morality outside religion. The traditional Igbo see custom, morality and religion as being interrelated. "Custom laid down the code of law which established the nature of right-doings, it established penalties and taboos against malefactors. Moral sanctions were mainly religious sanctions".[340]

2.3.3. IGBO SENSE OF COMMUNITY

The Igbo people have many proverbs to express the sense of community and its preeminence. For example, the Igbo say: "Ofu osisi anaghi eme ofia" (one tree does not make a forest). The Igbo see great strength in unity and solidarity. Individualism and disunity are not welcomed. The community has its own being defined by common blood inheritance. The life of a member of the community is, therefore, interwoven with the others through the common

---

[337] Mbiti J.S., *African Religions and Philosophy,* op. cit., pp. 2 - 3.
[338] Ibid., p. 4.
[339] Idowu E.B., *African Traditional Religion, A Definition*, op. cit., p. 146.
[340] Okafor F.C., *Africa at Crossroads,* New York, 1974, p. 25, in Onwubiko O.A., *Wisdom Lectures on African Thought and Culture*, op. cit., p. 31.

blood which they share and through the web of ritual, social and economic interdependence which practically exist and which tie them together as a community.[341]

There is one thing which all kinsmen share in common and which binds them together, and that is the common blood they share by virtue of a common descent and ancestry. This is the backbone of all kinship relations and the great spirit of brotherhood which pervade all communal activities. To the Igbo man, community is *"Umunna" –* brethren.[342] It is, therefore, logical that the being of the community, that is, the members of the community, the totality of the legacy of the ancestors and which, in a sense, is identical with the being of the ancestors, is larger than and superior to that of any one individual who only partakes of the totality of the blood of the group. Hence, the community takes precedence before any individual member. Therefore, no matter how great a man is, he can never win judgment against his clan.

The individual must respect the judgment of the community no matter how unfavourable the judgment may be to the individual. The community is given pre-eminence over the individual. The individual has meaning when he identifies himself with the community. Without the community, the individual has no identity. However, it is pertinent to say that the community consciousness which is found in Igbo traditional setting does not stifle or exterminate individuality. Individuals might have rights, but they had them only by virtue of the obligations they fulfill to the community. In this way, individual lives out his or her individuality by being useful to his or her community. The autonomy of the individual person, therefore, is upheld among the Igbo, but individualism, which breeds anarchy and encourages hooliganism is unacceptable in Igbo society. The individual person has the widest scope to enrich his personality without prohibition by the community. The human rights which were put into writing in modern times, had long been enshrined in Igbo culture. The individual person's recognition in the Igbo community is based on what is called "egalitarian principle" which ensures that no one person or group acquires too much control over the life of others. Individuality in Igbo context is that which gives all citizens an equal opportunity to achieve success.[343]

Igbo social anthropology reveals that a person is not a "thing" to be used by a community but a person in a community of persons. A person needs a community and vice versa. None should exist at the expense of the other, and that

---

[341] Nwala T.U., *Igbo Philosophy*, op. cit., p. 207.
[342] Ibid., p. 207.
[343] Uchechukwu Dine G.E., *Traditional Leadership as sample of African democracy among the Igbo of Nigeria*: *Christian Evaluation;* Snaap Press, Ltd., Enugu, Nigeria, 2007, op. cit., p. 31.

is why the Igbo world (spirit and material) is very dynamic and change-oriented. Tradition is a constitution of the people. The Igbo constitution refuses to "absolutize" the individual at the expense of the community and vice versa.

It is the community that gives meaning to the individual achievement and success. This is because what the individual may call success is attained through the security and help of the community. The community practically is the custodian of the individual; therefore, the individual must always cooperate with the community. When the individual decides to stay alone, having no contact with his or her community, not cooperating with the community, then the individual is acting like a person that has no origin and identity.

The Igbo emphasize community life and communalism as a living principle of which the basic ideology is community identity. Its aim is to produce and present an individual as a community culture-bearer. Culture[344] is a community property and must therefore be community-protected.[345] The identity of the individual is not emphasized at the expense of the community identity. The community togetherness and cooperation are seen by the Igbo positively rather than being negative. It is regarded as a blessing rather than a curse. Hence, the Igbo regard their living together not as an unfortunate mishap warranting endless competition among them but as a deliberate act of God to make them a community of brothers and sisters jointly involved in the quest for a composite answer to the varied problems of life. Hence, in all they do they always place man first and their actions are usually joint community-oriented actions.

The relationship between the community and the individual is complementary in nature. The community needs the individual and the individual needs the community. The people uphold the need for community as well as the individual in society. The type of community which not only discourages isolationism but also imposes psychologically the need for person to person involvement of

---

[344] Culture is a term of virtually limitless application. It can even refer to everything that is produced by human beings as distinct from all that is part of nature. It can be seen also as a set of meanings, values and patterns which underlie the perceptible phenomena of a concrete society, whether they are recognizable on the level of social practice (acts, ways of proceeding, tools, techniques, costumes and habits, forms and traditions), or whether they are the carriers of signs, symbols, meanings and representations, conceptions and feelings that consciously or unconsciously pass from generation to generation and are kept as they are or transformed by people as the expression of their human reality. Cf., Obasi S., *Evangelization and Modernity: Cultural Issues as Missiological Imperative in Ecclesia in Africa*, Hamburg, 2008, p. 33.
[345] Onwubiko O.A., *Wisdom Lectures on African Thought and Culture*, op. cit., p. 21.

individuals, explains the significance of the Igbo concept of "Ikwu na ibe" (people of one's next of kin). No one person can escape the observation of the community members who form part of him in time of peace and in time of trouble. An Igbo individual separated from the Igbo community is like a fish out of water, which loses its normal life flavour and dies away. There is this sense of brotherhood in the community that makes it not to be shameful or to be considered repugnant to ask one's neighbours for help. If a person finds himself or herself in difficulty, it is not unusual for him or her to call for help from his/her clan members and other relatives.[346] This explains why a community may have poor people but it may not have beggars. A beggar is considered here as someone who is not accommodated in the elastic means of the community's life and resources. He is outside the community and does not receive community security and love. He is like a child without family care and love.

The Igbo man views his community in relation to other communities, just as he views his family in relation to other families, and his person in relation to other individuals in the community. "A successful man does not merit respect if he fails to help the members of his family especially the young to make their own success. In a similar manner, a community that is evidently lagging behind in comparison with others soon becomes an object of derision to its members, even if the individuals in the community are very successful."[347] The Igbo solidarity attitude to work is another factor which makes it impossible for them to have beggars in their communities. "When a job had to be done, the whole community turned out with supplies and music and proceeded to sing and dance its way through to the successful conclusion of each particular chore. In this way work was converted into a pleasurable productive pastime."[348]

In the 1960s, Julius Nyerere of Tanzania proposed the philosophy of "ujamaa". "Ujamma" can be likened to the Igbo extended family system. The idea behind this philosophical ideology is solidarity. This solidarity is such a vital value that individuals cannot but work and identify with it. The rights and duties of individuals appear as elements of corporate rights and duties so that the solidarity of the unit is emphasized but not at the expense of the individual's private interests that ultimately do not disrupt the community. The philosophy or principle of good becomes whatever makes for the community welfare.

---

346 Mbiti J.S., African Religions and Philosophy, op. cit., p. 138.
347 Oguejiofor J., *The Influence of Igbo Traditional Religion on the Socio-Political Character of the Igbo,* op. cit., p. 20.
348 Okafor F.C., *Africa at Crossroads,* N.Y., 1974, p. 22, in Onwubiko O.A., *Wisdom Lectures on African* Thought *and Culture,* op. cit., p. 23.

2.3.4. THE SENSE OF HUMAN RELATIONS AND HOSPITALITY

The sense of human relations is one of the cultural values that is strongly alive in Igbo traditional setting. We categorize this relation into two types: Internal and external relations. Internal deals with relationship within family setting, within clan or town. External relation deals with the inter-tribal, that is, outside one's clan, outside one's town. Inter-community relationship realized in the interaction between individuals of different communities is different from the intra-community relationship based on inter-personal relationship realized in a definite community.

The art of dialogue and conversation is a cherished value in African (Igbo) human relations. People freely discuss their problems and look for suggestions and solutions together. The unwillingness to talk to people about either private or public affairs can be interpreted as bad manners or sign of enmity. The Igbo people believe that he who discusses his affairs with others hardly runs into difficulties or makes mistakes in execution of his plans.[349] We must, however, note that discussions must respect individual's sentiments. Hence, conversations that may cause misgivings are avoided. This Igbo sense of accommodation accounts for why, in traditional Igbo culture, the weak and the aged, the incurable, the helpless, the sick were affectionately taken care of in the comforting family atmosphere. The comforting family atmosphere is provided by the extended family system. It is a system that ultimately rested and still rests on philosophy of "live-and-let live" otherwise known as "the eagle-and-kite" principle. It is a principle which defines rights, duties, responsibilities and obligations towards the less fortunate, those incapacitated in one way or another.

The Igbo sense of human relation is reflected in their sense of hospitality, in the way they welcome strangers. The Igbo easily incorporate strangers and give them lands to settle, hoping that they would go one day, and the land would revert to the owner. In Igboland, one cannot opt out of his original community completely. So, they did not imagine that others could.

The Igbo have symbolic ways of expressing welcome. These are forms of presentation of kola-nuts, traditional gin, coconuts, "Nzu" (chalk). These are given to a visitor to show that he is welcome and safe. Among the Igbo, the basis of hospitality is the generally accepted principle that a guest must not harm his host and that when he departs, he should not develop a hunch back on the way home. In general, the Igbo are friendly people. They treat strangers with a lot of affection and hospitality. They also expect others to treat them the same way. This is why they easily integrate into any community they find

---

[349] Onwubiko O.A., *Wisdom Lectures on African Thought and Culture,* op. cit., p. 27.

themselves because of this belief in peaceful co-existence. This is evident in Nigeria even today. Among the tribes in Nigeria, the Igbo are the most travelled and have adapting capability. This is easily noticed when we look at the number of Igbo living in diaspora. The number is astonishing when compared with the number of other tribes of Nigeria living abroad.

2.3.4.1. CHALK-STONE (NZU) AND KOLA-NUT (OJI); SYMBOLS OF ACCEPTANCE, HOSPITALITY AND FRATERNITY IN IGBO CULTURAL SETTING

"Nzu" is the Igbo name for chalk-stone. It is normally soft in nature and white or grey in color. "The chemical component of *nzu* consists of nearly pure calcium carbonate (CaCo3) which comes from sedimentary rock. It has marine origin"[350] In Igbo culture and tradition, "nzu" is regarded as a symbol of purity. We have up to five elements, namely: Water, "nzu", wine, "kola-nut" and the sacred "Ofo" that are used in the ritual consecration of the morning; which can be regarded in modern terminology as morning prayer and thanksgiving. Among these five elements, "nzu" stands out as the third significant element.

In Igbo traditional setting, "nzu" and "kola-nut" are the first things a host presents to his guest. "It is wrong or mischievous to ascribe "nzu" or its presentation to a guest as having element of idolatry or heathen practices. In practical terms, when it is presented (more often with kola-nut) to a guest, the host picks up the chalkstone, "nzu," and with it in his hand, he begins to invoke the spirits of the ancestors, of the land, his father's ancestors and the Supreme deity, to descend and hear him make supplications and prayers."[351]

When a host prays or makes entreaties, he makes some markings on the floor with "nzu". The pattern or marks made on the floor are peculiar to individuals. We do not have a prescribed system of marking with "nzu". If, however, the host finishes his prayers and markings, he drops the "nzu" on the floor for his guest. He does not pass the "nzu" hand to hand but rolls it on the floor to the guest or next person present. There is a reason for this kind of practice. Igbo affirms:

> "Nzu", in its purity and sanctity, carries with it some element of luck, and luck being abstract attribute of nature which is not transferred hand to hand, "nzu" must be rolled on to each individual for him or her to pick his or her "luck".[352]

---

[350] Igbo P.C., *Elements of Igbo Culture and Tradition*, op. cit., p. 43.
[351] Igbo., p. 46.
[352] Ibid., p. 43.

It is germane to state here that we have an aspect of the application of "nzu" that has changed with time; this change came into scene, perhaps due to modern civilization. The practice is thus:

> The smearing, applying or rubbing the powdered "nzu" on the eyelids of either the host or the guest; in modern times, this practice has been backtracked because, according to some sources, it makes one look like a native doctor just returning from an oracle.[353]

However, the initial practice of rubbing the powered "nzu" on the eyelids was seen as being advantageous to the people in pre-colonial days when slavery and kidnapping were being practised. In the distant past when kidnapping for slavery and slave trade was prevalent, when those in the practice of kidnapping see somebody with the "nzu" painting on eyelids, they automatically assume that he was from a strong man's house and as such untouchable.

The sanctity and purity of "nzu" in Igbo culture and tradition is seen from the fact that a person in a mourning period keeps off the practice of making those strokes of marking both on the floor or rubbing the "nzu" powder on eyelids. The category of mourners that must abstain from this practice within the mourning period include one who had just lost a spouse, one who had just lost a father or mother, and one who had just lost a very close relation of the first instance. A woman is also restricted from making those markings on the floor; rather she is by the tradition allowed to make the mark at the back of her palm.[354] "Nzu" is known to be medicinal.[355]

2.3.4.2. KOLA-NUT

Kola-nut is the produce of the kola tree. Kola, which is also called cola, is a common name for approximately 125 species of tropical trees of the same family as cocoa. The most common of the Igbo kola-nut is a pod-like receptacle seed of about 2.5cm long with mottled brown of a reddish grey. A typical and fully developed Igbo kola will bear not less than three cotyledons, and most often, not more than seven or eight. Another species called "Oji ugo" of the

---

[353] Ibid., p. 47.

[354] Igbo P. C., *Elements of Igbo Culture and Tradition*, op. cit., p. 47.

[355] Medicinal uses of "nzu" abound: pregnant mothers usually make water solution of "nzu" and rub it on their pregnant stomach. It is believed that this solution is absorbed by the unborn baby for the well-being of the baby. This same water solution of "nzu" is applied on a skin with heat rashes, and if added unto it, some other medicinal leaves, it cures a lot of other skin infections. If mixed with some other preparations "nzu" is believed to have the potency of curing measles. "Nzu" is elaborately used in "Ozo" title taking in Igbo culture and tradition. A water solution of "nzu" is rubbed all over the body of an intending initiate at certain stage of the ceremony of "Ozo" title taking. Cf., Igbo P.C., op. cit., pp. 47 - 48.

same size and shape but with yellow color is of high cultural value. This brand of kola-nut is often rare and symbolizes royalty and purity – attributes of spiritual beings, kings, affluent and titled men.[356] The Igbo believe that the living do not eat the kola-nut alone, whenever it is broken. The ancestors and the gods do participate in the eating of it. Adibe explains this thus:

> The common sacrificial food eaten with the spirits in Igbo mystical experiences are throwing of pieces of kola-nuts - oji on the ground and pouring some drops of wine on the ground for the spirits to partake in whatever ceremony about to be performed. These religious rituals are symbolic of communion and expected reciprocal love to and with the favorable spirit.[357]

2.3.4.3. THE SPIRITUAL SYMBOLISM OF KOLA-NUT (OJI IGBO)

Kola-nut serves as a means of unity among Igbo people. God revealed this nut to them as a means of bringing people together. Kola-nut is a symbol of reconciliation and unity. In any event that kola-nut is presented, it plays a supreme role of securing people's trust to deal freely with one another. It creates awareness, secures commitment to custom and strengthens trust. "Whoever presents or shares kola-nut with a guilty conscience invokes the righteous judgment upon himself."[358]

The Igbo see Kola-nut as a symbol of life. Thus, they say: "onye wetalu oji wetalu ndu" (he that brings kola-nut brings life). Kola-nut is the first thing a host offers to his guest after normal greetings or introduction. It shows the value and respect one has for his visitor. This gesture of welcome and hospitality is pigeonholed in the presentation of kola-nut to a guest by the host. The Igbo culture provides rules and reasons for every bit of her life and conduct. Thus, if a brother or friend visits one another, he must be presented with kola. The latter is a sign of welcome and second stage of reception after greetings.[359] Kola-nut is a divine nut. He who refuses to bring out kola-nut denies not only the kola-nut but also the blessing and the thanksgiving that go with it. However, he who brings kola-nut or eats it with evil mind brings condemnation to himself.

If one has a guest and does not have kola to offer him or her, one must confess this and then seek to present wine or something else he can easily afford without contradicting his conscience. If there is nothing immediately to suffice for

---

356 Ibid., p. 50.
357 Adibe G.E., *Igbo Mysticism: Power of Igbo Traditional Religion and Society*, Mid-Field Publishers Ltd., Nigeria, 2009, p. 170.
358 Ibid., p. 87.
359 Ibid., p. 90.

kola, for instance, at nighttime, one might push the lack of kola to darkness of the night as the Igbo people say: "abali ewerela oji" (the night has taken the kola-nut); or one can simply say: "kam jide gi ugwo oji" (let me owe you the presentation of kola-nut).

If one does not offer his visitor kola-nut and at the same time fails to acknowledge the reasons why he cannot do so, this has implications. This symbolically means that the guest is not welcomed by the host. It is always better not to present kola than to do so with anger, constricted heart, animosity or mischief. A kola so served creates more harm or bias than remorse. In religious ritual "oji" (kola-nut) is used as an introductory part of the general ceremony. "oji" is a sign of acceptance, unity of life and love. It equally symbolizes hospitality.

Opata also asserts that *"oji* – (kola-nut) serves as a symbol of good will and hospitality on interpersonal relationship; a symbol of peace and love on communal relationship."[360] Ekwunife demonstrates the unity, the cultural and spiritual symbolism that is in the presentation of kola-nut (oji). He states thus:

> Oji (kola-nut) is used in the ritual prayer for consecrating the day. It is also used in beginning meetings and other ritual purposes. But two warring parties or enemies cannot share Igbo kola until peace is established between them.[361]

Igbo commentators like Adibe, Igbo, Opata, just to mention but a few, believe that "the number of lobes *oji* (kola-nut) has, after it has been broken, indicates some sacred significance and some mystical meaning for those present that would participate in the eating".[362] Thus, a kola-nut with one lobe is regarded as dumb kola-nut and should not be eaten by pregnant women. A kola-nut with two lobes is regarded as bad omen, abomination and an aberration. Such kola-nut is often thrown away and should not be eaten by anybody. A kola-nut with three lobes is called "oji okike", (the creative deity or symbol of fecundity). It can again be called "oji Ikenga", which is symbol of achievement. A kola-nut with four lobes is a symbol of the four market days. It is regarded as a conventional kola-nut. When kola-nut has five lobes, the sharer takes the fifth lobe as his good luck symbol while the rest share the remaining four. "The kola-nut with six lobes: The sixth lobe is thrown away and treated as if only five. The

---

[360] Opata D.N., *Essays on Igbo World-View,* Nsukka: Ap Express Publishers, 2001, pp. 100 - 104, in Adibe G.E., Igbo Mysticism: *Power of Igbo Traditional Religion and Society,* op. cit., p. 170.

[361] Ekwunife A.N.O., *Consecration in Igbo Traditional Religion,* Snaap press, Enugu, Nigeria, 2003, p. 86.

[362] Adibe G.E., *Igbo Mysticism: Power of Igbo Traditional Religion and Society*, op. cit., p. 171, Igbo P.C., Elements of Igbo Culture and Tradition, op. cit., p. 50, Opata D.N., *Essays on Igbo World-Views,* Nsukka, Ap Express Publishers, op. cit., p. 67.

kola-nut with seven lobes: is regarded as the ultimate which signifies perfection. This is sent to the oldest man in the village who would offer sacrifice to village deity for some celebration to be observed. The tiny central lobe of "oji" symbolizes the presence of the invisible world with its beings in the midst of the visible. It is this presence that makes the Igbo world think in a perpetual interaction between these two worlds".[363]

The Igbo kola-nut (oji Igbo) expresses and communicates signs of unity, fraternity, acceptance, achievements, productivity, wealth, joy and sorrow of every family. It expresses also the unity and diversity of the Igbo world; hierarchy, authority, royalty and purity, wholeness of human being; fullness of life and perpetual presence of the spirits among men. It signifies hospitality, kindness, good faith and communion. All these attributes are summed up in the reflective dictum of the Igbo saying: "onye wetalu oji wetalu ndu" (he that brings kola-nut brings life).

Kola-nut has four principal rituals attached to it. They are:

1. Presentation of kola-nut (iche oji) and donning the kola-nut (imaba oji akwa),

2. blessing or consecration of kola-nut (igo oji),

3. breaking of kola-nut (iwa oji),

4. distribution of kola-nut (ike oji).

2.3.4.4. PRESENTATION OF KOLA-NUT (ICHE OJI)

In most cases this is done by the host. The host presents the kola-nut to his guest as Igbo custom and tradition demand. A guest may present a kola-nut to his host, but this is in an extraordinary situation. Normally, a guest does this when he has the intention of asking for a favour from his host. But we have to note here that this is different from "iche oji"– presentation of kola-nut.[364]

---

[363] Ekwuife A.N.O., *Consecration in Igbo Traditional Religion*, Jet Publishers, Enugu, Nigeria, 1990, in Igbo P.C., *Element of Igbo Culture and Tradition*, op. cit., p. 50.

[364] In the instant case the host takes away the kola-nut brought by the guest and presents (chee) his own kola-nut to the guest, saying "oji abia" (kola has come). If the host has a relation or kinsman around, assisting in playing the host, he directs the kinsman to show the kola-nut to the guest. The kola-nut often goes with chalkstone, "nzu" and a small amount of money, from the smallest denomination to any amount so desired by the host. This money is called "Mma oji" (kola-nut knife) or "imaba oji akwa" (donning the kola-nut). This practice of putting money is not common in all parts of Igboland. "Nzu" is passed round for individual markings on the floor. Then the guest would say to the host that "oji eze di eze na aka" – meaning literally that "the king's

2.3.4.5. "MMA OJI" (KOLA-NUT KNIFE) OR "IMABA OJI AKWA" (DONNING THE KOLA-NUT)

This is the tradition of putting some money – any amount, in the kola-nut and chalkstone saucer for one's guest. "It is pertinent to say that this practice is not common in the whole of Igboland; some areas practice it while some do not."[365]

2.3.4.6. BLESSING OF KOLA-NUT (IGO OJI)

Before kola-nut is blessed, the host requests the guest to remove the "mma oji" if there were any and one kola-nut (oji lue uno) if there were more than one kola-nut.[366] We present below an example of prayer said before the breaking of kola-nut.

Eze kere elu, kee ala, taa oji - Creator of heaven and earth, eat kola-nut.

Amadioha taa oji - *"Amadioha"[367]* eat *kola-nut.*

Ala Ezuhu taa oji - *Ezuhu* land eat kola-nut.

---

kola-nut is in the King's hand". But the true meaning of this manner of speaking is that the blessing and consecration of the kola-nut is the exclusive reserve of the host".

It is germane to note that there is another dimension to this. For instance, if it were to be in a public gathering, say, a gathering of Igbo people of diverse classes and communities, the presentation of the kola-nut falls on the person hosting the gathering, while the "igo oji" (the consecration) falls on a titled man or oldest man from the city where the gathering is taking place. They look for "a son of the soil" for the consecration as a mark of respect for the people of the city. Cf., Igbo P. C., *Elements of Igbo culture and Tradition,* op. cit., pp. 52 -53.

[365] In a very strict sense, the practice of "mma oji" was an exclusive preserve of full "Ozo-titled" men. In other words, if a guest comes to one's house and the host wants to honor or welcome the guest with kola-nut, and if the host shall include money "ego oji" (mma oji), it must be for a full "Ozo -titled" man. This tradition further stresses the good relationship existing between the giver and the receiver; a relationship which further enabled the "Ozo" titled man to eat and dine with his host. Cf., ibid, p. 53. This practice of putting money "ego oji" (mma oji) is not done today except when an "Ozo-titled" man pays someone a visit. In some parts of the Igboland it is now generalized to every visitor.

[366] This extra kola-nut, "oji lue uno", which is literally translated "when kola-nut gets home" means that when the guest gets home, he would remember from where the kola-nut came. So "oji lue uno" is an incomplete sentence whose full sentence is "oji lue uno okwue onye chere ya" meaning "when the kola-nut gets home it says who presented it". Cf., Igbo P.C., op. cit., p. 53. The ritual process of the blessing of kola-nut, begins with ablution of hands with water by both the host and the guest. This ablution ritual signifies spiritual ablution before the blessing of kola-nut. Having cleansed themselves, the host then picks one of the kola-nuts and begins to pray. He reverently expresses his desires to the gods, the ancestors and the deities of the land. Cf., Ekwunife A.N.O, *Consecration in Igbo Traditional Religion, op. cit. p. 9*, in Igbo P.C., *Elements of Igbo Culture and Tradition,* op. cit., p. 54.

[367] "Amadioha" refers to the god of thunder.

Ndi nwe ezi[368] *taa oji* - Founders of this habitant, eat kola-nut.

Agwu isi[369] *taa oji - Agwu isi* eat kola-nut.[370]

2.3.4.7. BREAKING OF KOLA-NUT *(IWA OJI)*

The act of breaking the kola-nut is normally done by the host or by the eldest man around who has prayed over the kola-nut. This can also be done by the host or the guest when the occasion warrants.[371]

2.3.4.8. DISTRIBUTION OF KOLA-NUT *(IKE OJI)*

"Ike oji" (distribution of kola-nut) is usually done by the host. The host will pick his "aka oji" (the main lobe of the kola-nut) and leave the responsibility of cutting the kola-nut into pieces and distributing it to the youngest in the gathering.

---

[368] "Ndi nwe ezi" refer to the ancestors of the land.

[369] "Agwu isi" refers to local deity.

[370] Cf., https: www.vanguardngr.com/2012/what-is-this-about-kolanut-in-igboland, accessed 22.4.2018.

[371] The main breaking of the kola-nut into its natural cotyledons remains in the hands of the elder who is around. It should be pointed out that the Igbo customs forbid a woman from "igo oji" or "iwa oji" (the blessing of a kola-nut or breaking of it) Cf., Igbo P.C., *Element of Igbo Culture and Tradition*, op. cit. p. 54. But a woman can present a kola-nut or distribute it after it has been blessed and broken and can partake in the eating of it. But a woman is totally forbidden from the blessing or breaking of the kola-nut.

CHAPTER THREE

3. THE IMPACT OF WAR ON HUMAN SPIRITUALITY: EVIDENCE FROM NIGERIA-BIAFRA WAR

3.1. INTRODUCTION

We have experienced from history that wars bring about a lot of changes, which include material changes, spiritual changes as well as psychological changes. Churchill asserted that "there is nothing wrong in change, if it is in the right direction. To improve is to change, so to be perfect is to have changed often."[372] The world learnt a lot of lessons from the first and second world wars. War in any form is not a pleasant experience thus:

> European nations began World War 1 with a glamorous vision of war, only to be psychologically shattered by the realities of the trenches. The experience changed the way people referred to the glamor of battle; they treated it no longer as a positive quality but as a dangerous illusion.[373]

The lessons and experiences which the world has gone through during war times, act today as guiding principles to the leaders of different countries of the world; who make every effort to seek for resolutions and peace when there are misunderstandings between nations or groups. Therefore, Eisenhower asserts:

> If men can develop weapons that are so terrifying as to make the thought of global war include almost a sentence for suicide, you would think that man's intelligence and his comprehension ... would include also his ability to find a peaceful solution.[374]

The Igbo generally do not like violence "per se" as we have earlier stated. The Igbo abhor shedding of blood in any form. "War was only taken to as a last resort; that is when all formal and normal courses of action to search for peace had failed."[375]

Many Nigerians and non-Nigerians have written a lot about Nigeria-Biafra war which started in 1967 and ended in 1970. Some commentators like Madiebo Alexander, Obiezuofu-Ezeigbo Chiemenem, Ezeani Emefiena, Frederick Forsyth

---

[372] Cf., churchillcentral. com/quotes., accessed 17.6.2017.
[373] Cf., *Postrel Virginia,* brainyquote.com, accessed 5.6.2017.
[374] Eisenhower D. Dwight, brainyquote.com., accessed 5.6.2017.
[375] Cf., Onwubiko, O.A; *Wisdom Lectures on African Thought and Culture*, op. cit., p., 29.

Offodile Chudi, Chinua Achebe,[376] just to mention but a few, have written books in which they narrated and analyzed the events of the Nigeria-Biafra war. The Nigeria-Biafra war brought a major turning point in the political history of Nigeria and in particular the Igbo people.

In this chapter we shall take the Igbo people as our case study. It is an obvious fact that any country that has experienced war never remained the same. That is the situation of Nigeria and in particular the Igbo people. A major change which this war has brought is in the area of spirituality of the Igbo people, which we will discuss in this chapter.

During the Nigerian civil war, some Igbo soldiers who fought on Biafra side "sought the use of protective ogwu (charms) in one form or the other."[377] After the war, the belief in charms and amulets among the Igbo was not strong as it was before the war. Many Igbo who believed in the power of charms, amulets and talisman discovered, during the war, that they were not efficacious as many believed they were. The war was a moment of test for the effectiveness of charms, amulets and talisman as well as for the "dibias" (native doctors) who prepared them. It was also for some a moment of test for the deities in which some Igbo believed that they existed and had powers. Many were really disappointed, because those things which they believed in (for example some of the *alusi* – deities) could not help or protect them during the war. The number of believers of Igbo Traditional Religion reduced drastically after the war. This and many more we shall discuss in this chapter.

The colonization of the Igboland by Britain was another moment of test for the belief in the deities and their powers. Many Igbo traditionalists strongly believed that when the gods are offended, the offender must not go unpunished unless necessary sacrifice, purification or atonement were made by the offender. During the colonization of Igboland, the Igbo resisted the introduction of foreign rule and ideology with radical destruction of their traditional way of life. The attachment of the Igbo to their traditional faith was fanatical and it was a traumatic experience cutting them off from the very source in which

---

376 Madiebo A.A., *The Nigerian Revolution and the Biafran War*, Fourth Dimension Publishing Co., Ltd, Enugu, Nigeria, 1980; Obiezuofu-Ezeigbo C. E., *The Biafran War and the Igbo in Contemporary Nigerian Politics*, Pan Negro Continental Ltd., Lagos Nigeria, 2007; Ezeani E., *In Biafra Africa Died: The Diplomatic Plot, 3rd edition*, Veritas Lumen Publisher, England, 2014; Forsyth F., *The Making of an African Legend: The Biafra Story*, Penguin Books Ltd., England, 1969; Offodile C., *The Politics of Biafra and the Future of Nigeria*, Safari Books Ltd, Ibadan, Nigeria, 2016; Achebe C., *There was a Country: A Personal History of Biafra*, Penguin Books, England, 2012.
377 Nwala T.U., *Igbo Philosophy,* op. cit., p. 89.

their life existence and survival had meaning. It was as if their world was coming to the end.[378]

Many questions may come to our mind as we discuss the issue of Nigeria-Biafra war. Some of these thought-provoking questions we may try to answer as we discuss the issue in this chapter. The questions are:

1. When and how did Nigerians notice that there may be a civil war in Nigeria?

2. What were the causes of the civil war in Nigeria?

3. Was the prevention of the war impossible?

4. How did the war start?

5. What were the parts played by other countries?

6. What prompted the people of Eastern Nigeria to secede?

7. Would there have been a war if the North had seceded as they had earlier planned to do?

8. If the Westerners (Yoruba) had not joined the Northerners (Hausa) against the Igbo of the East, would there have been a civil war in Nigeria? What prevented the Yoruba people from taking a neutral ground?

9. If the outcome of "Aburi" accord was obeyed by the parties involved in that accord, could there have been a civil war in Nigeria?

10. Who first declared war and took arms against the other, Nigeria or Biafra?

---

[378] At Agulu (Agulu is a town in Igboland) for instance when the British expeditionary force was advancing on the village, the native crier (the *okwu-ekwe*) who saw them approaching began to summon (in a poetic manner) the whole village to rise to the occasion and defend their town, their civilization and religion. He was heard shouting and charging the young warriors of Agulu, invoking the power of their goddess. "Haba, ekwewala" – O! Haba, don't allow this! "Haba ekwekwala" – O! Haba don't allow this! And no doubt, the people had an unflinching faith in the power of their goddess (Haba) to defend their town and confidently they marched out to beat back the invaders. When finally, the men with superior weapon won, some of the natives were taken as war prisoners. While in prison many refused to eat the whiteman's food, regarding it as an abomination, and fearing that their goddess "Haba", might punish them if they did. Those who ate the whiteman's food went straight, on their return, to "Haba" stream to wash their mouths and purify themselves. What a great show of faith. Even in the face of military defeat and humiliation, hunger and pain of death, the people still kept their faith. Cf., Nwala T.U., *Igbo Philosophy*, op. cit., pp. 35 - 36.

11.   What was the major motivating factor for the Biafra determination to fight on and what was the Nigerian government's primary reason to have Biafra as part of Nigeria?

12.   What major effects did the war have on the Igbo people?

3.2. THE CAUSES OF NIGERIA–BIAFRA WAR: REMOTE AND PROXIMATE

3.2.1. REMOTE CAUSES

3.2.1.1. THE TRAITS OF THE IGBO PEOPLE

One of the alleged causes of the Nigeria-Biafra war was the character or behaviour of the Igbo people which were often than not misinterpreted by other Nigerians. Can one really discover or describe the character exhibited by a group of people or a nation? In line with this Oguejiofor questions:

> It is obvious that in describing the spirit of a people, one is describing their dominant assumptions, the underlying sentiments that inform their beliefs, customs and practices. How does one get near to objectivity in such a description? Are there really attitudes or traits which are shared by people as numerous as the Igbo people? Is one therefore not falling prey to sweeping generalizations and unscientific stereotyping? Certain clarifications are therefore necessary.[379]

It is germane to say here that what we are outlining as the characters of the Igbo people are what have been said or written about them by persons from different backgrounds. They include foreign traders, colonialists, anthropologists, missionaries, historians and commentators both Nigerians and foreigners. These behaviours or traits we are going to present here do not necessarily mean that it is the way the Igbo see themselves. These traits are the way others see the Igbo. Their interpretations may be right or wrong. But one thing is clear; the interpretation of the character of the Igbo by others molds the way they treat and relate to Igbo people.

It is necessary to point out that one should not fall into the temptation of classifying one character trait as being negative or positive. This is because they can be good or bad, depending on their development in the individual concerned. For example, intelligence is a quality desired and admired by all, but it can also turn dangerous when possessed by antisocial elements. Nwabueze captures the mental picture of what we are describing here. He asserts:

---

[379] Oguejiofor J., The *Influence of Igbo Traditional Religion on the Socio-Political Character of the Igbo*, op. cit., p. 14.

The best in the Igbo character excites fear in others while the worst in him excites resentment and hatred. And he is endowed by nature with a rather liberal measure of both. His best is singularly good, his worst singularly bad.[380]

3.2.1.2. PIGHEADEDNESS

Pigheadedness is one of the characters that some see in the Igbo. I would not like to interpret pigheadedness as a negative character. Pigheadedness can mean astuteness, stubbornness or ambitiousness. These can be positive or negative depending on how one applies them. Echeruo affirms that:

> "Headstrong" and "ambitious". No two words can better define that quality in Igbo character which has been its primary source of strength and disaster. The Igbo are headstrong people – sensible but headstrong.[381]

What the outside observer might see easily in the Igbo is their headstrongness. The manifestation of this traits in the Igbo to the outside observer assumes more acuity when the person is not accustomed to the Igbo character and comes from a background which helps little to improve his adaptation or comprehension. It is therefore not surprising that a good number of colonialists saw little more than stubbornness of the Igbo. We will later explain this in detail.

Most probably, it was the pigheadedness of the Igbo that made it difficult for the colonialists to establish effective control of the Igbo interior. It was easier for the colonial master to have northern Nigeria under his control by simply signing a treaty with the Emir or defeating his army in a single war. But with the Igbo, the story was different. "The British in Igboland had to engage town after town and village after village for the simple reason that each of these constituted a city state, with an independent government which recognized no exterior master."[382]

One can assert that the Igbo people really gave the colonial master tough time. The colonial master misunderstood the Igbo's pigheadedness as an inclination to disobedience, outward readiness for confrontation and a sign of indisposition for external governance. This misunderstanding of the Igbo's trait by the

---

[380] Cf. Nabeel B., *The Igbo in the Context of Modern Government and Politics in Nigeria*, Owerri, Ministry of Information, 1985, p. 6, in Oguejiofor, J., *The Influence of Igbo Traditional Religion on the Socio-Political Character of the Igbo,* op. cit., p. 14.
[381] Echeruo M.J.C., *A Matter of Identity*, Owerri, Nigeria, Ministry of Information, 1979, p. 13, in Ogbuejiofor J., *The Influence of Igbo Traditional Religion on the Socio-Political Character of the Igbo,* op. cit., p. 15.
[382] Oguejiofor J., *The Influence of Igbo Traditional Religion on the Socio-Political Character of the Igbo,* op. cit., p. 15.

colonial master led to so many other things which may have destined the Igbo's fate in Nigeria, especially their political life, social life, economic advantages and religious life.

The description of Igboland as lawless by some colonial officials may have originated from their lack of goodwill or even willingness to study the people they were colonizing. This led them to many grievous errors including the imposition of chiefs on a people who generally did not recognize chiefs in their traditional political organization. It was of the pigheadedness of the Igbo people that made it unease for the colonial administration to take a firm root in Igboland until the beginning of the twentieth century. The colonial master applied several "military expeditions"[383] in order to conquer and subjugate an unwilling people – the Igbo.

We shall later evaluate how this confrontation and pigheadedness of the Igbo towards the colonial master affected the Igbo as a people. We shall explain this when we discuss amalgamation of Nigeria. Suffice it to say that it really placed the Igbo in an unenviable position in the political life of Nigeria which exists up till today.

3.2.1.3. HARD WORK AND DESIRE FOR ACHIEVEMENT

Hard work and desire for achievement are qualities found in human beings in many cultures of the world. Many have asserted that the Igbo people possess and exhibit this character. One of the earliest of such observations was that of

---

[383] Among such expeditions were the "Aro" Expedition (1901 - 1902), the "Ezza" patrol (1905); the "Ahiara" Expedition (1906). In many cases, military action against the people was so severe, involving massive burning, destruction of lives and property and mass imprisonment of the adult males. At "Ahiara Mbaise", for instance, the entire village of "Niche" was virtually razed to the ground. Some of those attacks were reprisal actions. However, they were all part of the measure adopted to bring the areas under British colonial control. The major targets were major centers of cultural influence and power in the area. Hence, the "Ibini Ukpabi" (or Long Juju Oracle) of the "Aro", the "Igwe-ka-ala" of "Umunne-oha", the "Kamalu of Ouzo", the "Agbala of Awka", the "Haba of Agulu", just to mention but a few; were all major targets of the colonial onslaught. British confrontation and eventual conquest of the Igbo was not however, an easy one. Even the British administration of the area was marked by bloody encounters, suspicion and tension that continued to prevail even long after the initial military conquest. The introduction of such political and administrative control mechanisms like the Indirect Rule (which was already successful in Northern Nigeria), the appointment of warrant chiefs, complicated matters. Popular revolts dogged British colonial domination of Igboland. There were, for example, revolts against introduction of taxation; against appointment of artificial unwanted warrant chiefs with no roots in the culture of the people; against British administration's inability to maintain a healthy economic environment (e.g., revolt against the low price of palm produce). These revolts often flared into serious disturbances and bloody clashes. One such historical revolt was the famous Aba women's Riot of 1929. Cf., Nwala T.U., *Igbo Philosophy,* op. cit., pp. 34 - 35.

Olaudah Equiano, who published in 1789 a book entitled: "The Interesting Narrative of the Life of Olaudah Equiano or Gustavus Vasa the African." Concerning the Igbo's attitude to work, Equiano wrote:

> We (the Igbo) are all habituated to labor from our earliest years. Everyone contributed something to the common stock, and as we are unacquainted with idleness, we have no beggars. The benefits of such a mode of living are obvious. The West Indian planter prefers the slaves of Benin or Eboe (i.e. Igbo) to those of any other part of Guinea for their hardiness, intelligence, integrity and zeal.[384]

There is, of course, hardly any culture that does not in certain ways encourage hard work as a human weapon for the domination of nature. But the testimony of many writers has confirmed a somewhat extraordinary concern of the Igbo people for hard work. In 1881, the British vice-consul on the then oil river protectorate described the Igbo as "exceedingly industrious people".[385] Ojukwu attests to this by saying: "the Igbo desire for achievement is somehow singular; given that the Igbo people give deference to achievement not linked to inherited positions."[386]

The desire for achievement is among the major reasons why they are feared and being resented by other tribes in Nigeria. It is also pertinent to state that the Igbo do not concern themselves with the achievement and pursuit of wealth which has no moral basis. This is because "wealth acquired under dubious circumstances does not earn respect; it has to be earned through hard work, under conditions of integrity and without deceit."[387] The hatred that the Igbo experience today from other major tribes of Nigeria partly comes from their ability to work hard and their desire for achievement. Forsyth explains that:

> Ironically it is their hard work and their success that have contributed to make the Igbo so unpopular in Nigeria, and notably in the North. Other characteristics are adduced to explain the antipathy they manage to generate; they are uppity and aggressive say the detractors; ambitious and energetic say the defenders. They are money-loving and mercenary says one school; canny and

---

[384] Equinano O., *Equiano's Travels*, P. Edwards (ed.), London, Heinemann, 1967, p. 7, in Oguejiofor J., *The Influence of Igbo Traditional Religion on the Socio-Political Character of the Igbo,* op. cit., p., 18.

[385] Ibid., p. 18.

[386] Odumegwu-Ojukwu E., *Because I am Involved*, Spectrum Books Ltd., Ibadan, Nigeria, 1989, p. 95.

[387] Okigbo P., *Reconstruction of Political Economy of Igbo civilization*, Owerri, Ministry of Information, 1987, in Oguejiofor J., *The Influence of Igbo Traditional Religion on the Socio-Political Character of the Igbo*, op. cit., p. 19.

thrifty says the other. Clannish and unscrupulous in grabbing advantages, say some; united and quick to realize the advantages of education say others.[388]

3.2.1.4. COMPETITIVENESS AND AMBITIOUSNESS

Competitiveness and ambitiousness may be seen by some as negative traits. These traits can be positive or negative depending on how they are developed in the individual concerned. In recent times, these traits have been developed enormously in Igbo communities and have helped immensely in the development of Igboland. This competitive spirit of the Igbo is seen in every Igbo community. Every Igbo community has a deep consciousness of its position in relation to the neighbouring communities. Every community aims at being the best among others. In the area of community development, morality, education, social development, politics, just to mention but a few, all communities work hard in order not to lag behind. In the past, these traits (competitiveness and ambitiousness) which are supposed to be positive were somehow put into negative usage. This was visible in inter-community violence or wars.

The spirit of competition directed to negative usage was also noticed within Igbo communities in which sections were often at loggerheads with one another in the process of balancing out the use of power and the administration of justice. The competitiveness and ambitiousness of the Igbo have been nurtured and structured positively in many communities. Thus, age-grades were formed and titled societies were instituted. Therefore, there are certain things which a healthy and normal person is expected to achieve at the appropriate period with the members of his age grade; such things like getting married and title taking. When one fails in this area, it is taken that one has lived below the community's expectations. Without minding the shortcomings of these attitudes, the spirit of competition and ambition has helped the Igbo as a group, individuals, and communities in self-development. The gaps in society caused by Northern apathy towards modernization could not be filled by the British alone. Before and after Nigerian Independence, "there were posts for clerks, junior executives, accountants, switchboard operators, engineers, train drivers, waterworks superintendents, bank tellers, factory and shop staff, which the Northerners could not fill. A few, but only a very few Yoruba from the Western region of the South went to north for the new jobs. Most were filled by the more enterprising Easterners. By 1966 there were an estimated 1,300,000

---

[388] Forsyth F., *The Making of an African Legend: The Biafra Story*, Richard clay (The Chaucer Press) Ltd, Great Britain, 1977, p. 108.

Easterners, mostly Igbo in the Northern region, and about another 500,000 had taken up jobs and residence in the West."[389]

These traits of the Igbo have been misinterpreted and misunderstood by other tribes in Nigeria, and because of this the Igbo people have been derided and hated. The Igbo drive, versatility and aggressive competitiveness sometimes make some to accuse them of being domineering and abrasive. Their rugged individualism is at times exaggerated to make others see them as selfish and acting with callous indifference. Their self-confidence, courage and boldness are at times displayed in ways which others interpreted as pride, arrogance and exhibiting a superiority complex. Their love of freedom, progressiveness, independent-mindedness at times expose them to be accused by others of being undisciplined, disrespectful, confrontational and culturally being insensi-tive. Their intelligence and shrewdness sometimes provoke the accusation of craftiness and deceit. Their spirit of accommodation and adaptability, adven-turism, innate receptivity to new ideas at times make others to accuse them of being without principles, unpredictable and slippery, if not unreliable. Their larger-than-life attitudes at times are being interpreted as being exhibitionistic. This is what some will call Igbo tendency towards expansiveness and self-dramatization.

3.2.1.5. ADAPTABILITY

Among all the tribes of Nigeria, the Igbo are known to be the most adaptable. More than any other ethnic group in Nigeria, the Igbo are said to have spread in incomparably larger numbers all the world. They also contribute immeasur-ably in the economic and social development of their adopted places of resi-dence. Everywhere else in Nigeria outside their home land, the Igbo have set-tled in large numbers confronting the harsh conditions of life in their undaunt-ed efforts to earn a living and to contribute to the economic and social devel-opment of the areas.

The difference in the degree of assimilation of the Igbo could be easily dictated from that of the other tribes of Nigeria. "In the West the Easterners' assimila-tion was total; they lived in the same streets as the Yoruba, mixed with them in all social occasions, and their children shared the same schools. In the North, at the behest of the local rulers, to which the British made no demur, all Southerners, whether from East or West, were herded into *Sabon Garis*, or strangers' quarters, a sort of ghetto outside the walled towns. Inside the *Sabon Garis* ghetto, life was lively and spirited, but their contact with their Hausa

---

[389] Forsyth F., *The Making of an African Legend: The Biafra Story*, Penguin Books, Ltd., England, 1969, p. 19.

compatriot was kept at the wish of the latter to a minimum. Schooling was segregated, and two radically different societies co-existed without any attempt by the British to urge gradual integration."[390]

3.2.1.6. ECONOMIC INDIVIDUALISM

Economic individualism does not mean here lack of brotherhood, selfishness and lack of spirit of accommodation and unwillingness to help one another. Rather, it means self-independence and the spirit of hard work. Mutual help is not lacking and has never lacked among the traditional Igbo, both in the tillage and weeding of their farms, in erecting living houses and in repairing them in directing or instructing an inexperienced person how to get about in the pursuance of his business and in the training of personnel for skilled jobs. However, over and above assistance accorded to the individual, he is expected to be able to fend for himself, especially if he is blessed with good health. A mature and married adult is expected to fend for his family.

Economic individualism and independence are thus another impetus to hard work. In Igbo traditional society, children were trained in working with their parents. They continued to do so until the approach of adulthood. They were then given their own portions of land and yam seedlings and were expected to develop them through their efforts. The same procedure largely applied to those sections of Igboland which specialized in other professions other than farming. Economic individualism as one of the traits of the Igbo encourages hard work and self-reliance among them. An Igbo man will never like to depend on another for anything for so long. He can depend on another for a short time in order to learn but will never make himself a beggar or perpetual servant.

3.2.1.7. THE DEMOCRATIC NATURE OF THE IGBO PEOPLE

The Igbo were originally democratic in their system of governance. They did not learn it from the western world. That was why the indirect rule applied by the colonial master in Igboland did not succeed. In line with this, Leith-Ross asserts:

> So natural did it seem to find autocracy in some form or other wherever one went in Africa that it was impossible even to imagine a democracy absolute as that of the Igbo.[391]

---

[390] Forsyth F., *The Making of an African Legend: The Biafra story*, op. cit., p. 19.

[391] Leith-Ross S., *African Woman*, London, Routledge and Kegan Paul, 1939, p. 67, in Oguejiofor J., *The Influence* of *Igbo Traditional Religion on the Socio-Political Character of the Igbo*, op. cit., p. 23.

Democracy, whether primary or representative, is hallmark of the Igbo traditional political systems. Within the village Republican Assemblies, all adult male participated on equal footing. When it becomes necessary to hold consultations (*igba izu*) in order to reach a consensus, the assembly may ask each family, kindred, various relevant groups (such as the youth, the titled men, etc.), to nominate their representatives to form a committee to deliberate and propose a consensus. In such situations, we hear such calls as "ezi obula", "onuama obula", "ndi nwoke", "umuokoro-obia", "ndi echiri echi", etc., "nye anyi otu madu" – (every family, every kindred, the men, the youth, titled men, please give us one person from among you). Unanimity or consensus, all the rigorous processes and compromises ("igba izu"– period of consultation) involved in the process are efforts made to accommodate the wishes of the majority, as well as those of the minority. In short, they are designed to arrive at what may be abstractly called the general will of the people or community.

Unanimity or consensus becomes imperative since the Igbo conceive of politics and government not as a means whereby the stronger or the many impose their will on the rest, but as the process of regulating normal life among brothers and sisters. The democratic spirit checks the apparent or possible excesses of seniority, status, number and achievement. This is further strengthened by the Igbo principle of equality and equivalence. This democratic spirit of the Igbo became obvious when the colonial master imposed indirect rule theory on the Igbo. Although it functioned well in the Northern region, it failed notably in the eastern half of the south, the land of the Igbo.

The British were so concerned with the idea of regional chiefs and the indirect rule that they could not even consider the nature of the people involved, on which this type of administration would be imposed. The Aba women riots of 1929 (Aba is in the heartland of the Igbo) were partly caused by the British who imposed rulers on the Igbo whom the people refused to accept. It was not difficult to impose measures on the Northerners. They were accustomed to implicit obedience, but it did not work in the East. "The whole traditional structure of the East makes it virtually immune to dictatorship, one of the reasons for the women riot in Aba in 1929. Easterners insist on being consulted in everything that concerns them".[392]

Power and Authority belong to all, but by virtue of seniority and ontological status, degree and capacity of knowledge, moral, spiritual, intellectual qualities and economic status, some members exercise greater authority and influence than the others. This was thought necessary in order to ensure an effective

---

[392] Forsyth F., *The Making of an African Legend: the Biafra story*, op. cit., pp. 18 -19.

political system. We often hear the Igbo saying: "onye obula bu eze n'obi ya " (everyone is king in his compound or chamber). Or "Igbo enwe eze" (the Igbo have no Kings or rulers). These common expressions point to the republican nature of the traditional communal Igbo society. These expressions are most often misunderstood and misinterpreted by others. This does not mean that the Igbo do not have rulers.

Almost all the towns in Igboland have their kings, but their system of governance is democratic and not otherwise. Abiola agrees to the above assertions. He states:

> The political system of this tribe (Igbo) was very, subtle and complex, based on the principle of village democracy. It was decentralized. It is also democratic, for everyone had the right to contribute to decision taking. Each village was the architect of its own fortune. Members of each village were bound together in their strict belief in the common ancestry. These village members formed a type of government mainly concerned with their corporate existence. Laws and regulations were formulated to guide their standard of behaviors.[393]

The actual organ of government in the village was the "village council' consisting of the leaders who were their compound's mouth-piece as well as the earthly representatives of the families' ancestors. The village council was in turn an earthly council voicing out the laws already sanctioned by the ancestors. These included laws against misbehaviour which were punished with the highest punishment of the land. Beside the village council, the system of age-group features most in the political structure of the Igbo society. The senior age-group looked after the maintenance of peace and order, as well as providing army commanders to ward off external trouble. The junior age-group catered for the community's sanitation and other necessary matters. The very senior age-group catered for other social affairs not touched by the junior age-group. It can be observed that the Igbo system of government was based on the principle of village democracies. It was segmental and strictly subject to the control of religion. It respected the institution of age-groups as well.

The Igbo were and are in the forefront of unity and development in Nigeria. "They have been everything to the Nigerian nation. They were great freedom fighters when some wanted independence postponed; they were great proponents of the one Nigeria."[394] The Igbo contribute immensely in all aspects of human and infrastructural development in Nigeria. "They played heroic and

---

[393] Abiola E.O., *A Textbook of West African History (A.D. 1000 to the Present Day), revised and enlarged, Molayo* Standard Press and Bookshops co. (Nig.) Ltd., 1984, p. 170.
[394] Uwalaka J., *The Struggle for an Inclusive Nigeria: Igbos to be or not to be? A treatise on Igbo Political Personality and Survival in Nigeria,* Snaap Press Ltd., Enugu, Nigeria, 2003, p. 4.

pioneering role in national development; built roads to make many remotest parts of Nigeria accessible, brought the light of Education to many areas that had no interest in education, brought the light of the Christian gospel to many corners that were under the stranglehold of superstition, demonism and moral turpitude, founded towns where there were dreaded forests and brought markets to economic deserts."[395] The traits of the Igbo portray them as being radical, overassuming and inconsiderate. But in many cases, this is rather a misjudgment of them. Uwalaka laments:

> This is how the Igbo man came to be feared, dreaded, derided, hated, suspected by other Nigerians and eventually suffered a great massacre that shook Africa and the world. It was a black and bloody chapter in the history of the Igbo man and marked a dramatic reversal in fortunes of the Igbo man in Nigeria.[396]

It was the traits of the Igbo that made some Nigerians to misinterpret the coup of January 1966 as an Igbo coup, which we shall later discuss. Another charge which is levelled against the Igbo is clannishness. Achebe explains that:

> He (the Igbo) is accused of unduly favoring his kindred and running to their defense at all times. He is supposed to have a tribal caucus where decisions are made and conspiracies hatched to advance Igbo interests.[397]

Unless one understands the hidden agenda in the Amalgamation of Nigeria, one may not understand the problems the Igbo have gone through and are still going through today in Nigeria, and finally, one will never understand the political structure in Nigeria and why there was a civil war in Nigeria.

3.2.1.8. THE COLONIZATION AND AMALGAMATION OF NIGERIA

Before we discuss the amalgamation of Nigeria, it is pertinent that we show the background (the colonization) on which the amalgamation was actualized. One may argue that the issue we are about discussing (the Colonization and Amalgamation of Nigeria) has nothing to do with the modernization of the spirituality of the Igbo people, which is the topic of this work. But of course, it has a lot to do with it. Unless we understand how Nigeria became one country through her amalgamation, we may not understand how the civil war in Nigeria started, what caused it, how the war affected the Igbo people in general, their spirituality, and the problems of Nigeria then, and today.

---

[395] Ibid.
[396] Ibid., p. 5.
[397] Achebe C., *The Trouble with Nigeria,* Heinemann Educational Books, England, 1984, p. 47.

3.2.1.8.1. COLONIZATION OF NIGERIA

By 1884, Britain, France, Germany and Leopold of Belgium were seriously competing for colonies in Africa. But by far, the most explosive issue that arose from the scramble was the rivalry over the Congo. Portugal's claim over the Congo supported by Britain was opposed by Leopold and France. Fearing that the rivalry might degenerate into war, Bismarck summoned a conference in Berlin of the Powers concerned with the scramble to discuss their claims to African territories and to reach agreement on a peaceful way of partitioning the continent among themselves.

Since rivalry over the Congo and the Niger territories dominated the conference, it is often called the Berlin West African conference. It sat from 15th November, 1884 to 30th January, 1885. The chief powers at the conference were France, Britain, Germany, Portugal, and King Leopold of Belgium representing his International African Association for the Congo. It should be noted that there were no African representatives at a Conference that was to decide the fate of Africans.

3.2.1.8.2. THE RESOLUTIONS OF THE BERLIN WEST AFRICAN CONFERENCE

The conference decided among other things:

(1)   That any power claiming territories on any part of the African coastline should formerly notify the other powers taking part in the conference.

(2)   That any such claims to territories must be backed by effective occu pation; that is, by the establishment of an effective degree of authority or administration in the area concerned before such claims could be recognized as valid.

(3)   That there should be freedom of trade in the Congo basin and freedom of navigation for the peoples of all nations on the Niger and Congo rivers.

(4)   Free access into the interior of Africa by traders, missionaries and other agents of all countries should be guaranteed by the occupying powers so that the slave trade would be finally eradicated and the material and moral benefits of European civilization extended to Africans.[398]

---

[398] Onwubiko K.B.C., *School certificate History of West Africa, Bk. Two,* Africana Educational Publishers, Nigeria, 1973, p. 230 - 231.

It is a known fact that Nigeria was a British colony. The Federation of Nigeria, as it exists today, has never really been one homogeneous country, for its widely differing peoples and tribes. It was Britain during the process of colonization and amalgamation of Nigeria that brought all the tribes of Nigeria together and cemented them into one country called "Nigeria".

It is pertinent that we survey the stages by which this great political union came to be. In 1900, Flora Shaw, former colonial correspondent, who later became the wife of Lord Lugard came up with the name "Nigeria". Before the year 1914, there was no country in the world known by the name Nigeria. On the other hand, for hundreds of years, there existed within the geographical space known today as Nigeria, peoples and nations identified as Yoruba, Igbo, Tiv, Hausa, Benin and so forth.[399]

3.2.1.8.3. LAGOS COLONY (NIGERIA) - 1861

The first move made by Britain in colonizing Nigeria was the annexation of Lagos in 1861. It was the first step taken by Britain in the 19th century to acquire economic and political domination over the people of Nigeria.

3.2.1.8.4. OIL RIVERS PROTECTORATE - 1885

Britain progressed in her move in colonizing Nigeria by the establishment of a British protectorate over the Oil River in 1885 as a result of increasing rivalry with other European powers in the area. The British government was unwilling at that time to undertake the heavy financial burden of administering the area in spite of the stipulations of the Berlin West African Conference on "effective occupation". But in 1891, it created a skeleton administration by the appointment of a commissioner and Consul-General who resided at old Calabar. Consuls and Vice-Consuls were also appointed to the various rivers. In 1893, the area of the Protectorate was extended inland to Lokoja and the Benue and renamed the Niger Coast Protectorate. Then in 1897, following the British occupation of Benin, that area west of the Niger became part of the Niger Coast Protectorate.

3.2.1.8.5. COLONY AND PROTECTORATE OF LAGOS - 1888

Certain events made British occupation of Yorubaland necessary. These were the adverse effects of the Yoruba wars on trade with Lagos which led to increasing interference in the affairs of Yoruba states by the Lagos administration, and the threat of French encroachment on Yorubaland. As a result of the

---

[399] Ezeani E., *In Biafra Africa died, the Diplomatic Plot, (3nd Edition),* Veritas Lumen Publishers, London, UK, 2014, p. 15.

French threat, the Lagos government signed a treaty with the "Alafin" of Oyo in 1888 by which he placed all Yorubaland under British protection. By 1896, all Yorubaland south of Ilorin was under the control of the Lagos government; Lagos and Yorubaland were administered as the Colony and Protectorate of Lagos.

3.2.1.8.6. COLONY AND PROTECTORATE OF SOUTHERN NIGERIA - 1906

On 1st January 1900, an important administrative advance was made when the Niger Coast Protectorate was renamed the Protectorate of Southern Nigeria, and the Consul-General became the "High Commissioner". Then, on 1st May 1906, this Protectorate was merged with the Colony and Protectorate of Lagos as the "Colony and Protectorate of Southern Nigeria" with Lagos as headquarters.

3.2.1.8.7. THE PROTECTORATE OF NORTHERN NIGERIA - 1900

The hinterland of Nigeria north of Lokoja was being administered formally on behalf of the British government by a chartered company – The Royal Niger Company. The British Government had declared a protectorate over areas claimed by the company in 1887. Then on January 1st, 1900, British government took over direct administration of the area from the Royal Niger Company and named it the Protectorate of Northern Nigeria with Lugard as its first High Commissioner.[400]

3.2.1.8.8. COLONIZATION AND ITS ADVERSE EFFECTS ON NIGERIA

The colonization of Nigerian tribes altered the course of their political history. It ended (though for a time) the long period of independence of the Nigerian tribes and replaced it with European foreign rule. This imposition of foreign rule was so humiliating and irksome to the Nigerian tribes. Therefore, it was strongly resisted, more specially in Eastern Nigeria.

In many areas, European occupation was accompanied by the elimination of Nigerian rulers and leaders by death or deportation or their replacement with stooges who tried to cooperate with the occupying power. For example, in Sokoto – Nigeria, "the Sultan was forced to flee and later killed in battle. The imperialists rather preferred to rule directly through willing Nigerian agents."[401]

---

[400] Onwubiko K.B.C., *School Certificate History of West Africa, Book two,* Africana Educational Publishers, Nigeria, 1973, pp. 254 -256.
[401] Ibid., p. 244.

The net result of this interference in the internal affairs of Nigerian tribes was the breakdown of tribal authority as the chiefs lost their powers over their people. This in turn resulted in the breakdown of law and order which the imperialists were forced to restore by more killings of the people in the name of pacification. Worse still, colonization ignored ethnic groupings. When the colonial masters wanted to unite the tribes through the process of amalgamation, they ignored totally the differences that existed and still exist up till today among the tribes. This resulted to a lot of problems Nigeria had in the past and is still having up till today.

3.2.1.8.9. SOCIAL EFFECTS OF COLONIZATION

The social evils resulting from the colonization were no less serious. Atrocities committed upon the Nigerian tribes during the period of colonization disorganized the tribes' social life and led to depopulation in many areas. This was particularly the case in Eastern Nigeria where resistance was stiff and long and the British colonial army were ruthless on the tribes of Eastern Nigeria.

The superiority of European weapons of warfare such as the Maxim-gun inspired Nigerian tribes with profound respect for the European and all he stood for. The result was that tribes developed an inferiority complex and began to copy blindly European culture and ways of life, and to despise African traditions and customs.

3.2.1.8.10. ECONOMIC EFFECTS

Most important of all were the economic injustices and cruelties meted out to the Nigerian population by the imperialist power. First, they regarded their colonies as "possessions" to be used mainly for the economic benefit of the powers that owned them. This led to the ruthless exploitation of Nigerian labour, lands and other resources for the benefit of the imperial powers. In some areas, the lands of the natives were seized and the natives were at the same time used to develop them. The worst economic injustice was the looting of invaluable Nigerian works of art. Many of these famous treasures are now scattered throughout the museums of the world.

It must be pointed out that during the colonial era, the colonial powers made no effort to establish secondary industries for the local processing of agricultural products. So, Nigeria continued to be the market for the manufactured goods of Europe and the producer of raw materials of Europe's industries. Again, there was no effort made by the colonial master to plough back some of the huge profits they made into the economy of the colonies.

3.2.1.8.11. POSITIVE EFFECTS OF COLONIZATION

We have stated above the negative effects of colonization on Nigerian tribes. It is germane to say that we have also the good side of colonization.

1. SECURITY AND POLITICS:

Politically, the colonization did immense good to Nigeria. The occupation or colonization of Nigerian tribes by British authority brought to an end the era of tribal wars, of fear and insecurity which had plagued many communities for long.

Many Nigerian tribes that had long remained separate and hostile to one another were brought together under one government by the colonial powers. The inhabitants of these new states were made to adapt the European idea of the state. In this way, the modern states of Nigeria are the products of colonization and amalgamation.

2. SOCIAL:

The partition laid to rest the evil ghost of the internal slave trade and slavery. When the British Government took over the administration of Northern Nigeria from the Royal Niger Company in 1900, one of the first laws it made for the protectorate was the slave-dealing proclamation of 1901 which abolished the legal status of slavery, prohibited slave-dealing and declared all children born after first April 1901 to be free. In 1902, an expedition destroyed the long "Juju" of "Arochukwu" in Eastern Nigeria where slave-dealing was still going on. In this way, this evil practice which had for many centuries laid waste large parts of West Africa was eradicated.[402]

3. HEALTH AND EDUCATION:

In the fields of health and education, Nigeria has gained enormously by European rule. Europeans have brought scientific methods of healing and preventing diseases through the establishment of hospitals and dispensaries, and through inoculation and vaccination. Attention has been given to research in tropical diseases. In 1899, Britain opened schools for Tropical Medicine at Liverpool and London. Even though medical facilities were grossly inadequate in Nigeria, the foundations for future development had been laid.

The greatest contribution of the colonial powers was perhaps the introduction of Western education to Nigeria. It is needless narrating here how Nigeria and the Igbo in particular have benefited from Western education. The adoption of

---

[402] Onuwubiko K.B.C., *School Certificate History of West Africa, Bk., two*, op. cit., p. 247.

English for the spread of education in Nigeria has helped various Nigerian tribes which have many dialects not only to be able to communicate with one another but also with other peoples of the world.

4. INFRASTRUCTURAL DEVELOPMENT:

The establishment and development of towns or urban communities was another contribution of colonial powers in the social sphere. The impact of these urban centers upon the social, economic and political life of Nigerian states has been tremendous. The introduction of modern means of transportation was another major development brought by the colonial master.

5. DEVELOPMENT OF AGRICULTURE:

In the development of agriculture, the colonial powers perhaps for selfish economic reasons, have contributed immensely by promoting the production of cash-crops such as groundnuts, palm oil and kernel, cotton, coffee, rubber, cocoa and so on. The colonial masters established schools for teaching improved methods of agriculture and introduced new varieties of crops and animals. In these ways, they stimulated interest in agriculture.

6. COMMERCE AND ECONOMY:

Among the valuable economic changes introduced by the colonial governments was the legal tender – coin currency. This replaced the barter system and cumbersome currency of iron bar and cowries which had prevailed for long in Nigeria. The first silver coins were introduced by the British in their colonies from 1886. In 1912, the West African Currency Board was set up to supply currency to British West African colonies. In 1915, it issued various denominations of coins and currency notes, after which came the commercial Banks – the Bank of British West Africa in 1890s and the colonial Bank in 1917.[403]

3.2.1.8.12. THE APPLICATION OF INDIRECT RULE BY THE COLONIAL MASTER

One may ask of how the colonial master managed or ruled the colonies and protectorates under his care before it later metamorphosed into "Nigeria" as we know it today. The colonial master introduced indirect rule, as a system of governance by which he ruled the colonies and protectorates under his care. Adigwe asserts that:

---

[403] Onwubiko K.B.C., *School Certificate History of West Africa, Bk two, 1800 - Present Day*, op. cit., p. 249.

Indirect rule as a theory of government originated in the nineteenth century. Before it was introduced into Nigeria; the Dutch had adopted it in Java. The introduction of the system of government into Nigeria was accomplished by Lord Lugard who was the governor of Nigeria from 1914 to 1916.[404]

Indirect rule is a system of local administration in which the essential features were the preservation of traditional political institutions and their adaptation under the tutelage and direction of the colonial master's administration, to the requirements of modern units of local government. In simple terms, it may be defined as a system of administration under which traditional rulers were allowed to rule their people under the supervision of the colonial master.[405] Abiola defines indirect rule as: "the art of ruling a group of people through the assistance of some agents. It is a policy of ruling through the traditional chiefs."[406]

3.2.1.8.12.1. THE COLONIAL MASTER'S APPLICATION OF INDIRECT RULE IN NORTHERN NIGERIA

Surprises are often expressed as to why Lord Frederick Lugard should appoint Africans to take part in running of the affairs of the colonies. But if we were to read the mind of Lugard, and considering the outcome of this system, it does not take time to know the basic reasons behind this. Certain circumstances made the colonial master to adopt indirect rule in Northern Nigeria. First, the colonial master was confronted by an acute shortage of trained European staff to help him run the administration of the vast territory which he had conquered. We have to recall that during this period, very few Europeans were prepared to come to West Africa which was described as "the white man's grave", owing to its poor climate and the presence of deadly insects like mosquitoes and tsetse flies. Lugard saw nothing bad in continuing with the existing African system of government which needed very few British hands.

In addition, it was Lord Lugard's considered opinion that before any British administration could succeed in West Africa, the African traditional rulers must be brought in. This, in his opinion, was due to the type of power being wielded by these rulers over their subjects. This was more noticeable among the Hausas, the Tivs, the Edos and the Kanuris. Lord Lugard did not see anything wrong in the appointment of the few British officials then available to him. They

---

[404] Adigwe F., *Essentials of Government for West African;* University Press PLC, Ibadan, Nigeria, 2011, p. 183.
[405] Ibid., p. 259.
[406] Abiola E. O., *A Textbook of West African History (A.D. 1000 to the Present Day), revised and enlarged,* op. cit., p. 164.

worked behind the scene in the running of the affairs of the people, making changes appear all the time, as if they came from the chiefs.

In fact, Lugard resorted to this system because the British government felt reluctant to get herself heavily involved in any financial responsibilities to the colonies. This was due to the willful declaration of independence towards the second half of the eighteenth century by the American colonies which formerly belonged to her. She therefore found it senseless to nurse a colony only to see it declaring itself independent. Under this situation therefore, Lugard realized that before he could successfully run the affairs of the Protectorates, he must evolve a system which could make the protectorates themselves finance their own administration, instead of becoming a burden to the British taxpayers. This point, no doubt, explains why this system was adopted first in Nigeria and later in other parts of the world.

It was Lugard's honest belief that any system of government in West Africa must be made beneficial to both the Europeans and the Africans. The best way to achieve this, Lugard thought, was by adopting a system of government that would combine African institutions with the British political beliefs. As we have earlier remarked, even if the European staff were available, the funds available were too small to finance large-scale direct administration. Thus, shortage of staff and funds made direct administration impossible at the time. In line with this, Van Gorder states: "In the north, the British relied on caliphates to maintain political oversight because they did not have the interest, manpower, or financial resources to dedicate to the region."[407]

In northern Nigeria, the colonial master was helped out of this difficulty by the existence of large Fulani emirates which had institutions that were easily adaptable to a system of indirect rule. In addition to this, social conditions in Northern Nigeria at the time easily suggested the adoption of a system of indirect rule, for, in a predominantly illiterate community where people cannot readily learn through the radio and the press about the daily activities of government, indirect rule recommends itself as the best system of administration. The colonial master took advantage of the existing political set-up and so retained the Fulani Emirs and chiefs in their positions as the governing class. These native rulers were, however, to be advised or directed by British administrative officers – Residents, District officers and Assistant officers attached to their courts.

---

[407] Van Gorder A.C., *Violence in God's Name, Christian and Muslim Relations in Nigeria*, African Diaspora Press, Houston, USA, 2012, p. 97.

In other words, the colonial master and his assistants ruled the Emirs (the traditional rulers) while the Emirs ruled their people, and British officers were to interfere in the government of the emirates mainly to check abuses of powers. The Emirs were allowed to continue to collect taxes for the emirate treasury. Part of the revenue collected was sent to the central government of the protectorate for use in the general development of the territory while the remainder was kept for local development projects such as markets, schools, railways, roads, agriculture, health services and for the payment of salaries of local emirate staff.

The Emirs continued to administer justice through the Emirate courts while British officials regulated punishments. The chief features of the system in the North therefore were the Emir and his court, a native treasury and a native court all under the control of the Emir whose government was supervised by British officials operating in the background. On the whole, the system proved successful in the Northern emirates of Nigeria where the colonial master had merely taken over and consolidated the Fulani administrations with their highly centralized organization and their hierarchy of officials for the maintenance of justice, law and order and their well-developed procedures of tax assessment and collection. Its success here enabled Britain to control the territory cheaply and effectively.[408]

But Michael Crowder would argue that "indirect rule at least in theory, did not mean government of Africans through their chiefs. In Practice indirect rule laid heavy emphasis on the role of the chief in the government of African people, even for those peoples who traditionally did not have political leaders as distinct from religious leaders."[409] This has sown some seeds of discord in Nigeria especially in northern Nigeria, where politics has never been separated from religion and this pushes the practice of democracy in Nigeria to uncomfortable position. Sometimes, in these areas, where politics is not separated from religion, the practice of bureaucracy is decorated as democracy even up till today.

3.2.1.8.12.2. INDIRECT RULE IN WESTERN NIGERIA

The colonial master saw the Yoruba colonies headed by the *Oba* who traditionally owed some allegiance to the *Alafin* of "Oyo" as a set-up similar to the Northern emirates under the Sultan of *Sokoto*. So, using the *Oba* as *Emir*, he imposed his system of indirect rule in the West. But it did not prove successful

---

[408] Onwubiko K.B.C., *School Certificate History of West Africa, Bk. two, 1800 - Present Day*, op. cit., p. 260 - 261.
[409] Crowder M., *West Africa under Colonial Rule*, Ethiopia Publishing Corporation, Benin City, Nigeria, 1976.

as in the North. One reason for this was that the colonial master tried to re-store supreme authority in Yorubaland to the *Alafin* of "Oyo" whose influence was steadily declining through the 19th century. Most of the already independent Oba of Yorubaland were not prepared to accept this situation.

Secondly, in *Egbaland* where there was an influential class of Western educated elite and where the British Government had signed a treaty in 1893 granting a quasi-independent status to *Abeokuta,* the colonial master disregarding the 1893 treaty, brought "Abeokuta" under the protectorate government in 1914. Then, he extended indirect rule to *Egbaland*. This roused a great deal of resentment and protest especially from the educated class who began to suspect British intentions. In 1918 the protests built up into a serious riot.

Thirdly, the British thought that the Yoruba Oba possessed autocratic powers as the Fulani Emir. But the powers of the Oba were limited for they could not act without the consent of the council of traditional title-holders. So, the British could not control the people by controlling them.

3.2.1.8.12.3. INDIRECT RULE IN EASTERN NIGERIA

The introduction of Indirect Rule in Eastern Nigeria in 1928 proved a complete failure unlike in Northern Nigeria where it was successful. There are certain reasons why it was a complete failure in the Eastern Nigeria. In the first place, in Igboland, the units of society were too small to shoulder the responsibilities expected of an Emirate in the North. Again, because of the Igbo system of village democracy and the egalitarian nature of its society, there was an absence of traditional authorities able to command the obedience of their people. Moreover, by the time of its introduction in Eastern Nigeria, many of its people were already used to British ideas of direct administration to a considerable degree owing to the inland extension of British protectorate authority since 1893.

However, the colonial master tried to solve the problem of the absence of traditional rulers by creating 'warrant chiefs' which Achebe calls "a deeply flawed arrangement that effectively confused and corrupted the Igbo democratic spirit."[410] By so doing, the colonial master gave them powers unknown before in Igbo society. With their arbitrary powers and control of the courts, the Warrant Chiefs became tyrants and most unpopular. "The use of these unpopular chiefs to introduce taxation in the East led to the first women riots

---

[410]Achebe C., *There Was A Country, A Personal History of Biafra*, Penguin Press, USA, 2012, p. 2.

in Nigeria, known as 'Aba women riot' in 1929."[411] The main targets of attack of this riot were the chiefs and the native courts.

3.2.1.8.12.4. FURTHER ADVANTAGES AND SHORTCOMINGS OF INDIRECT RULE

On the credit side, it has been claimed that Indirect Rule served a useful purpose in enabling the British to extend their control over Northern Nigeria and in helping to win the confidence of the people in Northern Nigeria. This success

---

[411] Towards the end of 1929, a certain warrant chief "Okugo of Oloko" near Aba following directives from the British administration began to assess the taxable wealth of the inhabitants of the village, and in the process counted women, children and domestic animals. Rumor quickly spread that the counting of women was the preparation for the taxation of women, for the original poll tax of 1927 had been preceded by a census the purpose of which was not made known to the people at the time of the counting.

Like wild fire, the rumor about the impending taxation of women spread, soon the women of Aba and Owerri Divisions were up in arms against the British Administration and the Native Authorities. In the ensuing riot, shops were looted, native courts and their documents were burnt down and Europeans and unpopular warrants chiefs were attacked. It looked like a miniature French Revolution with the peasant women rising against the new oppressive aristocracy of warrant chiefs and their European supporters. The riots spread to Calabar and Opobo by December 17th 1929. Troops were called in to help the police in quelling the disturbances and in the process fifty unarmed women were killed and about the same number wounded. This figure came of course from official sources. It is most likely that many more must have been killed or injured. The riot was however provoked not only by the fear of taxation of women but also by the low prices for farm products.

The significant thing about the riots which were spontaneous was that they had shown how illiterate women were able through their age-group societies to organize themselves far more effectively than the local British administrators who were completely ignorant of the structure of indigenous societies. An official commission of inquiry was set up to investigate the causes of the riots and make recommendations. Two Africans – Sir Kitoye Ajasa and Mr. Eric Moore – prominent Nigerian barristers were members.

The report of the commission was a condemnation of the system of Indirect Rule as applied to Eastern Nigeria. It recommended a reorganization of the system to base it more closely on the customs of the people. The out-come was that anthropological surveys of the area were conducted and the reorganization which followed was based on the natural social organization of the people. But the warrant chiefs remained. It was not till the 1940s that an enlightened system of local government was introduced.

It should be noted that in 1925 a similar movement, though not as violent, had been organized by Igbo women in almost the same area as Aba riots. It was what Coleman described as "a nativistic religious movement… allegedly a response to a miraculous message from "Chukwu" (God). Bands of women marched up and down the country denouncing such innovations as British currency and native courts and demanding a return to the customs of olden times. Perhaps it is this trait in Igbo women and the egalitarian and fearless nature of the Igbo people in general that have earned them such description as "the most troublesome of West African peoples" by the British colonial administrators. It was a tragic misunderstanding of the Igbo. Cf. Onwunbiko K.B.C., *School Certificate history of West Africa, 1800 – Present Day*, op. cit., pp. 263 -264.

was possible because the British made use of the existing local Northern administrative set-up which commanded the respect of the people.

It has been testified that Indirect Rule is an easy and cheap way of ruling illiterate communities who cannot easily understand the daily acts, laws and intricate set-up of a modern system of government. The system preserves native institutions, integrates them in the machinery of the central government, and above all, trains native rulers in the art of government at a higher level. In spite of the above credit given to Indirect Rule, there were a lot of lacunas found in this system of governance applied in Nigeria by the colonial master. First, its effects on Nigeria have been disruptive rather than integrative. In fact, it complicated the task of welding the diverse elements of Nigeria into a strongly united Nigerian nation.

By Indirect Rule, the British colonial administration encouraged a parochialism which has been difficult to eradicate especially in the former regional and central parliaments of the country. In Northern Nigeria, British officials undermined the unity achieved by the Jihad by their policy of building up the independent power of the Emir to the extent that the emirate was moving towards a separate independent state. In short, Indirect Rule was anti-unity and anti-national in practice. Secondly, it is clear from the available evidences that Indirect Rule was a system for retarding progress in self-government and perpetuating European rule rather than for preparing Nigeria for self-rule. It excluded educated Nigerians from participating in the government of their own people. This was why the educated class in Nigeria were so critical of it.

On the other hand, the extension of European rule in Nigeria brought about increase in trade and wealth, and therefore in standards of living. Nigeria needed modern amenities – railways and better roads, medical services, education and other social services. Indirect Rule has been found to be hopelessly wanting and incapable because of its very nature. Again, the system was in fact a subtle way of imposing a petty British autocracy on the people under the guise of training Nigeria's traditional rulers for eventual self-government. At a point, it became clear that the Emir and Chiefs held office at the pleasure of British officials and represented the colonial administration rather than their people.

Lastly, it has been observed that one of the serious shortcomings of Indirect Rule was that it was not of universal application. The system which Lugard devised for the Northern emirates of Nigeria could not easily be applied to southern Nigeria without modifications; and in Eastern Nigeria, it was a downright failure. It was not a universal formula for the planning of the advancement of Nigerian colonies.[412] In short, one can safely conclude that the system in Igboland was a bundle of failure and misadventure. It was the result of a complete ignorance of the people's traditions, as well as the deliberate discontinuance of the wishes and aspirations of the governed.

3.2.1.9. THE AMALGAMATION: THE PROCESS THAT GAVE BIRTH TO WHAT IS TODAY CALLED "NIGERIA"

Before the year 1914, there was no country called "Nigeria". Nigeria as a nation is a brain child of 1914 amalgamation. The idea of Nigeria was first conceived in the year 1897 when Lady Lugard spoke of "Niger Area". This dream became a reality when Nigeria was born in 1914 by the amalgamation of the people of the South and the North, thus the present country called Nigeria was formed. Some of the major problems that Nigeria is having as a nation did not start today. It started before her amalgamation and its independence. Her problems increased and were cemented after amalgamation in 1914. Unless we know this background, we will not know the root of Nigeria's problems that started before amalgamation and grown out of proportion after amalgamation. Akinjide agrees to the above assertions. He states thus:

> Nigeria is a complex country. The problem of Nigeria did not start yesterday. It started about 1894. Lord Lugard came to Nigeria about 1894 and many people did not know that Major Lugard was not originally employed by the British government. He was employed by companies. He was first employed by East Indian company, by Royal East African company and then by the Royal Niger company. It was from Royal Niger Company that "Nigeria" was transferred to the British government.[413]

Therefore, many have concluded that the interest of the Europeans in Africa and indeed in Nigeria was more of economic interest rather than something else. In the spirit of the Amalgamation, the colony and protectorate of Southern Nigeria and the Protectorate of Northern Nigeria were united as the Colony and Protectorate of Nigeria on January 1st, 1914. Lord Lugard became its first Governor General. One may ask: What was the spirit behind the amalgamation? What were the reasons behind this union? Or was it done only for the sake of it? In answering this questions, Onwubiko states:

---

[412] Onwubiko K.B.C., *School Certificate History of West Africa, 1800 – Present Day*, op. cit., 268 - 270.

[413] Akinjide R., *"The Amalgamation of Nigeria was a Fraud"*, Paper presented on 3rd February 2012 in Nigeria.

> Lugard's amalgamation of Nigeria was motivated by the need to pool together the resources of the North and South and to develop the trade of the North by providing it with an outlet to the sea.... The amalgamation has given a great advantage to Nigeria. A common economy, transport, communications, standard time, common federal civil service and General Orders, a common legislature and a common national assembly are some of the abiding benefits of the amalgamation.[414]

All these benefits Lugard had in mind when he championed this political union called amalgamation. However, the amalgamation of Nigeria has received strong criticisms from different angles. Some said it was not the best option for Nigeria. According to Akinjide "the Amalgamation of Nigeria was a Fraud"[415] Onwubiko argues that the amalgamation was not done in a proper order. He affirms:

> The amalgamation was not a complete amalgamation. The Nigerian Council set up in 1914 legislated only for the south; while transport and communication, customs and exercise and the Supreme Court were unified, education, public works, health, agriculture and local government were not. It is some of these shortcomings which have plagued Nigeria unity to the present day and so retarded the full development of West Africa's giant nation into full-fledged world power.[416]

The criticisms of amalgamation of Nigeria come from all sections of Nigeria, not only from the South but also from Northern Nigeria as well. The *Sardauna* of *Sokoto*, the "de facto" ruler of the Northern Nigeria before his death in 1966, questioned the unity of Nigeria as early as 1964. He said: "sixty years ago there was not a country called Nigeria. What is now Nigeria consisted of a number of large and small communities all of which were different in their outlooks and beliefs.... These many and varied communities have not knit themselves into a complete unit."[417] It is clear to many Nigerians that the federation of Nigeria, as it exists today, has never really been one homogeneous country. It consists of many tribes that have different cultures, languages, mentalities and so on, and yet they have not found any basis for true unity. Like many other African nations, Nigeria was an artificial structure initiated by the British which had neglected to consider religious, linguistic, and ethnic

---

[414] Onwunbiko K.B.C., School *Certificate History of West Africa 1800 – Present Day,* op. cit., p. 256.

[415] Akinjide R., *"The Amalgamation of Nigeria a Fraud",* Paper presented on 3rd Feb. 2012, in Nigeria.

[416] Onuwubiko K.B.C., *School Certificate History of West Africa 1800 – Present Day,* op. cit., p. 257.

[417] Quoted in Martin P. Mathew, *Nigeria: Current Issues and Historical Background,* New York, Science Publishers, Inc., 2002, in academia. edu., accessed 12.6.2017.

differences. When Nigeria won independence from Britain in 1960, the population was estimated to be 60 million people consisting of nearly 300 differing ethnic and cultural groups.[418] Frederick Forsyth, an assistant diplomatic correspondent who covered the Biafran side of the Nigeria-Biafra war states that:

> It is necessary to understand how Nigeria was formed by Britain out of irreconcilable people, how these peoples came to find that, following British rule, the differences among them, far from shrinking, became accentuated, and how the structure left behind by British was finally unable to contain the explosive forces confined within it…. In fact, through all the years of the pre-colonial period Nigeria never was united, and during the sixty years of colonialism and the sixty-three months of the First Republic only a thin veneer hid the basic disunity.[419]

The colonial master knew all these facts and yet preferred to ignore them and went ahead to unite what many called 'unfortunate marriage' that could not have taken place. Nigeria was called "a mere geographical expression not only by the British who had an interest in keeping it so, but even by its nationalists when it suited them to retreat into tribe to check their more successful rivals from other parts of the country."[420] This unfortunate yet obvious fact notwithstanding, the former colonial master had to keep the country one in order to effectively control his vital economic interests concentrated mainly in the more advanced and 'political unreliable' south. Thus, for administration convenience, Northern and southern Nigeria became amalgamated. "Thereafter the only thing these people had in common became the name of their country. That alone was an insufficient basis for true unity."[421]

One can rightly say that the amalgamation had a 'hidden agenda' which was for the interest of the colonial master. Under normal circumstances, the amalgamation would have united the different tribes together. But rather than uniting them, it created more disunity among them. "This 'marriage' (amalgamation) should not have been as it brought about ethnic clashes and rivalries even till this present time."[422] What is deceptive and questionable are the reasons why the colonial master accepted this union – amalgamation for Nigeria. For the colonial master:

---

[418] Cf., newworlddencylopedia.org/entry/Nigerian-Civil-War, accessed 18.7.2017.

[419] Forsyth F., *The Making of an African Legend: The Biafra story,* op. cit., pp. 9 and 13.

[420] Achebe C., *There was a country: A Personal History of Biafra,* op. cit., p. 5.

[421] Madiebo A.A., *The Nigerian Revolution and the Biafran War,* op. cit., p. 3.

[422] Eze-Uzomaka P., (ed.), *Nigerian Peoples and Cultures,* Parakletos Immunnis Drive, Nigeria, 2008, p. 72.

Northern Nigeria is poor and they have no resources to run the protectorate of the North. They have no access to the sea; the South has resources and they have educated people. It was not the policy of the British government to bring the tax payers' money to run the protectorate, it was in the interest of the British tax prayer that there should be amalgamation. After the amalgamation, the colonial master consciously did not encourage cross-fertilization of culture and contacts between the North and the South. Therefore, between 1914 and 1960, that's a period of 46 years; the colonial master allowed little or no contact between the North and the south because it was not in the interest of the colonial master that the North be allowed to be 'polluted' by the educated south.[423]

However, in Ojukwu's view, the Northern and Southern Nigeria interacted with one another before and after the Amalgamation in 1914. Therefore, Ojukwu said that:

It would be wrong, for anyone to say that the various peoples (the North and the South) had no contact with one another, because sporadic commercial and social contacts had, for centuries, been in existence, though politically and culturally, each group had remained distinct and separate.[424]

One sees no reasons for uniting as one country different tribes who do not understand themselves; they do not have one language, culture, tradition, mentality, etc. For the colonial master, such a genuine union without a hidden agenda, if allowed to develop, would have amounted to a major threat to the very economic interests he was striving to protect. "It was to remove this unwelcome threat that the colonial master introduced the divide and rule system of government for Nigeria."[425] The important aspect of this system is its emphasis on the differences among the peoples, while encouraging social apartheid. As a result, there was division, hatred, unhealthy rivalry, and pronounced disparity in development among the various peoples of the country. The colonial master, determined to ensure a continued uninterrupted economic exploitation of the country even after independence, recognized that this could only be done not by keeping the country one but by ensuring that the effective political and military powers were left in the hands of that part of the country that they could trust, (the North).[426] The military power was regarded as being necessary to ensure a stable government of such a big country as Nigeria, made up as it is of diverse and heterogeneous elements.

---

[423] Akinjide R., *"The amalgamation of Nigeria a Fraud"*, Paper presented on 3rd Feb, 2012 in Nigeria.
[424] Ojukwu E.O., *Because I am Involved*, op. cit., p. 16.
[425] Madiebo A.A., *The Nigerian Revolution and the Biafran War,* op. cit., p. 3.
[426] Ibid., p. 4.

This is where the traits of the Igbo betrayed them. The colonial master did not trust the Igbo (from the south) because they are clever, astute, industrious and ambitious. When one reflects on the basis on which the amalgamation of Nigeria was carried out, one would find a lot of lacunas in it. In 1900, the colonial master created the Southern Nigeria; in 1903, he created northern Nigeria; and in 1914, Nigeria was formed. But when we look at these components which the colonial master purported to have brought together, we will discover that they were all treaty based. There was a treaty with "Dossunmo" of Lagos. There was also a treaty with the "Oba" of Benin; the "Empires" and the "Obong" of Calabar. But by the time of the amalgamation, the colonial master did not call the nations with which it had treaty for consultation. He did not consult with the "Oyo", the "Egba", the "Efik", the "Igbo" the "Ibadan" the "Bini", the "Tiv", "Olorin", the "Sokoto Caliphate" etc. (These are different tribes in Nigeria). He used his military power to bring together the incompatible. At independence, the colonial master did not even call back to the nations with whom they had signed treaties to know whether they wanted to be one. And when he left, and left Nigeria to determine its destiny, the incompatible could not agree and this led to the Nigeria-Biafra war.[427]

In the actual fact, the Igbo entered the Nigerian amalgamation in 1914 with some handicap or some disadvantages, because the Igbo appeared to have the least exposure and interaction with other civilizations and developed kingdoms, and empires. The Igbo "entered" Nigerian history with relative disadvantages in relation to other major ethnic nationalities. Apart from the fact that unlike the Hausa-Fulani of the North and the Yoruba of the West, the Igbo never established any contagious national kingdom or empire in the whole of their history – a fact which limits elite capacity for mobilization and sustainable followership and major index of groups survival.

The Igbo were among the last batch of people to be touched by dominant external influences. While a greater part of Northern Nigeria had already been exposed to Islamic culture and civilization with the accompanying attribute of a centralized theocratic order, clearly defined political structure and the availability of centers of learning, and while the Yoruba of the West had already become Christian proselytizer, educationists and publishers in the mid-19th century, the initial Western presence in the whole of Igboland only became complete between 1910 and 1920. But regardless of this, the characters of the Igbo did not disappoint them. Forsyth states that:

---

427 Nzimiro I., *A study of Mobility Among the Igbos of Southern Nigeria; kinship and Geographical mobility 1965*, pp. 117 - 118, in Uwalaka J., *The struggle for an Inclusive Nigeria: Igbos to be or not to be?* op. cit., p. 7.

Ironically, in view of their (Igbo) later speedy development and progress which finally enabled them to overtake the other ethnic groups of Nigeria in terms of European-style development, the Ibos and the other peoples of the East were regarded as being more backward than the rest in 1900.[428]

Between 1945 and 1960, the Igbo manifested their character for which they are known. They were able to cancel out their difficulties in almost all section of national life, educationally, intellectually, economically and became the leading lights in the Nationalist struggle for independence.[429] The assertive nature of the Igbo made the colonial masters to detest and hate them while endearing themselves to the Northerners whose obedience was unquestionable. It has been said that the Igbo people are more outgoing and relate better than any other tribe in Nigeria. They are the most travelled among the tribes in Nigeria. Hence, Obiezuofu-Ezeigbo says:

It was easy for the Igbo to live in the West and the North because of their easy assimilation of the ways of life of their host. In the West, they lived among the people in the same house. While in the North, because of the British homo-segregation policy, which the Northerners had absorbed wholesale, and their religion, which made them to put their wives in the purdah, Easterners as well as the Westerners were herded to Sabon Garis (which means strangers quarters). This separation made contact between Hausas and other tribes minimal, which indeed pleased the colonial master. Inside the Sabon Garis' ghetto; life was kept at the wish of the latter to a minimum. Schooling was segregated and two radically different societies co-existed without any effort at proper social integration by the British.[430]

As we have seen so far, one can rightly say that the amalgamation of the North and south of Nigeria in 1914 was the beginning of some of the major crisis we have in Nigeria then, and till today. Onwubiko affirms the above statement. He asserts:

Lugard aimed at creating in Nigeria one administrative unit but he did not intend to create a Nigerian nation. So, he pursued a policy of isolating the North from the South – a policy which his successors maintained. For instance, the North was excluded from the Legislative Council until 1947. Thus, it can be

---

[428] Forsyth F., *The Making of an African Legend: The Biafra Story*, op. cit., p. 16.

[429] Nwankwo A., *Igbo: Identity and Affirmation, Sunday concord News Paper, Nigeria*, 17th, September 2000, p. 9, in Uwalaka J., *The struggle for an Inclusive Nigeria, Igbos to be or not to be?* op. cit., p. 2 - 3.

[430] Obiezuofu-Ezeigbo., C.E., *The Biafran War and the Igbo in Contemporary Nigerian Politics*, op. cit., p. 5.

said that Lugard sowed the seeds of the separatist tendency which has till to-day plagued Nigeria unity.[431]

Lugard was partly responsible for the backwardness of the North in education and other social services. His policy of excluding European Christian missionaries from the Muslim North – a policy faithfully followed by British officials until recent years insulated that part of the country from the beneficial and progressive missionary influences to which the south largely owes its advances over the North today. Forsyth explains that "the concern of the Emirs and their courts, like that of most feudal potentates, was to remain in power in conditions as unchanging as possible. To this end they set themselves against the biggest challenge to their own conservatism – change and progress. The obvious forerunner of these two is mass-education. It was no accident that in Independence year 1960 the North with over half of Nigeria's 50 – million population had 41 secondary schools against the South's 842; that the North's first university graduate qualified just nine years before independence. Western education to the Emirs was dangerous, and they did their utmost to confine it to their own offspring or those of the aristocracy."[432]

In Southern Nigeria, it was a different story. The South being open-minded and was ready for cross-fertilization of cultures and ideas, was invaded by an avid thirst for education in all its forms. "By 1967 when the Eastern Region (the Igbo) tried to pull out of Nigeria, it alone had more doctors, lawyers and engineers than any country in Negro Africa. Missionary work in the North which might have eased that area into the twentieth century was effectively stopped to discourage Christian apostolic work north of the Kabba line."[433] Forsyth maintains that "the amalgamation was an imposition on Nigeria. This was manifested when the North made it quite clear and has maintained this attitude ever since, that it did not want amalgamation with the South. The North agreed to go along only on the basis that (1) the principle of separate regional development should be enshrined in the new constitution, and that (2) the North should have nearly fifty percent of the seats in the legislature (North 9, West 6 and East 5)."[434]

No one could have captured the truth about this irreconcilably forced relationship better than the man who cobbled together the demonic incongruity himself, the British colonial master Fredrick Lugard. On the eve of the amalgama-

---

[431] Onwubiko K.B.C., *School Certificate History of West African 1800 – Present Day,* op. cit., p. 272.
[432] Forsyth F., *The making of an African Legend: The Biafra Story,* op. cit., p. 18.
[433] Ibid., pp. 17 and 18.
[434] Ibid., p. 20.

tion of the two British protectorates of South and North of Nigeria, Lugard said that: "The South and North are like oil and water that do not mix."[435] The opposition of the North to amalgamation with the South was given voice in numerous statements by their leaders. In 1947 (the year of the inauguration of the Richards Constitution), one of the representatives from the North, Mallam Abubakar Tafawa Balewa, later to become Prime Minister of Nigeria said:

> We do not want our southern neighbors to interfere in our development …. I would like to make it clear to you that if the British quit Nigeria now at this stage the Northern people would continue their interrupted conquest to the sea.[436]

During various regional conferences in the past before independence, the Northern delegates claimed fifty percent representation for the North at the central government, and at the general conference at Ibadan in January 1950 the Emir of Zaria and the Emir of Katsina announced that "unless the Northern Region is allotted fifty per cent of the seats in the central legislature, it will ask for separation from the rest of Nigeria on the arrangements existing before 1914. They got their wish, and Northern domination of the center became an inbuilt feature of Nigerian politics."[437]

The North also demanded and obtained the loosest possible form of Federation and made no secret of their deep conviction that the amalgamation of North and South in 1914 was an error. The expression of that conviction runs right through Northern political thinking from the end of the Second World War to independence. In March 1953, the Northern Political leader, Sir Ahmadu Bello,[438] told the House in Lagos: "The mistake of 1914 has come to light and I should like it to go no further".[439]

---

[435] Ebiem O., *Nigeria, Biafra and Boko Haram, Ending the Genocides through Multi-State,* Gen Computers, Nigeria, 2014, p. 47.

[436] Forsyth F., *The making of an African Legend: The Biafra Story*, op. cit., p. 20.

[437] Ebiem O., Nigeria, Biafra and Boko Haram, Ending the Genocide through Multi-State, op. cit., p. 47.

[438] Sir Ahmadu Bello, the Sardauna of Sokoto, first Premier of Northern Nigeria, was born on 12th June 1909 in "Rabbah", near Sokoto. His father, Ibrahim, the chief of Rabbah, was a grandson of Usman Dan Fodio, the Fulani religious leader who founded the Sokoto Empire at the beginning of the nineteenth century. After primary education in Sokoto, he attended Katsina Higher College where he was a contemporary of Sir Abubakar Tafawa Balewa. For three years he taught at Sokoto Middle School. Later, he became district head of Rabbah. Following a local government course in England, he was appointed secretary to the Sokoto Native Authority. Like many of his contemporaries among the small elite in Northern Nigeria, he quickly became involved with politics, participating actively in the rapid political changes that preceded Nigeria's independence.

All said and done, Lugard did not envisage self-government for Nigeria. He planned for perpetual British colonialism. His system of Indirect Rule, his hostility towards educated Nigerians in the South and his system of education for the North which aimed at training only the sons of chiefs and emir as clerks and interpreters show him as one of Britain's arch-imperialists.

3.2.1.9.1. THE AMALGAMATION: THE FORERUNNER OF UNBALANCED POLITICAL STRUCTURE IN NIGERIA

3.2.1.9.2. THE FORMATION OF PIONEER POLITICAL MOVEMENTS AND POLITICAL PARTIES IN NIGERIA

Post-independence nationalist movements in Nigeria were carried on through well-organized modern political parties. These parties were led by new generation of nationalist leaders who had considerable mass support. In spite of this, there was a serious lacuna in the formation of political parties in Nigerian politics starting from post-independence era till today. In line with this, Madiebo maintains that:

He was one of the founders of the N.P.C. (Northern Peoples' Congress) in 1949. His princely background in a feudal North gave the "Sardauna" – a title which means war leader – automatic leadership of the party. He became successively regional Minister of Works, of Local Government and Community Development. He was appointed in 1954 the first Premier of Northern Nigeria. By this time, the fact that his party controlled the vast and dominant Northern region had made him the most powerful political figure in Nigeria. Imperious in manner and gifted with a keen political sense, Sir Ahmadu Bello was to dominate Nigeria's political life until his death in January 1966.

 Although his predominant image is one of feudal Moslem religious leaders he was really first and foremost a politician. His conservatism and near-ostentatious attention to religion were carefully cultivated attitudes calculated to appeal to the realities of the Northern Nigeria of his time. His personal private life and the basic enlightenment of his policies on education and industrialization in the North do not reveal a man opposed to change. By temperament, he was a natural leader, born in a ruling family, he was ambitious for power. He preferred to keep direct personal control of the North. 'I would rather be called the Sultan of Sokoto than the president of Nigeria' he was quoted as saying as late as 1965.

As the leader of the N.P.C., which controlled the federal government from independence in 1960 until the military coup in 1966, it was normally his place to assume the post of federal Prime Minister. This he left to his deputy, Sir Abubakar Tafawa Balewa, whose activities in Lagos he guided all the time by remote control. Personally charming, Sir Ahmadu was admired by many, feared by many more and respected by all. His attachment to the old North, however, and his undisguised attempt to use region as a base for controlling the whole of Nigeria made him unpopular in the rest of the country. The assassination of this gifted and certainly the most forceful Nigerian politician of his time was a direct attempt to dislodge a man whose grip on the lever of power appeared so strong that it led many idealistic progressive to think that it would be permanent as long as he lived. Cf., Uwechue R., *Reflections on the Nigerian Civil War, Facing the future*, Wordsmithes Printing & Packaging, Nigeria, 2003, pp. 190 - 191.

[439] Forsyth F., *The making of an African Legend: The Biafra Story*, op. cit., p. 21.

The growth of nationalism and the subsequent emergence of political parties were based on tribal rather than national interests, and therefore, had no unifying effect on the people against the colonial master.[440]

As we have earlier mentioned, the colonial master not only amalgamated the Northern and Southern Nigeria which had nothing in common, but also to an extent prevented the North from having cross-fertilization of cultures and ideologies with the South and the outside world. This instituted tribalism which reflected also in the formation of political parties in Nigeria.

The first republican political parties were formed on a wrong foundation. They were founded on the substratum of tribalism and not on the ideology of nationalism and one Nigeria. For example, when the North formed a political party, the Northern leaders called it Northern Peoples' Congress. That was in accordance with the dictum and policies of Lugard. When Aminu Kano formed his own party, it was called Northern Elements Progressive Union (NEPU) not Nigerian Elements Progressive Union. It was only Awolowo and Zik who took another direction in the formation of their political parties. Dr. Nnamdi Azikiwe formed (NCNC) – National Council of Nigeria Citizens; while Chief Obafemi Awolowo[441] formed (AG) – Action Group. In line with the above assertions Obiezuofu-Ezeigbo states:

---

[440] Madiebo A.A., *School Certificate History of West Africa, 1800 – present day*, op. cit., p. 4 - 5.

[441] Chief Obafemi Awolowo, former leader of the Action Group, was born at "Ijebu-Remu" on the 6th of March 1909. The son of a Yoruba farmer, he was one of the truly self-made men among his Nigerian contemporaries. During a checkered career as a teacher, shorthand typist, businessman, newspaper reporter and then trade unionist, he studied in his spare time, gaining a bachelor's degree in commerce in 1944. He entered Nigerian politics briefly before going to England to qualify as a lawyer in 1947. On his return he plunged into politics and in 1951 founded the Action Group. After serving in various ministerial capacities, he became premier of the Western Region in 1954. At independence in 1960, he quit that post to become leader of opposition in the Federal Parliament. A tussle for power between him and his deputy, Chief S.L. Akintola, who replaced him as premier of the Western Region, and his rigid opposition to the N.P.C., that controlled Federal Government, brought an alliance of his enemies which soon led to his trial and imprisonment on charges of treason in 1963. He was released by General Gowon soon after the military coup of July 1966.

A popular leader among the progressive in pre-war Nigeria, Chief Awolowo attempted in vain to bring about a last-minute reconciliation between General Gowon and General Ojukwu. On this account he led a peace delegation to Enugu (Ojukwu's capital) in early May 1967. When Biafra seceded and war broke out, he gave his support to General Gowon and was appointed to the highest civilian post in the Federal Military Government, the vice-presidency of the Federal Executive Council. Strong-willed, austere and single-minded, Chief Awolowo, who had published a number of books on Nigerian politics and constitution, was perhaps the boldest and certainly one of the most ruthless of Nigeria's politicians. Cf., Uwechue R., *Reflections on the Nigeria Civil War, Facing the Future,* op. cit., p. 196.

The 1959 election showed the line of power struggled that would follow. The Eastern region was dominated by the National Council of Nigeria Citizens (NCNC) headed by Dr. Nnamdi Azikiwe. This party was hitherto a national party, partly because of the tribal appeal of the other parties, concentrated more in the Eastern region. Action Group (AG) was designed and nurtured for the Western region and was headed by Chief Awolowo. While the Northern Peoples' Congress (NPC) was formed for the Northerners and was headed by the Sarduana of Sokoto.[442]

In line with the above explanations, Ozigbo summaries the formation of the political parties in Nigeria thus: "The new breed Yoruba politicians put their priority on Yoruba interests. They rallied around their main political party (Action Group) which had arisen in 1951 from the 'Egbe Omo Oduduwa' (children of Oduduwa Society) which was born in 1947. Their ethnic oracle was Chief Obafemi Awolowo, the founder of both the Egbe 'Omo Oduduwa' and the Action Group. The foremost Northern elite stood by the motto of their own leading political party (the Northern People Congress) which professed 'one North, one people'. Their flag bearer was Sir Ahmadu Bello, the Sardauna of Sokoto. Most Eastern political Leaders dreamed and worked for a truly one Nigeria, even after 1952. The National Council of Nigeria Citizens (NCNC) had arisen in Lagos on 24th August, 1944 as a national party. Ethnic pressures from western and northern Nigeria forced the NCNC to become a largely Igbo political party. The history of the NCNC is written large in the political philosophy of probably its foremost leader, Dr. Nnamdi Azikiwe."[443]

We can see that the formation of political parties in Nigeria was based on individual interest and ethnic sentiments rather than national interests and common good. These individual and ethnic interests, rather than the common good, have become a chronic cancer that has eaten deep into the political system of Nigeria even up till today. It did not start today. It started before Nigeria got her independence in 1960.

Akinjide summarizes the political structure of Nigeria designed by Amalgamation thus: "Northern Nigeria was to represent England, Western Nigeria like Wales; Eastern Nigeria to be like Scotland. In the British structure, England has permanent majority in the House of Commons. There was no way Wales can ever dominate England, neither can Scotland dominate Britain. But they are very shrewd. They would allow Scottish man to become Prime Minister. They

---

[442] Obiezuofu-Ezeigbo C.E., *The Biafran War and the Igbo in Contemporary Nigeria Politics*, Pan Negro Continental Ltd., Lagos, Nigeria, op. cit., p. 10.
[443] Ozigbo I. R. A., *A History of Igboland in the 20th Century*, Snaap Press Ltd., Enugu, Nigeria, 1999, p. 15.

would allow a Welsh man to become Prime Minister in London but the fact remains that the actual power is rested in England. In fact, the so-called Amalgamation of Nigeria in 1914 was a complete fraud. It was not done in the interest of the whole Nigeria."[444]

The political struggle and the consequent drifting apart of the various peoples of Nigeria went on over the years unchecked, to an extent that the Federal Parliament was reduced to an inter-tribal battlefield. Sporadic physical violence erupted from time to time between the various peoples of Nigeria to mark the end of each phase of the rapid drift towards total disintegration of the country.

The contraption called Nigeria and the unity called amalgamation imposed by the colonial master were seriously tested by inter and intra-tribal, regional and sectional disagreements on a number of issues and the struggle for political powers and control. The centrifugal forces of maladministration, nepotism, corruption, economic mismanagement, blatant rigging of elections, political intolerance and ethnic competition, also crept into the polity along with the attendant instability. This resulted devastatingly in the breakdown of law and order in most places especially in the Western region.[445] All this culminated in the first military coup in the life of Nigeria as a nation, on 15th January, 1966.

3.2.2. THE IMMEDIATE CAUSES OF NIGERIA-BIAFRA WAR

3.2.2.1. THE FIRST MILITARY COUP IN NIGERIA – 15th JANUARY, 1966 AND ITS INTERPRETATIONS

It is obvious that many factors contributed to the first military coup in Nigeria. Ezeani summarizes the main factors as thus:

1. High level corruption in the government, 2. violent political crisis in Yoruba land in Western Nigeria, 3. Tiv riots – which in comparison with Yoruba crisis, was inconsequential.[446]

Ex-Biafran officer by name, Ifeajuna Emmanuel, claimed to have engineered the first military coup in Nigeria. For him the reasons for the coup were thus:

---

[444] Akinjide R., *"The Amalgamation of Nigeria a Fraud"*, Paper presented on 3rd Feb., 2012 in Nigeria.

[445] Enoch O., *The major task of Nationhood, Nigerian Vanguard Newspaper,* Sept. 29th 2009, p. 29.

[446] Ezeani E., *In Biafra Africa Died: The Diplomatic Plot, 3rd edition,* Veritas Lumen Publisher, England, 2014, p. 23.

The elections held in October 1965 in Western Nigeria proved the last straw of iniquity that broke the crooked back of the Government. Those who caused the confusion stayed on. They said they were prepared to rule even if only one man survived. We could not wait to see our people die to one man. We could not wait to see the nation destroyed because of evil men. Why should evil men not go? [447]

Apart from the reasons already given above, why the military took over power on 15th January, 1966, the inability of the then Prime Minister, Sir Abubaka Tafawa Balewa[448] and his government to rescue the situation at that time also

---

[447] Ifeajuna E., 1960, Indictment, Unpublished Work on why he engineered the first military coup in Nigeria, in Ezeani E., *In Biafra Africa Died: The Diplomatic Plot,* op. cit., p. 27.

[448] Sir Abubakar Tafawa Balewa was born in 1912 in the small town of "Tafawa Balewa" in Bauchi Province of North-Eastern Nigeria. After primary education in Bauchi, he went to Katsina Higher College for five years, qualifying in 1933 as a teacher. He taught at Bauchi Middle School until 1945, then spent a year at the Institute of Education of London University and on his return was appointed Education Officer for Bauchi Province.

As one of the few educated people of his time in the North, he quickly became involved in the politics of that region. Constitutional development in Nigeria brought the need for indigenous legislators and he soon became a member of the first Northern House of Assembly from which he was elected to the Nigeria Legislative Council in Lagos in 1946. A further constitutional change made him in 1952, as Minister of Works, one of the first group of central government ministers. In 1954, he was appointed Minister of Transport. Rapid constitutional development on the eve of independence brought further changes. Thus, as a parliamentary leader of the N.P.C. (Northern Peoples' Congress), the biggest party in the federal parliament, he was appointed in August 1957 as the first Prime Minister of Nigeria. After the 1959 eve-of-independence elections, Sir Abubakar became on 1st October 1960, the first Prime Minister of independent Nigeria. Surviving a stormy federal election in 1964, he was reappointed Prime Minister, a post which he retained until his assassination in January 1966. Sir Abubakar's period of six years as the head of the government of independent Nigeria weighed heavily on the frail figure of this quiet man. In Nigeria's turbulent and complex politics, he remained a cool figure preoccupied with the problem of holding together the country's 250 ethnic groups.

As the head of the federal government, Sir Abubakar controlled Nigeria's foreign policy. Outside Nigeria as within it, he was guided by the same sense of moderation. Opposed to extreme and hasty Pan-Africanism, he is remembered as stating at the inaugural meeting of the O.A.U. at Addis Ababa in 1963 that he did not believe in the "African personality" – the firebrand African nationalism as defined by Kwame Nkrumah of Ghana.

Although he was Nigeria's federal Prime Minister, on the purely party-political plane, he was always number two in his own party, N.P.C. Under the shadow of Sir Ahmadu Bello, the party's imperious and aristocratic chief, he never really had a free hand in ordering the affairs of the federal government. Much of the weakness of which his government was frequently accused came from his subordinate status in which his personal opinion and judgment were constantly interfered with by his party boss.

A devout Moslem, popularly known as "Balewa the good", Sir Abubakar was a simple man. He was born a commoner, belonging to the small "Jere" tribe (a branch of the Hausa ethnic group) and throughout his life reflected the humility and native shrewdness that this background gave him. His assassination was perhaps the most regretted in Nigeria, where few people had any-

contributed to the coup of 1966. The Balewa Government was inefficient. It failed completely to find solutions to the problems of the nation. Gradually, life became more and more unsafe. Motorists were waylaid, killed and their vehicles set on fire. Political opponents were killed and their houses burnt, but Balewa pretended that all was normal and under control throughout the country.[449] Thus, six-year-old Nigeria, unhealthy since its birth on 1st October, 1960, had, by January 1966, shown some terminal symptoms. The symptoms were summarized thus:

> A politicized 1962 census; the political anarchy in the Western Region; the bloody Tiv riots; a partially boycotted 1964 general elections; and other social ills such as ethnic chauvinism, endemic corruption, nepotism, economic stagnation, wanton arson, political thuggery, and an incompetent leadership at the center.[450]

The tribalism, corruption and sectionalism which we have earlier talked about, that entered into the political life of Nigeria after the amalgamation were noticed also in the Nigerian Army. Madiebo laments that "the result of this system was that standards fell within the Army and soldiers became politically conscious... the criterion for promotion and advancement in the Army was based more on political considerations than on efficiency or competence... This situation forced some southern officers who were politically conscious to identify themselves openly with political parties and politicians in order to gain military promotions and appointments without any hindrance. Junior officers joined in the bitter struggle for military success through politics – a massive exercise which reduced the Army and its promotions to a ridiculous farce. It could be described as a football pool in which rich dividends were paid out to successful stalkers." [451]

This led to the first military coup planned by a group of five young officers led by Major Chukwuma Nzeogwu and the majority of these planners were of Igbo origin. They tried to overthrow the federal and regional governments. They succeeded in the North where they killed the Premier, Alhaji Sir Ahmadu Bello. In the West, the Premier, Chief Akintola was killed and in Lagos the Federal Prime Minister Alhaji Sir Abubakar Tafawa Balewa and his finance minister

---

thing against him as a person. He was killed for what he represented officially – the head of a government that had become unpopular with Nigeria's progressives. Cf., Uwechue R., *Reflections on the Nigerian Civil War,* op. cit., pp. 188 - 189.

[449] Ademoyega A., *Why We Struck, the story of the first Nigeria coup,* Evans Brothers (Nigeria Publishers) Limited, Ibandan, Nigeria, 1981, p. 91.

[450] Ojo O., *Olusegun Obasanjo, in the Eyes of Time, A Biography of the African Statesman,* U.S.A., Pine Hill Press Inc., 1997 in Ezeani E., *In Biafra Africa Died: The Diplomatic plot,* op. cit., p. 27.

[451] Madiebo A.A., *The Nigeria Revolution and the Biafran War,* op. cit., pp. 10 -11.

Chief Festus Okotie-Eboh were killed. In the East, the coup failed. In Lagos, the loyal troops under the command of Major General Aguiyi Ironsi,[452] General officer Commanding the Nigerian Army, succeeded in foiling the coup.[453]

The list below shows the officers involved in the coup as well as their ethnic backgrounds.

1.   Major Kaduna Nzeogwu (Igbo)

2.   Major Adewale Ademoyega (Yoruba)

3.   Major Emmanuel Ifeajuna (Igbo)

4.   Major Timothy Onwuatuegwu (Igbo)

5.   Captain Emmanuel Nwobosi (Igbo)

6.   Major Chris Anuforo (Igbo)

---

[452] General Johnson Thomas Umunakwe Aguiyi Ironsi was born in March 1924 at "Umuahia" in Eastern Nigeria. After primary education partly in the East and afterwards at Kano in Northern Nigeria, he joined the Nigeria army as a private in 1942. By 1946, he had risen to the rank of company sergeant-major. In 1948, he went to Camberley Staff College in England and returned a year later as second lieutenant of the Royal West African Frontier Force. He served first at Accra (Ghana) before being posted to Lagos. Promoted to captain in 1953 and major in 1955, he served as equerry to Queen Elisabeth II during the royal visit to Nigeria in 1956. Promoted to lieutenant-colonel in 1960, he was appointed commander of the fifth battalion of the army stationed in Kano, and later in the year was placed at the head of the Nigeria contingent of the United Nations' force in the Congo. Here he displayed considerable personal valor, enhancing his reputation as a soldier.
From 1961 to 1962, he was the military attaché to the Nigerian High Commission in London during which period he was promoted brigadier. After a course at the Imperial Defense College, he returned to Congo in 1964 as commander of the entire United Nations peacekeeping force. He returned to Nigeria in 1965 and was promoted to major-general and, as the most senior indigenous officer, became head of the Nigerian army.
The coup of January 1966 brought the army to power and as its head, Ironsi became the head of the Nigeria government. He was first and foremost a soldier. Neither particularly gifted in, nor really interested in politics, his regime was marked by indecisive action and was overthrown easily after barely seven months. Although power was handed to him the leader of the forces loyal to the Balewa administration, the government he inherited was a poisoned gift. Acute political differences and tribal distrust made his position untenable. As an Igbo, governing in the charged atmosphere that followed the coup, the Hausa-Fulani North distrusted him. His attempts at conciliation only made his overthrow easy for his opponents. Cf., Uweche R., *Reflections on the Nigerian Civil War, Facing the Future*, op. cit., pp. 193 -194.
[453] Adedeji A., *"The Imperative of true Federalism," Daily Champion News Paper, Nigeria*, 16th April, 2001, p. 36.

7.   Major Humphrey Chukwuka (Igbo)

8.   Major Don Okafor (Igbo)

9.   Captain Ogbo Oji (Igbo)

10. Captain G. Adeleke (Yoruba)

11. Lt. Fola Oyewole (Yoruba)

12. Lt. R. Egbiko (Esan)

13. Lt. Tijani Katsina (Hausa Fulani)

14. Lt. O. Olafemiyan (Yoruba)

15. Capt. Gibson Jalo (Bali)

16. Capt. Swanton (Middle Belt)

17. Lt. Hope Harris Eghagha (Urobo)

18. Lt. Dag Warribor (Ijaw)

19. Second Lt. Saleh Dambo (Hausa)

21. Capt. Ben Gbulie (Igbo).[454]

The President, Dr. Nnamdi Azikiwe, was not in the country when the coup took place. He was on tour in Europe. Under the law, Senate President, Nwafor Orizu became Acting President during his absence and had all the powers of the President. The Acting President, Nwafor Orizu, made a nationwide broadcast, after he had briefed President Nnamdi Azikiwe on the phone the decision of the Cabinet, announcing the Cabinet's "voluntary" decision to transfer power to the armed forces. Major General Johnson Aguiyi-Ironsi then made his own broadcast, accepting the "invitation". On 17th January, Major General Ironsi established the Supreme Military Council in Lagos and effectively suspended the Constitution. It is pertinent to say that it was at the command of Major General Ironsi that the coup plotters of Jan. 1966 were put in prison.

3.2.2.2. WAS THE COUP OF 15th JANUARY, 1966 AN IGBO COUP?

Some people from the North and the West of Nigeria alleged that the coup of 15th January, 1966 was an Igbo coup. Their argument was based on the fact

---

[454] Cf., en.wikipedia.org/wiki 1966-Nigeria-coup., accessed 12.4.2017.

that firstly, the majority of the soldiers who carried out the coup were of Igbo origin. The key plotters were almost Igbo, and secondly, that only very few Igbo statesmen and soldiers were killed during the coup when compared with the victims from the Northern and Western Nigeria.

From the ethnic consideration, the alleged "Igbo coup" of January 1966 was, for all intent and purposes, a pro-Yoruba coup to the extent it was an anti-Igbo coup. This hypothesis is supported by the following arguments. Firstly, the coup was plotted in order to forestall the Yoruba land from being destroyed by the North as earlier planned. Secondly, the coup plotters agreed to hand over power to a prominent Yoruba politician, Obafemi Awolowo.[455] Some commentators argued that the 15th January, 1966 coup was structurally anti-Igbo because it "dismissed an Igbo President, Igbo President of the Senate, Igbo Foreign Minister, Minister of Education, Transport and Aviation. That Coup also dismissed Igbo Premiers in two out of the four regions of the federation. The endgame was to install Chief Obafemi Awlolowo, a Yoruba Prime Minister.[456]

The former secretary to Chief Obafemi Awolowo who spoke to the Guardian newspaper of Nigeria, on the 20th anniversary of the death of Awolowo in 2007 was not of the view that the coup of January 1966 was an Igbo coup. He asserts:

> People were told that it was an Igbo coup but that is not correct. It is a very interesting part of the Nigerian story. In the first place, there have been many serious lies that have been told by our leaders in the last 45 years of Nigeria's history. Our leaders have not been bold enough to tell us the truth … the interesting part of the Nigerian story and Awolowo's story would have been explained in the book written by Chukwuma Ifeajuna. It would have been clearer

---

[455] It was on record that the coup plotters of 1966 wanted to hand over the administration of the country to Awolowo a politician from the West. If the coup plotters had such a thought in mind, how could one then say that the coup of Jan. 1966 was an Igbo coup and for the interest of the Igbo alone. In line with this, Ebiem asserts: Having concluded that the socio-political situation in the country had so deteriorated to an almost irretrievable level, the soldiers decided that the best thing to do was to remove those in the helm of power who could not manage effectively the situation and bring in someone who they believed could. Though Awolowo was not a detribalized Nigerian politician, his administrative records and qualities were never in doubt. The soldiers were impressed with his abilities as a Yoruba ethnic leader and thought he could do well as a national leader. Even Emeka Ojukwu who would later lead Biafra in a bid for self-determination and independence was impressed with Awolowo's administrative capabilities and said so in his tribute to Awolowo on his demise in 1987. He described Awolowo as the best President that Nigeria never had. Cf., Ebiem O., *Nigeria, Biafra and Boko Haram, Ending the Genocide through Multi-State*, op. cit., p., 73.

[456] Cf., Okocha E., *Blood on the Niger: An Untold story of the Nigerian Civil War.*, Nigeria Sunray Publications Ltd., in Ezeni E., *In Biafra Africa Died: The diplomatic plot*, op. cit., pp. 34 - 35.

what actually happened. That book said that the plan of the coup makers was to release Awolowo from jail and make him their own leader.... If that book had been published early, the story that it was an Igbo coup would have been debunked and it would have been a different ball game.[457]

Even if the coup was carried out by 90% of the Igbo soldiers, was it only for the interest of the Igbo people? What the coup plotters had in mind in carrying out the coup was it not for the interest of Nigeria as a whole and not just for the Igbo people alone? Emeka Odumegwu Ojukwu, the late Biafran leader, says:

> It is said that the 1966 coup that failed was strictly an Igbo coup; but then the irony of history is that it was the late General Aguiyi Ironsi, an Igbo who single-handedly dismantled the coup in Lagos, while my humble self, another Igbo man rendered it immobile in the north.[458]

Those who alleged that the coup of 1966 was an Igbo coup have not inquired to know why the coup plotters struck; what was their intention? The intention of the coup plotters was to replace the old politicians with what they called "honest progressives" who would work under military supervision thereby removing corruption and other ills that had entered the political system of Nigeria at that time. Their intention was not just to take over power for their selfish purposes. The majority of Nigerians, both the Northerners and the Southerners, knew the intentions of the coup plotters and gave their consent to it.

> The January coup was widely acclaimed all over the country including the Northern Region, where top civil servants celebrated its success, and apparently happy ending by holding parties both in their homes and in public places.[459]

Ojukwu,[460] an Igbo officer, who later became the governor of Eastern Region and the leader of Biafra did not know about the planned coup until it took

---

[457] Available at: http://www.nigeriavillagesquare.com /forum/mainsquare/9449-1966-coup-plotters-planned-hand-over-power-awo.html, and http://nigeriaworld.com/articles/2007/may/089.html, accessed 12.12.2008, in Ezeani E., *In Biafra Africa Died: The diplomatic plot*, op. cit., p. 29.

[458] Cf., obindigbo.com.ng/2016/10-unforgettable-quotes-late-biafran-leader-odumegwuojukwu, accessed 6.7.2017.

[459] Madiebo A.A., The Nigeria Revolution and the Biafran War, op. cit., p. 27.

[460] Chukwuemeka Odumegwu Ojukwu was born in November, 1933, to a millionaire motor transport magnet, Sir Louis P.O. Ojukwu (1908 - 1966) of Nnewi, Anambra State, Nigeria. He read history at Oxford University England, after receiving his secondary education at Epsom college; an English public school. On his return from England in 1955 he joined the Civil Service as Assistant District Officer and later joined the Nigerian Army. He became a Lieutenant Colonel

place. When he heard about the executed coup, he had an encounter with Nzeogwu, the alleged leader of the coup planners.[461]

Ojukwu never took part in the coup of Jan. 1966 and never supported the coup plotters. One can discover that from his interactions with Nzeogwu which is narrated in the footnote. How then can one say that the coup was an Igbo coup; when the top military officers, like Ironsi, Ojukwu, Madiebo, just to mention but a few, did not know about the coup until it took place and were never in support of the coup. Or did the 5 Majors who carried out the coup represent the Igbo people? Definitely not!

Therefore, if we were to give the coup of 15th January, 1966 a democratic interpretation devoid of sentiments and emotions, one can say that the coup plotters had genuine intentions of carrying out the coup. And it can be said not to be an Igbo coup but a Nigerian coup for the interest of Nigerians in general.

---

and Quarter Master General of the Nigerian Army in 1963. A year later, he was appointed Commander of the 5th Battalion, Kano.

After the January 1966 coup, he became the military Governor of Eastern Nigeria at the age of 33. The following year, he assumed the Office of Head of the Republic of Biafra and was promoted to the rank of a General in 1969. He left Biafra on 9th January, 1970 and returned to Nigeria after receiving state pardon in June 1982. Cf., Forsyth, op. cit., in Ozigbo I.R.A., p. 182.

[461] Ojukwu narrated thus: "Immediately the January 1966 coup happened, I started phoning round to know what was happening. My Brigade Headquarters was in Kaduna; naturally, that was where I took my orders from. I phoned the headquarters, surprisingly it wasn't the brigade commander who answered the call but Chukwuma. I asked what was happening and why it was happening. I listened to all he had to say. Dissatisfied, I asked, 'on what basis is all this? He answered back rather sharply and impatiently. We had a hot exchange of word. I dropped the phone and tried to contact other commanders at their post only to discover that they had all fled. I was the only commander still at my post. It became clear to me that Nzeogwu was effectively in charge in Kaduna.

I phoned Kaduna again. This time it was Hassan Katsina who answered the call. I told him without mincing words that all the nonsense must stop. He was answering all my questions with the prefix, 'my commander says this, my commander says that… with obvious reference to Nzeogwu'. I said who the hell is your commander? In the absence of the other senior officers, I am the most senior officer around and I'm not taking orders from any junior officer. I told Hassan to call Nzeogwu to speak to me. When I was speaking with Nzeogwu later, he requested me to collect some money from the treasury. I said, no. Nobody goes to the treasury to collect money like that. And in fact, I wouldn't obey such order from a junior officer. Then, he said if I didn't cooperate, he would march on Kano and storm the place. I told him that that adventure would not succeed as his vehicles could not reach Zaria. Impatiently, he shouted down the line that he would attack by air. I told him that that was just a bluff since he had no bombs. He said he would use hand grenades. I laughed and told him that they would probably not explode and that even if they did, it would probably be a premature explosion. Then he said he would send an assassination squad. I told him his boys would just be picked up if they tried it." Cf. Ojukwu E.O., *Because I am Involved,* op. cit., pp. 161 - 163.

But one may argue that their "method of achieving their objectives was wrong and unethical."[462]

But why was the coup of January 1966 initially accepted by the majority of Nigerians and later turned out to be rejected by some who have accepted it initially? The coup was accepted by majority of Nigerians but when the coup was politicized and when the issue of tribalism was brought in, the whole story changed. The majority of Nigerians, Hausa, Yoruba and the Igbo, accepted the ideas and the intentions of the coup plotters of January 1966. They also accepted Ironsi's regime at the beginning but later some military personnel from the North took another direction of thought.[463] But one should bear in mind that:

> The immediate reasons for the first coup, in Nigeria however, concerned the nationwide disillusionment with the corrupt and selfish politicians, as well as with their inability to maintain law and order and guarantee the safety of lives and property. During the initial stages, Nzeogwu and his collaborators were hailed as national heroes. But the pattern of killings in the coup gave it a partisan appearance.[464]

Another point which opposes the motion that the coup was an Igbo coup is derived from the fact that the Westerners – the Yoruba were the beneficiaries of the coup and not the Igbo.

> Western Nigeria probably benefited most from this revolutionary turn of events. The military takeover ended a long nightmare of bloody riots which were triggered off by the rigged Western Nigeria Parliamentary elections. In the East, Midwest and Lagos, the entire people and press hailed the change

---

[462] But by killing Sir Ahmadu Bello, Nzeogwu and the other coup plotters had put themselves on a collision course with the religious, ethnic, and political ramifications of such an action, something they had clearly not thought through sufficiently. Cf., Achebe C., There *was a country,* op cit., p. 79.

[463] The new regime started well. It was backed by enormous popular support. All over Nigeria, including the North, people rejoiced at the end of the rule of the corrupt politicians and hoped for a new dawn. The last of the plotters of January had been brought peacefully out of their hiding places and were detained in their various regions of origin. Loyalty to the new regime was pledged by NPC of the North, the Action Group of the West and the NCNC of the East and Midwest, even though the politicians of these parties were out of power and some were detained. Support also came from the trade unions, the students' union and the Emirs of the North. Foreign correspondents noted the popularity. A columnist in the African World noted 'the favorable reception accorded to these constitutional changes by different sections of the Nigerian population clearly shows that the army movement was in fact a popular revolt by the masses. Cf., Forsyth F., *The Making of an African Legend: Biafra story,* op. cit., p. 44. Cf., hhtp://www.photius.com/countries/Nigeria/government/Nigeria_government_the 1966 coups civi-10021.html, accessed 17.7.2017.

with absolute joy and optimism for the emergence of a new Nigeria free from corruption, tribalism and nepotism.[465]

That the coup did not succeed in the East was not a planned act by the coup plotters. What we should bear in mind is that not all the Igbo officers were in support of the 1966 coup. For example, General Ironsi was among the officers that the coup plotters planned to kill. Ironsi was an Igbo. The plotters did not succeed because Ironsi was in control of the situation in Lagos at that time when the coup was taking place. So, it was acclaimed that Ironsi foiled the coup of 1966 in the south.

Attesting to the above submission, Madiebo says: "It appeared as if General Ironsi was successfully foiling the coup in Southern Nigeria, thereby forcing the young officers who started it to flee into hiding in panic and fear. Soon after this, what was left of the civilian regime quickly handed over full responsibility for the government of Nigeria to Ironsi."[466]

One of the props for the idea that the coup of 15th January, 1966 was an all-Igbo affair, aimed at bringing about Igbo domination of Nigeria, has always been that there was no coup in Enugu. Forsyth argues that "the evidence does not support this theory. Troops of the First Battalion, garrison Enugu, moved against the premier's Lodge at 2 am on the day of the coup. They surrounded it but waited for orders before attacking the house and its occupants. The commanding officers, Lieutenant-Colonel Adekunle Fajuyi, a Yoruba, was away on a course; the second-in-command, Major David Ejoor, a Midwesterner, was in Lagos. The troops not predominantly Igbo as has been suggested but largely Middle-Belt infantrymen from the Northern Region, crouched round the house as dawn rose and waited for orders. Meanwhile Ifeajuna and Okafor were speeding across the country to give those orders...."[467]

Forsyth argues further that "no man did more to foil the coup of 15th January, 1966 than the Army G.O.C. Major-General Ironsi, an Igbo from Umuahia. In Lagos, General Ironsi had taken command of the army and had restored order, but it was not that which put him later in power. It was the reaction of the population as much as anything else that made quite plain to all that the reign of the politicians was at an end. This public reaction, often forgotten today, gives the lie most firmly of all to the idea that the January coup was a factional affair."[468] It is pertinent to note here that "Aguiyi Ironsi was also on the list of

---

[465] Madiebo A.A., The Nigerian Revolution and the Biafran War, op. cit., p. 27.
[466] Ibid., p. 22.
[467] Forsyth F., *The Making of an African Legend: The Biafra story,* op. cit., pp. 39 – 40.
[468] Ibid; p. 41.

those to be murdered. Ironsi got wind of the plot and mounted a successful resistance in Lagos ultimately breaking the back of the coup."[469] It was an act of God's providence that Ironsi escaped being killed by the coup plotters.[470]

It is a known fact that the chief plotter of the 15th January, 1966 coup in Nigeria did not organize it only with the Igbo soldiers. Madiebo argues that:

> Judging from the soldiers in the Brigade Headquarters, it was very striking that Nzeogwu executed his coup almost entirely with soldiers of Northern Nigeria origin. His medical attendants, driver, escorts and guards were all Northern soldiers and he only ate meals prepared by his Northern batman. Nzeogwu was an Igbo man.[471]

Forsyth also supports the above argument.[472] But how can one explain the Igbo dominance in the composition of the coup plotters of 15th January, 1966 in

---

[469] Achebe C., *There Was a Country,* op cit., p. 80.

[470] It seems he too was destined for death that night. Earlier he had been at a party given by Brigadier Maimalari and had gone on to another party on the mail boat Aureol, moored at Lagos docks. When he returned home after midnight his telephone was ringing. It was Colonel Pam, to say there was something afoot. Minutes later Pam was dead. Ironsi put down the phone as his driver, a young Hausa soldier, came in to say there were troops driving through the streets. Ironsi moved fast. He jumped into his car and ordered the driver to take him straight to Ikeja barracks, the biggest barracks in the area and home of the Army Headquarters. He was stopped by a road block of Ifeajuana's soldiers who pointed their guns at him. Ironsi climbed out, stood up straight and roared "GET OUT OF MY WAY". They moved. At Ikeja (Lagos) he headed for the regimental sergeant-major's quarters and rallied the garrison. From Ikeja he sent out a stream of orders throughout the morning. Troops loyal to him and the Government took over. Major Ejoor, reporting to him just before dawn was ordered to get back to Enugu and resume command as fast as he could. Ejoor went to nearby Ikeja airport, took a flight, and headed for Enugu airport.
Ejoor arrived in Enugu, took over the garrison and withdrew the troops around Dr. Okpara's home. At 10 am the same troops stood guard of honor as a fearful Premier said good-bye at the airport to President Makarios of Cyprus who had been finishing a tour of Nigeria in Enugu. Later Dr. Okpara was allowed to leave for his hometown of Umuahia. In the Midwest dissident troops arrived at the Premier's Lodge at 10 am but were withdrawn on orders from General Ironsi at 2 pm. The coup had failed. Ifeajuna and Okafor arrived in Enugu to find Ejoor in the saddle. They hid in the house of a local chemist. When Okafor was arrested; Ifeajuna fled to Ghana, later to return and join the other plotters in prison. In Lagos, General Ironsi had taken command of the army and had restored order, but it was not that which put him later in power. It was the reaction of the public as much as anything else. Cf. Forsyth F., *The Making of an African Legend: The Biafra story*, op. cit., pp. 40 41.

[471] Madiebo A., *The Nigerian Revolution and the Biafran War,* op. cit., p. 20.

[472] In Kaduna the group leader was the left-leaning and highly idealistic Major Chukwuma Nzeogwu, an Igbo from the Eastern Region who had lived all his life in the North and spoke Hausa better than Igbo. On the eveing of 14th Jan. 1966, this brilliant but erratic chief instructor at the Nigerian defense Academy of Kaduna led a small detachment of soldiers, mostly Hausas, out of town ostensibly on routine exercises. When they arrived at Sir Ahmadu's splendid resi-

Nigeria? Osaghae tries to explain this by stating that perhaps why there were more Igbo in the group that carried out the coup is because:

> Coup planning and execution usually involves a close-knit core of officers, and 'federal balance' does not usually come into play – concern with balance would be likely to endanger the success of the coup and the lives of the plotters.[473]

We should also bear in mind that during the coup, some Igbo were killed and not only the Hausa and Yoruba. Another fact which supports the argument that the coup of January 1966 was not an Igbo coup is the statement made by Ademoyega who was one of the coup plotters of January 1966. He says:

> If the Gowon government had released the whole lot of us detained by Ironsi, (after the coup failed) surely, Nzeogwu and the remainder of us would have returned to the places of our choice in Nigeria. Not one of us would have been involved in Biafra.[474]

The above statement points to the fact that the coup plotters of January 1966 did not carry it out in the name of the Igbo. Neither did they carry it out bearing in mind the interest of the Igbo alone. Achebe also argues that "although 'superficially' it looked as if it was an Igbo coup. However, when one investigates little deeper one would discover some complicating factors. Nzeogwu was Igbo in name only. Not only was he born in Kaduna, the capital of the Muslim North, he was widely known as someone who saw himself as a Northerner,

---

dence Nzeogwu told the soldiers they had come to kill the Sardauna. They made no demur "they had bullets… if they had disagreed, they could have shot me," he said later. They stormed the gate killing three of the Sarduana's guards and losing one of their own number in the process. Inside the compound they shelled the palace with mortars; then Nzeogwu tossed a hand grenade at the main door, coming too close in the process and injuring his hand. Once inside, Sardauna was shot along with two or three house servants. Elsewhere in Kaduna another group entered the house of Brigadier Ademolegun and shot him and his wife while in bed. A third group killed Colonel Shodeinde, the Yoruba second-in-command at the Defense Academy. With that the bloodshed in the North was over.

In the afternoon of 15 January, Nzeogwu broadcast from Kaduna Radio telling his listeners, 'our enemies are the political profiteers, swindlers, men in high and low places that seek bribes and demand ten percent, those that seek to keep the country permanently divided so that they can remain in office as Ministers and VIPs. The enemies of the country are the tribalists, those who practice nepotism, those that make the country look big for nothing before international circle'. Later he said privately: 'our purpose was to change our country and make it a place we could be proud to call our home not to wage war… Tribal considerations were completely out of our minds at this stage.' Cf., Forsyth F., op. cit., p 37.

[473] Osaghae E.E., Nigeria *Since Independence, Crippled Giant*, London, Hurt and Company, 1998 in Ezeani E., *In Biafra Africa Died: The diplomatic plot,* op. cit., p. 35.

[474] Ademoyega A., *Why We struck, the story of the first Nigeria coup,* Evans Brothers Publishers, Nigeria, 1981, p. 201.

spoke fluent Hausa and little Igbo, and wore the Northern traditional dress when not in uniform. In the end the coup was foiled by the man who was the highest-ranking Igbo officer in the Nigerian army, Major-General Aguiyi-Ironsi."[475]

3.2.2.3. WAS THE COUP OF JANUARY 1966 A MISTAKE? COULD NOT THE REVOLUTION HAVE TAKEN ANOTHER STEP INSTEAD OF A BLOODY COUP?

The motives of the coup plotters may be good and morally justified but the means they took in attaining their objectives may be said to be unjustified. We have mentioned earlier in this work that the Igbo abhor shedding of blood. No human being in his right senses will accept a bloody coup in the name of revolution. Insofar as the intention of the coup plotters of January 1966 might be in order, nobody would support any bloody coup planned and carried out like the one of January 1966. Offodile explains that:

> The Igbo people were politically content to a reasonable extent and did not particularly need a coup in 1966. Even if they were dissatisfied, why kill Ahmadu Bello or Tafawa Balewa? They were not creating problems directly for the Igbo. The crisis point was in Western Nigeria, where Chief Obafemi Awolowo, the leader of the Action Group Party and the leader of opposition in the federal parliament had been convicted of treasonable felony and was serving a prison term at the Calabar prison.[476]

Some of the coup plotters of 1966 coup in Nigeria argued that rather than many dying, let a few die that the whole nation might be saved from the hands of bad men. The coup plotters did not consider other possibilities of restructuring Nigeria other than revolution through a bloody coup. The alleged leader of that coup, Major Patrick Chukwuma Kaduna Nzeogwu, in his radio message after the coup said that:

> The aim of the Revolutionary Council is to establish a strong united and prosperous nation, free from corruption and internal strife. Our method of achieving this is strictly military but we have no doubt that every Nigerian will give us maximum co-operation by assisting the regime and not disturbing the peace during the slight changes that are taking place.[477]

---

[475] Achebe C., *There was a Country,* op. cit., p. 80.

[476] Offordile C., *The Politics of Biafra and the Future of Nigeria*, Safari Books Ltd., Ibadan, Nigeria, 2016, p. 32.

[477] Cf., How Nzeogwu's 1966 coup changed Nigeria forever, waidigbenro.wordpress.com/2016/01/15/how-nzeogwus-1966-coup-changed-nigeria-forever, accessed 15.7.2017.

The above statement confirms that the coup plotters of January 1966 over-ruled other possible avenues of restructuring Nigeria other than a bloody coup which nobody in his or her normal senses would support.

After the coup, which was alleged to be led by Major Nzeogwu, an Igbo man, 8 other coups had taken place; some were bloody, others were not. To the knowledge of majority of Nigerians, the Igbo did not take part in the organization and the execution of these coups. Do we then conclude that these coups were Hausa coups or Yoruba coups? Do we also conclude that they were for the personal interest of Hausa people or for the personal interest of the Yoruba people? Apart from this, one may question the reasons why these coups have taken place. Going down the memory lane, let us examine these coups.

1. THE JULY 1966 COUP

This coup is popularly known as Nigerian counter coup. It took place in July, 1966. Major General Gowon was the leader of the coup. General Ironsi's regime was overthrown and the then Military Head of State, Ironsi, was murdered by the coup plotters. This coup was seen as a retaliation by the Hausa to the Igbo for the coup of 15th January, 1966 which they claimed to be an Igbo coup.

2. THE 1975 COUP

In this coup General Yakubu Gowon, the then Head of State, was ousted in a palace coup on 30th July, 1975 which brought then Brigadier Murtala Muhammed to power as Head of State.

3. THE 1976 COUP

This is popularly and allegedly known as the "Dimka Coup", this bloody and aborted coup led to the assassination of General Murtala Muhammed. Upon General Muhammed's death, and then the foiling of the coup, Lt General Olusegun Obasanjo became the Head of State.

4. THE 1983 COUP

The Nigerian military coup of 31st December, 1983 was led by a group of senior army officers who overthrew the democratically elected government of President Shehu Shagari. Participants included Major General Ibrahim Babangida and Muhammadu Buhari, Brigadiers Ibrahim Bako, Sani Abacha, and Tunde Idiagbon. Major General Buhari was appointed Head of State by the conspirators.

5. THE AUGUST 1985 COUP

This was a palace coup led by the Chief of Army Staff, Major General Ibrahim Babangida, who overthrew the administration of Major General Muhammadu Buhari.

6. THE ALLEGED VATSA COUP OF DECEMBER 1985

Hundreds of military officers were arrested; some were tried, convicted and eventually executed for conspiring to overthrow the Babangida administration. The conspirators were alleged to have been led by Major General Mamman Jiya Vatsa.

7. THE 1990 COUP

Major Gideon Orkar staged a violent and failed attempt to overthrow the government of General Ibrahim Babangida.

8. THE 1993 COUP

Facing pressure to shift towards a democratic government, Babangida resigned and appointed Ernest Shonekan as interim President on 26th August, 1993. Shonekan's transitional administration only lasted three months, as a palace coup led by General Sani Abacha took place. In September 1994, Abacha issued a decree that placed his government above the jurisdiction of the courts, effectively giving him absolute power.[478]

The aims of the coup of 15th January, 1966 were made known to the public. Majority of Nigerians accepted the revolution at that time. One may argue that the way the revolution took place was not accepted by some people. Apart from the coup of January 1966, which we have earlier stated the aims and the intentions of its plotters, one may question the aims and purposes of the other coups which took place after that.

If 15th January, 1966 coup in Nigeria has been alleged to be an Igbo coup, with mistakes attributed to it, Nigeria would have learnt from the mistakes of the past. But instead of learning from the mistakes of the first coup in Nigeria, some Nigerians decided and agreed to continue making the same mistakes which they have condemned in the past.

The same ills which the coup plotters of 1966 coup wanted to eradicate, namely: maladministration, nepotism, corruption, economic mismanagement, blatant rigging of elections, political intolerance and negative ethnic competition;

---

478 Cf., wikiwand.com/en/militarycoupsinNigeria, accessed 20.5.2017.

were they not in the increase after that coup and up till today in Nigeria? Of course, they are. One can argue that, had it been the coup of January 1966 was successful, all these ills enumerated above would have been eradicated. But one cannot be sure of that. All we know is that the ills are on the increase in Nigeria today. Therefore, one concludes that the problem of Nigeria is not only with the rulers but also with the system itself. When the system is right, it will never give room to these ills mentioned above.

The Amalgamation of Nigeria was made on a false foundation. Therefore, the amalgamation gave room to the above-mentioned ills. Sometimes the military believe that coups can solve immediate problems of a nation. Coups do not solve problems but instead create them. The military would have looked for a way to solve the problem of Nigeria rather than coup plotting. It appears they did not look for other alternatives.

The amalgamation of Nigeria in 1914, which united the different tribes into one nation gave room for mutual suspicion among the tribes; and this has continued to linger up till today. In order to explain more and to give us a mental picture of what we are saying about the hidden agenda of the amalgamation, let us look at the military establishments and installations in different parts of Nigeria before the January 1966 coup.

MILITARY ESTABLISHMENTS AND INSTALLATIONS IN NIGERIA BEFORE THE COUP OF JANUARY 1966

NORTHERN NIGERIA

3rd Battalion	Kaduna
5th Battalion	Kano
1st Field Battery (Artillery)	Kaduna
1st Field Squadron (Engineers)	Kaduna
88 Transport Regiment	Kaduna
Nigeria Military Academy	Kaduna
Ordnance Deport	Kaduna
44 Military Hospital	Kaduna
Nigeria Military Training College	Kaduna

Reconnaissance Squadron and Regimental

Headquarters	Kaduna
Nigeria Air Force	Kaduna
6th Battalion (while under formation)	Kaduna
Ammunition Factory	Kaduna
Recruit Training Depot	Zaria
Nigeria Military School (NMS)	Zaria

WESTERN NIGERIA

4	Battalion	Ibadan
2	Field Battery (Artillery)	Abeokuta
2	Reconnaissance squadron	Abeokuta

EASTERN NIGERIA

1ST	Battalion	Enugu

There were no military units in Midwestern Nigeria and those in Lagos were either administrative or ceremonial. Both the 2 Field Battery and 2 Reconnaissance squadron at Abeokuta in Western Nigeria were moved there from Kaduna in 1965, after the political coming into being of Sardauna-Akintola alliance.[479] How do we explain the installation of almost 90% of the Military Base in Nigeria being concentrated in the northern part of the country alone? "To some military officers of Southern Nigeria origin this concentration of military establishments in one part of Nigeria did not appear as a mere coincidence."[480] It was all a planned act.

Mainasasa criticized Madiebo for making the above assertions. He said that Madiebo "listed a number of military installations in Nigeria and minor ones such as the Boy's Company or the Nigeria Elementary Military School Zaria which were open to all Nigerian school children, but cleverly omitting some

---

479 Madiebo A.A., *The Nigerian Revolution and the Biafran War,* op. cit., pp. 9 - 10.
480 Ibid., p. 10.

installations sited in the South."[481] Mainasasa listed the ones in the West which he said Madiebo forgot to mention. But he failed to give not even a single one located in the East which in his thinking Madiebo would not like to mention. Mainasasa thus states:

> The omissions included a whole artillery or reconnaissance squadron located in Abeokuta, in the former Western Region; the Federal Guard, an elite unit based at Obalende, Lagos; the Military Hospital Yaba, which was better equipped than the one in Kaduna, the headquarters of all the military installations located in Yaba, Lagos including the Main Ordinance Depot which indented, procured and distributed all material and other needs of the Nigerian Army; the Myong Barracks, the newly built Ikeja Cantoment and the Ammunition Depot.[482]

In criticizing Madiebo, Mainasasa did not make any disparity between military installations, military schools and hospitals. He grouped all of them under military installations. Mainasasa went further in his criticism of Madiebo and asserts:

> Another point to remember is that the location of federal projects is done on an overall basis. It is unfair to single out military installations and to ignore other institutions. By January 1966 all the Federal educational institutions of higher level were located in the South i.e., the Universities of Ibadan, and Lagos, King's College, Federal Emergency Science School at Victoria Island, Lagos. Almost all major infrastructural facilities such as seaports, railway headquarters, electricity power installations and most of the tarred roads were in the south.[483]

Here Mainasasa failed again to make a distinction between the South-East and South-West. All the areas he mentioned above belong to South-West which are Yoruba areas. Up till today we have only two functional seaports in the whole of Nigeria which are located in Lagos and Port-Harcourt respectively. It was recently that one international Airport was located in the South-East.

3.2.2.4. THE COUNTER-COUP OF 29TH JULY, 1966; THE MASSACRE OF THE IGBO AND ITS CONSEQUENCES

After the counter coup of 29thJuly, 1966 in which Major General Ironsi, the then Head of State and Fajuyi the Governor of the Western Region were kidnapped from the government house at Ibadan and later shamefully murdered,

---

481 Mainasasa A. M., *The Five Majors – Why They Struck,* Hudahuda Publishing Company, Zaria, Nigeria, 1982, p. 15.
482 Ibid., p. 15.
483 Ibid., p. 16.

the northern military soldiers and their politicians imposed on Nigerians without any consultation from other regions of the country, Lt. Col. Gowon, as the new Head of State. This was how the counter coup of July 29th 1966 started.[484]

---

[484] General Ironsi was dining on the evening of 28 July with Lieutenant-Colonel Fajuyi, Military Governor of the West, at the latter's residence in Ibadan. Ironsi had just completed his nationwide tour. With them was Colonel Hilary Njoku, the Igbo commander of the Second Battalion based at Ikeja outside Lagos. The coup started with a mutiny at Abeokuta Barracks in the Western Region where a Hausa captain led a group of troops into the officers' mess at 11 pm and shot three Eastern officers, a lieutenant-colonel, a Major and a lieutenant. They then besieged the barracks, disarmed the Southern soldiers among the guard, seized the armory and armed the Northerners. They also sounded the call to action, which brought the garrison from its sleep to line up on the parade ground. The Southern soldiers were singled out and locked up in the guardroom, while the Northerners made a house-to-house search for those not present. By daybreak most of the Southern officers and senior N.C.O.s had been rounded up.
 They were led out of the guardroom at dawn and shot. Meanwhile the mutineers had apparently telephoned the adjutants (both Northerners) of the Second Battalion act Ikeja and the Fourth Battalion at Ibadan to inform them of the news. But at 3.30 am an Igbo Captain among the prisoners at Abeokuta escaped; he telephoned to Army Head-quarters in Lagos. He reported what he thought was a simple mutiny. At A.H.Q. the man in charge in the absence of Ironsi was his Chief of staff, Lieutenant-Colonel Gowon.
It was he who now took charge. Whether he did so to better the direction of the coup and the massacres that it entailed, or whether he tried to prevent it, is till hotly debated. He claims he had nothing to do with the coup, but his subsequent behavior would appear to cast doubt on this and he may have been a not-too-hesitant accomplice.
 The news also reached General Ironsi. The three officers conferred shortly after midnight and agreed that Njoku should return to Lagos in a civilian vehicle and in mufti to take over control and counter the 'mutiny'. He left in order to return to his chalet and change. Once outside he noticed troops dismounting from two parked Land rovers. They gave him a burst from Sten guns, and he ran off, wounded in the thigh. Later, after treatment at Ibadan hospital he traveled back to the East disguised as a priest, while patrols scouted the West for him and roadblocks had orders to shoot on sight. It was the tenacity of the hunt for Eastern officers, and the duration of it long after Colonel Gowon had taken over supreme control in the name of the mutineers, that cast doubts on both the political aspect of the coup and Gowon's innocence of events.
 In fact, the Southern troops in Ironsi's bodyguard had been disarmed before midnight by the Northern counterparts who had been stiffened by twenty-four extra Northern troops sent from the Fourth Battalion headquarters in Ibadan. This battalion, after the death of Colonel Largema in January, had been under the command of Colonel J. Akahan, a Tiv from the North. The newly arrived party was commanded by Major T. Danjuma, a Hausa, who is now second-in-command of the First Division of the Nigerian Army and Garrison Commander of Enugu. Inside the house Ironsi and Fajuyi heard the shooting and sent down Ironsi's Air force A.D.C., Lieutenant Nwankwo, to find out what was going on. (Ironsi's Army A.D.C., Lieutenant Bello, a Hausa, had quietly disappeared, although there is no evidence to connect him with the coup). Downstairs Nwankwo was arrested and his hands tied. After waiting almost till dawn Colonel Fajuyi descended to find out what had happened to Nwankwo. He too was arrested. Finally, at 9.00 am Major Danjuma went upstairs to find General Ironsi and arrested him. He too was brought downstairs.
 Among those who knew what happened after that, only Lieutenant Nwankwo has ever given testimony. From the Federal Government side, a discreet veil was drawn over everything. What followed then was Nwankwo's evidence.

If Nigeria needed somebody to replace Ironsi who was murdered during the counter-coup, it was not Gowon. Gowon was not the highest-ranking soldier at that time in the Nigerian Army. Ojukwu, the then governor of the Eastern Nigeria in Peace accord held at Aburi in Ghana, made it clear why the Eastern Region of Nigeria refused to recognize the leadership of Gowon as the new Head of State. Ojukwu based his objection on the fact, *inter alia*, that:

> No one can properly assume the position of Supreme Commander until the whereabouts of the former Supreme Commander, Major General Aguiyi Ironsi, was known. He therefore asked that the country be informed of the whereabouts of the Major General and added that in his view, it was impossible, in the present circumstances, for any person to assume any effective central command of the Nigerian Army.[485]

Ademoyega, a Yoruba, one of the January 1966 coup plotters asserts that:

> It was clear that Ojukwu had not recognized Gowon as the Supreme Commander for two reasons. The first was that the death of General Ironsi had not been officially announced, and consequently, the post of the Head of State and Supreme Commander had not yet become vacant. Secondly, Gowon was not rightfully entitled to the headship of the Government. In the order of seniority, after Ogundipe and Adebayo, there were still three other Lieutenant-Colonels before Gowon. These were Imo, Effiong and Njoku, all from the Eastern Region.[486]

Gowon was said to have headed the counter-coup of 29th July, 1966. The question one may ask is: What lessons could Nigerians ought to have learnt from

---

All three men were stripped and flogged with horsewhips. After being put into separate vans the convoy set off with Major Danjuma leading. At the Mokola road junction where the roads divide, one going to Oyo town and the other to Letmauk Barracks, garrison of the Fourth Battalion, the convoy split. Danjuma headed back to Letmauk after giving whispered orders to Lieutenant Walbe, the commander of General Ironsi's escort. The rest of the convoy proceeded. After ten miles the three detainees were ordered down and made to march along a narrow footpath in the bush. They were stopped and were beaten and tortured again so badly that they could hardly walk. After being pushed on they came to a stream which in their weakened state they could not jump across. They were carried over the stream and a few yards down the path, where they were laid face down and given another beating. At this point Nwankwo had managed to untie the wire round his wrists and made a dash for it. He got away. The other two men, nearly dead from their sufferings, were finished off with bursts of Sten gun. Later the police found their bodies and buried them in Ibadan cemetery, from where they were taken six months later and laid to rest in their respective home towns. (Cf., Forsyth F., *The making of an African Legend: The Biafra story*, op. cit., pp. 53 – 55).

[485] Cf., info@emeagwali.com, official Record of the Minutes of the Meeting of Nigeria's Military Leaders held at Aburi Ghana, accessed 21.7.2017.

[486] Ademoyega A.A., *Why we struck, the story of the first Nigeria coup*, op. cit. p. 181.

the counter coup? What corrections did the counter coup plotters want to impact?

We have to recall that Ironsi became the Military Head of State in 1966, after the coup of Major Nzeogwu and his group in which Ironsi was said not to have taken part. This was proved by the fact that Ironsi took part in foiling the coup of January 1966. Before this coup, Ironsi was the highest in rank in the Nigerian Army. It was through the approval of the military council that Ironsi became the Head of State. In line with the above assertion one begins to ask the reason behind Gowon taking up the position of the Head of State when he was not the highest-ranking officer in the Nigerian Army and was not approved by the Supreme Military Council of Nigeria. In the midst of this state of confusion, many Igbo, military personnel, civilians both men and women were murdered in broad day light and even children were not spared.

By the end of August 1966, civilians of Southern Nigeria origin became the main targets of the mass killings all over the country. This was perhaps because there were no more soldiers to be killed and yet the killings simply had to go on somehow. Very soon the majority of Easterners from all walks of life were back in Eastern Nigeria and many more were still returning daily.[487] The counter coup and the massacre of the Igbo were seen by many as a revenge for the first coup of 15th January, 1966 in which some of the Northerners and a few of the Southerners were killed. Some commentators explained the counter coup of 29th July, 1966 as a coup motivated by ideas of righteous revenge for the deaths in 15[th]January, 1966 of three senior army officers of Northern birth. Forsyth argues that the above reason given by the Northerners for carrying out the counter coup is not convincing. He states:

> It seems far more likely that the key to the motives of the officers who mutinied in July is to be found in the code word that triggered the operation – 'ARABA'. It is the Hausa word for 'secession'; and although there was undoubtedly a strong element of revenge inside the movement and the subsequent activities of its perpetrators, their political aim was to fulfill the longstanding wish of the Northern people and quit Nigeria once and for all.[488]

Forsyth analyzing and comparing the 15th January and 29th July, 1966 coups states:

> The two coups were utterly different. In the first coup there had been a fiery zeal to purge Nigeria of a host of undoubted ills. It was reformatory in motivation; blood-shed was minimal - four politicians and six officers. It was extro-

---

[487] Madiebo A.A., The *Nigerian Revolution and the Biafran War*, op. cit., p. 81.
[488] Forsyth F., *The Making of an African Legend: The Biafra Story,* op. cit., p. 52.

vert in nature and non-regional in orientation. The July coup was wholly regional, introverted, revanchist and separatist in origins and unnecessarily bloody in execution.[489]

Ojukwu also comparing the two coups emphasizes that:

> It is important to note the difference between the second military intervention that propelled General Gowon to power and the original coup, planned and badly executed by Ifeajun, an intervention that propelled General Ironsi to power. Ironsi did not revolt against any constituted authority. His government was legally and formally vested and given specific order to restore peace. The second intervention, on the other hand, was a revolt, it was illegal, it was unconstitutional and it succeeded partially. The eastern resistance to it carried on until the end of the civil war.[490]

The Northerners claimed that the then Head of State, Ironsi, did not bring the coup plotters of January 1966 to book. They accused him of taking part in plotting the coup and his government involving herself in tribalism. But contrary to these allegations on Ironsi, Forsyth described Ironsi thus:

> Despite his honesty, General Ironsi was not a politician; he was totally devoid of cunning and showed little aptitude for the intricacies of diplomacy necessary inside a highly complex society. He was also on occasion ill-advised a common fate of military men in government. Nevertheless, he did nothing to merit what happened to him.[491]

General Ironsi, in forming the government headed by him, made several appointments which give a clue to his attitude towards the concept of one Nigeria. He named Lieutenant-Colonel Yakubu Gowon, a Northerner, his Army Chief of Staff and right-hand man; (who later gave orders for his execution). Mallam Hamsad Amadu, a young relative of the Sardauna of Sokoto, became his private secretary. His personal escort were composed mostly of Hausa soldiers commanded by another Young Hausa, Lieutenant W.G. Walbe, a fact which may later have cost the General his life. The only appropriate word that qualifies the massacre of the Igbo in the North and some part of Western Nigeria is "Genocide". The resumed killings brought with it an influx of refugees into Eastern Nigeria from all over the Federation of Nigeria. They came back by air, land and see in pathetic and shocking conditions. Most of them had one or the other part of their bodies either broken or completely missing. Thousands of children arrived, some with severed limbs and many others emasculated. The adults bore the full brunt of the killings and very few arrived from the North

---

[489] Ibid., p. 52.
[490] Ojukwu E.O., *Because I am Involved,* op. cit., p. 9.
[491] Ibid., p. 45.

unharmed. Many whose limbs were not severed, brought them back shattered and had to be amputated anyway. Some had their eyes, nose, ears and tongues plucked out.

The highlight of this horror was the arrival in Enugu of the headless corpse of an Igbo man. Women and children below the age of fifteen were raped and many of them came back in stretchers. The remaining Eastern Nigerian soldiers in Lagos came back by air. They arrived either naked or in underpants and the big gashes on their bodies showed they had been thoroughly beaten and tortured. There was hardly a single family in Eastern Nigeria which did not suffer a loss through these massacres.[492]

As could be expected, tempers were extremely high, particularly when those who managed to come back told their stories of carnage and atrocities. From Kano came the story of how Easterners who had assembled at Kano international airport in an attempt to fly away to safety were rounded up by Northern troops and killed. In Jos the mobs were said to have combed out all Easterners. All of them including men, old women and children, were either killed or maimed. Young women were raped until some of them collapsed and died. Some pregnant women they said had their wombs cut open and their unborn babies brought out and publicly executed. In Zaria, there was an attempt to imitate the system tried out in Sokoto in May, 1966. Most of the Igbos were hounded into a Church, and there, rather than burn the Church down, their assailants were sent in with machetes and other weapons to cut them down.[493] Before the Aburi accord was held, it was on record that the Easterners (the Igbo) have been the foremost advocates of one Nigeria. Forsyth affirms that:

> Far more important, and often overlooked, was a complete volte-face in Eastern thinking on the question of the future form of Nigeria; previously the Easterners had been the foremost advocates of one Nigeria, had put more effort into the realization of this concept than any other ethnic group, and had constantly promoted its cause at the political level. But between 29th July and 12 September the East swung through 180 degrees. It was not, for them, a happy experience, but one which they felt was dictated by recent events.[494]

---

492 Madiebo A.A., *The Nigerian Revolution and the Biafran War*, op. cit., p. 84.
493 Ibid., pp. 84 - 85.
494 Forsyth F., *The Making of an African Legend: The Biafra story*, op. cit., p. 74.

3.2.2.5. THE EFFORTS MADE BY THE EASTERN REGION TO RECONCILE WITH OTHER REGIONS OF NIGERIA

3.2.2.5.1. THE ABURI ACCORD

As tension mounted high and as civil war became apparently forthcoming, measures were made by the then Governor of Eastern Region, Lt. Col. Ojukwu, and the new Head of State Lt. Col. Gowon to resolve the existing issues and to avert the possibilities of the situation resulting into a civil war. At the height of killings of civilians, officers and men of Igbo extraction, the political impasse between Col. Gowon and Lt. Col. Ojukwu became extremely sour. The most annoying and surprising thing about this massacre of the Igbo by the Northerners was that the Federal government of Nigeria under the leadership of Gowon knew of it and practically did nothing to control the situation. Achebe states:

> What terrified me about the massacres in Nigeria was this: If it was only a question of rioting in the streets and so on, that would be bad enough, but it could be explained. It happens everywhere in the world. But in this particular case a detailed plan for mass killing was implemented by the government – the army, the police – the very people who were there to protect life and property. Not a single person has been punished for these crimes. It was not just human nature, a case of somebody hating his neighbor and chopping off his head. It was something far more devastating, because it was a premeditated plan that involved careful coordination, awaiting only the right spark.[495]

Therefore, a meeting point for a dialogue to take place between the two personalities became necessary. But this dialogue became exceedingly necessary. It also became difficult, as the Igbo from the Eastern region refused to attend any meeting in Lagos for fear of being inflicted with bodily harm or outright elimination by the rampaging Northerners. With the breaking down of communication between Lagos and the East, the countdown to civil war began. It was the unavoidable drift towards civil war that made the Ghanaian Head of State, General Ankrah, to arrange for a meeting of the Supreme Military Council to be held at Peduase Lodge in Aburi Ghana on 4th and 5th January, 1967.

During this peace conference, many troubling issues were brought up, discussed and resolutions reached; among them were:

1. To renounce the use of force as a means of settling the Nigerian crisis.

---

[495] Achebe C., *There Was a Country,* op. cit., p. 82.

2. To agree to exchange information on the quantity of arms and ammunition available in each unit of the Army in each Region and in the unallocated stores, and to share out such arms equitably to the various commands.

3. To reaffirm their faith in discussions and negotiation as the only peaceful way of resolving the Nigerian crisis.

4. Resolution that there should be no more importation of arms and ammunition until normalcy was restored.

5. The immediate resumption of the Ad Hoc Committee to work out a constitutional future for Nigeria.

6. The payment of salaries until the 31st of March, 1967 of all staff and employees of Government and statutory corporations and any others who were forced to leave their posts as a result of the disturbances.

7. The setting up, in the meantime of a committee to look into the problem of rehabilitation of displaced persons and the recovery of their property.

8. The repealing of all decrees which tended to over-centralize power at the expense of regional autonomy. This would be followed by the enactment of a decree before the 21st of January, to restore the Regions to their political position prior to January 15, 1966. [496]

3.2.2.5.2. FAILURE OF ABURI ACCORD AND ITS CONSEQUENCES

It was said that the meeting in Aburi began and ended in a most cordial atmosphere and members unanimously issued a second and final communiqué. But what about the implementation of the resolutions at the conference? The Aburi Conference was successful only in Ghana, the place of the conference, as all the parties that attended the Conference agreed upon most of the issues discussed. They were all very happy at the end of the Conference, as they believed that all the thorny issues that led to the drift were successfully trashed out. However, the euphoria of this perceived successful outing was short lived. As soon as the aircraft that conveyed the parties to the East and Lagos touched the tarmac, it seemed like the air which was polluted with hatred and mistrust blew the two combatants resulting in the immediate change of countenance and reasoning. They started to sing different tunes from what were agreed upon in Aburi Ghana.

When the Federal Permanent Secretaries saw what had been conceded to Ojukwu, the Governor of the Eastern Region, they raised their objections. Lt.

---

[496] Cf., info@emeagwali.com, official Record of the Minutes of the Meeting of Nigeria Military Leaders held at Aburi, accessed 5.8.2017.

Col. Gowon reinterpreted what had been agreed in Aburi while Lt. Col. Ojukwu quickly rejected Gowon's version of interpretation.[497] Ojukwu did all he could to see that the issue at hand was resolved. Ademoyega states that:

> Ojukwu scored all his points at the meeting. If Gowon were to be faithful to the resolutions, the Nigerian Civil War might have been averted. But as was usual with him, as soon as Gowon stepped down in Lagos, he gave his ears to the Federal Civil Servants and to his Northern masters, who advised him that he had conceded too much to Ojukwu. There and then, he was prepared to dishonor his own word and break the terms of the Aburi agreement.[498]

From every indication, Gowon was given advice by some federal senior civil servants, most of whom were acting on foreign advice, to reject the Aburi Accord which they alleged not to be in favour of the Federal Government. "Gowon buying their idea rejected almost all the resolutions made at Aburi. As a follow-up, Gowon enacted Decree no. 8 which gave him power to declare a state of emergency in any Region irrespective of the wishes of the Governor of that Region. Later, Gowon published these as the official outcome of the Aburi conference. The above measures were clear indications that Gowon was no longer giving much consideration to the possibility of a peaceful solution. Rather he was rapidly preparing the ground for the use of force."[499] There were every indication that Northern leaders never had any intention of implementing the accord at Aburi. Madiebo notes that "no objective person would dispute the fact that it was the failure to respect the terms of the Aburi Accord that led to the war."[500]

This action of Gowon complicated and jeopardized the unity of Nigeria. From thenceforth, things were never the same. The Eastern Nigeria Government, then absolutely helpless, passed a couple of Edicts to protect the interests of its people and avoid a total economic collapse of the Region. These Edicts were meant to serve as temporary relief while a more permanent solution was being sought. Foremost among these Edicts were the Registration of Companies Edicts, the Revenue Collection Edict and the Court of Appeal Edith. As punishment for these measures taken by the government of the Eastern Region, Gowon's administration imposed economic sanctions on the Eastern Region.

One begins to wonder why Gowon made an accord in Aburi which he knew he would not implement or rather was convinced not to implement. One of the

---

[497] Omotoson K., *Just Before Dawn*, Spectrum Books Ltd., 1988, in Obiezuofu-Ezeigbo, C.E., *The Biafran War and the Igbo in Contemporary Nigeria Politics.*, op. cit., p. 63.
[498] Ademoyega A., *Why We Struck, the Story of the First Nigerian Coup*, op. cit., p. 186.
[499] Madiebo A., *The Nigerian Revolution and the Biafran War*, op. cit., p. 93.
[500] Offodile C., *The Politics of Biafra and the Future of Nigeria*, op. cit., p. 49.

main reasons why Aburi accord failed was lack of trust from both parties that were involved in the accord. There was mutual suspicion between Nigerian Government and the Government of the Eastern Region. When Aburi accord failed:

> Many people realized that the period of negotiations had indeed come to an end. Nigeria was like a spaceship geared for a journey to hell. The switch had been turned on in January 1966 and now nothing could stop her headlong rush along the appointed course.[501]

There was no doubt that the Conference had failed for three main reasons, all blamed on the Northern Oligarchy. The first was the sudden capitulation of the Northern delegation who made a proposal that conflicted with their own original memorandum especially at a time when such a new proposal could not be entertained, much less accepted. The second was the renewal of the atrocities even in its fiercest form. The third was their refusal even to honour the few agreements already reached since August 10th with respect to the removal of Northern troops from the West. It was obvious even to outside and impartial observers that some Northerners were hell bent on having everything their own way.... Oddly enough, the Northerners were asking for closer association of Nigeria, while at the same time they were mercilessly burning, killing and maiming a good part of the community of Nigerians. It was an inconceivable contradiction between wish and practice and between desire and doing which seemed purely fictional but could be made real in a community of savages.[502]

As a result of the deteriorating situation, Colonel Ojukwu convened a meeting of the Advisory Committee of Chiefs and Elders at Enugu, on the 26th of May, 1967 to acquaint them with the latest developments and seek their decision. He gave the Committee three options as alternative solutions to the crisis:

1. To accept the terms of the North and Gowon and thereby submit to domination by the North; or

2. to continue the present stalemate and drift; or

3. ensure the survival of the people by asserting their autonomy.

After due consultations were made, the Advisory Committee gave Ojuwu a reply. Therefore:

---

[501] Amadi E., *Sunset in Biafra,* Cox and Wyman Ltd, Britain, 1973, p. 20.
[502] Ademoyega A., *Why We Struck, the Story of the first Nigeria Coup,* op. cit., in Obiezuofu-Ezeigbo C.E., *The Biafran war and the Igbo in Contemporary Nigerian Politics.,* op. cit., p. 132.

On the 27th of May, the Consultative Assembly mandated Col. Ojukwu to declare, at the earliest practicable date, Eastern Nigeria a free sovereign and independent state by the name and title of the Republic of Biafra. Lagos' reaction to this was swift and immediate for Gowon at once announced a new constitution for Nigeria based upon the division of the existing four Regions into twelve states. By this arrangement, the Eastern Region was unilaterally split into three states: Rivers, East Central and South Eastern States.[503]

3.2.2.5.3. THE EASTERN REGION DECLARATION OF THE STATE OF BIAFRA

With the failure of Aburi Accord, every other effort of reconciliation between the Federal Government of Nigeria and the Government of the Eastern Region also failed. It is germane to ask whether Ojukwu, then Governor of the Eastern Region, single handedly moved for secession of the Eastern region from Nigeria. Why did he opt for secession? Was secession the only option left, suitable and safer for the Igbo at that time? We will try to answer these questions in due course.

With the people's minds thus prepared for war, demonstrations were organized and held all over the Eastern Region demanding immediate action against Nigeria. Everywhere the cry on everybody's lips was "Ojukwu Nyeanyi Egbe" (Ojukwu give us guns). Finally, on the 30th May, 1967, the Governor of Eastern Nigeria declared Eastern Nigeria an independent and sovereign state of Biafra. In doing this, he was merely acting in accordance with the mandate given to him earlier by the people. The mandate had authorized him to do so at the earliest practicable date.[504] On 30th of May 1967, diplomats and journalists were called to the State House, soon to be renamed Biafra Lodge, to hear Colonel Ojukwu read the Declaration of Independence. Here is the text:

Fellow countrymen and women, you, the people of Eastern Nigeria: Conscious of the supreme authority of Almighty God over all Mankind; of your duty to yourselves and posterity; aware that you can no longer be protected in your lives and in your property by any government based outside Eastern Nigeria; believing that you are born free and have certain inalienable rights which can best be preserved by yourselves; unwilling to be unfree partners in any association of a political or economic nature; rejecting the authority of any person or persons other than the Military Government of Eastern Nigeria to make any imposition of whatever kind or nature upon you; determined to dissolve all political and other ties between you and the former Federal Republic of Nigeria; prepared to enter into such association, treaty or alliance

---

[503] Madiebo A. A., *The Nigerian Revolution and the Biafran War*, op. cit., pp. 93 - 94.
[504] Ibid., p. 94.

with any sovereign state within the former Federal Republic of Nigeria and elsewhere on such terms and conditions as best to protect your common good. Affirming your trust and confidence in me; having mandated to proclaim on your behalf and in your name, that Eastern Nigeria be a sovereign independent Republic,

NOW THEREFORE I, LIEUTENANT-COLONEL CHUKWUEMEKA ODUMEGWU OJUKWU, MILITARY GOVERNOR OF EASTERN NIGERIA, BY VIRTUE OF THE AUTHORITY, AND PURSUANT TO THE PRINCIPLES RECITED ABOVE, DO HEREBY SOLEMNLY PROCLAIM THAT THE TERRITORY AND REGION KNOWN AS AND CALLED EASTERN NIGERIA, TOGETHER WITH HER CONTINENTAL SHELF AND TERRITORIAL WATERS SHALL HENCEFORTH BE AN INDEPENDENT SOVEREIGN STATE OF THE NAME AND TITLE OF 'THE RPUBLIC OF BIAFRA.'[505]

With these words, the Eastern Region of Nigeria entered into a self-stated independence, and the word 'Biafra' entered the contemporary political vocabulary – in the view of most political observers at that time, only temporarily. "There were sentiments and deep feelings that dominated the people of Biafra which actually started after the massacre of the Igbos in the Northern and Western Nigeria."[506]

---

[505] Forsyth F., *The Making of an African Legend: The Biafra Story,* op. cit., pp. 98 - 99.

[506] Firstly, there was a deep sense not of rebellion, but of rejection, and this feeling lasts until today. For the Biafrans, they did not leave Nigeria but were chased out of it. They firmly believe that the impulse of separation came from the Nigeria side. For most of them it was the shattering of the illusions of their lifetime that after being the foremost of the 'one Nigeria' actors and thinkers, it was finally they who were not wanted. The subsequent attempt of Nigeria to hammer them back into the country has always appeared illogical – among other things. They are convinced that there is no place for them inside Nigeria as equal citizens with the Nigerians; that the latter do not want them as people, but only their land for the oil it bears and the riches it can produce. They are convinced that it was the Nigerians, not they, who broke the bond that links the contractual society whereby the citizens have a duty of loyalty to government, which government repays with a guarantee of the protection of life, liberty and property. They remain convinced the only role they could ever play in Nigeria henceforth would be that of victim in the first instance and work-slaves ever after; ironically, despite protestations to the contrary from General Gowon (he had in the meanwhile promoted himself to Major-General), the behaviour of the Nigerian Arm, numerous statements from senior Lagos officials, and the propaganda from Kaduna, far from assuaging this fear, have completely confirmed it.
Secondly, the Biafrans felt and still feel an utter mistrust for anything that Nigerian government may say or promise to do. This manifested itself immediately before the civil war started and during the war itself. Here again precedent gives succor to their belief, for General Gowon repeatedly showed that he cannot impose his will on his army or air force commanders, nor they theirs on the troops in the line. Repeated pledges from Gowon that the soldiers would behave decently, that the air force would desist from bombing civilian centers, have turned out to be hot air. As a result, all peace proposals based on a 'Hand over your guns and then we'll be nice

3.2.2.5.4. WAS SECESSION THE BEST OPTION FOR THE IGBO PEOPLE AT THE TIME IT WAS DONE?

Many commentators have put forward arguments for and against the secession of the East from Nigeria before the civil war of 1967. Some also argued that it was untimely done, and that the decision was rather too early to have been carried out. Among those who hold this view is Madiebo. He argues:

> The mandate had authorized Ojukwu to move for secession at the earliest practicable date. The question was whether the date chosen was 'the earliest practicable date'. Almost all the senior army officers thought the answer to that question was an unqualified 'No'. The thought of being independent of Nigeria was simply glorious but to make this a reality was going to be a miracle; yet there was universal jubilation.[507]

Some critics point out that the declaration of the state of Biafra was the brain child of Ojukwu and his closest allies in order to fulfil his long-time ambitions. For example, Gowon, the then Nigerian Head of State, gave this as his major reason for fighting a war against Biafra. Speaking to a Time correspondent - "Friedel Ungeheuer", Gowon justified his declaration of war against Biafra thus: "I know that the world opinion thinks of me as a monster. But the war is not against the Ibos. It is against the personal ambitions of Ojukwu and his rebel gang."[508]

If the war against the Igbo according to Gowon was fought against Ojukwu's personal ambitions and his rebel gang, one may question the justification of such a war. If it was fought only to punish one man and his group for their am-

---

to you' promise from the Federal side have met with complete disbelief. As for future constitutional guarantees of safety inside Nigeria, lately offered by Gowon and heavily backed by Britain, the Biafrans reply that they had these guarantees in the constitution of Nigeria before, but they did not change anything during 1966. This mistrust makes any peace proposal by the Nigeria regime highly unlikely to succeed.

Thirdly the Biafrans were possessed of a deeply held conviction that the advent of the Nigerian Army into their land would mean the execution of another pogrom of such massive proportions that it would constitute genocide, that in the planning of the Northern rulers (hence of the Lagos Government) the Biafrans were destined for extinction once and for all, and that the North, avid for the oil royalties of the coast, would continue Balewa's promised 'interrupted march to the sea' over their dead bodies. Outside, this fear was contemptuously put down to 'Ojukwu's propaganda', particularly in British Government circles. The subsequent months, far from robbing this fear of its base, confirmed it in the eyes of the most Biafrans without a word being necessary from Colonel Ojukwu. Cf., Forsyth F., *The making of an African Legend: the Biafra Story,* op. cit., pp. 99 - 101.

[507] Madiebo A. A., *The Nigerian Revolution and the Biafran War,* op. cit., pp. 94 -95.

[508] Times Newspaper, 23rd August, 1968, p. 27 in Ezeani E., *In Biafra Africa Died: The Diplomatic Plot,* op. cit., p. 45.

bition, should a nation be destroyed because of the sin of one man and his group? The argument of Gowon on why he led Nigeria into war against the Eastern Region has a lacuna. But whatever opinion one may have against Ojukwu, why he led Biafra into war against Nigeria, one thing we should bear in mind is that:

> If Ojukwu, had chosen to co-operate with Gowon against the wishes of the Eastern people, could have kept his fortune, enjoyed a high position in Nigeria and probably still kept his Governorship of the East, not as a popular leader but as a hated quisling surrounded by Federal Army soldiers. Alternatively, if power had been his motivation, he could have bided his time, intrigued with other Southern leaders among whom he had considerable standing, nursed into being a new southern Army, and led his own coup at later date. With his acumen he would probably have been more successful as a coup leader than those who led the previous two insurrections.[509]

Contrary to Gowon's view, Obiezuofu-Ezeigbo holds that:

> The declaration of independent state of Biafra had for a long time been on the lips of every Biafra. It was a spontaneous feeling as a result of common bond occasioned by horrendous experience in the hands of the Northerners. What the people were awaiting was the pronouncement from the leader and a legal tooth to back it up. It was therefore ridiculous to hear many people say that Ojukwu declared independence of Biafra out of selfish reason and ambition to rule Biafra as a Head of State. Had it been another man other than Ojukwu, he would have done the same, as there was no room enough to maneuver out of the spontaneous wishes and desires of the people. In fact, if he had refused to declare the independence, he would have been toppled by those busy body soldiers who staged the 15th January, 1966 coup detained in the Eastern Region. They would have used Ojukwu's inability to declare independence which was the popular wish of the people.[510]

Ayandele blaming Odumegwu Ojukwu for the civil war in Nigeria states: "If an individual ever decided the course of events in any country. Odumegwu Ojukwu did – by pushing Nigeria inexorably in the direction of civil war."[511] The anti-Biafra school also holds that "one important case the Nigerian Government had against Biafra hinged on the Igbo annexing other ethnic groups in the East to Biafra. For this reason, the Nigeria Government had a duty to res-

---

[509] Forsyth F., *The Making of an African Legend:* The Biafra Story, op. cit. p. 101.
[510] Obiezuofu–Ezeigbo C.E., *The Biafran War and the Igbo in Contemporary Nigerian Politics*, op. cit., p. 92.
[511] Ayandele E.A., *The Educated Elite in the Nigerian Society*, Ibandan Nigeria, 1973, I.U.P., in Ezeani E., *In Biafra Africa Died:* The Diplomatic Plot, p. 45.

cue them".[512] But one would recall that the Easterners (Igbo) were not the first in Nigeria to move for secession. In his autobiography, 'My Life', Bello recalled the strong agitation for "secession by the North and added that it looked very tempting."[513] The Pro-Biafra camp gives one major reason why the Igbo opted for secession. Ezeani asserts that "almost all pro-Biafra commentators agree to one major factor, which necessitated Biafra secession. This factor is pogrom."[514]

In agreement with the pro-Biafra argument, Effiong, the second in command of the then Biafra nation, stated after the civil war that "throughout history, injured people have had to resort to arms in their self-defense where peaceful negotiations failed. We were no exception.... We have fought in defense of that cause."[515] In the same line of thinking, Achebe reflecting on the Nigeria-Biafra war affirms that "the absence of a concerted plan to address the eruption of violence throughout Nigeria against Easterners, mainly Igbos, and the inaction around the refugee problem amplified the anger and tensions between the then federal government, led by Lieutenant-Colonel Yakubu Gowon, and the Eastern Region. Calls in the East for independence grew louder, and

---

[512] Cf. Ezeani E., *In Biafra Africa Died: The diplomatic Plot,* op. cit., p. 45.

[513] Demonstrating civil servants in Kaduna carried banners proclaiming: "Let there be secession". In the same city colonel Hassan called a meeting of all the Northern Emirs, and many arrived with clear mandates from their people at home asking for secession of the North. In Zaria the Emir was mobbed by crowds begging for secession. After the meeting the Emirs sent Ironsi a secret memorandum telling him in effect, to abrogate the Unification Decree or they would secede. General Ironsi replied by going to great lengths to explain that the decree involved no changes of boundary, and that indeed it hardly changed the *status quo* at all; he pointed out that it was a temporary measure to enable the army, accustomed to a unified command, to rule; and that there would be no permanent changes made without the promised referendum. The Emirs declared themselves satisfied. Cf., Forsyth F., *The Making of an African Legend: The Biafra Story,* pp. 50 - 51.
It came as a surprise that by 1953 the North had modified its views on separatism to a structure which would give the regions the greatest possible freedom of movement and action, a structure which would reduce the power of the center to the absolute minimum. This system of government can be called confederation.
What the Northerners were demanding, and apparently with the will of the overwhelming body of Northern opinion behind them, was a confederation of Nigerian states. This was what Colonel Ojukwu, Military Governor of the Eastern Region, asked for at Aburi, Ghana, on 4 January 1967, after about 30,000 of the Eastern people had been killed and about 1,800,000 driven back to the East as refugees. Even then, he only asked for it as a temporary measure while tempers cooled. Cf., Forsyth F., *The Making of an African Legend: The Biafra Story*, op. cit., p. 22.

[514] Ibid., p. 46.

[515] Major General Philip Effiong, the Biafran second in command, broadcast announcing, the end of the Nigeria-Biafra war, January 12th 1970, in Ezeani E., In Biafra Africa Died: The Diplomatic Plot, op., cit., p. 46.

threats from the federal government grew more ominous, in a vicious cycle."[516]

Majority of Nigerians witnessed how the Easterners were massacred[517] in the Northern part of Nigeria and in some parts of Western Nigeria. Was that not enough for the Igbo to defend themselves? Almost 97% of the people killed during the crisis in Nigeria which later developed into a civil war, knew nothing about the January, 1966 coup that was organized and carried out by the military. Soyinka affirms what seems to be the major reason for the secession of the Igbo. He asserts:

> It would be a distortion of history an attempt to trivialize the trauma that Igbo had undergone to suggest – as some commentators have tried to do – that it was the lure of the oil wealth that drove them to seek a separate existence. When a people have been subjected to a degree of inhuman violation for which there is no other word but genocide, they have the right to seek an identity apart from their aggressors.[518]

---

[516] Achebe C., *There was a Country,* op. cit., p. 85.

[517] In some of the major massacres against the Igbo organized and carried out by the Northerners, the police and the army not only joined in but in many cases actively led the killing gangs, spear-heading the looting of the victims' properties and raping of their womenfolk. The massacre at the airport near the Fifth Battalion's home city of Kano was outstanding. A Lagos-bound jet had just arrived from London, and as the Kano passengers were escorted into the customs shed, a wild-eyed soldier stormed in, brandishing a rifle and demanding 'Ina Nyamiri' – Hausa language for 'where are the damned Igbos'? There were Igbos among the customs officers; they dropped their things and fled, only to be shot down in the main terminal by other soldiers. Screaming the blood curses of a Moslem Holy War, the Hausa troops turned the airport into a shamble, bayonetting Igbo workers in the bar, gunning them down in the corridors, and hauling Igbo passengers off the plane to be lined up and shot. From the airport the troops fanned out through downtown Kano, hunting down Igbos in bars, hotels, and on the streets. One contingent drove their land rovers to the rail-road station where more than 100 Igbos were waiting for a train and cut them down with automatic weapon fire.
The soldiers did not have to do all the killing. They were soon joined by thousands of Hausa civilians, who rampaged through the city armed with stones, cutlasses and other dangerous weapons. Crying 'heathen' and 'Allah' the mobs and troops invaded the Sabon Gari (strangers' quarter) ransacking, looting and burning Igbo homes and stores and murdering their owners. All night long and into the morning the massacre went on. Then, tired but fulfilled, the Hausas drifted back to their homes and barracks to get some breakfast and sleep. Municipal garbage trucks were sent out to collect the dead and dump them into mass graves outside the city.
The death toll will never be known, but it was at least a thousand. Cf., the correspondent of Time magazine, 7 October 1966 in Forsyth F., The *Making of an African Legend: The Biafran Story*, pp. 78 - 79.

[518] Soyinka W., *You must set Forth at Dawn,* USA., Random House, 2006, in *Ezani E., In Biafra Africa Died:* The *Diplomatic Plot,* op. cit., p. 47.

Some commentators who are among the proponents of anti-Biafra state that the Igbo went to war against Nigeria because of economic purposes; that they went to war in order to possess and secure the crude oil deposited in their Region. Obasanjo for example, was quoted as telling the Niger Delta people when he visited them at the early days of his second tenure as the President of Nigeria that "the Igbos went to war because of the crude oil."[519] But when one analyzes the situation critically, one will notice that what Obasanjo accused the Igbo of, was what the Nigerian Government under the leadership of Gowon fought for. The war against the Igbo was fought in order that the Federal Government under the leadership of Gowon could control the rich oil deposit in the Eastern Region. Obiezuofu–Ezeigbo states that:

> It is a notorious fact that the Igbos were defeated in the oil war waged against them by the Federal Government of Nigeria under Gowon administration. The Federal Government fought the Igbos not really because they wanted Igbos in their midst but because they wanted the territory in which the Igbos occupied which laid the golden eggs for Nigeria.[520]

The story would have been totally different had it been that the Eastern Region were not blessed with rich oil deposit. Nigerian government would not have fought that war against the Igbo people. The Nigerian government would have allowed Biafra to be an independent country. "It has been postulated that if the Biafrans had had as their homeland a region of semi-desert and scrub they would have been allowed to depart from Nigeria with cries of 'Good riddance 'in their ears."[521]

3.2.2.5.5. LACK OF PREPARATION BY BIAFRA FOR A WAR

It is a known fact that any war that is not prepared for cannot be won. Numerically, the Northern Region and the Western Region put together outnumbered the Eastern Region. Also, in terms of weapons and ammunition they were superior to the Eastern Region. When we consider the number and strength of trained soldiers of both sides, the Northern and the Western Regions put together were superior to the Eastern Region. So, when we are talking of preparation for war, we should also consider the true condition of Biafra at that time before the war started. We have to note that:

> Despite the deadly propaganda that emitted from the Eastern regional en-
> clave and the enthusiasm of the people, inwardly, the fears of the outbreak of

---

[519] Obiezuofu–Ezeigbo C.E., *The Biafran War and the Igbo in Contemporary Nigerian Politics.*, op. cit., p. 78.
[520] Ibid.
[521] Forsyth F., *The Making of an African Legend: The Biafra Story*, op. cit., p. 109.

war still gripped the people and authorities. The authorities had believed that differences between the Lagos authorities and the Eastern government authorities would cease after verbal exchanges arising from the propaganda. These beliefs informed the attitude of the government of the Eastern region's inadequate preparations for war.[522]

Those commentators who accused Ojukwu, the Biafran leader, of pulling Eastern Region out of Nigeria and leading Biafra into war against Nigeria have to rethink and consider what Ojukwu said, what he had in mind before the war started. Ojukwu said that he was doing his best to avoid a situation in which secession would become necessary. Ojukwu was quoted to have said even as late as March 1967 that he did not plan to pull Eastern Region out of Nigeria. Ojukwu asserted:

> My threat to take unilateral action to implement the Aburi agreement has been interpreted to mean a decision to secede. That interpretation appeared to me far-fetched. There is no doubt that if I find myself compelled to take such an action, the repercussion will be serious for the country and where we go from here will depend on the attitude of other parts of the country particularly the North and Lagos. But the situation can be avoided if my friends decide to play fair.[523]

From the above statement by Ojukwu, we can conclude that Ojukwu had no intention of seceding Eastern Region from Nigeria nor had he the intention of leading Biafra into war against Nigeria. Those who have accused him of doing so should reconsider their position. For Ojukwu, war was the last resort; he never intended it. He said:

> We went into the war because we had no choice except to defend ourselves from extermination. Right from the start, it was an unequal war. Against the 150 rifles with which we started Lagos had the whole armament belonging to the Nigeria Federation accumulated over many years. With no allies on our side and deprived of the economic opportunity of earning foreign exchange, we had a fight against a deadly foe supported by the imperialist power of Britain, Russia and United States of America.[524]

Ojukwu made a lot of propaganda indicating how prepared Biafra was for a war against Nigeria, if the massacre of the Igbo did not stop and the Aburi Accord failed to stand. He made it quite clear that Biafra had to defend herself against any attack. But all the propaganda made by Ojukwu was to put fears

---

[522] Obiezuofu-Ezeigbo C.E., *The Biafran War and the Igbo in Contemporary Nigeria Politics,* op. cit., p. 101.
[523] Oyewole F., *Reluctant Rebel,* Rex Collings Ltd., London 1975, p. 18.
[524] Ojukwu E.O*., Because I am Involved,* op. cit., p. 353.

into the mind of Nigeria government. When Ojukwu was making the propaganda such as: "the grass would fight for Biafra; no force in black Africa could subdue Biafra by air or by sea etc.,"[525] these propagandas were only offensive propagandas without military backing. At the time when Ojukwu was making these propagandas, the preparation of Biafra for any surprise attack by the Nigerian soldiers was zero. It was never intended that Biafra should go on the offensive, certainly at that stage with an army that was outnumbered and heavily outgunned by the opposing side.[526]

Ojukwu's propaganda instead of frightening the Federal Government into seeking a peaceful resolution of the problem facing Nigeria and the Eastern, increased the tension between Nigeria and Biafra. "Unfortunately, the boasts boomeranged and hardened the Federal Government's resolve; its preparation for the war became thorough."[527] Analyzing Ojukwu's intention of using propaganda to force Nigeria into a peaceful resolution of the problem that existed between Nigeria and Biafra, Obiezuofu-Ezeigbo states that:

> it was unfortunate for Ojukwu to believe that things would normalize after the battle of words with Gowon. Ojukwu failed to go down the memory lane. If he had done so, he would have discovered that the Northerners were acting out the script prepared by their leaders even before the January 15th 1966

---

[525] Despite his propaganda, Ojukwu still had faith that his friends in the North and Lagos would play fair. However, his friends in the North and Lagos took his propaganda seriously and prepared for a show down with him. While the negotiation was still going on, the Federal Government engaged in a serious recruitment of soldiers and importing arms into the country. The recruitment and the importation of arms into the country were not done in secret, because Ojukwu was aware of this. His reaction to the Arm build-up was reflected in the letter of protest dated February 16th, 1967 where he accused Gowon of violating Aburi's agreement by recruiting soldiers and importing ammunition into the country. Cf., Ojukwu E. O., *Because I am Involved*, op. cit. p. 312.
In the same vein, Gowon knew the unpreparedness of Ojukwu and had told his officers and men that Ojukwu had no weapons. This may had informed his pronouncement that he was only taking a police action against Ojukwu. The Nigerian soldiers who were the first to encounter the Biafran army believed that Ojukwu had no arms at all and it was going to be a walkover on Biafra. On the first contact of Biafra and Nigerian soldiers at "Garken Afikpo" – road. Madiebo says: "fighting began with each enemy battalion poised against two platoons of Biafran army. After two hours of intensive exchange of fire, the Nigerian army turned around and broke into run towards their starting line. They were obviously surprised and for that reason suffered heavy casualties and conceded a number of prisoners of war." Cf., Madiebo A. A., *The Nigerian Revolution and the Biafran War*, op. cit., p. 126.
[526] Cf., Oyewole F., op. cit., p. 24. in Obiezuofu-Ezeigbo C.E., *The Biafran War and the Igbo in Contemporary Nigerian Politics*, op. cit., p. 102.
[527] Obiezuofu-Ezeigbo C.E., *The Biafran War and the Igbo in Contemporary Nigeria Politics,* op. cit., 103.

coup. The script was to annihilate and wipe out the Igbo race who they considered to be an obstacle to their continued march to the sea.[528]

Lack of preparation by Biafra for a war was seen in various aspects. In the areas of acquisition of ammunition, Biafra was not prepared. Even though there was a government statement before the war that no country in Black Africa could defeat Biafra by air, land, or sea, Biafra still started the war with practically nothing, and could not improve on that situation right to the end. "The Biafran Army had nothing other than old bolt-action rifles made available by government civilian agents. A few machine guns were issued at the scale of about one or two per company. In the way of support weapons, only the First Battalion had 6 x 81mm and 6 x 3' mortar barrels, inherited from the Nigeria Army. For these, the bombs available were extremely limited. Other units had to rely entirely on local devices as substitutes for support weapons. They fortified their defenses with ditches, mines and armored vehicle traps."[529] From all indications, Ojukwu knew that Gowon and the Nigerian government were preparing seriously for war against Biafra. This reflected in the letter Ojukwu wrote to Gowon, which dated February, 16th 1967. In that letter, Ojukwu said:

> Contrary to the decisions at Aburi, recruitment into the army has continued with publicity in different parts of the country except the East, contrary to the agreements, you have proceeded to appoint ambassadors without reference to the Supreme Military Council; contrary to the agreements, purchase and importation of arms have continued...[530]

One may be tempted to ask what Ojukwu did when he had all this information and knew what Gowon and the Federal government were planning. Why did Ojukwu keep quiet? Why did he not start doing something and getting prepared for any attack from the Nigerian government? In line with the above question, Obiezuofu-Ezeigbo reacts this way. He questions:

---

[528] Ibid.

[529] The Biafran Army despite its gallant efforts, was forced into fighting defensive battle throughout the war and no Army can win a war through defensive battle. The little money available for the purchase of military stores and weapons was wasted by those civilians who were responsible for all military purchases during the war. Rifles arrived either in unserviceable condition or with the wrong caliber of ammunition. Most of the artillery guns and mortars were unserviceable when they arrived in Biafra. For the very few that were serviceable the shells and bombs for them often arrived without fuzes! Inadequate preparations for a possible war on the Biafran side was also seen in the area of early recruitment and training of officers and men before the outbreak of hostilities. One of the reasons behind this lack of preparation was the attitude of the old Nigerian officers then on the Biafra side who thought that soldiering was the exclusive preserve of those officers who were trained in Sand Hurst and Moors in Britain. Cf., Madiebo A. A., *The Nigerian Revolution and the Biafran War*, op. cit., p. 382.

[530] Ojukwu C.O, *Because I am Involved*, op. cit., p. 313.

One wonders why Ojukwu with full knowledge of the massive recruitment and importation of arms by Nigeria kept quiet. Did he believe that grass would fight for Biafra as he used to say in his propaganda? It was indeed a shame that the Eastern Region leadership with all the officers and men it could boost of before the hostility which was superior in all respects to that of Nigeria was still wallowing in delusion that only their propaganda would subdue Nigeria without the use of soldiers and equipment.[531]

One should not level all the blames on Ojukwu, the leader of Biafra, for lack of preparation for the war against Nigeria. We should have in mind that U.S.A, Russia and Britain were supporting Nigeria against Biafra, most probably because of economic interest they had in Nigeria which perhaps Biafra could not have given them. Even if Biafra had all the money needed for importation of good weapons and ammunition, she was seriously handicapped from doing so. This is because she was deprived of foreign currency and was cut off from having international trade and interactions. She only managed to get few weapons and ammunition most probably from France. So, the situation was very difficult for Biafra. We said earlier in this work that Ojukwu and the Biafran government were not anticipating any war against Nigeria. Ojukwu thought that the whole issue could be settled amicably. One would say that the war came as a surprise to Biafra.

3.2.2.5.6. DISARRAY, LACK OF MUTUAL TRUST AND PLANNING IN THE BIAFRAN ARMY

There was crisis of confidence and mutual suspicion in the Biafran Army immediately before the war started. "The dangerous situation notwithstanding, there appeared to be very little that was being done in the Eastern Region in the way of preparing to resist any further attempt to carry the massacres into the Region. It appeared as if the Military authorities were much more concerned with the threat to their offices by the presence of many senior military officers in the Region than with that posed by the apparent determination of some sections of the country to exterminate a whole tribe".[532] We have to recall that majority of the soldiers that took part in the first coup of January 1966 came from the Eastern Region. So, there was fear that this same group might carry out another coup within the Eastern Region.

This unfortunate state of affairs resulted in the complete exclusion of all Armed Forces personnel from all national policy-making bodies throughout the

---

[531] Obiezuofu-Ezeigbo, *The Biafran War and the Igbo in Contemporary Nigerian Politics,* op. cit., p. 98.
[532] Madiebo A. A., *The Nigerian Revolution and the Biafran War,* op. cit., pp. 86 -87.

period of the war, probably as a means of ensuring the security of the Military Governor.... The military got news of what was going on either from the civilians or through the telephone. Thus, the news of the Aburi Conference, the Ad Hoc Constitutional Conference and even the very declaration of independence came to the Army as a surprise over the national radio network.[533]

This situation in the Biafran Army worsened the inadequate preparation that already existed for any surprise attack from the Nigerian Army against Biafra. Many officers in the Biafran Army, who saw what was going on, threatened to resign from the Army. The officers were not happy about the state of lack of preparation of the Biafran army and the exclusion of many officers from the administration of affairs of things in the Biafran Army. Madiebo describing the states of affairs in the Biafran army states thus: "the army in Eastern Nigerian, therefore, had more than enough reasons to be of very low morale indeed. Most of the soldiers came back in rags, having lost all they had, and there was no prospect of replacements. Wherever they went, it seemed they were unwanted because the civilian refugee problems were overwhelming and demanded immediate action."[534] This mutual suspicion and lack of preparation in the Biafran Army contributed a lot to the failure of Biafra. It has been suggested that:

> This crisis of confidence between Ojukwu and the Army may well be the reason why he leaned entirely on the civilians for all military purchases including weapons. These weapons, when they arrived in Eastern Nigeria were hidden in villages around Nnewi, under arrangement outside military control.... The army ignorant of what was available to it at any given time, could not plan in advance. In addition, this system proved to be a colossal waste of money because a good percentage of these weapons were unserviceable.[535]

3.3. THREE DAYS' PROPOSED POLICE ACTION THAT TURNED INTO THIRTY MONTHS OF UGLY WAR

Gowon the then Head of State of Nigeria boasted that he would take a police action against Biafra rather than engaging in a war with her. For him, Biafra was too weak and small to engage herself in a war with the almighty Nigerian forces. Therefore, he called the action he would take against Biafra – "police action". To have a mental picture why Gowon made the above statement – "police action" against Biafra, let us discuss the strength of both sides – Nigeria and Biafra in terms of weapons, soldiers and external support.

---

[533] Ibid., p. 87.
[534] Ibid., p. 89.
[535] Ibid., op cit., pp. 90 - 91.

Never in modern history has a war been fought between armies of such disparity in strength and firepower as the Nigeria-Biafra conflict. On the one hand has been the Nigerian Army, a monstrous agglomeration of over 85,000 men armed to the teeth with modern weapons, whose government has had uninhibited access to the armories of at least two major powers and several smaller ones, which have been endowed with limitless supplies of bullets, mortars, machine-guns, rifles, grenades, bazookas, guns shells and armored cars. These have been supported by numerous foreign personnel of technical experience who have concerned themselves with the efficiency of radio communications, transport, vehicle maintenance, support weapons, training programs, military intelligence, combat techniques and services. To these have been added several scores of professional mercenaries, Soviet non-commissioned officers for operation of the support weapons, and replenishment of lorries, trucks, jeeps, low-loaders, fuel, transport planes and ships, engineering and bridge building equipment, generators and river-boats. The war effect of these machines has been backed by a merciless air force of jet fighter and bombers armed with cannon, rockets and bombs and a navy equipped with frigates, gun-boats, escorts, landing craft, barges, ferries and tugs. The personnel have been lavishly supplied with boots, belts, uniforms, helmets, shovels, pouches, food, beer and cigarettes.[536] From the Biafran side, the story is different. The military force was made up of volunteer force representing less than one in ten of those who had presented themselves at the recruiting booths for service. Weapons and ammunition were the major problem for Biafra.

Forty percent of the Biafran fighting manpower was equipped with captured Nigerian equipment including an assortment of highly-prized armored cars taken when their crews were caught unawares and ran away. Also contributing to the firepower have been homemade rockets, landmines, anti-personnel mines, stand-cannon, booby-traps, and Molotov cocktails, and to the defense have been added devices such as tankpits, treetrunks, and pointed stakes. Without new vehicles for a year and half, Biafrans struggled, kept on moving basically on repaired, patched, cannibalized transport and home-refined petrol. Spare parts have been either taken from wrecked vehicles or machine-tooled. [537]

Biafra was forced into war by Nigerian Army. We are not going to recall all the stories of Nigeria-Biafra war. But we have to narrate areas during the war, where Biafra proved Gowon wrong, who stated that he would use "police action" against Biafra. Within few months of the declaration of independence of

---

[536] Forsyth F., *The Making of an African Legend: The Biafra Story*, op. cit., p. 144.
[537] Ibid., p. 115.

Biafra, a remarkable array of forces had ranged themselves to crush the new country. General Gowon launched the Federal Army behind the slogan 'to keep Nigeria one – is a task that must be done'. Phrases like 'one Nigeria', 'to preserve the territorial integrity of Nigeria' and 'crush the revolt' were soon bandied about, though little constructive thought appears to have been done by anyone to consider a lasting solution beyond the slogans. It was Nigerian Military force that shot the first shot of the war. Fighting started on 6 July 1967, with an artillery barrage against "Ogoja", a town near the border with the Northern Region in the north-east of Biafra. Many analysts did predict that Biafra would fight a defensive war. But to the ultimate surprise of many, Biafra made several offensive attacks.

On 9th August 1967, Biafra struck in earnest with an offensive attack that shook observers both in Biafra and Lagos. Starting at dawn a mobile brigade of 3,000 men they had carefully prepared in secret, swept across the Onitsha Bridge into the Midwest. In ten hours of daylight the Region fell, and the towns of Warri, Sapele, the oil center at "Ughelli", "Agbor", "Uromi", "Ubiaja", and "Benin city" were occupied by Biafra. Of the small army of the mid-west nothing was heard; nine out of eleven senior officers of that army were "Ika-Igbo", first cousins to the Igbo of Biafra, and rather than fight them welcome the Biafran forces.

The capture of the Midwest changed the balance of the war, putting the whole of Nigeria's oil resources under Biafran control. Although she had lost about 500 square miles of her own territory in three small sectors at the perimeter, she had captured 20,000 square miles of Nigeria. More importantly, the whole of the Nigerian infantry was miles away opposite "Nsukka", with the broad Niger separating them from the road back to the capital and helpless to intervene. For the Biafrans, the road to Lagos was open and undefended. Colonel Ojukwu hoped that an alliance of two of the three Southern regions would swing the West into agreement and force the Federal Government to negotiate.

 After a week it appeared this was not going to happen, and Colonel Ojukwu gave order for a further advance westward. On 16th August 1967, the Biafrans reached the "Ofusu" river bridge which marks the border with the Western Region. Here there was a brief scrap with Nigerian troops, who then withdrew. Inspecting the Nigerian dead, the Biafrans were elated; the Nigerian soldiers were from the Federal Guard, Gowon's own bodyguard of 500 Tivs, normally garrisoned in Lagos. If Gowon had had recourse to use these, it was reckoned, there must be nothing else available.[538] Realistically speaking, Nigerian forces had underestimated Biafran Army. Nigerian government believed that they have won the war before the war started in 1967. They never believed that Biafra would ever fight an offensive battle. This shock has never left them up till today.

On 20th August 1967, the Biafrans stormed into "Ore," a town on crossroads thirty-five miles into the West, 130 miles from Lagos and 230 miles from Enugu. This time the Tivs facing them took a worse beating, and disconsolately pulled back in disorder. To observers at the time it appeared that barely ten weeks after the Arab-Israeli war another military phenomenon was to be witnessed with tiny Biafra toppling the government of the enormous Nigeria. A sudden motorized push at that time along any one of three major roads available would have put Biafran forces deep into the Yoruba heartland and at the gate of Lagos. Such was the order Colonel Ojukwu gave. Nigeria got support of some of the world powers. Without these supports, she would not have survived the onslaught of the Biafran soldiers.

It was later learned from sources inside the American Embassy that on 20th August 1967, the Westerners were teetering on the verge of going over to a policy of appeasing the Biafrans to save their skins; that Gowon had ordered his private plane to be made ready, the engines warmed and a flight plan prepared for Zaria in the North; and that the British High commissioner Sir David Hunt and the American Ambassador Mr. James Matthews had had a long and serious talk with Gowon as a result of which the nervous Nigerian Supreme Commander agreed to carry on.[539]

News of this intervention reached Colonel Ojukwu within a week and caused anger among British and American citizens in Biafra, who felt their ambassadors were playing fast and loose with their safety, for if the news had got out to the Biafran public their reaction could have been violent.[540] It would be an act of omission narrating Nigeria-Biafra war without mentioning "Abagana" battle.[541] The "Abagana" ambush was the biggest ever fought battle in Igboland area between Nigerian forces and the Biafran forces.

---

[538] Forsyth F., *The Making of an African Legend: The Biafra Story,* op. cit., pp. 118 - 119.
[539] Ibid.
[540] Ibid., p. 119.
[541] The Nigerian Second Division main force at Abagana finally made move towards Onitsha. It was a formidable and extremely terrifying force moving in a convoy of 96 vehicles and carrying stores and men. In front of this convoy were a saladine and a ferret armored car, while two other ferret armored cars brought up the rear. The first reaction of the Biafran troops immediately they saw the convoy was to take flight and run to cover in desperation. The Nigerian force

Gowon decided to stay on and save his government from collapse and ensured the continuation of the war. Had he fled, there seems little doubt the West would have swung over, and Nigeria would have developed into a confederation of three states. Biafran suspicions since that day have been that the carrot that tempted Gowon and his fellow minority men to stay in power was the pledge of British and American aid. Certainly, the aid flowed hard and fast from that date.

The taking over of some parts of mid-west of Nigeria by Biafra opened Nigeria's eyes to the fact that they were fighting a war. Nigeria underestimated Biafra from the first day of the war. Biafra took advantage of this once-for-all opportunity and got the war in her grasp. But she allowed it to slip. In fact, "Ore" was as far as the Biafran forces could reach. A remarkable about-turn took place. Unknown to all, the commander of the Biafran forces in the Mid-west of Nigeria was a traitor.[542]

---

was so strong that Biafran troops stood absolutely no chance of halting it. The Nigerian troops move started 1600 hours and by 1800 hours the entire convoy and Nigerian soldiers with it had been destroyed. This is how the battle was fought:

When the convoy approached the Biafran troops around "Ifite-Ukpo" junction, Major Uchendu very wisely allowed the advance party of armored vehicles to pass. He then attacked the main convoy from the front, middle and rear. The leading lorry was knocked out and blocked the road and was quickly set on fire. None of the vehicles, therefore could move forward, and being very bulky, could not make their way back; neither could those behind move up, for the whole road became completely jammed up with vehicles. Biafran troops then completely surrounded the 96 vehicles loaded mainly with ammunition and stores and prevented the troops in them from dismounting. The Nigerian forces were helpless and in less than one hour, all the Nigerian soldiers were either killed or had escaped, leaving Biafran soldiers with all the vehicles and their stores. Major Uchendu feared that a very desperate counterattack would be launched by the Nigerian soldiers almost immediately, which he was definitely not strong enough to beat off. To ensure that this unbelievable catch was not recovered by the Nigerian soldiers, he ordered that all the vehicles and their stores be set ablaze.

While the vehicle burnt, a counterattack of a strong company led by two ferret armored cars was launched by the Nigeria troops from "Abagana". Biafran troops were too happy and excited to abandon the vehicles at any cost. After one hour of very desperate battle, the Nigerian company was virtually destroyed together with one of the armored vehicles. The rest fled back in the direction of "Abagana" town. The expected Nigerian counterattack had come and gone and the Biafran troops were now faced with the task of trying to put out the fire, so that they could salvage some ammunition and stores. At that stage, only few lorries had not burnt and the amount of ammunition recovered from them was more than what the Biafran army got in any period of two months. Very few federal soldiers survived this ambush, and those who did were found walking dazed and aimless in the bush. Cf., Madiebo A.A., *The Nigerian Revolution and the Biafran War,* op. cit., p. 225.

[542] Victor Banjo was a Yoruba and had been a Major in the Nigerian Army, imprisoned by General Ironsi for allegedly plotting against him. His prison had been in the East, and he was from there, released by Colonel Ojukwu at the outbreak of the war and offered a commission in the Biafran

Army. He joined Biafra rather than go home to the West and face the possible danger of revenge from the northerners ruling there. Why Colonel Ojukwu chose the one senior Yoruba in the Biafran Army to command the forces destined to march into Western Nigeria, he has never revealed, but the two men were known to have been close friends, and Colonel Ojukwu had implicit trust in him. With the rank of Brigadier, Banjo commanded 'S' Brigade when it moved into the Mid-west.

According to his own confession, when he was later unmasked; he planned to enter into talks with the leaders in the West, notably chief Awolowo. He discovered the hideout in Benin City of the Mid-west Governor Colonel Ejoor, though he did not report this to Ojukwu, who wished to talk to Ejoor. Instead he asked Ejoor to act as intermediary between himself and Awolowo, but Ejoor declined to take the risk.

Banjo said later he relayed messages using the sideband radio of the British Deputy High Commission in Benin. A British official communicated the message in German to another official in the High Commission in Lagos. The message was passed on to Chief Awolowo. The plot Banjo later revealed was typically Yoruba in its complexity. In conjunction with two senior Biafran officers, who also had political ambitions, he was to cause the ruin of Biafra by withdrawing the troops from the Mid-west on a variety of pretexts, arrest and assassinate Ojukwu. As a Nigerian hero he would then re-enter his home Western Region with all his past forgiven and forgotten. He added that the second part of the plot, which was to come later, was that he and Awolowo were to rally the newly recruited Yoruba Army to his standard, and depose Gowon, leaving the Presidency of Nigeria for himself, and permitting Awolowo his long-desired premiership. It seems unlikely that the Gowon government was informed of his postscript. Banjo managed to recruit into his scheme Colonel Ifeajuna, also released from prison, a Moscow-trained Communist officer called Major Philip Alele, a Biafran Foreign Service official called Sam Agbam, who did some of the negotiation between the two sides while out of Biafra, and several other junior officers and functionaries. In Enugu Colonel Ojukwu, although frustrated by the lack of action in the west, continued to trust Banjo and accepted his assurances of administrative difficulties, man-power shortage, lack of enough guns and ammunition, and so forth. It was true that Nigerian forces had grown stronger within few weeks. With a crash recruiting program putting into uniform after a brisk one-week training course such diverse elements as college students and prison inmates, the Nigerians had formed first one fresh brigade and then another.

At this point Banjo decided to strike directly at Colonel Ojukwu. He conferred in the Mid-west with Ifeajuna and Alele, and they worked out the final arrangements for the assassination, which was to take place coincidentally with Banjo's presence in Enugu, where he had been summoned to explain what he was doing in the Mid-west. None of the three seemed to realize time had run out for them. Amazingly they had broached their plan to a number of other officers and civilians, without any attempt to check first to see if those people would not remain loyal to Ojukwu. In fact, many did, some met Ojukwu and informed him about the plot. Ifeajuna and Alele were summoned separately to the state house where Ojukwu coldly confronted them, then ordered their arrest. Banjo was also summoned but arrived with a strong escort of men loyal to himself, whom he wished to accompany him wherever he went. He was persuaded they could stay at the gate, while he went in alone but armed. He agreed. While he was waiting in the ante-room Colonel Ojukwu's police A.D.C., a shrewd young Inspector, went out to the guard posse with a bottle of gin. After passing it round, he invited them to come to his house nearby and sample some more. They agreed and trooped off. Inside state house Ojukwu's men observed their departure, then swung their automatic guns at Banjo. He was disarmed, then ushered in to see the Head of State. It was six hours to the time Colonel Ojukwu would have been killed. It was impossible to keep the sandal quiet as the main culprits freely confessed their parts and the smaller fry were arrested. The effects of this incident on the Biafran army were traumatic; and swift demor-

3.3.1. THE INTERVENTION OF THE OAU (ORGANIZATION OF AFRICAN UNITY) AND OTHER BODIES

The Organization of African Unity (OAU) made some efforts to intervene and resolve the problem that existed between Biafra and Nigeria. In the view of Achebe:

> The umbrella body of sovereign African nations lacked credibility in this effort … as it harbored a strong one Nigeria bias from the very beginning of the war. The OAU's initial attempt to bring about peace talks – with meetings slated for Kampala, the capital of Uganda, in May 1968, and Addis Ababa, Ethiopia (at the OAU headquarters), in July 1968 were ineffectual, and quickly disintegrated into fiascos of confusion.[543]

Other attempts were made by the OAU, but those could not change the situation. Most African countries adhered to the doctrines of the Organization of African Unity, which supported Nigeria for the same reasons espoused by the great powers: "allowing Biafra to secede would result in the destabilization of the entire continent."[544] That was the stand of the OAU throughout the civil war in Nigeria.

However, there were a few prominent nations in Africa that openly declared support for the Biafran cause for humanitarian, ethical and moral reasons. "Tanzania's Nyerere, one of the few survivors of the cold war tussle on the continent and a towering African statesman of the era, saw Biafra's attempts to secede through the lens of 'the Jews seeking a homeland following the Holocaust in Nazi German and elsewhere in Europe".[545] Other African countries that supported Biafra included Zambia, Gabon, Ivory Coast. The Commonwealth Secretariat arranged for peace talk in Uganda for 21st May, 1968. On 20th July, 1968, Nigeria and Biafran delegates at OAU conference at Niamey, Niger, arranged for peace talks to be held in Addis Ababa Ethiopia (4th – 6th August, 1968). The talks ended in failure.

In September, 1968, the six-member OAU consultative committee appealed for end of fighting and urged Biafra to renounce secession and Nigeria to grant all Biafrans a general amnesty. The OAU reaffirmed its faith in the unity and

---

alization set in. Although torn by his one-time friendship with Banjo, and a relation by marriage to Alele, Colonel Ojukwu was heavily pressured by his army colleagues to the view that examples had to be made to stop the rot. He gave his assent. The four ringleaders were tried by special tribunal, sentenced to death for high treason and shot at dawn, on 22nd September 1966. Cf., Forsyth F., *The Making of an African Legend: the Biafra Story,* op. cit., pp 120 - 123.

[543] Achebe C., *There was a Country*, op. cit., p. 96.

[544] Achebe C., *There was a Country*, op. Cit., p. 97.

[545] Ibid., p. 97.

territorial integrity of Nigeria. It will be recalled that Pope Paul VI made an unsuccessful effort to resolve the Nigeria-Biafra conflict at Kampala on August 1, 1969. Nigeria turned down offers of mediation from Switzerland, Austria, Sweden and Yugoslavia.[546] Nigeria insisted on Biafra's unconditional surrender while Biafra was prepared to accept nothing short of full independence. Nigeria's insistence that Biafra should renounce secession and accept the 12 states structure was unacceptable to Biafra. In all this quest for peace, the OAU stood behind Nigeria.

3.3.2. THE PEACE CONFERENCES

The eighteen months of the war between July 1967 and December 1968 were punctuated by three peace conferences, all of them abortive. Their failure surprised no one, least of all those on the Biafran side. What we have to bear in mind is that:

> The prerequisite of any peace conference, if it is to be successful, is that both parties must 'ipso facto' be persuaded that the conflict in progress is no longer susceptible to a military solution within their grasp, and that a negotiated solution is not only desirable but in the long run inevitable.[547]

In addition to the above conditions for a successful conflict resolution and peace agreement, "ought that those on the outside of the conflict, should do all in their power to bring both parties to an agreement. For any power outside the conflict to profess a desire to see a peaceful and negotiated solution on the one hand while providing one of the partners with a reason for failing to come to share that view is hypocrisy."[548] All these conferences failed because of a number of reasons. Biafra proposed agreement on a ceased fire, and more prolonged talks on the terms of the future nature of association between Biafra and Nigeria. On the other hand, Nigeria countered with a seven-point agenda which amounted to discussing the ways and means of organizing Biafra's total and unconditional surrender. While the conference was still in progress, Britain continued to supply arms to Nigeria. This also contributed to the failure of the conferences.

---

[546] Ozigbo I.R.A., *A History of Igboland in the 20th Century*, Snaap Press, Enugu, Nigeria, 1999, p. 160.
[547] Forsyth F., *The Making of an African Legend: The Biafra Story,* op. cit., p. 241.
[548] Ibid.

3.3.3. THE PART PLAYED BY THE WORLD POWERS AND NON-GOVERNMENTAL ORGANIZATIONS

We cannot overlook the international politics that took place during this war. There were five major outside influences on the Nigerian civil war, namely, Great Britain, the United States of America, France, Russia and non-governmental organizations. Britain's role in Nigeria-Biafra war was the most visible, influential and contentious. After initially refusing to sell arms to either side, the British openly sided with the Federal Military Government of Nigeria.

When evaluating British Government policy towards the whole question of the Nigeria-Biafra war, two schools of thought emerge: one claims that the policy was in fact the absence of a policy, the hopeless outcome of a mish-mash of stupidity, apathy, indifference, callousness and ignorance in high places. The other maintains there was a policy from the start, that it was one of total support not for the Nigerian people but for the regime presently in power in Lagos. It was carefully masked from public view. The stupidity of the politicians, the ignorance and apathy of the general public and the men controlling the mass-communication media were used either in the furtherance or the dissimulation of that policy. As an increasing amount of research into the growing pile of documentation available takes place; it is becoming plainer that the evidence supports the latter view.[549]

Forsyth goes further to emphasize that:

> the British leadership should privately wish to see a single and unified Nigeria so long as this was practically feasible is not blameworthy; but what happened was that in its total determination to see a single economic unit no matter what the cost in suffering to the people of the country, through the grossest interference in the internal politics of the country, the British government chose to ally itself not with the people or their aspirations, but with a small clique of army mutineers. The fact that this clique has shown itself throughout to be largely unrepresentative of Nigerian grass-roots opinion, far from changing the 'Support' policy has merely hardened it until a point where British government policy is so inextricably entwined with the survival of the present Nigerian regime as to be publicly committed to total complicity in anything that regime may do.[550]

British public did not know the true facts of Nigeria-Biafra war in time. It took the British public a full year from the outbreak of the war to acquire even a hazy and largely uniformed outline of what was going on. But seeing through

---

[549] Cf., Forsyth F., *The Making of an African Legend: The Biafra Story,* op. cit., p. 156.
[550] Ibid., p. 157.

press and television that people were suffering appallingly, the British public reacted. In the next six months it did everything it could within constitutional limits to change the Government's policy over arms to Nigeria and to donate assistance to Biafra. The British public reacted in different ways to help alleviate the sufferings of the Biafran masses; they organized meetings, committees, protests, demonstrations, riots, lobbies, sit-ins, fasts, vigils, collections, banners, letters sent to everybody in public life capable of influencing other opinions, sermons, lectures, films and donations.

Young people even volunteered to go out and try to help; doctors and nurses did go out to offer their services. Some even offered to take Biafran babies into their homes for the duration of the war; some volunteered to fly or fight for Biafra. The donors are known to have ranged from old age pensioners to the youths. "While considerably less mobilization of parliamentary, press and public opinion in Belgium and Holland managed to bring the government of those countries to modify their policy of shipping arms to Lagos, the efforts of British popular opinion failed to budge the government by one iota. This is not an indictment of the British public but of the Wilson Government."[551] French aid to Biafra had the most direct impact on the war. Uwechue contends that:

> France aid to Biafra had the most direct impact on the war. France became involved in Biafra as a result of the pressure exerted on her by respected African leaders and by French public opinion at home.[552]

Most historians agree that French support for Biafra was not enough for her to succeed in creating an independent state. France did more harm than good by raising false hopes and by providing the British with an excuse to reinforce Nigeria. The Soviet Union (USSR) supported Nigeria and supplied her ammunition. The UNO was also in support of Nigeria. Thus, Nigerian government had world recognition as the "bona fide" ruler of the entire Nigeria.

One would not fail to remember at this point the generous heart and compassion of the American public. When the plight of the suffering children on both sides of the Nigeria and Biafra came to the notice of the American public through their press, their contribution exceeded that of all other countries even on a pro rata basis of population. But another side of the story was that the reaction of the American masses could not change the attitude of the US government in support of Nigeria in terms of supply of arms and other helps. So, the government of the United States "guided by the dead hand of States

---

[551] Forsyth F., *The Making of an African Legend: The Biafra Story*, op. cit., p. 186.
[552] Uwechue R., *Reflections on the Nigerian Civil War: Facing the Future*, New York: Africana Publishing Corporation 1971, p. 98.

Department, remained steadfast in its support of Nigeria regardless of the danger this might have on Biafrans ."[553] Mercenaries fought on both sides of the war because the pay was attractive. Those soldiers of fortune came from Rhodesia, South Africa, Egypt, France, Britain, Germany, Italy and USA. In Biafra, some signed six months contracts and trained the commando guerrilla brigade to help Biafra. Among the Nigerian mercenaries were Egyptian, Rhodesian and South African pilots.

3.3.4. APPLICATION OF PROPAGANDA AS AN INSTRUMEN OF WARFARE

Propaganda was applied by Nigeria and Biafra during the war. The war was fought as much in the airwaves as in the war fronts. It was fought in radio, television and newspapers. The fighters were reporters, editors and newsmen. Propaganda also known as psychological warfare is a necessary instrument of warfare. It is another arm of war – the soul of war reporting.

Both Nigeria and Biafra freely indulged in it but all admitted that Biafra had an edge on Nigeria. It was essentially a war of words between the Radio/TV Nigeria and the Radio/TV Biafra. As Television laboured under serious constraints, the propaganda boiled down to a contest between the Federal Radio Corporation (later FRCN) assisted by Radio Kaduna and Radio Biafra (Voice of Biafra). The Biafrans were characterized as secessionists and rebels. Nigeria's main arena of propaganda was the news-talks. "Nigeria's justification for the war was to keep Nigeria one. Nigerians were urged to actively support the federal government. The BBC relayed Nigeria's propaganda news bulletin as a show of support for Nigeria."[554]

Biafran propaganda aimed at raising the morale of Biafran soldiers and civilians alike. It projected the war as a struggle for survival and security which Nigeria had brazenly denied the Biafrans. It saw Nigeria's prosecution of the war as aimed at genocide – the annihilation of Biafrans. That was most visible in the oppressions and imposed sufferings of the war, the food shortages, starvation, bombings and the total blockage of Biafra by Nigeria. Even though the reporting on the war was often inaccurate, the people readily associated themselves with the position of the Radio Biafra. The war was reported as being that of Muslim (Nigeria) versus Christian (Biafra). The civil war was not a religious war, contrary to Biafra's propaganda. It was not Muslim North versus Christian East. Biafra insisted there was jihad against her people and tended to regard all Northern soldiers – Christian and Muslim alike as Hausa. Most Northern soldiers from the Middle Belt were Christians and non-Hausa.

---

[553] Forsyth F., The *Making of an African Legend: The Biafra Story*, op. cit., p. 236.
[554] Ozigbo I.R.A., *A History of Igboland in the 20th Century,* op. cit., p. 163.

Nigeria openly declared that starvation was an instrument of warfare and vowed neither to lift the blockade on Biafra nor to allow the international relief agencies to operate freely in Biafra. She hired foreign pilots to strafe and bomb civilian targets – homes, hospitals, markets, etc. Radio Biafra so emphasized the issue of genocide that most Biafrans believed it. It portrayed the federal troops as vandals.[555]

3.3.5. BIAFRANS' LIFE STYLE DURING THE WAR

The Nigeria-Biafra conflict created a humanitarian emergency of epic proportions. Millions of civilians – grandparents, mothers, fathers, children, and soldiers alike – flooded the main highway arteries between towns and villages fleeing from the areas of chaos and conflict. They traveled on foot, by truck, by car, barefoot, with slippers, wheelbarrows, many in worn-out shoes. Some had walked so long their soles were blistered and bleeding. As hunger and thirst grew, so did despair, confusion, and desperation. Most were heading in whatever direction the other was headed, propelled by the latest rumors of food and shelter spreading through the multitude like a virus. Refugees were on the move in no specific direction, anywhere, just away from the fighting. As they fled the war zones, they became targets of the Nigerian air force. The refugees learned to travel at nights and hide in the forests by day. The Igbo accommodated one another during the war. They manifested the virtue of hospitality which they are known for. In chapter two of this work, we talked about the extended family system which is one of the practices embedded in the Igbo culture; the Igbo through this practice supported one another during the war.

Many Igbo were uprooted from their homes and brought into safer areas, where they really had no relatives, no property; many of them lived in school buildings and camps. Most of these camps were often hastily constructed tent villages set up beside bombed-out Churches, in football and sport arenas, or in open fields in the forest. They generally lacked electricity, good drinking water, or other basic necessities of life. Occasionally, the more established camps had sturdier shelters on the premises of abandoned schools or colleges or built near freshwater streams or little rivers.

Life in the camps varied in quality. Some of the better organized camps provided water, shelter, food, basic health care – mainly vaccinations for children against the most prevalent diseases and treatment of common bacterial infections – and education. Other camps could only be described as deplorable, epidemic-ridden graveyards. In these camps, the combination of poor sanita-

---

[555] Ibid., p. 164.

tion, high population density, and shortages of supplies created a bitter cock-tail of despair, giving rise to social pathologies and psychological traumas of all kinds – violence, extortion, and physical and sexual abuse.[556]

3.3.6. BIAFRAN'S WARTIME TECHNOLOGICAL ACHIEVEMENTS AND INNOVATIONS

The saying which goes that necessity is the mother of inventions truly manifested itself in Biafra during the Nigeria-Biafra war. As Biafra came increasingly under pressure, Biafrans made effort to find solution to their problems. A number of directorates were constituted to cater for the various aspects of national need. There were directorates for food supply, transport, fuel, housing, manpower utilities, propaganda, etc. Each directorate was charged with some specific assignments. A National Guidance Committee coordinated the assignments.

The Directorate for Food Supply mounted a national land Army whose task was to attack the land with hoes to produce food and in so doing fight hunger. The greatest technological impact was made by the Research and Production Unit (RAP). Constituting this group were Biafran scientists, technologists, technicians and craftsmen drawn from the University, Research and Technical establishments, Colleges of Technology, the public service and the Private sector. Initially, those scientists clustered around Enugu and Port-Harcourt. With the fall of Enugu and increasing recognition of the scientific efforts of the group by the government, Umuahia became the center of the research efforts. The RAP was formally born with its headquarters at Umuahia.

A number of workshops were set up for specific groups with production targets. There were Weapon and Equipment Workshops; Chemical Materials Workshops; Mechanical Engineering and Design Workshops; Metallurgy for Furnaces, Crucibles and Castings Workshops; Electronics and Electrical Workshops; Petroleum extraction and Refinery Group; Biological Processes and Productions Group, etc. There were interactions and integration between these workshops and groups. They all functioned under one overall direction and control. Weapons and equipment workshops produced an array of military hardware such as: Guns – automatic rifles, double barrels, pistols, bullets, cartridges and grenades, Mortars, shells, explosives, ground-to-air rockets; Landmines and anti-tank weapons (Biafran beer, foot-cutter, coffin, Ojukwu bucket, flying *Ogbunigwe*), shore batteries and anti-aircraft guns; Tanks and

---

[556] Achebe C., *There was a country,* op. cit., p. 170.

armored vehicles often converted from bulldozers and harvesters; Battery reactivators.

The chemicals and materials group used available local materials like lead, sulphur and brine. The petroleum and Refinery group replicated the Port-Harcourt refinery twice at "Uzuakoli" and "Amandugba" and set up numerous mini refineries. The biological processes and products group produced vaccines, alcoholic beverages, food packs, soap, mosquito repellants, etc. They produced tons of edible salt per day and bagged it for distribution. Army boots and helmets were manufactured too.

The Airport and road development unit designed, built and maintained the "Uli" and "Uga" airports. These airstrips were large enough to take heavy aircrafts. The radio control tower at "Uli" was mounted on wheels. The landings and takeoffs were at night between 10pm and 4 am.[557]

3.3.6.1. "OGBUNIGWE" (MASS KILLER) THE BRAINCHILD OF BIAFRAN TECHOLOGICAL ADVANCEMENT

As the economic blockade fashioned against Biafra by Gowon intensified, Biafran scientists were compelled by this situation to make more inventions in order to sustain the young nation and make some progress in the ongoing war. "Perhaps no more important instrument of war lay at the disposal of the Biafrans than the bomb called "Ogbunigwe". Gordian Ezekwe, Banjamin Chukwuka Nwosu, and the less well-known technician Willy Achukwu were among the group of originators of this notorious weapon. "Ogbunigwe" would later become widely adopted and manufactured by the RAP engineers. The bomb was a complex three-chamber apparatus that usually included delayed action devices containing a propellant, an explosive substance – often gunpowder in an igniting base – and scraps of metal for maximal effect. "Ogbu-nigwe" bombs struck great terror in the hearts of many Nigerian soldiers and were used to great effects by Biafran army throughout the conflict."[558] The Biafran scientists and Engineers proved to the world that Biafra and in fact African continent can develop their own technology. Achebe asserts that:

> We were told, for instance, that technologically we would have to rely for a long, long time on the British and the West for everything. European oil companies insisted that oil industry technology was so complex that we would

---

[557] Ozigbo I.R.A., *A History of Igboland in the 20ᵗʰ Century*, op. cit., pp. 169 - 170.

[558] Arene E.O., *The "Biafran" Scientists: The Development of an African Indigenous Technology (Lagos, Nigeria*: Arnet Ventures, 1997); Bayo Onanuga, *People in the News, 1900 – 1999: AS Survey of Nigerians of the 20ᵗʰ Century* (Lagos, Nigeria: Independent Communications Ltd; 2000) in Achebe C., *There Was a Country,* op. cit., p. 157.

never in the next five hundred years be able to figure it out. We knew that was not true. In fact, we learned to refine our own oil during the two and a half years of the struggle, because we were blockaded. We were able to demonstrate that it was possible for African People, entirely on their own, to refine oil. We were able to show that Africans could pilot their own planes.[559]

But what happened to Biafran technologies after the war? It would be sad to know that:

The Biafran technologies were generally crude but they worked. The inventiveness and adaptability exhibited by the scientists were immense and commendable. Biafra was able to achieve these technological advancements independently without any foreign help. Regrettably, these war-time technological outfits were allowed to decay at the end of the war.[560]

3.3.7. THE VIOLATION OF THE RULES OF WAR

Rules of war can be defined as "a body of customs, practices, usages, conventions, protocols, treaties, laws and other norms that govern the commencement, conduct, and termination of hostilities between belligerent states or parties."[561] Countries, individuals or groups sometimes use violence to settle disputes. This has happened in the past and is still happening today. All cultures have always had the idea that there has to be limits to violence, if wars are to be prevented from descending into barbarity. For example, there are rules protecting non-combatants, prisoners and the wounded. These rules are set out in international humanitarian law. Even wars have limits. Attacking civilians who are harmless constitutes a war crime and, in modern society today, using chemical weapon is against the rules of war. Nigerian soldiers violated the rules of war with impunity during the Nigeria-Biafra war. Obiezuofu-Ezeigbo recalls that:

Markets were mostly the targets of the Nigerian jet fighters and bombers. The ways they went about it showed that they knew the market days and the location of the popular markets in Biafra. One wonders if their target was the civilians or the soldiers. The number of people who were killed by jet fighters and bombers in different markets were far greater than what were killed in the battlefield.[562]

---

[559] Morrow, "Achebe C., *An Interview", Conjunctions; in There Was a Country*, op. cit., p. 156.
[560] Ozigbo I.R.A., *A History of Igboland in the 20th Century*, op. cit., pp. 169 - 170.
[561] Cf., legal-dictionary.thefreedictionary.com/Rulesofwar, accessed 12.9.2017.
[562] Obiezuofu-Ezeigbo, C. E., *The Biafran War and the Igbo in Contemporary Nigerian Politics*, op. cit., p. 139.

The indiscriminate air bombardment by the Nigerian air force was interpreted as an attempt to exterminate Igbo race. Anyasodo narrates his personal experience, how the Nigerian Military violated the rules of war during the Nigerian civil war. He states:

> There was this amorphous Nigerian bomber aircraft with a white pilot which comfortably flew very low on Afo umuohiagu market; that was in 1969. In this raid more than 3,000 lives were destroyed, about 90 percent of them were women who went to the market to find some food for their children. They were mostly women because all the able-bodied men were in the war front. I supervised the mass burial of the victims of this heavy bombardment as captain commanding the Engineering squadron. I gave the order that the caterpillar assigned to the erect obstacles along Aba-Owerri road be used first to bury these dead bodies. The sight was too awful for words.[563]

The widespread killing of Biafran civilians was unimaginable. The explanation that it was difficult to differentiate between soldiers and civilians cannot hold water. "These massacres were witnessed by numerous foreign residents."[564]

---

[563] Professor Chika Anyasodo who was in London for the Igbo language conference, London 2012, narrated this story to Emefiena Ezeani on Thursday, March 22, 2012 during their discussion on Nigerian history and politics, in Ezeani E., In Biafra Africa Died: The Diplomatic plot, op. cit., p. 135.

[564] New York Review, 21st December, 1967: In some areas outside the East which were temporarily held by Biafran forces, as at Benin and the Mid-western Region, Igbos were killed by local people with at least the acquiescence of the Federal forces. About 1,000 Igbo civilians perished at Benin in this way.

Washington Morning Post, 27th September, 1967 states: But after the Federal takeover of Benin, Northern troops killed about 500 Igbo civilians in Benin after a house-to-house search.

London Observer, 21st January 1968: The greatest single massacre occurred in the Igbo town Asaba where 700 Igbo males were lined up and shot.

New York Times 10th January 1968: The code (Gowon's Code of Conduct) has all but vanished except from Federal propaganda. In clearing the Mid-west state of Biafra forces, Federal troops were reported to have killed, or stood by while mobs killed more than 5,000 Igbos in Benin, Warri, Sapele, Agbor and Asaba.

Asaba, referred to above in the Observer's report, lies on the western bank of the River Niger, and was a wholly Igbo township. Here the massacre occurred after the Biafran troops had crossed the bridge back into Biafra.

Later Monsignor George Rocheau sent down on a fact-finding mission by His Holiness the Pope, visited both Biafra and Nigeria. At Asaba, by then in Nigerian hands, he talked with priests who had been there at the time. On 5th April 1968 he was interviewed by the French evening newspaper "Le Monde", to whom he said: There has been genocide, for example on the occasion of the 1966 massacres... Two areas have suffered badly (from the fighting). Firstly, the region between the towns of Benin and Asaba where only widows and orphans remained, Federal troops

3.3.7.1. REFUGEES, HUNGER AND HUMANITARIAN AID

The refugee crisis in Biafra started with the massacre of the Igbo in the Northern and Western parts of Nigeria. The refugee crisis grew out of proportion during the war itself. It was the starvation in Biafra that really woke up the consciousness of the world to what was going on. The general public not only of Britain but of all Western Europe and America, though usually unable to fathom the political complexities behind the war news, could nevertheless realize the wrong in the picture of a starving child. It was on this image that a press campaign was launched which swept the western world, caused governments to change their policy, and gave Biafra the chance to survive.

But even this issue was fogged by propaganda suggesting the Biafrans themselves were 'playing up the issue' and using the hunger of their own people to solicit world sympathy for their political aspirations. There is not one priest, doctor, relief worker or administrator from the dozen European countries who worked in Biafra throughout the last half of 1968 and watched several hundred thousand children die miserably, who could be found to suggest the issue needed any 'playing up'. The facts were there, the press men's cameras popped, and the starvation of the children of Biafra became a world scandal.[565]

The most sympathetic and agonizing of this humanitarian crisis in Biafra was the blocking of all the avenues through which supplies could reach Biafra. Awolowo, one of the political giants in Western Nigeria has been quoted to have advised the Nigerian government and Gowon to make use of starvation as one of the instruments of warfare against Biafra. Nigerian government bought the idea of Awolowo and the world was shocked when its effects began to manifest. It was then clear that:

> With the blockade and the war, the supply of imported protein was cut off. While adults can stay in good health for a long time without adequate protein, children require a constant supply of it.[566]

Biafra made some efforts to look for some avenues to grow food crops and provide some basic needs for her people. The Biafran administration set up intensive chicken and egg-rearing farms to boost production of the available

---

having for unknown reasons massacred all the men. According to eyewitnesses of the massacre the Nigerian commander ordered the execution of every Igbo male over the age of ten years.
At Calabar in Biafra, more massacres took place. Mr. Alfred Friendly reported in the New York Times of 18th January: "Recently captured by Federal forces, soldiers were said to have shot at least 1000 and perhaps 2,000 Igbos, most of them civilians". Cf., Forsyth F., *The Making of an African Legend: The Biafra story,* op. cit., pp. 258 - 259.
[565] Ibid., p. 195.
[566] Ibid., pp. 196 -197.

protein – rich foods. They might have beaten the problem, at least for two years, had it not been compounded by the shrinking of their territorial area, the loss of the food-rich peripheral provinces, and the influx of up to five million refugees from those provinces.[567]

By mid-April of 1968, they had lost the Cross-River valley along most of its length and part of the south, the "Ibibio" homeland in the provinces of "Uyo", "Annang" and "Eket", and the land containing the richest earth in the country. At about this time reports from the International Red Cross representative in Biafra, Swiss businessman Mr. Heinrich Jaggi, from the Catholic Caritas leaders, from the World Council of Churches, the Biafran Red Cross, and the doctors of several nationalities who had stayed on, showed that the problem was getting serious. The experts were noticing an increasing incidence of Kwashiorkor, a disease which stems from protein deficiency and which mainly affects children. The symptoms are reddening of the hair, swelling of the joints and bloating of the flesh as it distends with water. Besides kwashiorkor, there were other illnesses like anemia and just plain starvation. The effects of Kwashiorkor, which was the biggest scourge, are damage to the brain tissues, lethargy, coma and finally death.[568]

As the war continued, the refugee crisis grew to unpredictable size and the problem of hunger also increased. The great majority of the civilian population fled from the fighting zone into unoccupied Biafran areas. By the end of February, 1968, there was an estimated one million refugees inside the unoccupied zone. The extended family system which had assisted the Easterners to absorb their refugees from the Northern and Eastern Nigerian eighteen months previously could not operate, since most of the refugees had no relatives with whom to stay. Most therefore huddled in shelters built in the bush on the outskirts of villages, while the Biafran authorities with the assistance of the Red Cross and the Churches set up a chain of refugee camps where the homeless could at least have a share of a roof and a meal a day. Many of these camps were set up in the empty schools, where most of the housing facilities were not adequate.

Forsyth, giving account of this refugee crisis, states that Caritas and the World Council of Churches, being organizations not operating on the Nigerian side of the fighting line, and not being required to go through procedural channels before bringing relief, decided to do it alone. They were purchasing abroad various quantities of food and medicines to fly into Biafra. They had no aircraft

---

[567] Ozigbo I.R.A., *A History of Igboland in the 20th Century,* op. cit., pp. 166 - 168.
[568] Ibid.

or pilots, and therefore came to an arrangement with Mr. Hank Wharton, an American freelance who flew in Biafra's arms shipments from Lisbon twice a week, to buy space on his aircraft. But the quantities that could be brought in in this way were tiny.[569]

The Red Cross organization made some efforts to send some amount of relief and wishing to ask for or buy their own aircraft and hire their own pilots, sent in repeated appeals from Geneva to the Nigerian Government asking for safe conduct for clearly marked Red Cross aircraft to fly in by day without getting shot down. These appeals were consistently refused by the Nigerian government. Nigerian government feared that the relief aircraft might carry weapons. Then it was suggested that Red Cross staff supervise the loading. Nigerian Government said no to that. Ojukwu also suggested that Nigerian Red Cross staff should accompany each relief flight right into the airport in Biafra in order to overcome the fears of Nigeria government. But the Nigerian government did not agree to this arrangement.

As starvation of the Biafrans continued during the war, Nigerian government offered Biafra a Greek gift.[570] The food crisis loomed in Biafra as a result of the economic blockade of Biafra by air, sea and land by Nigeria. In the first six months of the war, Biafra managed to cope with the decreasing food reserves. By 1968, the loss of many farmlands following Biafran's military retreats and concomitant refugee problem made food shortage increasingly worrisome. By the middle of that year, the problem assumed crisis proportion.

About 60 percent of the population of Biafra was then squeezed into about a quarter of Biafra's land. Much of Biafra's food producing areas in Abakaliki, Afikpo, Aba, Umuahia and Owerri sectors were lost to Nigeria. Industrial life in Biafra was at a standstill. Existing factories were bombed or closed down. Bia-

---

[569] Forsyth F., *The Making of an African Legend: The Biafra Story,* op. cit., p. 198.

[570] On 8th of July 1968, the Nigerian Foreign Minister, Mr. Okoi Arikpo, held a press conference in Lagos in which he proposed a land corridor. Food would be brought by ship into Lagos. From there it would be airlifted to Enugu, safely in Nigerian hands, and then convoyed by road to a point south of Awgu, captured the previous month by Federal forces. There the food would be left on the road in the hopes that Biafrans would come and take it. The proposal was hailed by the British government and press as a most magnanimous gesture.... There was enormous antagonism inside the country, not from Colonel Ojukwu but from the ordinary Biafrans, to the idea of taking any food at all by courtesy of the Nigerian Army. Many expressed the wish that they would prefer to do without food than take food handouts from their persecutors. Then there was the question of poison. There were incidents of people dying mysteriously after eating foodstuffs bought across the Niger in the Mid-west. An analysis of samples made at" Ihiala" hospital laboratory revealed that white arsenic and other toxic substances had been present in the food. Cf., Forsyth F., *The Making of an African: The Biafra Story*, op. cit., p. 202.

fra reverted to subsistence level. The trade level was nil. Markets were deserted for fear of air raids. A scourge for hunger, starvation and malnutrition set in particularly for children, nursing mothers and the aged. When the pictures of starving Biafran children burst on the world, the world community reacted, which we have discussed earlier. Biafrans owed huge thanks to the international relief agencies and acclaimed the saving roles of Pope Paul VI and the missionary priests of the Holy Ghost (C.S.Sp).

Despite the numerous relief centers, sick bays and relief kitchens, over a million children were also spirited away to Gabon and Cameroun. Pediatric care centers were opened in Libreville, Abidjan and Sao Tome to harbour Biafran children. The total scourge of starvation and disease made the war a real holocaust for Biafra. About 2 million Biafrans were estimated to have died of hunger. The population of Biafra was about 14 million at the inception of the war in 1967. The figure dropped to about 11 million at the end of the war in 1970. About 3 million Biafrans perished in the war.[571]The Church, in particular the Catholic Church made a lot of moves to alleviate the sufferings of the people and to initiate peaceful resolutions. It was on record that "the dioceses in Biafra carried on relief work, including flying in relief materials, medicine and Church personnel, and she had nothing to complain with reference to the Government."[572]

The universal Church also made efforts to resolve the Nigeria-Biafra crisis as we have earlier indicated in this work. Pope Paul VI invited to the Vatican City from 3rd - 7th February 1969 the Archbishop of Kaduna, Lagos and Onitsha, with one more Bishop from each Province, to meet for several days with officials of the Secretariat of States. Kaduna province: Archbishop J. McCarthy and Bishop Reddington of Jos. Lagos Province: Archbishop J. Aggey and Bishop McCoy of Oyo. Onitsha Province: Archbishop F. Arinze and Bishop Whelan of Owerri.[573]

3.4. THE END OF THE WAR

Whoever has experienced a war in his or her life time would not like to have a repeat of that experience. It is a known fact that during war battles both sides, the conquering army and the one being conquered would like the war to end as soon as possible. This is because definitely the both sides at war receive the pains and agonies of the war and most painfully the loss of human lives that are involved. This was the case of Nigeria-Biafra war. Increased hunger and

---

[571] Cf., Ozigbo I.R.A., *A History of Igboland in the 20th Century*, op. cit., pp. 166 - 168.
[572] Arinze F., *The Baton of Faith, Personal Recollections, Interview with Isizoh Chidi Denis,* Rex Charles and Patrick Ltd., Nimo, Nigeria, 2008, pp. 55.
[573] Ibid., pp. 55 - 56.

hardship were probably the greatest problems of Biafrans. With increasing hardship and declining military supplies, many Biafran soldiers began to desert the war fronts. Many Biafran civilians developed a double mind about the war. Biafra's second capital, Umuahia, had fallen to the Nigerians on 21st April, 1969. It was an omen of the worst calamity that was yet to come.

Biafra celebrated the second anniversary of its existence (May 31, 1969) with the *Ahiara Declaration* which proclaimed the political and moral philosophy of the State of Biafra. It was Biafra's war cry and code of conduct. The document spelt out what Biafrans were fighting for. Unfortunately, a cross section of the Biafran elites were not enamored by the socialist thrust of the *Ahiara Declaration.* The Declaration should have appeared much earlier in the Biafran struggle.[574]

With the defection of Dr. Nnamdi Azikiwe to Nigeria and the growing Nigerian successes in the war fronts, the fate of Biafra hung on a thread. In August 1969, Dr. Nnamdi Azikiwe had a stop-over in Lagos on his flight to Liberia from London. He was welcomed at the airport and invited to the Dodan Barracks for a discussion with Gowon. Interestingly, Gowon decided to accompany him to Monrovia to discuss with President William Tubman on the Nigeria civil war (18th August, 1969). On 28th August, 1969, Dr. Nnamdi Azikiwe formally declared his support for Nigeria and urged Biafra to renounce secession and seek accommodation with the Nigeria federal government. On 5th September, 1969, Dr. Azikiwe returned to Lagos and went on a series of tours throughout Nigeria – to all state capitals, to Enugu, Nsukka and Onitsha. In January 1970, Nigeria recaptured Owerri from the Biafrans.

On 9th January, 1970, Biafra's Emergency Cabinet decided that General Ojukwu the Head of State, should go to Ivory Coast and also meet the French President to plead with them for an urgent negotiation of peace settlement. That was the official information released by the Biafran government.[575] When the Biafran troops heard that Ojukwu had left the country, there was low morale in Biafran camps and Biafran soldiers started to lose hope in the war. The Nigerian troops closed in as Biafran defences collapsed. "There, on 12th January, 1970, the acting Head of State of Biafra, Major General Philip Effiong, yielded to pressure from Biafran troops to seek for peace. In a broadcast, Major General Effiong called on the Biafran forces to lay down their arms and stop fighting. The war thus ended unconditionally for Biafra, on 12th of January, 1970. Ojukwu got the news of Biafra's surrender in Abidjan, Ivory Coast. It has

---

[574] Ozigbo I.R.A., *A History of Igboland in the 20th Century,* op. cit., p. 161.
[575] Ibid., pp. 161 -162.

been claimed that Gowon officially ordered the federal troops in Biafra to stop fighting on 14th January, 1970."[576] But some hours elapsed before Nigerian troops carried out the order to stop fighting. "As a result, in the 72 hours that elapsed between 12th and 15th January, hundreds of unprotected Biafrans were killed, raped and beaten up by Nigerian troops. Gowon received the formal surrender of Biafra at the Dodan Barracks in Lagos. Major General P. Effiong led the capitulation team."[577] The war ended on 15th January, 1970.

One may accuse Dr. Nnamdi Azikiwe, the foremost Biafran Statesman of abandoning Biafra and going over to Nigerian side when his support was seriously needed in Biafra. But one ought to recall that Azikiwe made several unsuccessful attempts to reconcile Biafra and Nigeria. Withdrawing his support for Biafra and going over to Nigerian side may be seen as the only avenue to stop the war between Biafra and Nigeria. He would not have succeeded stopping the war had it been that he kept on supporting Biafra; Gowon and Nigerian officials would not have listened to him. Secondly, it was clear that Biafra was not making any progress in the war. Hunger and starvation became another war Biafra was fighting against and had no hope of winning. At this stage, everybody was looking for a saviour that would come and intervene. In my own opinion, Azikiwe decamped from Biafra in order to prevent more Biafrans from being killed in the battle field and also from hunger and starvation.

3.5. WHY BIAFRA WAS DEFEATED

Many commentators and writers on the Nigeria-Biafra war have asserted in their own views why Biafra failed to achieve a sovereign status despite the commitments, efforts, zeal and sacrifices made by its subjects towards achieving this dream. When we consider the number of Biafran soldiers against the ammunition and international support Nigeria got, it would have been the unimaginable happening, in fact a miracle, if Biafra had won the war. The truth about this issue is that Biafra never wanted in the first place to fight a war against Nigeria. She was pushed into war by the massacre of Biafrans by the Hausa-Fulani. We have to recall also that Nigerian forces were the first to attack Biafra. Madiebo affirms the above statement. He asserts that "the truth, as already mentioned was that no one expected a shooting war and whatever assistance the Army got was on compassionate grounds."[578]

Biafra thought that the Nigerian Government would be forced or persuaded to negotiate with her and resolve their problems without further violence. War

---

[576] Ozigbo I.R.A., *A History of Igboland in the 20th Century*, op. cit., p. 162.
[577] Ibid.
[578] Madiebo A. A., *The Nigerian Revolution and the Biafran War*, op. cit., p. 108.

was the last thing on her agenda. There are other reasons why Biafra did not win the war. Biafra made some mistakes before and during the war itself. What in fact strengthened the morals of Biafrans and made the war to last more than expected was the conviction of Biafra of the justness of her cause; she never doubted for one moment that justice would prevail eventually and victory would be hers. The faith in Biafra's ultimate victory was what kept Biafrans slugging it out for three years in spite of heartbreaking set-backs to the astonishment of the world. Biafrans felt that having been so unjustly treated, humiliated and massacred, God and the world community could not stand idly by and allow them to be exterminated in their homeland. But we all know that sentiments do not overshadow reality. It was therefore out of ignorance of this basic fact of life that Biafra made several grievous mistakes which contributed so much to her defeat. We normally say that prevention is better than cure.

> Igbos could have prevented the war by effectively challenging the counter coup of July, 1966 promptly rather than allow it to gain momentum. If that had happened, Biafra would not have had a war to lose in the first place.[579]

Biafra was so completely carried away by her total conviction in justness of her course, and her belief in the existence of a fair and just world conscience, that she took it for granted that justice would be done and her rights recognized just by bringing her case to the notice of the world. She therefore made no alternative arrangements or necessary preparations for an armed show-down with Nigeria. By the time she discovered rather belatedly, that world conscience is really not that effective in international politics, she was already in serious danger. One of the reasons generally accepted by many for the defeat of Biafra was the existence of crisis of confidence and trust in Biafra throughout the war. This crisis existed within the Army, between the Army and the civilians, between the Army and the government and, indeed, between the Biafran government and some of the foreign supporters. The initial detention of Dr. M. I. Okpara, former Premier of Eastern Nigeria soon after Ojukwu became Governor, the wartime unexplained mass detention of top ranking Biafran Army officers and civilians, and the appointment of Colonel Banjo, a Yoruba, to lead the invasion of Mid-west in 1967, were the most blatant manifestations of this lack of confidence and trust. Ojukwu in his book, 'Because I am Involved' explained why he chose Banjo, a Yoruba to lead the invasion of Mid-west. It was not based on his friendship with Banjo, as some might have suggested but rather to manifest the necessity of truthfulness, unity and the need to fight for a common good irrespective of tribes and irrespective of where one comes from. Ojukwu says:

---

[579] Ibid., p. 378.

> When I appointed Colonel Banjo to lead Biafra forces west across the Niger to Lagos, the appointment was to signify an east-west disposition not only for myself but of the entire Biafran people for solidarity in the Nigerian crisis. Thus, when today I call for a new understanding between the east and the west and between the north and the south, the call is not new. When I call for true unity in the country, the call is not evidence of a new Ojukwu strategy.[580]

Nevertheless, it was because of the lack of mutual trust by people pursuing the same aim that Ojukwu disregarded:

> The confidence of military experts and highly experienced political leaders who could have perhaps helped him save Biafrans from the greatest calamity that ever befell them. Biafran's foreign friends were not given sufficient information to enable them to plan and render a more meaningful military and diplomatic assistance to Biafra. Thus, within outside Biafra, ignorance of the true situation was universal with the disastrous consequences this had for the people of Biafra.[581]

There was dangerous class distinction among the soldiers. The old Nigerian soldiers in Biafran Army saw themselves as very superior to other soldiers. "They viewed themselves as an elite class, which they guarded jealously and resisted any encroachment by those they considered to be bloody "civilians". This they did without minding the expediency and the necessity of having more officers and men necessary for the prosecution of the impending war. Within the old Nigerian army, there was always an emphasis and distinction between the trained infantry, viewed as the elite class within the army and the administrative class, regarded as civilian in army uniform." [582]

Biafran authorities did not start the recruitment of the new soldiers and the buying of ammunition in time. This is because they did not see the possibility of the problem at hand resulting into a civil war. Had it been that necessary preparations for war started in time "this would not only help in smooth prosecution of the war but would also have reduced the war casualties among the newly recruited or conscripted officers and men of the Biafran army."[583] It is on record that at the early stage of the war, enthusiastic men turned out in large numbers to be recruited into the Army but were turned back by those old Ni-

---

[580] Ojukwu E. O., *Because I am Involved,* op. cit., p. x.

[581] Madiebo A. A., *The Nigerian Revolution and the Biafran War,* op. cit., p. 379.

[582] Amadi E., *Sunset in Biafra, op.* cit., p. 2, in Obiezuofu-Ezeigbo C. E., *The Biafran War and the Igbo in contemporary Nigerian Politics,* op. cit., p. 178.

[583] Obiezuofu-Ezeigbo C.E., *The Biafran War and the Igbo in Contemporary Nigerian Politics,* p. 179.

gerian soldiers. This was part of the set-back that Biafra experienced, which affected seriously the number of soldiers she made use of during the war.

Another secret which seriously affected the effectiveness of the Biafran soldiers, was that 70% of her soldiers were conscripted and given crash program training; majority of them were not well trained. This was because of lack of time. And some were unwilling to accept the training given to them due to the fact that they were conscripted; they were forced into this profession. The crisis of confidence, which we earlier mentioned, reflected in many aspects of the war. This reflected also in the procurement of Arms and Ammunition for Biafra. It was observed that:

> People who were not trained and knowledgeable in the use and operation of Arms and Ammunition were sent to procure Arms and Ammunition for Biafra. These amateurs purchased wrong Arms and Ammunition thereby wasting the scarce funds on the old Arms and Ammunition not necessary for the prosecution of modern warfare.[584]

Could it be said that Ojukwu, the leader of Biafra, trusted the civilians more than his soldiers and colleagues? It would be an exaggeration if we say so. From all indications, it seemed that Ojukwu had some fears over the old Nigerian soldiers who experienced the Nigerian coup of 1966. He was afraid that a coup might be carried out by the same old soldiers who were unpredictable. Ojukwu's fears actualized when Banjo and Ifeajuna who were among the old soldiers plotted a coup against him, which we have earlier indicated in this work. But one would ask: Had Ojukwu fears also over his friends and his confidants? Ojukwu, however, had a few military friends and perhaps confidants, but each one of them seemed to have a reason for being so close. In fact, the only known confidant and friend was Major Chude Sokei. He later performed top secret military and civil assignments both inside and outside the Region. There was Colonel Victor Banjo, a Yoruba, who was in detention in the Eastern Region for his role in the January coup. He was released and moved into State House to live with Ojukwu. Major Ifeajuna, also a released January 1966 coup detainee, was a close friend of Ojukwu with special privileges. He not only refused to accept any field appointment within the Army but was also accommodated at government expense in the Progress Hotel, Enugu while many senior officers lived in slums in the town.

There were also rumors that Ojukwu was trying to appease those privileged officers for personal reasons not unconnected with the January 1966 coup. If

---

584 Obiezuofu-Ezeigbo C.E., *The Biafran War and the Igbo in Contemporary Nigerian Politics*, p. 179.

these rumors were right, then these tactics failed woefully because the same privileged group in September, 1967, made unsuccessful attempt to overthrow the Governor.[585] The lack of confidence which Ojukwu had over some of his army officers was like an infection to majority of other Biafran soldiers, which made many soldiers to have low morale.

Most of the soldiers came from the Nigerian side down to Biafra in rags, having lost all they had, and there was no prospect of replacement. Wherever they went, it seemed they were unwanted because the civilian refugee problem was overwhelming and demanded immediate action. Lt Colonel David Ogunewe, the Commanding Officer of the first Battalion Enugu, made it clear that he did not want any Senior Officers particularly the colonels, to interfere in any way with the running of the Battalion which was the only Military unit in the region. He discouraged even visits to the Battalion by such officers. His fear was that unless he was careful, he might be displaced from his command by someone else. All senior officers realizing that they could neither go to Ojukwu nor to Colonel Ogunewe retired to a common house given to them at the independence Layout, Enugu. There they played cards and checkers all day completely disinterested in what was happening around.[586]

When the experienced soldiers were not involved in the affairs of planning of any war, one would rightly guess what would be the result of such an action – confusion, mistakes in planning, waste of energy and available funds. This was exactly what happened in Biafra. There were really big lacunas in the preparations if at all enough preparations were done; which many doubted from evidences given. It was clear that "lack of confidence and cooperation among the senior officers in Biafra contributed immensely to the inadequate planning and preparation for the impending war."[587]

Certainly, we may agree to the above assertion made, because the senior officers would not have done much when they were not totally absorbed in the Army by the military authorities of Biafra. Therefore, they would not have forced themselves into the planning of the war from outside, when they were not totally absorbed into the Biafran Army.

Biafran authorities did not make use of experts who were available in the preparation of the war and during the war. This was evident in many ways. For instance, whatever money Biafra ever had during the war was under the con-

---

[585] Madiebo A.A, *The Nigerian Revolution and the Biafran War*, op. cit., pp. 91 -92.

[586] Ibid., p. 89.

[587] Obiezuofu-Ezeigbo, C.E., *The Biafran War and the Igbo in Contemporary Nigerian Politics*, op. cit., p. 180.

trol of the Head of State, while the actual spending was the responsibility of one Mr. C.C. Mojekwu a lawyer. It goes without saying that better results could have been achieved with the little Biafra had, if financial experts were brought in, and credible accounts kept. This points to the question of purchases made for the Army during the war. Even though there was a government statement before the war that no country in Black Africa could defeat Biafra by air, land, or sea, Biafra started that war with practically nothing, and could not improve on that situation right to the end.[588]

 The Biafran Army, despite its gallant efforts, was forced into fighting defensive battles throughout the war and no Army can win a war through defensive battles. The little money available for the purchase of military stores and weapons was wasted by those civilians who were responsible for all military purchases during the war. Rifles arrived either in unserviceable condition or with the wrong caliber of ammunition. Most of the artillery guns and mortars were unserviceable when they arrived in Biafra. For the very few that were serviceable, the shells and bombs for them often arrived without fuses.

Despite this obvious waste of time and money, these civilians under Mr. Mojekwu continued to buy for the Army until the end of the war. The question many people ask is: Why did the Biafran authorities use civilians for their purchases instead of armed forces personnel who were most qualified for that. For the answer to this question, one's guess is as good as the other. If qualified personnel were used for those purchases, perhaps numerous aircrafts which could not fly as soon as they were paid for, would never have been bought. Biafra could have therefore made better use of the limited resources available to her to achieve better results in the battlefield. How could complete honesty be expected when all Biafran funds were raised and spent throughout the war under accounts opened in the name of individuals? [589]

Another reason for the defeat of Biafra in the war was the failure of Biafran leaders to involve the old politicians in the preparations and planning of the war and other logistics. Many of the old politicians were kept at arms-length before and during the war. Many of them were cramped into detention where they stayed throughout the war. In Nigeria, the story was rather different. The old politicians were carried along in whatever the government was planning or doing. For example, old politicians like Anthony Enahoro, Chief Awolowo and so many others played important roles that determined the final outcome of the war.

---

[588] Madiebo A.A., *The Nigerian Revolution and the Biafran War*, op. cit., 382 - 383.
[589] Ibid.

Ojukwu refused to involve the old politicians in the administration of Biafra who were well versed in the art of governance and diplomacy. His scornful attitude against them tilted the balance of many negotiations between Nigeria and Biafra in favour of Nigeria and resulted in many ways the sad story of Biafra's failures and sufferings. For instance, the issue of blockade by Nigeria and ceasefire were the areas in which the skillful talent of politicians and their diplomatic acumen were needed. "The Biafran unsuccessful persuasion of Nigeria to lift the blockade and agree to a ceasefire resulted in many deaths through hunger and other casualties of the war."[590]

The Biafran financial disaster, if not a total collapse as a result of the change in currency by Nigeria in January, 1968, was the most important single reason why she lost the war. "At the end of the financial chaos which followed in Biafra, she had lost over 50 million pounds which could have made a world of difference in her favour if properly utilized for the execution of the war. This should not have happened if prior arrangements were made to counter the move. After all, as far back as October, 1967, the common man in Biafra was already talking about a possible change of currency by Nigeria. As a result of that fantastic financial loss, Biafra found it difficult to support her Army at war."[591]

We have said a lot about how unprepared Biafra was for a war with Nigeria. But to put it more realistically and contrary to Biafra's propaganda, she had initially neither the men nor the arms to prosecute a successful war with Nigeria. All through the war, Biafra's grand strategy never aimed at defeating Nigeria but at holding her back for as long as possible to enable world conscience to be aroused in sympathy for Biafra. Biafra aimed at defending itself until Nigeria got tired and left her alone. It will be recalled that it was Nigeria that declared the war and attacked Biafra all through the 30 months of the war. It has already been shown that Biafra's forays into the Mid-west of Nigeria were mere diversionary tactics foiled by Banjo's ambition.

---

[590] Some of these unsuccessful attempts by Biafra were later achieved through Dr. Azikiwe, an old politician and elder Statesman of Biafra. Although some might have said many things against Azikiwe as regards his leadership of the Igbo and his attitude as an Igbo Statesman; we should also recognize some of the things he did in the favour of the Igbo. One would say that Dr. Azikiwe helped the free passage given to Biafrans after their defeat in the war. Through his diplomacy, he may have frustrated those elements in Nigeria who had canvassed for the trial of the Igbo leaders in Biafra and other elements that believed in the extermination of Igbo race. Cf., Madiebo A. A, T*he Nigerian Revolution and the Biafran War*, op. cit., p. 379.
[591] Ibid., pp. 381 - 382.

Nigeria was superior to Biafra in weaponry and armored support. Biafrans made less mistakes and were more careful in the use of their limited arms than the Nigerians. That enabled Biafra to slow down the Nigerian advance into Biafra with occasional serious setbacks. Nigeria's tactics in the war boiled down to three, namely, use of longer artillery range and mortar fire to scatter Biafran troops and civilians, then, use of armored vehicles to clear the way and finally move the troops to occupy and hold a particular area of Biafra. Nigeria was attacking and Biafra was mainly defending. One may ask how Biafra could have won the war, if she was always at the receiving end, fighting defensively instead of offensively.

Personal interest instead of common interest, personal ambition and deceit, were among the things that prevented Biafra from coming out victoriously from the war. One recalls the issue of 'saboteur'. This was seen in the action of Banjo and Ifeajuna who organized a coup against Ojukwu and Biafra. Obiezuofu-Ezeigbo states that "in addition to other factors responsible for the capitulation of Biafra is the concept of 'saboteur' in the war. This destructive concept rocked and disorganized the entire Biafran establishments. It created fears and witch-hunting; it eroded confidence and the fighting spirit of the Biafran soldiers. The term 'saboteur' was an offshoot of Victor Banjo's mad ambition for power. Its effects were the reversals in the Mid-western and Western operations. The results of these were overwhelming on the psyche of the Biafran populace. It was the most significant factor that caused the capitulation of Biafra. The term 'saboteur' was designed as a prelude to undermine the trust and confidence between the civilians and the fighting soldiers. It was the tacit acts of Banjo and his colleagues in crime that exploded the concept to such a magnitude and proportion that it became another weapon of the war that destroyed Biafra."[592]

After the deadly and disgraceful act of Banjo and his colleagues, the army of Biafra lost confidence and admiration it had hitherto enjoyed from the people. "It was difficult for the army to understand how Colonel Banjo, a Yoruba, who found himself in Enugu by chance could be the first Biafran to detect acts of Sabotage in the front lines from his office in Enugu. Yet, everyone believed him and gave him maximum assistance in his campaign without realizing his deceit."[593]

---

[592] Obiezuofu-Ezeigbo C.E., *The Biafran War and the Igbo in Contemporary Nigerian Politics*, op. cit., p. 184.
[593] Ibid., p. 185.

Before the Nigeria-Biafra war started in 1967, the entire citizens of Eastern Region of Nigeria saw themselves as one family having same ideology and many things in common. Gowon created 12 states out of the existing 4 states, thereby, splitting the then Eastern Region unilaterally into 3 states, namely, East Central, Rivers and South-Eastern states. The common ideology and thinking changed automatically among the member states that formerly formed the Eastern Region. It was clear that the creation of more states and the splitting of the former Eastern Region into 3 states was designed "to remove the possibility of a coordinated and effective resistance by the entire peoples of the South against the North. With the Ibo as the guinea pigs, the other Southern tribes heaved a sigh of relief and were too happy to call the war that followed – an Ibo rebellion."[594] In his analysis on why Biafra was defeated in her battle against Nigeria, Madiebo concludes thus:

> I think there was by far too much time and energy wasted in frequent struggles for power and position inside Biafra during the war. Those struggles intensified whenever there was a bit of stability in the war fronts. A situation like that should never have been allowed to exist during a war of survival. We posed as experts in everything and that brought about confusion and frustration. It also caused vital omissions in places where people left their jobs to do other people's jobs. If Biafran soldiers have learnt to stick to the jobs for which they were trained and given others a chance to do their own jobs, they would have learnt a useful lesson and probably would have won the war.[595]

Biafra was not prepared for the war she fought; that was why she lost. It is said that he who fails to plan has planned to fail. One thing about wars and competitions is that normally one side comes out victorious over the other. But sometimes it may not be the stronger, the better or the one that is fighting for one's right that wins. That is the case with Nigeria-Biafra war. Biafrans fought in the belief that it was the only way to protect themselves from possible extermination. Biafrans believed that they were fighting to ensure their very survival. It is true they lost the war, but they fought well enough and with sufficient determination to bring their grievances successfully to the notice of the entire world. Despite a negative world reaction, they made a significant impact which is a commendable achievement. What we are trying to say is succinctly summarized in the words of a French Deputy Ambassador, Raymond Offroy, who had this to say after visiting the Biafran enclave: "Before I came to Biafra, I was told that Biafrans fought like heroes. But now I know that heroes fight like Biafrans."[596] Biafra actually fought two battles: physical military combat with

---

594 Madiebo A.A., *The Nigerian Revolution and the Biafran War*, op. cit., pp. 388 - 389.
595 Ibid., p. 384.
596 Madiebo A.A., *The Nigerian Revolution and the Biafran War.*, op. cit., p. 387.

the Nigerian forces and fight against hunger and starvation which came heavily on the Biafran people, because of the boundary blockade mounted by Nigeria against her. In spite of the effects of hunger and danger of starvation, many Biafran soldiers fought the war sometimes on empty stomachs, believing that they would win because they were fighting for their freedom. Arinze explains that:

> Many Biafrans were living in the hope that their cause was just. These did not realize how difficult it was to win that war, or how short of arms and food Biafra and its army were. For example, when the Nigerian troops entered Awka from Enugu, it was difficult to persuade the Biafran population to evacuate the town. Many kept believing that the Biafran army could not be conquered. They did not know that the army was short of arms and ammunition. I was told that to get the people to move out, some Biafran soldiers were told to fire a few bullets into the air. But the people accused these of being saboteurs or of lowering the morale of people. When one Religious Sister heard me saying that Biafra army had neither enough food nor arms, she asked me 'shall we cook food at the feeding center and bring to the soldiers at the war front?' This innocent Sister had little idea of the magnitude of the problem. She was probably among the many Biafrans who believed that since they had suffered so much, God would not allow Biafra to be defeated.[597]

Biafra needed support from outside but could not get that because the world-powers were in support of Nigeria. Some countries who were not among the world-powers or some countries in Africa could not come out fully in support of Biafra because of the fears of the world-powers; what they might think of them. In view of this Arinze says that:

> In 1968 and 1969 I also heard from various sources that while a certain country in Western Europe had sympathy for Biafra, it could not accord it diplomatic recognition because another big power was against that, and that was because that country and their friend wanted Nigeria to remain as one entity. I was told that some European politicians who visited Biafra in 1969, were keeping a watchful eye on public opinion in their country which was pro-Biafra, and elections were coming. Moreover, President Charles de Gaulle of France, although apparently in favor of self-determination for Biafra, was not prepared to confront the British militarily on the issue. So, I presumed that, short of a miracle, Biafra could not win the war.[598]

---

[597] Cf., Arinze F., *The Baton of Faith,* op. cit., pp. 63 - 64.
[598] Arinze F., *The Baton of Faith, op. cit.,* p. 63.

CHAPTER FOUR

4. THE EFFECTS OF THE NIGERIA-BIAFRA WAR ON THE IGBO

4.1. INTRODUCTION

It is not wrong to say that the present Nigerian predicament is a direct off-shoot of the after-effects of the Nigeria-Biafra war. Within the context of the Nigerian predicament, the Igbo case is a little more complex. This complexity hinges on the peculiar experiences the Igbo had during and after the war; and the attendant psychological and political hang-over of that war. The federation of Nigeria has never been one homogeneous country, for it consists of more than 300 ethnic tribes. But the major ones are Hausa, Igbo and Yoruba. This unfortunate yet obvious fact notwithstanding, the former colonial master welded all these tribes into one country. Therefore, the only thing that all these tribes have in common is the name, Nigeria. Yet this is not a sufficient basis for true unity. We all know that when unity does not exist, division comes in. This separation and division were experienced in Nigeria-Biafra war. In this chapter we shall showcase the impact of the Nigeria-Biafra war on the Igbo, and on Igbo Traditional Religion and Spirituality. We shall also look at the impact the war had on the political and economic status of the Igbo.

4.2. THE IMPACT OF NIGERIA-BIAFRA WAR ON THE IGBO TRADITIONAL RELIGION AND SPIRITUALITY

The defeat of the Igbo in the Nigeria-Biafra war has affected them so much in what they are known for; their language, culture, spirituality, solidarity, boldness, dignity, outspokenness, just to mention but a few. The Igbo man has suffered so much in Nigeria because of this defeat. But we should know that defeat in a war does not remove from someone or from a nation the sense of the essence of living. It does not delete someone's name for which he or she is known; it does not destroy his or her spirituality; neither does it change completely his or her character or identity for which he or she is known.

But we ought to know that every war leaves its scars, deep psychological wounds, trauma, more so, when it does not overtly end in one's advantage. It induces some sense of despair and hopelessness, apathy and indifference, some defeatism and inaction. The Igbo fought a war of attrition and survival in which they not only faced the Nigerian federal might but also the conspiracy and might of the British colonial masters and the unusual cooperation of the two superpowers at the time, Soviet Union and the United States, and of course the Arab-Muslim connections. One can then imagine the hardship, suffering and horror which the Igbo man went through in that war as we have already narrated.

The war ended since 1970, but it left marks on the Igbo psyche and vision. It is true that it did nothing to the Igbo drive, hard work, enterprise, resilience, dynamism, versatility and will-to-be, yet it took a toll on her collective psyche, and her self-perception within the Nigerian polity, which have had disastrous political consequences for the Igbo man and Igbo nation.[599] When we talk of spirituality here, we refer to Igbo Traditional Religion and the flourish of this religion in Igboland. When the Nigerian civil war ended in 1970, evidence before us showed that the number of Igbo traditional religionists and the popularity of this religion have declined.

As we have mentioned earlier in this work, the war period became a litmus test for the activeness and efficacy of the minor deities in various towns of Igboland. During the war, many Igbo traditional religionists as well as the non-Igbo traditional religionists concluded that some of these minor deities (*alusi*) were neither active nor efficacious. Therefore, after the war many of the worshippers of these minor deities (*alusi*) were converted to Christianity, the shrines of some of the minor deities (*alusi*) were destroyed in some towns and villages and the worship and offerings to them stopped.

As we have earlier indicated, in Igbo Traditional Religion, we do not have those who spread the teachings of this religion. In other words, we do not have those who preach the tenets and teachings of this religion. One might ask how the existence of such a religion can be guaranteed in future, when the worshippers are not canvassing for new members. Before the civil war started, after the civil war and up till today, Christianity showed and continues to show love and charity to the Igbo people and Nigerians in general. Christianity preaches love and translates her preaching into actions. During the war, she cared for the sick and the wounded and gave them medications and nursing through the Red Cross Organization; the hungry and the naked were fed and clothed through the help of Caritas Organizations and other aid groups.

The Church made efforts to resolve the Nigeria-Biafra conflict and to prevent the war from prolonging. A lot of Igbo traditional religionists were converted to Christianity after the war. This is because it was Christianity that showed them love and care during the war crisis. In other words, Igbo Traditional Religion lost a lot of its members after the war. After the war, the missionaries who were working in Igboland were expelled and told to go back to their homeland.

---

[599] Arinze F., *The Baton of Faith,* op. cit., p. 56.

This meant that the indigenous priests had to carry the burden of the work of evangelization alone in Igboland and beyond. Francis Arinze, the then Archbishop of Onitsha (now Francis Cardinal Arinze) recalls the experience thus:

> The local priests presumed that the Irish missionaries who had faithfully remained in Biafra would be respected by the Nigerian troops and that, if anything, it was they (the local ones) who needed protection. The contrary turned to be the case. Most Irish priests working in the Archdiocese of Onitsha (not many left the country at this stage at the end of the war) gathered at Nnokwa. When they went to see the Nigerian military officers, they were given a rough reception. On 29th January 1970, some world radio stations announced that Irish missionaries in the former Biafra were rounded up and brought to Port Harcourt and thence to Lagos. Eventually they were tried and sentenced to six to twelve months' imprisonment with probable expulsion. It was a painful time for the Church in all the dioceses of former Biafra.[600]

The accusations levelled on the missionaries by the Federal Government of Nigeria under the leadership of Gowon were that:

> They insulted the sovereignty of Nigeria. They brought food inside the country without passing through Lagos. They preached for Ojukwu…. Let them go said Gowon. Go and run the Church with your own Nigerian priests.[601]

We have to note that the Church dissociated herself from the politics of the conflict of the civil war in Nigeria. But it initiated one of the most heroic relief operations to help the population that was dying by hundreds of thousands from starvation and diseases. In the critical phase of the war, many relief flights were flown by night to the local airport of Biafra at "Uli" which was the only Biafra's gateway to the outside world. But the Nigeria government under the leadership of Gowon interpreted the charity rendered by the Church differently. Baur states that after the Nigeria-Biafra war:

> The missionaries, mostly Catholic priests and sisters, were accused of having prolonged the war through their charitable help; they had to stand before a war tribunal; were fined and deported.[602]

Two major developments have characterized the Church in Nigeria since the end of the civil war, namely, the nationalization of schools and the vocations explosion. They affected more or less all Churches, but more visibly the Catho-

---

[600] Arinze F., *The Baton of Faith*, op. cit., pp. 67 - 68.
[601] Ibid., pp. 69 - 70.
[602] Baur J., *2000 Years of Christianity in Africa: An African Church History, 2nd Revised Edition*, Paulines Publications Africa, Nairobi, Kenya, 1998, p. 271.

lic Church and more evidently the Igbo Church.[603] Immediately after the civil war in Nigeria, when the Government took over schools in the former East Central State, the Catholic Church has continued to demand that schools be returned to their original owners. "Since then, also religious teaching has been relegated to the background in most schools. It was the view of most lovers of peace, progress and well-being of the Nigerian society that much of the indiscipline and moral decadence of the society result from the lack of necessary religious education in the schools."[604] One can see that the Nigeria-Biafra war ended in 1970 but there has been since then, a cold war being carried out against the Igbo. Arinze, narrating how the indigenous priests made a lot of sacrifices when the missionaries left, states:

> When the Irish missionaries were sent away, Onitsha had about 32 local priests and 3 of them were overseas. The total of missionary priests in 1967 was about 50. One can imagine how 32 priests, most of them rather young, were to cover what 80 priests did in 1967. Some local priests were put in charge of three parishes. One of the very energetic priests of the Archdiocese fainted after the gospel one Sunday because of over work. Another had to be brought to hospital after three Masses on a row.[605]

When the missionaries left Igboland, preaching of vocations to the priesthood was seen as a big challenge and ought to be intensified. For the work of evangelization to progress in Igboland, more priests were needed. Therefore, the preaching of vocations to the Catholic priesthood was carried to Catholics and Non-Catholics alike. Some Igbo traditional religionists were converted to Christianity. Some later became Catholic priests and some became Anglican pastors. These priests and pastors later converted some members of their families. In some cases, all the members of the priests' and pastors' families who were formally Igbo traditional religionists were converted to Christianity. The civil war dealt a heavy blow on Igbo Traditional Religion. The vocation explosion to the Catholic priesthood and religious life some years after the war can be attributed as a truly positive consequence of the civil war. Baur emphasizes that:

> Calamities have always fostered a religious outlook, but this war did something more: It banished all the missionary personnel, thus bringing about a situation that called for dedication on a Church that was now totally "ours".[606]

---

[603] Ibid.

[604] Nwosu V.A., ed., *The Catholic Church in Onitsha: People, Places and Events, 1885 - 1985*, Etukokwu press Ltd., Onitsha Nigeria, 1985, p. 284.

[605] Arinze F., *The Baton of Faith*, op. cit., pp. 75 -76.

[606] Baur J., *2000 Years of Christianity in Africa*, op. cit., p. 272.

The war experience and the constant and consistent threats and harassment to which the Igbo are exposed everywhere in Nigeria today have created in the Igbo psyche an emergency mentality. This perhaps explains one of the Igbo tendencies towards pragmatism and short-term results, which have promoted the politics of expediency among the Igbo. This has led the Igbo to the person-alized survival strategies, which at times affect negatively the overall interest of the Igbo, for the individual does not recognize anybody outside his chain of survival. Perhaps, it was Momoh who graphically captured this war-induced personalized survivalist attitude of the Igbo, when he said:

> The trauma of the civil war would have led many to insanity. But the Igbo people came into Nigeria after the war with a bang. They started from below and climbed out of the pit of utter despair… but something seemed to have been retained – memories of a war that saw the stark reality between saving your life and dying in saving the life of another. Self-preservation is built into the psyche of man and you cannot blame our brothers across the Niger for choosing themselves before others. They took their belongings alone with them as the pressure of the war increased. The time came to choose to lose the property or die with the property. They chose life and led their way out of harm's way with their wives and children and relatives. Then another time came when they had to choose between their own safety and the collective death of their families. They scattered each for himself…. Children, husbands and wives went in different directions. Families were totally dispersed…. If nothing else this self-preservation and the belief in self before any other has remained with our brothers across the Niger.[607]

Although the Nigeria-Biafra war induced personalized survival attitude in the Igbo, yet the Igbo witnessed a lot of heroic and altruistic actions and sacrifices of individuals and groups in Igboland. Perhaps, the greatest mistake which the Igbo had made since the end of the war was their failure to rehabilitate the Igbo psyche, to develop series of psychological and moral measures to reen-force the Igbo self-esteem, Igbo-affirmation, and Igbo consciousness, to reori-entate the Igbo from merely personalized survival strategy to include the Igbo survival as a group. Some countries or groups in history, who had suffered similar fate as the Igbo like the Jews, came out more united and more resolved to fight against future threats to their people.[608]

---

[607] Cf., Momoh T., *"Threat to Igbo Solidarity"*, *Vanguard 16th Feb., 2003*, p. 9, in Uwalaka J., *The Struggle for an Inclusive Nigeria: Igbos to be or not to be?* op. cit., pp. 68 - 69.
[608] Uwalaka J., The Struggle for an Inclusive Nigeria: Igbos to be or not to be? op. cit., p. 69.

4.2.1. ECONOMIC IMPACT

The war ended in January 1970 and left the Igbo and other Easterners within the 'Biafran' enclave, poor and dejected. A people who spent their treasures building up other people suddenly found themselves paupers without help; former landlords now found themselves without roof, despite the fact that the goal of the war which was survival could with some level of conviction be said to have been achieved. For at the end of it both belligerents saw war and were happy that it ended.

The war ended since 1970, but none of the promises made by Gowon have been realized in any appreciable or recognizable way. Rather the Igbo man in particular have been made to feel vanquished all these whiles. Even though physically the war did end, yet there appeared to have been more insidious, more perfidious, more destructive and dangerous 'war' against the Igbo, which has been classically called 'the Igbo question' in Nigeria. This is a 'war' against the people's psyche, against the people's self-consciousness, a war against the people's economic welfare, symbolized in the now widely used word marginalization. This consists in the official and calculated attempts by the powers that be to keep the Igbo poor, and deprived; keep them permanently and psychologically defeated; keep them subservient doing the masters bidding; keep them divided in order to manipulate them.[609] This war by other means which is going on today in Nigeria with the code name marginalization is total, economic, bureaucratic, political and structural. The marginalization of the Igbo predicament in Nigeria today was condemned by Dim Chukwuemeka Odumegwu Ojukwu, leader of the defunct Biafra. He lamented thus:

> The Igbos in Nigeria are not seen as a people. The Igbos are seen by other Nigerians as targets. All problems and darts are aimed at them. Deliberate policies are promulgated to subjugate and subdue the Igbo man. Look at the indigenization and nationalization program. The Igbos were a target group. The program was carried out at a time Igbos were just emerging from the throes of civil war. With only 20 pounds (N40) per adult did Igbos stand any chance to pick stocks in companies being indigenized? [610]

It has been on record that when Yoruba misunderstand themselves in the streets of "Idumota" and "Balogun" in Nigeria, Igbo are killed and Igbo shops are looted. When Hausa have a problem in Kano, Igbo die. When Hausa and Yoruba quarrel among themselves Igbo are killed. One can simply conclude that the Igbo are being treated this way because they were defeated in the Nigeria-Biafra war. One can really say that there is then the deliberate struc-

---

[609] Uwalaka J., *The Struggle for an Inclusive Nigeria: Igbos to be or not be?* op. cit., pp. 19 - 20.
[610] Cf., Sunday Vanguard Newspaper, Nigeria, Jan. 21st 2000, in Ibid., pp. 21 - 22.

tural imbalance devised to destabilize the Igbo, which was started by Gowon, who hurriedly split Nigeria into 12 states to break the bone of resistance in the East, and had since been imitated by other military governments, which sought credibility.

At the end of the frenzy of balkanization in 1996, Nigeria had 36 states most of which are liabilities to themselves and burden to the nation. Right from the beginning, the immediate post-first republic states creation was designed to impede the Igbo and limit their potentials. The 1966 exercise gave them one state, the East Central State, while the old North was split into six states and the old West was broken into Lagos and Western states. The minorities in the old East earned two states. The Igbo outside East Central State only found themselves as minorities in Mid-Western and Rivers, South-Eastern and Benue-Plateau states. Today, the mainland Igbo are chiseled in five states, while the Yoruba and Hausa/Fulani have seven and nineteen states muscles. In the disbursement of national resources, the Igbo shares pale to insignificance in comparison with the old West and the old North. This accounts for why the old Hausa-Fulani can produce over 30 appointees if taken two per states, the Yoruba about 18 appointees while the Igbo from heartland (South East) can only produce a maximum of 10 appointees. By the local distribution, the South-East has mere 95 local council areas as against 137 of the South West, 123 of the South-South, 112 form the North-East, 121 for the North-Central, and 186 for the North-West.[611]

The no victor and no vanquished declaration was only an expression that was never taken seriously. All actions and treatments towards the Igbo people show that they are being handled by Nigeria as those who were defeated in the battle field and have no rights to certain things in Nigeria. We shall explain this further when we discuss the political effect of the civil war on the Igbo. But suffice it to say that the hatred directed to the Igbo man by other Nigerians increased after the war. While Igbo were nursing the injuries of the war, there was every plan to hinder their progress economically and otherwise. Achebe asserts that:

> There were hardliners in Gowon's cabinet who wanted their pound of flesh, the most powerful among them being Chief Obafemi Awolowo, Federal Commissioner for Finance. Under his guidance a banking policy was evolved which nullified any bank account which had been operated during the civil

---

[611] Nnamani C., For Ndigbo let the future begin now, Address at the Odenigbo Forum Held in Eko Meridian Lagos, 17th March, 2001. Cf., Daily Champion Newspaper, March 6th Nigeria, 2001, p. 6 in Uwalaka J., *The Struggle for an Inclusive Nigeria: Igbos to be or not to be?* op. cit., p. 22.

war. This had the immediate result of pauperizing the Igbo middle class and earning a profit of 4 million pounds for the Federal Government Treasury.[612]

This action by the Federal Finance Ministry of Nigeria made every Igbo man to receive only 20 pounds, irrespective of any amount he might have had in the bank before the war started in 1967. But this particular financial action was never extended to other Nigerians who were not Igbo. This is why this action was seen by the Igbo as not being justified. It was rather seen as part of the punishment imposed on them because of the war they fought against Nigeria.

Again, the Indigenization Decree which followed soon afterwards completed the routing of the Igbo from the commanding heights of the Nigeria economy to everyone's apparent satisfaction. For any nation to grow economically, socially, politically and otherwise, she ought to carry all her citizens along this path of progress. This means that there ought to be an existing evidence of unity which has to be felt by all. When unity does not exist among the citizens of a country, what we would expect is imbalance in economic growth, social, political, cultural growths as well as imbalance in revenue allocations.

Actually, this unity that ought to exist, was well expressed in the Nigerian Anthem after independence, which among other things, said: 'though tribe and tongue may differ, in brotherhood, we stand.' Another stanza has it 'our flag shall be a symbol, where truth and justice reign'. These, for one, define the grand idea called Nigeria, and the country, which the founding fathers wanted to establish, a country founded on common brotherhood, truth and justice.[613] The early Igbo positive disposition in the construction of this Nigerian project contrasted sharply with the attitude of the leaders of the other two major tribes, the Hausa and Yoruba. Their utterances, which we have somehow mentioned earlier, betrayed this disposition. For example, in 1947, Sir Abubaka Tafawa Belewa (later to become the first Nigerian Prime Minister) said: "Since the Amalgamation of the Southern and Northern provinces in 1914 Nigeria has existed as one country on paper...."[614]

It is on record that similar comment like the one quoted above was made by Ahmadu Bello, the Sarduana of Sokoto (later to become the first Nigerian Premier of the Northern Region). He said:

---

[612] Achebe C., *The trouble with Nigeria*, Heinemann, England and Wales, 1983, op. cit., pp. 45 - 46.
[613] Uwalaka J., *The Struggle for an Inclusive Nigeria: Igbos to be or not to be?* op. cit., p. 49 - 50.
[614] Ibid., p. 50.

> Nigeria is so large and the people so varied that no person with any real intellectual integrity would be so foolish as to pretend that he speaks for the country as a whole.[615]

Other famous men in Nigeria made similar comments. For example, Awolowo, the post independent Yoruba political leader was quoted to have said that: "Nigeria is a mere geographical expression".[616] Even Gowon, who led the war against Biafra, in August 1966, said that "there is no basis for unity."[617] We have cited these statements to demonstrate the skepticism and veiled unacceptability of the unity of Nigeria by some Nigerian leaders.

Unfortunately, it appears that it is this legacy of skepticism, divisiveness, tribalism, nepotism and religious and ethnic bigotry that has endured, and for all intents and purposes, Nigeria has remained a political space, with no true national identity, no national consciousness, no national commitment and no true national loyalty. Even up till today, people are still posing the national question: to belong to Nigeria or not to belong? If to belong on what ground? How to renegotiate the corporate existence of Nigeria? Ojukwu who was one of the advocates of Nigerian unity asserts that:

> If we believe in unity, as I most certainly do, then we must accept that our survival can only be through unity, that without unity we shall perish. Then we must be prepared to approach the issue of unity and national solidarity realistically, selflessly, fearlessly and with a singularity of purposes. We must overcome old prejudices and entrenched interests and banish from every Nigeria, the atmosphere of insecurity. Whilst on this point I would add – a peaceful atmosphere under which combatants on both side of the civil war dead or alive are reconciled.[618]

If Nigerians really believe in the unity of Nigeria and want that unity to exist, they must be prepared to abolish ethnic ghettos in some of the cities which we have earlier mentioned in this work. Government must conscientiously set about to diffuse ethnicity in the body politic of Nigeria, blur those imaginary boundaries that separate citizen from citizen; encourage all Nigerians to feel at home anywhere in Nigeria; banish every action of authority that could be termed arbitrary as it undermines peoples' confidence in the institutions; devise laws, enter them into Nigeria statute books: laws whose purpose is to enhance unity and to protect and secure the unity acquired; de-emphasize ethnicity, where it is not possible, confine it to the realms of ceremony, cultur-

---

[615] Ibid.
[616] Ibid.
[617] Ibid.
[618] Ojukwu E., *Because I am Involved,* op. cit., p. 24.

al displays and sports, and discover new ways of avoiding the glaring injustice of the quota system. These are only few actions Nigeria needs to take if she truly believes in unity. In summary "there is no better way to unity than endeavors jointly undertaken and achievements jointly won."[619]

It is because of this lack of unity that exists in Nigeria and the hatred shown to the Igbo that led to the creation of economic hardship for the Igbo immediately after the war. Immediately after the civil war, some of the Igbo people who had lands and property in other parts of Nigeria, places like Northern Nigeria, Lagos and Port-Harcourt lost them. They were confiscated by the indigenes of those places; in spite of this, some still claim that there is unity and that Nigeria belongs to all. Ojukwu said:

> I will not comment on the absurdity of the situation in which a Nigerian citizen, whilst seeking to recover his property, within Nigeria, is considered to have abandoned it. Let it suffice merely to say that such a situation can only remain a constant strain on Nigeria critical national equilibrium and most certainly cannot enhance unity.[620]

Many Igbo who had businesses in Northern and Western parts of Nigeria lost them after the civil war. Many did not return to the locations of their businesses after the war because of the ugly experiences they had in those places immediately before the war started. It was impossible for many who were living in those places, when the war was about to begin, to carry their goods and personal belongings with them while leaving those places down to the East. Many practically lost everything they had for their livelihood.

After the civil war, almost all the Igbo who were civil servants lost their positions in Nigerian civil service to the Northerners and the Westerner. While they were most qualified for those positions, the Igbo were never recalled to their former positions in civil service after the civil war. They were replaced with the Hausa and the Yoruba. This takeover of the Igbo's positions in the civil service by others, in spite of Gowon's declaration of 'no victor, no vanquished' at the end of the war in 1970, was seen by many Igbo as an increasing hatred towards them by other Nigerians. They see it as an existence of cold war after the civil war has ended. To give us a mental picture why the Igbo were treated and are being treated this way, Isichei explains that:

> The hatred of the Igbo is centered mostly on their entrepreneurship, instead of being a virtue to be emulated by other tribes has become nightmare to other Nigerians who prefer to fan the embers of tribalism rather than engage

---

[619] Ibid., p. 22.
[620] Ibid., p. 23.

them in a healthy competition. Different tribes have different reasons for hating the Igbo. The Igbo are hated because they brought European goods into the market. They controlled the transportation system and maintained trade link between the other parts of the country; they were the middlemen…. An Idoma abhorred the Igbo because the Igbo man was the headmaster of the primary school. He was the teacher, he was the railway station master, he was the post master etc. The feelings of a lot of people about the Igbo in Idoma before the civil war were that they were the controllers of trade, administration, the school system etc. Before the crisis and the civil war, some of the Igbo traders in Idoma were buying their farm products from the farmers directly in their farms. Some of them would buy a whole plantation of corn or yams when the crop was still growing. They would pay the farmers very little for that.[621] Isichei in explaining the business acumen of the Igbo says that:

When Tsar Market was developing at this time, the Tiv welcomed Hausa traders but insisted on the exclusion of the Igbo. But Hausa themselves came to demand the admission of Igbo traders: Now they remembered that no large Nigerian market could (at that time) be fully effective without an Igbo contingent. (This is also evident in Nigeria today). Igbo had access to certain types of trade goods – especially European cloths and hardware – which were available only at much greater expense from other peoples. Igbo were also good carpenters and blacksmiths. Finally, there was the vast kinship-like network of Igbo between the trading outpost (such as Obudu), and the large market – centers (such as Onitsha). If a market is to be fully successful the Hausa said, it must have Igbo. The Tiv, however stood adamant: No Igbo…. The Tiv finally did allow Igbo to come to market.[622]

However, the Igbo maintain that they are not in business to exclude others from participating. It is through a healthy competition that economy thrived maximally. It is through a healthy competition that monopolies are broken and the prices of goods and services made affordable to everybody. It is through a healthy competition, that the natural and human resources are utilized optimally for the benefit of everybody. It is certainly not beneficial for people who do nothing but watch Igbo toil from morning till evening, to plan and devise methods within their idle time on ways of destroying the efforts of the toil. The arson designed against the Igbo also set back the economy of the Nation many years backwards. "It is therefore important for Nigerians to think positively towards accommodating healthy competition than designing methods of de-

---

[621] Isichei E., *History of West Africa since 1800*, op. cit., pp. 209 - 210, in Obiezuofu-Ezeigbo C.E., op. cit., p. 230.
[622] Ibid., p. 233.

stroying the foundation of healthy economic growth and turn around to blame government of the day as incompetent and inefficient".[623]

4.2.2. THE SOCIAL IMPACT

This Social impact of the civil war is not only experienced by the Igbo but also by other Nigerians. We are going to look at this from two dimensions: How the Igbo people related and interacted with other Nigerians before the civil war and after the civil war.

4.2.3. IGBO SOCIAL LIFE IN NIGERIA BEFORE AND AFTE THE CIVIL WAR

Following the introduction of Christianity in 1841; western education in 1858; western culture and British colonialism into Igboland in 1902; a new Igbo society that was ready and eager to interact more with other ethnic groups, religions and other cultures emerged. The Igbo society is still in evolution because aspects of tradition and modernity still contend and co-exist. Its social, political, economic and religious arrangements arguably stand somewhere between the old and the new.[624] Traditionally, Igbo communities lived in dispersed settlements. Family compound consisted of a collection of clay-walled and thatch-roofed houses, often fenced in with a wall. A number of such closely clustered compounds formed the village and several villages constituted the village-group or town. Most traditional towns were not large and had only several thousands of inhabitants each. "In 1890, the population of Igboland was estimated at 3 million."[625]

Besides modern improvement in physical structures like houses, roads, streets, electricity, etc., the Igbo village is easily recognizable. Impact of westernization is pronounced in the new building architecture, house furniture and home facilities. Improvement unions which date back to the 1930s and 1940s have given great boost to Igbo towns many of which now exhibit modernized structures and institutions like markets, schools, colleges, health centers, hospital, churches and post offices, pipe-borne water and electricity installations, cottage industries, and town halls. Cities have become integral components of Igbo society. They are largely influence of the colonial rule. As new administrative centers emerged, the tendency was for the accompanying colonial institutions (merchant house, daily markets, schools, missionary residences, etc.) to be converged at such centers. It was only a question of time before rural – urban migrations set in.

---

[623] Obiezuofu-Ezeigbo C.E., *The Biafran War and the Igbo in contemporary Nigerian politics*, op. cit., p. 233.
[624] Ozigbo I.R.A., *A History of Igboland in the 20th century*, op. cit., p. 116.
[625] Ibid., p. 116.

Before the Nigerian civil war, Igbo-Hausa-Yoruba relationship, integration and interaction of one another were not as bad as it became immediately after the war and today. The settler-indigene dichotomy has grown in recent years and it threatens the peace and stability of the nation. For example, the Jos crisis and other ethnic and religious crisis in Nigeria have caused many deaths. Okonkwo would argue that:

> The settler-indigene dichotomy can be resolved only when we remove the distinctions between indigene and non-indigene practiced throughout the country. The Nigerian constitution guarantees freedom of movement and out-laws discrimination based on ethnic group or state of origin.[626]

At this juncture, it would be pertinent to recall that some of the Igbo statesmen and personalities who played major roles in Nigeria politics and in Igbo leadership, were born in northern Nigeria. Some grew up there and equally had their early education there. For example, Dr. Nnamdi Azikiwe,[627] the first president of Nigeria, was born in Zungeru in northern Nigeria in 1904. He attended his early education at Onitsha, Lagos and Calabar before proceeding to the United States of America for his further education. This means that he

---

[626] Okonkwo R., *National Integration of Nigeria: The indigene issues, in Nigeria peoples and Cultures* edited by Eze-Uzoamaka P., op. cit., p. 316.

[627] Dr. Namdi Azikiwa former President of the Federal Republic of Nigeria, was born on 16th November 1904 at *Zungeru*, Northern Nigeria, of Igbo parents from Onitsha in Eastern Nigeria. After primary and secondary education in Nigeria, he studied history and political science in the United States. Returning to Africa in 1934, he spent three years as editor of the African Morning Post in Accra (Ghana). He settled in Lagos in 1937 and established a chain of newspapers, the most notable among which was the West African Pilot.

He entered politics and was a foundation member of the N.C.N.C. (National Council for Nigeria Citizens) of which he was first secretary-general, becoming its president in 1946. After holding various political and ministerial appointments, he became the first premier of Eastern Nigeria in 1954. First president of the national senate, he became at independence in 1960 Governor-General and Commander-in-Chief of the Federation of Nigeria. Following further constitutional change, he became president of the new Republic of Nigeria in 1963, a post he held till the military coup in January 1966.

In the confusion and insecurity which followed the coups and massacres of the Igbo in 1966, Dr. Azikiwe fled to his hometown in Eastern Nigeria where he was overtaken by the secession of Biafra. Never an enthusiast of secession, he served reluctantly in an undefined capacity on a number of missions abroad for the Biafran regime. Breaking with Ojukwu on the question of a negotiated settlement, he went into voluntary exile in London in September 1968. A year later, he came out openly for a peaceful settlement on the basis of a united Nigeria.

Blending academics with politics, Dr. Azikiwe is a very learned man who has published many books on African history and politics. He is the founder of the University of Nigeria at Nsukka, Eastern Nigeria. Popularly known as Zik of Africa, Azikiwe's career from the start has been marked by strong Pan-African flavor. It is perhaps this continental vision, more than anything else that ultimately decided his adherence to the principle of preserving one Nigeria. Cf., Uwechue R., *Reflections on the Nigerian Civil War: Facing the Future,* op. cit., pp. 194 - 195.

went through many cultures and lifestyles both in Nigeria and abroad. Emeka Odumegwu Ojukwu, the then Governor of Eastern Nigeria and the leader of Biafra during the war, was also born in Zungeru in northern Nigeria, in 1933. He had his early education in Lagos, the former capital of Nigeria. Patrick Chukwuma Kaduna Nzeogwu, one of the key plotters of the 1966 coup in Nigeria, was born in Kaduna in northern Nigeria. He attended his early education in Kaduna. Nzeogwu could be said to be more of Northerner than Easterner, because he was born in northern Nigeria, had his early education there and spent almost his life in the North. It is also on record that Nzeogwu conducted the coup of 1966 in Nigeria, almost entirely "with soldiers of Northern Nigeria origin. His medical attendants, driver, escorts and guards were all Northern soldiers and he only ate meals prepared by his Northern batman."[628]

This could be an indication that Nzeogwu trusted the northerners more and was at home in their midst more than he was in the midst of others. He was more of a Northerner, spoke Hausa better than Igbo, wore Hausa outfits more than Igbo outfits and his second name 'Kaduna' bore witness to the above assertions. In fact, he was more of Hausa than Igbo. From the birth background of the Igbo personalities given above, it indicates that their parents most probably had lived in those places these personalities were born. That was when the relationship of Igbo-Hausa-Yoruba had not degenerated, that is, before the civil war in Nigeria. The situation changed after the civil war. The relationship has gone sour. But in spite of this change of attitude, many Igbo are still living in Northern and Western Nigeria.

The evolution of the Nigeria state from colonial days to the present seems to be in the direction of smaller and smaller units and greater and greater division in it. With the enshrinement of the indigene-non-indigene dichotomy, it would seem Nigeria is moving toward the often warring, small units found in the pre-colonial period. As a modern state, Nigeria has to reverse the trend of dissolving into a failed state of small enclaves of indigenes. In many cases, countries that have experienced civil or external war, do have most often, after the war, increase in crime and violence. That was the situation of Nigeria after the civil war. "Violence is a disease, a disease that corrupts all who use it regardless of the cause."[629] After the end of the civil war in 1970, increase in crime and violence was experienced. Most outstanding of this violence are ethnic, religious and domestic violence.

---

[628] Madiebo A. A., *The Nigerian Revolution and the Biafran War,* op. cit., p. 20.
[629] Hedges C., https://goodreads.com.quotes/tag/violence, accessed 3.11.2017.

Throughout recorded history in West Africa, Nigeria seems to rank top among the list of nation-states that have witnessed the most perturbing and unprecedented upsurge of ethnic and religious disturbances in contemporary times. The situation has actually worsened in the post-war political democratic environment. It has remained a constant threat to peace in Nigeria. The vigour it has assumed in contemporary Nigeria has, therefore, continued to threaten the co-existence and co-habitation of the different ethnic nationalities in Nigeria. Suffice it to say that if positive and urgent measures are not taken to checkmate the rising upsurge in the near future, the much-orchestrated slogan 'unity in diversity' will, no doubt, be at stake. Incidentally, ethnic and religious conflicts and divisions arising from them are intertwining phenomena in contemporary Nigeria.

Ethnic and geographic divisions in Nigeria, translate also into religious differences in most cases. In its simplest form, while the Northern Nigerians are predominantly Hausa-Fulani and Moslems, the Southerners are largely Yoruba/Igbo and Christians. It seems all efforts in the past to check or control these types of conflict through administrative and bureaucratic machineries have failed to yield practical or desired results. Several lives have been lost, others maimed, many others displaced and properties worth billions of naira destroyed in the uprisings caused by ethnic and religious loyalties in the country…. If this is not effectively monitored and controlled in no distant time, the country might sooner or later degenerate into a state of anarchy and total disintegration.[630]

4.2.4. POLITICAL IMPACT

The political system and practice in Nigeria were not built on a good foundation. Ademoyea observes:

> Nigeria's political problems sprang from the carefree manner in which the British took over, administered, and abandoned the government and people of Nigeria. British administrators did not try to weld the country together and unite the heterogeneous groups of people. There was one evil that outlived British administration, namely, political non-advancement. When the British came, they forcibly rubber-stamped the political state of the ethnic groups of Nigeria and maintained that status quo until they left.[631]

---

[630] Cf. Anugwom E. E., and Oji P., *Ethnic and Religious Crises in Nigeria: A review of Past and Present Dimensions, in Religion and Societal Development, Contemporary Nigerian Perspective*, edited by Okwueze M.I., op. cit., pp. 143 -144.
[631] Ademoyega A., *Why We Struck, the Story of the first Nigeria Coup*, op. cit., p. 1.

Few years after the British left, the people of Nigeria resumed fighting for their political rights. It is important to note that the political mind-setting of the people of Northern and Southern Nigeria are not same. This is one thing the British colonialist did not understand and did not take time to study. This led them to make many mistakes when instituting political structure in Nigeria. Example of one of those mistakes is the indirect rule which we have earlier discussed. The indirect rule had serious negative impact in the formation of political structure in Nigeria. From this, we can easily understand why there was fundamental difference between the political aspirations of the leaders of the North and South. In the South, political leadership sprang from the people, that is, from grassroots. These people had been the custodian of their own civic rights before the British came. It was easy and natural for the common people to be active again, when political agitation for national freedom became a popular preoccupation of Nigerians in the 1940s.

In the North, however, the ruling class, made up of the sons and kinsmen of the Emir, took over the political leadership of the people. Unfortunately, they represented their own class interests, rather than the popular will of the masses. This happened because the British governed Nigerian indirectly through the traditional rules. In the South, they governed through the 'Oba', 'Obi' and 'Amanyanabo' who were relatively powerless amongst their peoples. "In the North, they governed through the Emirs whose sons and kinsmen were the Chiefs and Native Authority officials, who lorded it over the people. These emerged as the aristocratic political leaders of the 1940s. As a result, the true leader of the masses was hamstrung and held down."[632]

Up till today, there is no clear and distinct democracy in Northern Nigeria although people pretend there is. This is because the aristocratic political structure and leadership is still in existence. In the South, for example, in Igboland, the story is different. The Igbo people practised democracy before the coming of the Europeans to Igboland without even knowing what type of leadership they were practising. They practised democracy locally before ever it was introduced into Nigerian political system. That was why indirect rule did not function well in Igboland. They saw indirect rule as being in opposition to the local democracy they were practising before the advent of the colonial master.

The Igbo people normally say: "Igbo ama Eze" (The Igbo do not accept the kingship authority or autocratic governance). This implies the application of democratic principles in leadership. When we look carefully at how the political system and ideologies were structured and instituted in Nigeria, one can

---

[632] Ibid., pp. 3 - 4.

see that the colonial master knowingly or unknowingly instituted tribalism in Nigerian political life which continues to exist even up till today. Achebe laments:

> Nothing in Nigeria's political history captures her problem of national integration more graphically than the chequered fortune of the word tribe in her vocabulary. Tribe has been accepted at one time as a friend, rejected as an enemy at another, and finally smuggled in through the back-door as an accomplice.[633]

Affirming the above assertion, Madiebo says:

> The practice of democracy in Nigeria after independence was scuttled by politics of divide and rule, which was foisted on her by Britain. This type of politics resulted in acute hatred and tribalism in the administrative structure of the country. This manifested in election rigging, arson, murder and the coup that toppled that political dispensation.[634]

This tribalism in political structure, injected into the political bloodstream of Nigeria by the colonial master, was dangerously projected and popularized by the military coup of January 1966 (which was interpreted as Igbo coup) and got out of control after the Nigeria-Biafra war. Tribalism has done a lot of damage to Nigerian image, character and politics. During elections, people do not take the character and potentialities of the candidates to be elected into consideration rather their ethnicity. A Nigerian child seeking admission into a federal school, a student wishing to enter a college or university, a graduate seeking employment in the public service, a businessman tendering for a contract, a citizen applying for a passport, filing a report with the police or seeking access to many of the avenues controlled by the state, has to fill out a form which requires him to confess his tribe (or less crudely, and more hypocritically, his state of origin). But the self-conscious wish to banish tribalism in Nigeria has proved largely futile, because a word will stay around as long as there is work for it to do.

The political situation in Nigeria worsened after the civil war. One might have thought it could get better, but it did not. What worsened the situation was the mutual suspicion that existed after the civil war among the major tribes we have in Nigeria. In the First Republic democratic experiment, political parties were formed on ethnic lines. For instance, the Islamic and aristocratic Hausa-Fulani tribes of Northern Nigeria formed the Northern People Congress (NPC)

---

[633] Achebe C., *The Trouble with Nigeria*, op. cit., p. 5.
[634] Obiezuofu-Ezeigbo C.E, *The Biafran War and the Igbo in Contemporary Nigerian Politics,* op. cit., p. 295.

as their political party. In Western Nigeria, the predominantly Christian Yoruba formed the Action Group (AG) until their ranks were infiltrated with promises of power and money, and that succeeded in splitting them into many opposing political groups.

In Eastern Nigeria, where the Igbo people were in the majority, the main political party was the National Convention for Nigerian Citizens (NCNC). Other numerous tribes, some of them, more populous than many independent world nations, were used by major political parties at home and by other interested outside powers for power juggling exercises during the frequent political crises in the country. The Second Republic democratic experiment was also marred by same problems that ruined the First Republic. For instance, there were the Nigerian Peoples Party (NPP) predominantly populated by the Igbo; the Unity Party of Nigeria (UPN), basically a Yoruba party and the National Party of Nigeria (NPN), inclined towards the North. However, NPN was like the defunct NCNC because of its quasi-national spread.

There were also People's Redemption Party (PRP) and Great Nigerian People's Party (GNPP). Later, Nigerian Advance party (NAP) was registered to balance the equation of the three parties from the North and three parties from the South. Ironically, the leaders of the defunct parties of the First Republic headed the two major political parties in the South. Dr. Azikiwe, the former leader of NCNC was then a leader of NPP. Chief Obafemi Awolowo, the former leader of the Action Group (AG) was then a leader of UPN; while Shagari, a follower of Sarduana of Sokoto, became the leader of NPN by virtue of being the flag bearer of the party in the presidential election. Mallam Aminu Kano, former leader of (NEPU) Northern Elements Progressive Union, became the leader of PRP. It was indeed a return of the old politicians in a full swing.[635]

4.3. THE LESSONS OF NIGERIA-BIAFRA WAR, NIGERIA NEVER LEARNT FROM

Every Nigerian today, no matter his or her grievance and resentment, knows that physical war is no longer a solution to the problems in Nigerian, unless the unimaginable happens. Nigerians, in spite of their actions to the contrary, have known that there is no good war. Atofarati asserts that:

> The Nigerian civil war, unlike other wars across international boundaries, was a war of unification, a war of reintegration. The human aspect was paramount. It was a contradiction and complication not easy to resolve how to fight causing only limited destruction, how to inflict wounds and heal at the same time, how to subdue without fatal and permanent injuries, how to feed

[635] Obiezuofu-Ezeigbo C.E., *The Biafran War and the Igbo in Contemporary Nigerian Politics*, op. cit. p. 295.

and house civilian population without exposing troops to danger and risk of saboteurs and infiltrators, how to achieve surrender without inflicting permanent or lasting psychological humiliation.[636]

The question is: Have unification and reintegration, which Atofarati said the war was meant to bring, been achieved today? What worries majority of Nigerians today is that their leaders, past and present, after the civil war, have failed to live up to expectations. From the look of things, the leaders have not learnt any lessons from the civil war. In 2014, Nigeria was 100 years, old, after it was assembled by Britain in 1914 with the amalgamation of the South and North. Counting from the year 1960 when Nigeria got her independence from Britain, the country is already more than 50 years old. After all these years, it is surprising that Nigeria has made very little progress in the field of life, political, economic, cultural, social or educational compared to other countries of the world.

After more than 50 years of political independence, Nigeria cannot boast of the basic facilities, such as reliable electricity and good network of roads. These are things that are taken for granted in countries that one cannot compare with Nigeria in terms of wealth generation. Hence, Ezeani questions:

> What is wrong with Nigeria? Why is the country which takes the glory of being the giant of Africa unable to run even an airline with a single aircraft? Why can Nigeria not perform after it has killed Biafra it wanted the world to believe was the major obstacle hampering its progress? Why was the war-time Biafra better than the peace-time Nigeria in terms of national achievements, technological advancement and social cohesion?[637]

It is quite obvious that there are positive lessons to be learnt from the civil war. But why is it that the previous and the present leaders of Nigeria have refused to learn from these lessons.

> Nigeria is endowed with enormous human and material resources, and jet it is economically under developing and technologically crippled, why? Why has Nigeria not learnt from the Biafra experience?[638]

The answers to the above questions are not far-fetched. The Nigeria ruling elite is composed of many who lack vision and mission and do not truly believe in one Nigeria that is genuine. For this reason, they cannot distinguish between meritocracy and mediocrity, and so it does not matter who is in control provided the person is from a particular ethnic group. Sadly, though they cannot

---

[636] Atofarati A., africamasterweb.com/Biafranwar-causes.html, accessed 9.11.2017.
[637] Ezeani E., *In Biafra Africa Died., The Diplomatic Plot,* op. cit., pp. 185 - 186.
[638] Ibid., p. 186.

perform and move the country forward, they cannot allow any other person or persons who can perform to take charge of piloting the state's ship. Consequently, much of the country's human potential is constantly wasted.

It is hard to believe that Biafra, during the war that lasted for 30 months, was able to achieve, under the condition of war, what Nigeria could not achieve over the period of 56 years and up till today. Ojukwu explained how Biafra was able to feed her citizens to a greater extent, in spite of the physical and economic blockades fashioned and mounted by the Nigerian government. Ojkukwu said:

> I have therein described in some detail how the authorities responded to problems of food shortages by establishing a land army and cultivating practically every path of ground, industrialized the salt brines and clay deposits, replaced animal protein, which was in short supply, with hitherto untried vegetable protein which was abundant, created and managed a currency and monetary system through the central Bank of Biafra, and totally mobilized the population towards the war effort by an inimitable propaganda machine.[639]

Nigeria cannot boast of feeding her citizens today. She relies heavily on importation of goods and food items from abroad in order to achieve that. Ojukwu also narrated how Biafra was able to develop technologically during the war under duress, without any support from abroad. He says:

> I had also recounted the achievements of the Directorate of Research and Production (RAP) under the most severe difficulties, including frequent relocation, they produced, perhaps crude, but effectively usable military equipment and supplies (tanks, rockets, mortars, anti-aircraft guns, Ogbunigwe, land mines and anti-tank weapons) from purely locally found materials. They fabricated agricultural implements and tools, durable consumer goods including spares and equipment, communications and telephone systems (radio stations on wheels), they engineered and built under stress the Uli airport which was during the civil war period, the busiest airport in black Africa, next to Johannesburg in the number of aircraft handled, yet operated only between the hours of 10pm and 4am. They ensured a steady flow of water and electricity to the towns and rural areas that became temporarily the base of military operations. They created petroleum refining capacity everywhere so that Biafra had the most widely diffused petroleum refining technology in black Africa.[640]

Nigeria cannot today boast of steady power supply. It would be an understatement to say 'steady' power supply. What one would rather say is: 'Monthly or weekly power supply'. We cannot talk of water supply today in Nigeria

---

[639] Ojukwu E.O., *Because I am Involved*, op. cit., pp 65 - 66.
[640] Ibid., p. 66.

because that is a thing of the past. If Biafra was able to refine fuel during the war, why not Nigeria today? It is a shame that a country that has crude oil as one of her natural resources cannot refine it; rather it has to be sent abroad and refined and brought back to be sold at a higher price. All the above-mentioned achievements of Biafra are still lacking in Nigeria today. This is because Nigeria refuses to make use of Biafran personnel after the war and has blocked her mind from learning from the experiences of the civil war. Ojukwu was of the opinion that:

> Whatever was achieved in the area east of the Niger in those days can be duplicated if not battered anywhere in Nigeria under like conditions. Unfortunately, the tragedy of war was compounded by another of an almost equal dimension when – the post war 3Rs pronounced by the victor became the 3Ds experienced by the vanquished – demobilization, dismantling and devitalization. In carrying out this short-sighted policy, Nigeria lost an opportunity of developing the so much needed indigenous technology.[641]

Nigeria today cannot manage an airline. But Biafra built her airport by herself during the war. That airport became the second busiest airport in Africa. Today, Nigeria employs foreign contractors to build her roads, her airports, manage them and maintain them for her.

4.4. THE MASS KILLING OF THE IGBO: GENOCIDAL OR NOT?

Was there a genocide in Biafra or not? We have many comments as regards this question. But we have to understand what "genocide" means before we can say there was a genocide or not against the Igbo during the Nigeria-Biafra war.

4.4.1. THE ETYMOLOGY AND THE MEANING OF THE WORD "GENOCIDE"

In 1944, a polish-Jewish lawyer named Raphael Lemkin (1900 – 1959) sought to describe Nazi policies of systematic killing, including the destruction of European Jews. He formed the word 'genocide' by combining "genos"- from the Greek word for race or tribe, with – "*cide*", from the Latin word for 'killing'. In proposing this new word, Lemkin had in mind 'a coordinated plan of different actions aiming at the destruction of essential foundations of the life of national groups, with the aim of annihilating the groups themselves.[642] Genocide is thus defined as:

> Any of the following actions committed with intention to destroy a national, ethnic, racial or religious group: killing members of the group: causing serious

---

[641] Ibid., pp. 66 - 67.
[642] ushmm.org/w/c/en/article.php? accessed 15.11.2017.

bodily or mental harm to members of the group; deliberately inflicting on the group conditions of life calculated to bring about its physical destruction in whole or in part; imposing measures intended to prevent births within the group, or forcibly transferring children of the group to another group.[643]

In 1946, the United Nations' General Assembly adopted a resolution that 'affirmed' that genocide was a crime under international law but did not provide a legal definition of the crime. Two years later, the UN General Assembly adopted the Convention on the Prevention and Punishment of the Crime of Genocide which legally defined the crime of genocide for the first time. Though the term 'genocide' was not coined until 1944, acts of genocide have been committed throughout history. In ancient times, it was common practice for victors in war to slaughter enemies they conquered.[644]

There are certain incidents which occurred during the Nigeria-Biafra war from which one can verify whether or not genocide against the Igbo was carried out by Nigeria. Let us show some of those incidents. It was on record that during one of the incidents of Igbo massacre by Nigeria, Adekunle said:

> I want to see no Red Cross, no Caritas, no World Council of Churches, no Pope, no missionary, no UN delegation. I want to prevent even one Ibo from having even one piece to eat before their capitulation. We shoot at everything that moves and when our troops march into the center of Ibo territory, we shoot at everything, even things that do not move.[645]

Bestialities and indignities of all kinds were visited on Biafrans in 1966. In Northern Nigeria, numerous Biafran housewives and nursing mothers were raped before their husbands and children. Young girls were abducted from their homes, working places and schools and forced into sexual intercourse with sick, demented and leprous men. [646]

As we have mentioned earlier in this work, Awolowo, the then Nigerian Minister of Finance, was the person who suggested to the then Nigerian government to use starvation as a weapon of war. He said: "all is fair in war, and starvation is one of the weapons of war. I do not see why we should feed our enemies fat in order for them to fight harder."[647] Richard Nixon, one-time Presi-

---

[643] http://endgenocide.org/learn/what-is-genocide/ accessed 17.11.2017.

[644] history.com/topics/what-is-genocide, accessed 10.11.2017.

[645] Adekunle B., Commander, 3rd Marine Commander Division, Nigeria Army to French Radio Reporter, https://oblongmediadotcom.files.wordpress.com/2017/05/img6845-2.jpg, accessed 15.11.2017.

[646] Mr. Erif Spiff, Eyewitness, 1966, Washington Post editorial, July, 2nd, 1969.

[647] Awolowo O., Nigerian Minister of Finance, July 28th, 1969, https://oblongmediadotcom, accessed 16.11.2017.

dent of the United States of America, lamented when he noticed how the Igbo were massacred. He said:

> Until now efforts to relieve the Biafran People have been thwarted by the desire of the central government to pursue total and unconditional victory and by the fear of the Igbo people that surrender means wholesale atrocities and genocide. But genocide is what is taking place right now and starvation is the grim reaper. This is not the time to stand on ceremony or go through channels or to observe diplomatic niceties. The destruction of an entire people is immoral even in the most moral of wars. It can never be condoned.[648]

It was not only Awolowo who advocated mass starvation against the Igbo as a means of warfare. Some other people did, like Anthony Enahoro, the then Nigerian Commissioner for Information, at a press conference in New York, July 1968. He said: "Starvation is a weapon of war, and we have every intention of using it against the rebels".[649] It is on record that this massacre of the Igbo was not carried out only by the soldiers but also by the policemen on uniform and the civilians of Nigeria. One policeman was quoted to have said: "The Igbo must be considerably reduced in number".[650]

One word now describes the policy of Nigerian military government towards secessionist Biafra: 'Genocide'. It is most unfortunate, but it is the only word which fits Nigeria's decision to stop International Red Cross and other relief agencies from flying food to Biafra.[651] As we have mentioned earlier in this work, civilians took part in this massacre of the Igbo. "In some areas in the East, Igbos were killed by local people with at least the acquiescence of the Federal forces, 1000 Igbo civilians perished in Benin in this way".[652]

One of the greatest single massacres occurred in the Igbo town of *Asaba* where "700 Igbo male were lined up and shot as terrified women and children were forced to watch".[653] There were other cases of Igbo massacre which were on record, for example, "The Nigerian troops killed or stood by while mobs killed more than 5000 Igbo in *Warri, Sapele, Agbor,* (New York Time, 10th January, 1968). Again, there has been genocide on the occasion of the 1966 massa-

---

[648] Nixon R., during the Presidential Campaign, September 9th, 1968, ibid.

[649] https://oblongmediadotcom.files.wordpress.com/2017/05/img 685-2.jpg.

[650] Lagos policeman quoted in New York Review 21st, December, 1967. Cf., https:// oblongmediadotcom.files.wordpress.com/2017/05/img 6845-2.jpg.

[651] Washington Post editorial, July 2, 1969. Cf., https://oblongmediadotcom.files.wordpress.com/2017/05/img.

[652] Max Edward Reporter, reporter on the ground – New York Review, 21st December 1967. Cf., ibid.

[653] London Observer, 21st January, 1968. Cf., ibid.

cres. The region between the towns of *Benin* and *Asaba* where only widows and orphans remained, the federal troops having, for unknown reasons, massacred all the men. (Paris Le Monde, 5th April, 1968). In Calabar, Nigerian forces shot at least 1000 and perhaps 2000 Igbos, most of them civilians. (New York Times, 18th January, 1968)".[654] The refugee camps were not spared in this massacre. "650 refugee camps which contained about 700,000 haggard bundles of human flotsam waiting hopelessly for a meal, outside the camps, was the reminder of an estimated four and half to five million displaced kwashiorkor scourges, a million and half children, suffered from it; that put the forecast death toll at another 300,000 children. More than the pogroms of 1966, more than the war casualties, than the terror bombings, it was the experience of watching helplessly Biafran children waste away and die that gave birth to, a deep and unrelenting loathing. It is a feeling that will one day reap bitter harvest..."[655] Senator Kennedy of America spoke up when he saw this genocidal killing of the Igbo. He said:

> The loss of life from starvation continues at more than 10,000 persons per day over 1000,000 lives in recent months. Without emergency measures now, the number will climb to 25,000 per day, within a month and 2,000,000 deaths by the end of the year. The New Year will only bring greater disaster to people caught in the passion of fratricidal war, we cannot allow this to continue or those responsible to go free.[656]

In Washington Post, it was boldly written and reported that "the Nazi had resurrected just here as Nigerian forces".[657] But one may ask how the Nigerian government under the leadership of Gowon did react to this allegation of genocide against the Igbo. It would be shocking to notice that the Nigerian government regarded all the incidence of massacre and genocidal slaughter of the Igbo during the Biafra war as a mere propaganda. The New York Times carried an article headlined 'Observers report that no Nigerian genocide', dated Lagos, Nigeria, December 6. This went further to report:

> Neutral military observers of the Nigerian civil war said here today that they have concluded that Biafra's charges that Nigerian troops were engaged in genocide were unfounded. The observers said that Ibos, the predominant tries of Biafra, had 'a real fear that they will be killed if they fall into the hands

---

[654] https://oblongmediadotcom.files.wordpress.com/2017/05/img.

[655] Forsyth F., January 21st 1969. Cf., https://oblongmediadotcom.files.wordpress.com2017/05/img, accessed 18.11.2017.

[656] Senator Kennedy *appeals to Americans, Sunday, November* 17th, 1968, in https:// oblongmediadotcom.files.wordpress.com2017/05/img.

[657] Washington Post, editorial July, 2nd, 1969. Cf. ibid.

of the Federal Troops, but this is dispelled by the treatment they receive when they encounter Federal Troops'.[658]

What a remarkable bit of ambiguity. The observers said the Federal Military Government was protecting Igbo and their property in conquered areas (prison is a form of protection too). This statement is really funny and ought not to be taken seriously. The world remembers Rwanda's genocide; yet before Rwanda's, there was Biafran genocide. Just as the geographic name of Biafra which has been in existence from time immemorial has been deliberately erased from the map of the world, so is Biafra genocide expunged from the world record of genocides. Victors are known to rewrite war histories and most often these are not histories but mosaics of myths and falsehoods.

In a letter written in 1969 by nine Professors from United States of America and addressed to four US Senators, these Professors, confounded by the gratuitous human brutality taking place in Biafra, implored for action to "avert the worst crime against humanity since World War II,"[659] and that was the true description of Biafra; 'the worst crime against humanity since World War II' and yet Biafran genocide is not found in the International record of world genocides. This speaks volumes about the hypocrisy which characterizes international relations and politics.[660]

4.5. IF BIAFRA HAD WON THE WAR

The Igbo complain of being marginalized politically and economically. They claim that there is no equity and justice in the distribution of Nigeria revenue allocation. Some Nigerians who are not of Igbo origin complain same thing. The marginalization of the Igbo in today's Nigeria has been well documented and is well known to merit repetition here. However, since this forms the crux of the Igbo predicament in Nigeria today and the clearest example of the failure of Nigeria to heal the wounds of the civil war, and give the Igbo a sense of belonging, it would be necessary to highlight some cases of this marginalization. What do we actually mean here by marginalization? "Marginalization is

---

[658] Cf., Speech by Mr. Maxwell Cohen, Lawyer, Member of the International Law Committee of the American Bar Association; advisor to the Biafran Government on the United Nations Genocide Convention: An Eyewitness to Genocide in Biafra on the Occasion of the First International Conference on Biafra, In New York, December, 7, 1968, in Ezeani E., *In Biafra Africa Died: The diplomatic Plot,* op. cit., p. 145.

[659] Keil C., et al, *"Biafra", The New York Review of Books, vol. 12,* no. 1, January 16th 1969, in Ezeani E., op. cit., p. 147.

[660] The reader will learn more about the current topic by watching the audio-video in the Internet link: http://www.youtube.com/watch?feature=player_embedded&v=rZeELnOiHAW, accessed 15.3.2012, in ibid.

the relegation of a people to an unimportant position in a group. Such people do not count when serious decisions of national interest are being taken. The people are out maneuvered to play third and fourth fiddle."[661] There are many examples given by prominent people in Nigeria on how the Igbo are marginalized in Nigeria. Okadigbo, one-time Senate President of Nigeria said:

> Current marginalization of Igbos is a continuation of the war that ended over 30 years ago. Destruction of property of strangers wherever it may be in Nigeria, be it Lagos, Kano or anywhere is a continuation of the war; burning down of markets just because people from other places are making some profit, that is war. Failure to promote people from Igboland for jobs which they are qualified or removing them from their jobs just because they are Igbos that is continuing that war. Failure to give Igbo a place in Nigeria military in proportion to their population and ability is part of that war.[662]

The Igbo economic, bureaucratic and political reverses have a common origin; they are traceable to the Nigerian civil war, 1967 – 1970. About this, so much has already been written. It suffices to direct attention to only three very revealing areas. The first, the most devastating occurred during the civil war with the creation of a new federalism in Nigeria based on state. The inequalities and injustices of state creation carried out by successive Nigerian governments was a planned act to put the Igbo people in less advantaged situation in all federal institutions because of federal character principle based on quota system.

Secondly, as a result of the civil war, the Nigerian armed forces became afraid of Igbo officers and men. Although some of them were reabsorbed after the civil war through the 'no victor, no vanquished' policy, yet they lost so much seniority and were psychologically ill-equipped to play any significant roles in the events which later unfolded as the military later exercised commanding influence in the politics of 1970 – 1979 and 1983 – 1990.

Thirdly, the Igbo emasculation can also be seen from population manipulation, boundaries adjustment and gerrymandering in the delineation of federal constituencies and senatorial districts.[663] The Igbo are treated in this way because they are seen by Nigeria as people who were defeated in the civil war. Had it been that Biafra won, the story would have been different. Earlier in this work, we enumerated the achievements of Biafra during the war. Had it been that Biafra succeeded in her effort to secede from Nigeria:

---

[661] Uwalaka J., *The Struggle for an Inclusive Nigeria: Igbos to be or not to be?* op. cit., p. 20.
[662] Cf., Okadigbo C., *Vanguard Newspaper, Nigeria,* Jan. 21st 2000 in Uwalaka J., *The Struggle for an Inclusive Nigeria: Igbos to be or not to be?* op. cit., p. 20.
[663] Cf., Ekwueme A., *Address to the World Igbo Summit,* Vanguard Newspaper, Nigeria, June, 21st 2000.

Biafra would have become a model to all other African states. By now the Western's discourse and reference to 'Black man's natural inferiority' may have been a part of history. In addition to being renowned for its technological progress, Biafra would have also produced an alternative to the Western party politics democracy, the practice of which has been tearing apart and destroying many African nation-states to this day.[664]

The defeat of Biafra has been seen by many Africans as disadvantage to Nigeria and to Africa in general. This deprived Nigeria and the entire Africa the healthy competition that would have existed if Biafra had succeeded in having her independence. This competition that would have been initiated by Biafra in the areas of economic, technological and political advancement was prevented by the defeat of Biafra. Kanu laments that:

> The loss of Biafra robbed Africa of what would have been a world power technologically, economically and politically. It is most unfortunate that Nigeria could not imbibe and absorb any lesson from the scientific and technological innovations in Biafra. That is why 50 years after, along with the underpinning problems of faulty foundational structure, the country can hardly generate electricity or refine crude oil…. It is also unfortunate that Nigeria in real terms, did not learn anything from the war itself.[665]

It is on record that some countries in Europe and America and even in Africa did not support the secession of Biafra out of Nigeria. This is because "Biafra was being equated to Japan because people, especially those in government already saw the potentials for Biafra to emerge as big as Japan if they succeeded in seceding out of Nigeria. Why would Europe prefer to support an African pariah rather than an African hope? In their conception, one Japan in Asia was a problem for Europe and another 'Japan' in Africa, if allowed to emerge, would be too much for Europe. Would not our world be richer if we have many Japans on earth?"[666]

The Biafra tragedy has been seen today by many as Africa's double tragedy, for Biafra would have played a leading role not only in the process of mental decolonization of Africans, restoration of the dignity of the Black but also in the cultural, political, economic and technological advancement of the African continent. Biafra was defeated in the civil war which lasted for the period of 30 months, but the ideology for the sovereign state of Biafra was not defeated. An ideology is difficult to be defeated by physical war. After a period of 51

---

[664] Ezeani E., In Biafra Africa Died: The Diplomatic Plot, op. cit., p. 198.
[665] Kanu aks Federal Government to absorb Biafran scientists; http: www.vanguardngr.com/2011/03/Kanu-asks-fg-to-absorb-biafran-scientists, accessed 12.12.2017.
[666] Ezeani E., *In Biafra Africa Died, The Diplomatic Plot,* op. cit., p. 213.

years Nigeria-Biafra war was fought, Nigeria has witnessed within these years many insurgents which put a question mark on the governance and unity of Nigeria.

Who would have believed that many years after the end of Nigeria-Biafra war, in spite of all attempts political, literary and psychological, to make Biafra a mere historical hiccup or footnote that it will once more become a subject of intense discussion? Biafra, an opprobrious name for some, dead name still for some others, a name of intense emotion and delight for many Igbo, a word uttered with trepidation by many, has once more reemerged with full force. The once trumpeted dead six letter word, now adorn the frontpage captions in the national dailies, attracting commentaries in the international media, and evoking nostalgic feeling and equally provoking hateful reactions in some quarters.[667]

4.5.1. MASSOB (MOVEMENT FOR THE ACTUALIZATION OF THE SOVEREIGN STATE OF BIAFRA)

One of the freedom-fighting movements that Nigeria has witnessed as regards Biafra is MASSOB (Movement for the Actualization of the Sovereign State of Biafra). This movement was formed by Indian trained lawyer, Ralph Uwazurike. Uwazurike founded MASSOB in 1999 in the aftermath of the Nigerian election that produced President Olusegun Obasanjo.[668] The group kicked off at Uwazurike's Temple of Peace residence, Lagos, and recorded a high rise in membership in its first few weeks. What was the idea behind the formation of MASSOB? "The Movement for the Actualization of the Sovereign State of Biafra had the intention of actualizing the failed   Biafra project as a Sovereign nation state."[669]

The leader of the group, Ralph Uwazuruike, vowed to declare the new Republic of Biafra on 27th of May, 2000. This announcement by Uwazuruike aroused an air of expectation even that of foreboding, and uneasiness. Some palpable fear

---

[667] Uwalaka J., *The Struggle for an Inclusive Nigeria: Igbos to be or not to be?* op. cit., p. 108.

[668] Uwazurike is well educated with degrees in politics and law. When he took the decision to launch MASSOB in 1999, the timing was crucial. He was either genuinely bitter or he decided to exploit the collective bitterness of the Igbo at that time for political advantage. It is possible that he had long planned to renew the agitation for Biafra and found the perfect opportunity in 1999, following Ekwueme's defeat (an Igbo politician) and Obasanjo's (a Yoruba man) ascendancy. 'Actually, there was tribal politics that went underground in that election'. Whatever be the case, it must be stated that contrary to popular myth that Ojukwu was behind the formation of MASSOB, it took Uwazurike a great deal of effort, long after the formation of MASSOB, to get close to Ojukwu. Cf., Offodile C., *The Politics of Biafra and the Future of Nigeria*, op. cit., p. 199.

[669] Uwalaka J., *The Struggle for an Inclusive Nigeria: Igbos to be or not to be?* op. cit., p. 108.

and uncertainty seem to hang in the air. There have been vigorous contrasting reactions bordering on the emotional and sentimental; on the joyful and the hateful, the rational and irrational; the audacious and the fearful; the hilarious and the offensive; the prudent and the provocative; the crude and the refined. This is understandable. After all, Biafra meant and still means many things to many people. There is no doubt that the Nigeria-Biafra war left a big wound in the mind and heart of many Igbo. War and hunger claimed many lives, many families were ruined. For this people, Biafra is not a hated idea. But reliving the experience of the war is something that should not be contemplated upon. Fear of wars, or even rumors of conflicts seem to dominate a great part of the lives of many Igbo.

So, one would anticipate, Uwazuruike's MASSOB scared and terrified many Igbo. There was fear of association. A good number of Igbo organizations, prominent Igbo sons and politicians and even communities came out with advertisements and press conferences to denounce Uwazuruike for fear of being associated with his project or to clear themselves of many suspicions of being associated with it; for fear of reprisals if the project turned sour. Who will blame them? Is Nigeria not a place where families and communities are sometimes punished or denied legitimate rights or amenities because they do not vote for the party in power; or because their sons or daughters are in opposition parties? Many that wanted to avoid such unmerited implications and harassment distanced themselves from Uwazuruike's adventure.

The reactions to 'Uwazuruike's MASSOB' have been characterized by extreme emotionalism and sentimentalism evidenced in the extreme euphoria of the faithful and extreme denunciation of the detractors and opponents. And when emotion takes over reason, the clarity of thought is obscured and objective analysis is compromised. In such situation, fancy can be taken for the fact, rhetoric for the reality, rumor takes over actuality. When one studies carefully the Movement for the Actualization of the Sovereign State of Biafra (MASSOB), one would see that 'Uwazuruike's Biafra' taken within the bounds of reason, determined by what is possible within a democratic set up, where there can be clash and disagreement over ideas and methods, without compromising the right and freedom of any opponent to express his view, even against mine and within the limit of the law, does not merit all the exaggerated emotions. The day I deny my opponent the right to express his views, and to uphold his claims, by the same action I put my right and freedom in jeopardy.

MASSOB was prompted by bad leadership and unfulfilled promises of 'no victor no vanquished'. When the leaders of a country do not have the future of their youths at heart, what result and reaction does one expect from the youths? This is the main reason for many insurgents in Nigeria today. When the leaders have failed to perform and lead well, the youths might tell them that they are not performing and they, the leaders, are planning to waste the youths' generation. Uwazuruike and his followers belong to the age bracket one can generally describe as the youths although of varying generations. When we talk of an unfulfilled citizenry, the first group of victims of this callous and bad situation is of course the neglected youths. The predicament of many youths in Nigeria has become an open sore staining the image and dignity of the Nigerian nation. The Nigerian youth is a victim of ineffective leadership and official misdirection. Youths are people laden with potentialities and they require a properly ordered society to develop them. They require well articulated policies which embody the yearnings of the youth: good education, good economic infrastructures. They ask for a society that provides them with opportunities to manifest and maximize their talents. But with a society like that of Nigeria saddled with corruption, lack of planning, visionless leaders, we have a youthful generation without direction and completely marginalized youths with stalled ambitions, frustrated and disappointed. The Nigerian society has become a graveyard of wasted talents. Of grave concern is also the fact that the Nigerian youths have become victims of an unwholesome political environment characterized by violence, hooliganism, lawlessness, manipulation, corruption. The situation is rubbing over on many young men who are now engaged in many dangerous and deviant behaviours, like armed robbery, cultism, prostitution, fraud, assassination, etc. This is really a sad situation. Soyinka laments and thus says:

> It is immoral in us to transfer to a new generation a degraded environment — physical, economic and moral that is degraded to a degree, that even a miraculous generation of geniuses will find it beyond their power to regenerate without a violent upheaval. We cannot live in an environment that robs youths of its capacity to choose.[670]

The Movement for the Actualization of the Sovereign State of Biafra can be seen as protest against persistent injustice and Igbo marginalization. The Igbo man has been subjected to persistent and unabated injustice. In spite of Gowon's promise after the war, of no victor, no vanquished, in spite of his promises of reconciliation, reconstruction and rehabilitation, nothing serious has actually been done by almost all regimes till date to bring about the three "Rs." The Igbo man seems to have been drawn to the Nigeria door and kept in the cold, without any welcome. He remains a discriminated, a suspected and an alienat-

---

[670] Soyinka W., *"Youth and the Nation": A shared responsibility,* This Day Dec. 2002, p. 14, in Uwalaka J., *The Struggle for an Inclusive Nigeria: Igbos to be or not to be?* op. cit., pp. 125 -126.

ed person in his country. You look in vain to find his name at the decision level of the armed forces, the same with the police, except for occasional token representation. You look in vain for any federal industries or any meaningful economic infrastructures in Igboland; you have to answer a Yoruba name or Hausa name before you can have a meaningful chance of ascending the highest office in the country.[671]

4.5.2. INDIGENOUS PEOPLE OF BIAFRA (IPOB)

Another movement that has risen in recent times is a group known as "Indigenous People of Biafra (IPOB)." Two groups claim to this movement. Nnamdi Kanu leads one of the groups and the other group is led by His Majesty, Honorable Justice Eze Ozobu (OFR), the former Chief Judge of Enugu State and the traditional ruler of "Aguobu Owa" in Enugu State. They used to be one group with the same objective, the realization of Biafra by peaceful means, until Kanu group decided to take a different approach. Kanu is the motivating force behind IPOB. The philosophical foundation for its formation and existence was, however, provided by a London based solicitor, Emeka Emekesiri. It is on the basis of a fundamental difference in strategy that the camps went their separate ways with each holding on tenaciously on the name IPOB. Emekesiri advocated the use of customary law to organize and govern the Indigenous People of Biafra based on provisions of the Nigeria constitution. He mounted a legal challenge in Nigeria courts for the right of self-determination of the remnants of the Indigenous People of Biafra not consumed in the war between Nigeria and Biafra. Emekesiri's ideology holds that "just as Bakassi Peninsula was removed from Nigeria by judicial power, it is our strong legal opinion that Biafra shall also be removed from Nigeria by judicial power."[672]

4.5.3. "BOKO HARAM"

Another insurgent that arose in Nigeria is "Boko Haram". But "Boko Haram" is quite different from the other movements we have discussed in this work. This is because from all indications it is a terrorist group. On 28th December, 2010, the Islamist group, "Boko Haram", openly declared war against peoples of other religions in Nigeria. This group had exploded several bombs in the city of Jos and carried out multiple other killings in Kano, Bauchi, Maiduguri and other places in Nigeria.

---

[671] Uwalak J., *The Struggle for an Inclusive Nigeria: Igbos to be or not to be?* op. cit., pp. 127 - 128.

[672] Emekesiri E., *What the Igbos want in* Offodile C., *The Politics of Biafra and the Future of Nigeria,* op. cit., p. 201.

4.5.3.1. THE ETYMOLOGY OF THE WORD "BOKO HARAM", ITS MEANING AND IDEOLOGY

"Boko" stands for "book" in Hausa, the dominant language spoken in northern Nigeria. "Haram" is the Islamic/Arabic word for forbidden. A loose translation would be "books are forbidden", and in this case "Western civilization books". "Boko Haram" is a fundamentalist jihadist group, which believes that Western education and civilization are corrupting the Muslims of Nigeria and they are on the mission to purify the religion and create an Islamic country in Northern Nigeria. This group wants to build a society, a separate political state in Northern Nigeria that is ruled by sharia and free from all corrupting agents such as Christians and all institutions that represent Christianity.[673]

"Boko Haram" which has "jihad" in its full name has been consistent and has used jihad in spreading the teachings of Mohammed in Nigeria. Most of the defenders of this group continue to defend them by saying that "Boko Haram" is fighting and killing people because of injustice and bad leadership that have resulted in impoverishing the Northerners in Nigeria. The counter argument by those who believe the contrary has always been that if there had been injustice and bad leadership in Nigeria, the North should be held accountable. Nigeria as an independent state has existed for more than fifty years and Northern Muslims have ruled the country for more than 85% of that period. Therefore, if the North has been unjustly treated and impoverished, it has suffered so by the hands of its leaders. [674] On December 28, 2010, Abu Mohammed also known as Abubakar bin Mohammad Shekau, one of the leaders and spokesperson for Boko Haram had declared:

> I want to tell the Muslims in this country Nigeria and the whole world that they need to know that this is a war between Muslims and non-Muslims; it is not similar to the wars of the pre-Islamic era, it is not a war for financial gains, it is solely a religious war. We did not start this war to end in one week, or one month or one year. Only when we are completely annihilated and nobody chooses to continue with our struggle may be, that could be the end. Or we establish a system where Islamic religion has the final say or Islamic religion determines everything, that will be the end of this war.[675]

He went further and boasted that:

> We are ready for anyone willing to face us, whether it is a group or even the government; because we know who supports us - God the creator of the uni-

---

[673] Ebiem O., *Nigeria, Biafra and Boko Haram, Ending the Genocide through Multi-State*, op. cit., p. 114.
[674] Ibid.
[675] Cf., *Who are Nigeria's Boko*, bbc.com/news/world-africa, accessed 16.11.2017.

verse, Allehn Akbar. Therefore, we are warning every Muslim who – believes in the religion of Islam that he should never help a non-Muslim in this war. If he helps any Non-Muslim and in so doing, a fellow Muslim suffers due to that, he should know that he is a dead person.[676]

Shekau issued a chilling message in one of his appearances, which provided a major insight into what his leadership of the group will bring. He said: "I enjoy killing anyone that God commands me to kill the way I enjoy killing chickens and rams."[677] In Nigeria, the percentage of Christians is about 67%. So, we can see that the above declaration of war is directed to the Christians. The percentage of the Igbo who are Christians is about 98% and these Christians are spread all over Nigeria. So, this war declared by "Boko Haram" affects the Igbo greatly. Since this declaration, more bombs have exploded in Abuja, followed by some more in Jos with several religiously motivated killings, lootings and burnings. Many critics have repeatedly claimed that the tragic thing about the situation is that in the midst of all these attacks on people of other religions and their property, some Nigerians have been sponsoring this group.

Actually, "Boko Haran" came into prominence in 2009 when there was a violent confrontation between the group and Nigeria's security forces and ever since has remained constantly in the news. Some members of the group were killed during the clash, and their leader Mohammed Yusuf was among those killed. After the clash, the group went underground for about one year and resurfaced as a deadlier jihadist sect. They started by throwing bombs and drive by shooting into beer parlours and gardens in Maiduguri and quickly spreading to other northern cities in Nigeria. They have successfully carried out bombing of Churches and Christians, police stations, media houses, the headquarters of United Nations in Nigeria, etc. The Igbo would not have experienced "Boko Haram" had it been they succeeded in having Biafra. The Boko Haram sect has vindicated Odumegwu Ojukwu and proved the venerable Obafemi Awolowo wrong about Biafra. Awolowo fought to 'keep Nigeria one' but it is now clear that the task had always been only one-sided. The North obviously did not get that memorandum and so did not share the same objective.[678]

In April 2014, "Boko Haram" drew international condemnation by abducting more than 200 schoolgirls from Chibok town in Borno State Nigeria, saying it would treat them as slaves and marry them off – reference to an ancient Islamic belief that women captured in conflict are considered war booty. "Boko Ha-

---

[676] *Who are Nigeria's Boko*, bbc.com/news/world-africa, accessed 16.11.2017.
[677] Ibid.
[678] Ezeani E., *In Biafra Africa Died: The Diplomatic Plot*, op. cit., p. 230.

ram" switched tactics, starting to hold on to territory rather than retreating after an attack. In August 2014, Mr. Shekau declared a Caliphate in areas under "Boko Haram's" control, with the town of "Gwoza" as its seat of power. He says:

> We are in an Islamic Caliphate, flanked by masked fighters and carrying a machine gun. We have nothing to do with Nigeria. We don't believe in this name.[679]

Later, Mr. Shekau formally pledged allegiance to the Islamic State of Iraq and Syria (ISIS) group, turning his back on al-Qaeda. ISIS accepted the pledge, naming the territory under "Boko Haram's" control as the Islamic State of West Africa Province and as being part of the global caliphate, it was trying to establish. But by March 2015, "Boko Haram" had lost all the towns under its control as regional coalition made up of troops from Nigeria, Cameroon, Chad and Niger was formed to fight it. Once again, "Boko Haram" retreated to the Sambisa forest, where the Nigerian military pursued it, freeing hundreds of captives.

In August 2016, the group apparently split, with an "ISIS" video announcing that Mr. Shekau had been replaced with Abu Musab al-Barnawi, believed to be a son of "Boko Haram's" founder. Mr. Shekau disputed this, insisting he was still in charge. And in a big surprise, 21 of the Chibok girls, seen as prized asserts for Mr. Shekau, were freed in October 2016 following talks involving the militants, the Nigerian, Swiss governments and the International Committee of the Red Cross. And while many fighters have been killed and weapons seized, some analysts say it is too early to write off "Boko Haram." "Boko Haram" has outlived other militant groups in Northern Nigeria and has built a presence in neighbouring states where it has carried out attacks and has recruited fighters.[680] "Boko Haram" has a force of thousands of men. "Central Intelligence Agency (CIA) officials have estimated around 9,000 cells that specialize in bombings. Through its raids on military bases and banks, it has gained control of vast amounts of weapons and money."[681]

4.5.4. NIGER DELTA AVENGERS

The Niger Delta Avengers (NDA) is a militant group in Nigeria's Niger Delta area. The group publicly announced its existence in March 2016. This is another movement that arose in Nigeria due to poor governance and corruption. The NDA have attacked oil producing facilities in Niger Delta Nigeria, causing

---

[679] *Who are Nigeria's Boko*, bbc.com/news/world-africa, accessed 16.11.2017.
[680] Ibid.
[681] Ibid.

the shutdown of oil terminals and a fall in Nigeria's oil production to its lowest level in twenty years. The attacks caused Nigeria to fall behind Angola as Africa's largest oil producer. The reduced oil output has hampered the Nigeria economy and destroyed its budget, since Nigeria depends on the oil industry for nearly all its government revenues.

The NDA declared that its aims are to create a sovereign state in the Niger Delta and have threatened to disrupt Nigeria's economy if their aims are not met. The NDA claims its members are young, well-travelled... and educated in East Europe. The group has criticized the President of Nigeria, Muhammadu Buhari, for having never visited the delta and his detention of the Biafran independence activist Nnamdi Kanu.[682]

What gave rise to the agitation of the Niger-Delta Avengers is the claim that their environments are being polluted by the oil companies, and the Niger-Delta people receive no compensation neither from these companies nor from the Federal Government of Nigeria. Worst still, there is no evidence of dividends of democracy in their area. For them, the Federal Government of Nigeria has interest only in taking oil that is deposited in their area but has no interest in developing their area. This made them to live in poverty while the Federal Government of Nigeria is enriching herself with the oil deposited in their area.

4.6. POST WAR RECONCILIATION, REHABILITATION, RECONSTRUCTION AND THE EXTENT THEY WERE CARRIED OUT

Before the civil war, the Igbo people were the engine of economic activities in various parts of Nigeria, in the townships and rural areas. They were the traders, craftsmen, engineers, mechanics, teachers, etc. They are known for their entrepreneurship and thrift. They save and invest wherever they are. They, like true believers in Nigeria, built their personal houses where they are. They make everywhere their home.

During the pogrom against the Igbo in the North and other parts of Nigeria, and at the outbreak of the civil war, they rushed in millions back to Igboland, empty handed, completely dispossessed. Millionaires became overnight paupers; people who were living in palaces, with housing estates came back begging for pen-houses and huts to lay their mats to sleep. In many places, some could not find any such generosity; owners of fleet of cars, came back with not even something resembling a child's bicycle; men with chains of investment came back with nothing to start life with. Many who left their villages for years

---

[682] Niger Delta Avengers, en.wikipedia.org/wiki/Nigeria-Delta-Avengers, accessed 15.11.2017.

without contact came back to the utter scorn and derision of their kinsmen. Of course, as should be expected, many of these victims committed suicide, some died out of heart attack, some became bedridden and many lost their children to malnutrition and kwashiorkor. At the end of the war, property belonging to the Igbo were confiscated as abandoned property in some states in Nigeria. It was a horrible experience and tragic indeed.

The war ended since 1970, but it left marks on the Igbo psyche. The Nigeria government knew after the war that a lot of damage have been done to the Igbo. It was obvious that they lost many lives, property and businesses. They lost also their position in Nigeria. When one wants to destroy the civilization of a nation, there are 3 ways to achieve that:

1. Destroy family structure,

2. destroy education and

3. lower the importance of the role models in the society and their references.

During the war in Nigeria, formal education in Igboland could not move on. Schools were closed throughout the 30 months that the war was fought. The students in Igboland suffered academic set-back. But when the war was over, what did the Federal Government of Nigeria do? The Federal Government worsened the situation by taking over to their custody all the schools built by the missionaries and individuals, which belonged to the Mission and individuals.

> The Government announced over the radio that she has taken over all the schools and went ahead to appoint principals for these schools and also claimed all the school property.[683]

After some years, the result of this action of the Federal Government began to manifest. The standard of education in Nigeria began to fall. Adequate attention was not given to teachers. They were not paid good salaries; gradually they began to lose their high esteem which they have acquired over the years. Nobody wanted to become a teacher any more. Teaching profession in primary and secondary schools became a profession for women alone; very few men were teachers. It is sad to say that this situation has not changed up till today. Commenting on this, Baur says that:

---

[683] Arinze F., *The Baton of Faith,* op. cit., p. 79.

The nationalization of the schools was Nigeria's plan to be completed by 1974, and it affected all Churches in Nigeria. Yet Catholic Igboland felt itself hurt in a special way, on account of the loss of her most capable teaching staff.... However, twenty years later the main complaint raised was that corruption and youth delinquency had increased intolerably on account of the lack of a religiously-based moral education in the schools. The state should either provide full opportunities for such an education or, as the best remedy, give back the schools to the Churches.[684]

Before the civil war, teachers were envied, they were paid good salaries and when due. Many young people wanted to become teachers. But after the civil war, dedicated teachers began to disappear in the society; emphasis on role models reduced; many youngsters began to despise education; academic and moral values began to fall. As we have mentioned earlier in this work, by the time Nigeria declared war on Biafra in July 1967, the Igbo had attained a high degree of economic prosperity, modern industrial growth, educational advancement and social sophistication. All these collapsed during the 30 months of brutal warfare. Biafra unconditionally surrendered fearing the worst consequences. They had forfeited all expectations of justice and rights as Nigerian citizens. The Nigerian government accepted the surrender and pledged there would be 'no victor and no vanquished' (no winners and no losers) in the new, united Nigeria.

The victorious Federal Government did not live up to its declarations and pledges. The defeated Igbo were not only largely left to fend for themselves but official efforts were made to hold them down, discriminate against them and marginalize them in the political, economic and social life of the nation. Nigeria had fought the war 'to keep Nigeria one'; it has since then remained one and disunited.

Therefore, the post-war policy of Rehabilitation, Reconstruction and Reconciliation, as it concerned Igboland, was grudging and hypocritical. Little genuine effort was made to assist the Igbo to rehabilitate themselves and to rebuild their war-damaged infrastructure. Rather than attempt a genuine reconciliation, a policy of systematic marginalization was pursued. The immediate concern in the first year after the war was to assist the Igbo in securing the basic needs of life, food, shelter and clothing. The first days after the surrender of Biafra were days of near anarchy and disorder. The millions of Igbo refugees bottled up in various axis of Igboland began to move back to their respective home towns, amidst untold harassments from the victorious Nigerian soldiers.

---

[684] Baur J., *2000 years of Christianity in Africa: An African Church History, 2nd Revised Edition,* op. cit. p. 272.

Property, services, women and girls were readily commandeered by the Nigerian soldiers. Contingents of the Nigerian army were posted to most cities and districts of Igboland.

This military occupation of Igboland lasted for several years. The occupying troops wreaked terror on the civilian population. They raped women and forced girls to marry them. The soldiers murdered any person who challenged their high-handedness. Many Nigerian officers and men took Igbo wives whom they married or regularized after years of enforced concubine. It was part of the price the Igbo paid for their defeat.[685]

4.6.1. REHABILITATION: FOOD AND SHELTER

It became necessary immediately after the war for the Biafrans to tackle the immediate problems of hunger, starvation, malnutrition, disease and lack of medication. Millions of Biafrans had come out of the war hungry, famished and physically battered. Many were gaunt, frail and sick as a result of the physical and mental sufferings undergone during the war. Food and medicine were in short supply. Money with which to buy food and drugs was not available.

The Biafran currency had become illegal tender once the Biafran Republic collapsed. The available food had to come from Nigeria and that had to be bought or donated. The Igbo were made to deposit their Biafran currency in the banks and a flat rate of N40 was paid to every depositor irrespective of the amount each person deposited. "For the first three months, Igbo hopes were on relief measures and supplies. Food, clothing and medicines were brought in by the National Commission for Rehabilitation, the Christian Council of Nigeria and the Nigerian Red-Cross Society. The supplies fell far short the need and only small portion of the people in need of help was reached."[686]

For reasons of insufficiency, logistics and graft, the relief materials did not often get to the people who needed them more. Large quantities of the material were stolen or diverted to unknown destinations. Besides, city dwellers received better attention than the millions in the rural areas who could not be easily reached. The federal government and affluent Nigerians were largely

---

[685] Cf., Ozigbo I.R.A., *A History of Igboland in the 20th century*, op. cit., p. 176.

[686] Nigeria rejected offers of food and assistance from countries and relief agencies it deemed unacceptable. Supplies from joint Church Aid were rejected. Thousands of tons of food and medicines (earlier meant for Biafra) were stockpiled in Sao Tome, but Nigeria would not accept them. Yet, shortages of food, shelter and money were extremely acute in Igboland in the first months after the war. Nigeria rejected the offers as being 'blood money'. Cf. Urhobo E., *Relief Operations in the Nigeria Civil War.*, Ibadan, 1978 in Ozigbo I.R.A., *A History of Igboland in the 20th century*, op. cit., 187.

indifferent to the physical plight of the Igbo people at the end of the civil war. It appeared they were not really interested in the recovery of the Igbo or their reintegration into the Nigerian state. The Igbo could not depend on relief supplies indefinitely. As the farming season arrived, every effort was made to re-engage in agriculture in order to produce food. There was acute shortage of agricultural input and farming implements. Seed yams, rice and maize seeds had to be found. Some quantities were supplied. Hoes, machetes, shovels, pick-axes were also provided, often by voluntary and non-governmental agencies.

The pre-war livestock and farm settlements that dotted the Eastern Region of Nigeria had all collapsed. For example, animal feeds, veterinary drugs and equipment were in very short supply; extension services, fishing nets, fertilizers, credit facilities, just to mention but a few, were no longer available. Lack of shelter was as acute as the scarcity of food. Many cities and towns in former Biafra lay in ruins. Relatively few residential buildings in the cities in Igboland remained habitable at the end of the war. The people on returning to their former homes had to erect make-shift structures that served them as temporary shelters and accommodations. Water supplies, dried pipes and bore-holes, water pumps tanks and wells were in urgent need of rebuilding. The time allocated for rehabilitation proper was as short as the relief supplies were inadequate. The Igbo quickly became less reliant on hand-outs and began to take their destiny into their own hands.

4.6.2. MEDICAL INSTITUTIONS

As one would expect, after the war, there were many wounded Ex-Biafran soldiers and civilians who needed medical attention and treatment. Many hospitals, health centers, maternity homes and dispensaries were also in ruins and overgrown with grasses. Efforts were immediately set in motion to reopen and clean them up. Often, doctors and nurses were not immediately available. So were the drugs. Patients slept on floor or on bare mattresses. The missionary expatriates were expelled from Igboland in May, 1970 for their alleged role of aiding Biafra with food, relief and medicines. Many of them were schools or medical staff.

The government and mission hospitals were rebuilt with generous donations from foreign relief agencies. The German aid organization, "Misereor" was most active in the repairs and re-equipping of the Catholic hospitals and other medical institutions. Some essential drugs were also supplied. New cottage hospitals and clinics were established in the bid to satisfy the growing medical needs of the people.[687]

4.6.3. RECONSTRUCTION OF OTHER INFRASTRUCTURE

The socio-economic base of the Igbo society (structures and infrastructure) appeared to have totally collapsed at the end of the Nigeria-Biafra war. Ruins and devastations were everywhere. The educational institutions at all levels, the industries, public utilities, health services, communication systems and financial institutions were severely battered and needed to be rebuilt. The air raids and bombings devastated Igbo lives and property. It must be emphasized that most of these reconstruction activities were fruits of self-help efforts by Igbo communities. They received little or no help from the Government. Hard-time and misery continued to be felt in Igboland for several years after the war. Recovery came slowly but steadily largely out of the dynamism and de-termination of the Igbo to survive.

4.7. CONCLUSION

It is obvious that the majority of the soldiers who plotted and carried out the coups of 1966 in Nigeria and those who fought in the Nigeria-Biafra war are no longer alive. But would Nigeria continue to live on her past mistakes? Is it not yet time Nigeria started living together in peace and forget the coups of 1966 and the Nigeria-Biafra war that was fought many years ago? It is clear that without peace no reasonable development can be achieved.

One obvious lesson Nigeria should learn from the war she fought is that wars do not solve problems but rather create them. My aim of making a short re-view of Nigeria-Biafra war in this work is neither to instigate anger in some people nor to insult. The target is that Nigeria should learn from her past mis-takes, correct her errors and create better future for her citizens.

Some Nigerians have written and advocated ways through which Nigerians can live together in peace and also ways through which Nigeria can solve the prob-lems that trouble her. Let us look at some of the proposals that some Nigerian statesmen have offered. Chinua Achebe in his book: "The Trouble with Nigeria" stated that one of the problems that confronts Nigeria is "tribalism". Achebe writes:

> Nothing in Nigeria's political history captures her problem of national integra-
> tion more graphically than the chequered fortune of the word tribe in her vo-
> cabulary. Tribe has been accepted at one time as a friend, rejected as an en-

---

[687] Ozigbo I.R.A., *A History of Igboland in the 20th century*, op. cit., p. 179.

emy at another, and finally smuggled in through the back-door as an accomplice.[688]

Ojukwu in his own assessment concludes that "tribalism is perhaps the one single factor that has nullified all efforts at evolving a national leadership in Nigeria, capable of fulfilling the nation's aspiration"[689] Tribalism became an issue in Nigeria because Nigeria is made-up of many tribes. It was through the mirror of tribalism that some Nigerians saw the coup of January 1966 as being carried out by one ethnic group; starting from then, many things that Nigeria executed were done based on tribal sentiment. Therefore, for Nigeria to achieve a true national integration, tribalism should be eradicated in her system. But how? Inter-tribal marriages should be encouraged by the parents and elders of all tribes in Nigeria; religious pessimism should be avoided and freedom of worship encouraged. In line with Achebe's national integration and true unity of Nigeria, Ojukwu asserts that:

> Nigeria needs unity; the definition of a nation includes: … a people who can together choose a leader; no Nigerian leadership can emerge until Nigeria comes into true existence; until Nigerians are prepared to modify, and sometimes to abandon their primordial attachments in favor of a new Nigerian relationship. Nigeria cannot unit, she cannot achieve unity without abandoning her fear of unity. She cannot fulfil her manifest destiny without achieving unity; without unity of purpose nothing in Nigeria can function with the requisite efficiency.[690]

In advocating for true integration and unity in Nigeria, Uwalaka states that this is possible when Nigeria is ready and determined to:

> Enthrone an inclusive Nigeria in which every citizen or component group, enjoy all the rights and privileges of belongingness, a sense which imposes a corresponding obligation to members. It is a Nigeria in which there are no official policies or action, to marginalize or exclude certain individuals, groups or cultures, and in which even unofficial or clandestine actions of private groups to do the same are officially combated.[691]

It is a Nigeria in which no one or group in society should be treated in any way and manner that would constitute any real threat to their security and survival. For this inclusivism to be real and operational, it must cover the three important areas in which a people's sense of belonging is immediately felt and experienced in the society. These are:

---

[688] Achebe C., *The trouble with Nigeria,* op. cit., p. 5.
[689] Ojukwu O.E., *Because I am Involved,* op. cit., p. 21.
[690] Ibid., pp. x - xi.
[691] Uwalaka J., *The Struggle for an Inclusive Nigeria: Igbos to be or not to be?* op. cit., p. 157.

1. **Political Inclusiveness**: This specifies that power is for all, so that no one or ethnic group or peoples is there merely to be ruled by the others, without the real possibility of having access to power and also involved in the process of conferring power.[692]

2. **Social Inclusiveness**: This specifies that no one or group should be treated as if they do not belong or not as a fellow man. Thus, the Nigerian society or state must not obstruct one's or any group's legitimate need for self-realization, that is, should not be alienated.[693] Indigenes cannot deprive non-indigenes of their constitutional rights. In the interests of national integration, economic development, peace and security in Nigeria, there must be equality before the law for all citizens and freedom of movement. Once a person settles in an area and pays his or her taxes, the person must be considered an indigene with all the rights under the law. Allowing indigenes to dictate rights for non-indigenes is against the best interests of the country. Nigeria must reverse its direction and move to greater national unity, rather than affirm the settler-indigene dichotomy.

For Nigeria to progress towards greater national integration and peace and stability in the country, there is need to amend the constitution to ensure that there is no legal distinction between indigenes and non-indigenes. Nigeria should ensure that there is freedom of movement and freedom from discrimination according to ethnic group or religion. For economic progress and equality and justice for all, the settler-indigene dichotomy must be ended.[694]

3. Economic Inclusiveness: This demands that the wealth in society in which all belong should be for all, so that one is entitled to a certain level of economic security, and one's survival and human dignity does not suffer a grave risk.[695] In his proposal for true unity of Nigeria as a nation and the eradication of tribalism in it, Ojukwu concludes thus:

> I am aware that there is no formula which can change our diverse society overnight and transform us into a nation. Yet, I believe our government should do more to encourage unity. Governments should de-emphasize ethnic origin in all official documents... There is no better way to unity than endeavors jointly undertaken and achievements jointly won. If Nigeria, there-

---

[692] Ibid., p. 158.

[693] Ibid.

[694] Okonkwo R., *National Integration of Nigeria: The indigene Issue in* Eze-Uzomaka P. ed., *Nigerian Peoples and Cultures,* op. cit., p. 320.

[695] Uwalaka J., *The struggle for an Inclusive Nigeria: Igbos to be or not to be?* op. cit., p. 158.

fore, has to fulfill her mission, succeeding governments must maximize their efforts to create avenues for joint endeavors.[696]

If Nigerians would be truly patriotic, according to Chinua Achebe, common-interest and not self-interest should be in their minds in whatever they are doing. When common interest is enthroned and tribalism, egotism, corruption, etc., are rejected in the Nigerian system, all will go well. Achebe emphasized that:

> True patriotism is possible only when the people who rule and those under their power have a common and genuine goal of maintaining the dispensation under which the nation lives. This will, in turn, only happen if the nation is ruled justly, if the welfare of all the people rather than the advantage of the few becomes the corner-stone of public policy.[697]

For Nigeria to progress as a nation, social injustice and cult of mediocrity should be uprooted in her system. The major objection to the practice of tribalism is that it exposes the citizens to unfair treatment and social injustice. Less advertised but no less damaging to social morality is the advantage which tribalism may confer on mediocrity. But that is not all. Let us take a hypothetical case where two candidates 'A' and 'B' apply to fill a very important and strategic position. 'A' has the right qualification of competence and character but is of the 'wrong' tribe, while 'B', less qualified, belongs to the right', tribe, and so gets the job. 'A' goes away embittered. 'B' throws a party and then messes up the Job. The greatest sufferer is the nation itself which has to contain the legitimate grievance of a wronged citizen and has to accommodate the incompetence of a favored citizen.[698]

The above example given by Chinua Achebe is a frequent experience in Nigeria. What Achebe tried to explain is that the denial of merit is a form of social injustice which can hurt not only the individuals directly concerned but ultimately the entire society. Corruption in Nigeria today can be seen as a cancer which has eaten deep into the Nigerian system. It seems that both the government and Nigerians themselves find it very difficult to get a solution to this problem. Obviously, this situation which has built up over the years will take some time to correct, assuming Nigerians want to do it peacefully. But to initiate change, the President of Nigeria must take, and be seen to take, a decisive first step of ridding his administration of all persons on whom the slightest wind of corruption and scandal has blown. When he can summon the courage

---

[696] Ojukwu O. E., *Because I am Involved,* op. cit., pp. 21 and 22.
[697] Achebe C., *The Trouble with Nigeria,* op. cit. p. 16.
[698] Ibid., p. 19.

to do that, he will find himself grown overnight to such position and authority that he will become Nigeria's leader, not just its President. Only then can he take on and conquer corruption in the nation. When the issues we have raised here are handled well and corruption is eradicated, if not completely, but at least to a reasonable level, Nigeria will surely make progress both in her governance and in her efforts of seeking national integration.

CHAPTER FIVE

5. MODERNITY AND IGBO TRADITIONAL RELIGION

5.1. INTRODUCTION

In discussing modernity, we are cognizant of the fact that the new has been a phenomenon of every age since man in his dynamism is always updating himself and his environment. Here, we have to understand "modernity" simply as the "new" against the "old" or the past. Here, we have to study modernity in reference to Igbo Traditional Religion which includes also Igbo culture and tradition. Our analysis of modernity will reveal the fact of its ambiguity or ambivalence. In other words, modernity holds out some encouraging qualities and some alarming short-comings or scandalous qualities both of which are offers of modernity.

It is in these offers of modernity that we see the changes and the effects that modernity has given to Igbo Traditional Religion and culture. However, for the sake of clarity and specificity, we shall trace and identify the modernity of our focus from post-colonial era, the advent of Christianity to Igboland and identify this modernity from the Western rooted enlightenment background. It is an obvious fact that the religions of the world have changed or modernized with the signs of time. Igbo Traditional Religion is therefore no exception. In this Chapter, we shall show and explain some of the encouraging qualities and some alarming short-comings or "scandalous" qualities both of which modernity has offered to Igbo Traditional Religion and culture and to humanity in general.

5.2. MODERNIZATION AND MODERNITY

The etymology of the term "modern" can be traced to the Latin word – "modo", meaning just now, in the sense of referring to the present and recent times as opposed to the remote past.[699]Hence, the modern must be understood against the background of the present being discontinuous with the past. The concept of modernity is rooted in the attempt to come to grips with the meaning and significance of the social changes occurring in Europe from the wane of Renaissance through the latter half of the nineteenth century, namely, the effects of industrialization, urbanization, and political democracy on essential rural and autocratic societies. Hence, the term "modernity" was used to capture the changes in progress and connote this new experience of

---

[699] Cf., The Oxford English Reference Dictionary.

the world by contrasting the "modern" with the "traditional". [700] In the traditional set-up, history was seen as a continuum where the present is continuous with the past. But modernity, on the contrary, refers to the world constructed anew through the active and conscious intervention of actors and the new sense of self that such active intervention and responsibility entailed.

> The single word "modern", with its variations – "modernization", "modernity" and "modernism", covers and attracts a great range of possible meanings and an inter-disciplinary convergence of definitions, namely, philosophical, political, anthropological, economical, etc.[701]

From the point of view of literary-aesthetic, for example, Alan sees modernity as a "concept structured in referential discourse with its object as the 'new', the fluid, ever-changing and dynamic nature of modern society."[702] Black takes modernization from historical standpoint as the "process, by which historically evolved institutions are adapted to the rapidly changing functions that reflect the unprecedented increase in human knowledge, permitting control over the environment that accompanied the scientific revolution."[703]

For Rogers, modernization is "the process by which individuals change from a traditional way of life to a more complex, technological advanced, and rapidly changing style of life".[704] This definition by Rogers agrees with Kumar's definition; which says that "modernization is a continuous and open-ended process."[705]Peter Berger, from the point of view of the sociology of knowledge, refers to modernization as the "transformation of the world brought about by technological innovations of the last few centuries, first in Europe and then with increasing rapidity all over the world. This transformation has had economic, social and political dimensions, all immense in scope."[706]

From the various definitions, it is simply understood that modernization is a process, while modernity is the resulting characteristics of the process in indi-

---

[700] Swingewood A., *Cultural Theory and the Problem of Modernity,* St. Martin's Press, New York, 1998, p. 138.

[701] Ibid., pp. 138 - 139.

[702] Ibid., p. 140.

[703] Black C., *The Dynamics of Modernization, A Study in Comparative History*, Harper and Row, New York, 1966, p. 7.

[704] Rogers E., *Modernization among Peasants: The Impact of Communication,* Holt, Rinehart and Winton, New York, 1969.

[705] Kumar K., *"Modernization and Industrialization"* in Encyclopedia Britannica, p. 280.

[706] Berger P., *Facing up to Modernity, Basic Books,* New York, 1977, p. 70.

viduals, institutions, countries, and cultures.[707] In other words, as the amount of knowledge in the world continues to increase because of constant research and in turn diffuses rapidly through efficient communication systems, what happens when this Knowledge is transformed into technology, which has increasing and unforeseeable effects on economic growth, on social systems, and on political decisions is what we call modernity. Invariably, the individual too is affected in his or her values, attitudes, beliefs, and behaviour.

It is remarkable that change takes place in any given culture all the time; it is, so to speak, natural, and the people are comfortable with it and understand it. But this happens not always. However, the trouble with modernization is that often the speed of the process of change leaves the people without an understanding of what is happening. The expression "the crisis of modernity" simply points to this fact that modernity is a problem, that traditional ways of life have been replaced with uncontrollable change and unmanageable alternatives. Put in other words, modernity is all about change through force outside our control. It is striking to note the impact of modernity on all the societies and institutions and its universality. One bitter truth, remains, everybody wants to be modern. In fact, Carrier would say:

> Insofar as modernity is opposed to tradition, a dichotomy between 'modern' and 'retrograde', is subtly set up in people's minds, and modernity thus comes to have a normative and idealized sense, since it is obvious that nobody wants to be considered retrograde.[708]

It is this very point of not wanting to be retrograde that makes everybody the agent or carrier of modernity. With this idea in mind, reality turns into a myth for modernity. Carrier is justified to call modernity "a new and totalizing mentality that involves every aspect of life, person and social, material and spiritual."[709] Wilfred asserts that "at the level of culture, we notice a dangerous trend toward transforming the whole world into a mono-cultural zone."[710]

Since modernity, according to the above assertions, opposes tradition and at the same time creates a new mentality in man that results to new set of meanings, symbols, insights and values which underlay specific ways of understanding, expressing and defining, it is rightly called a culture. This finds support in

---

[707] Cf. Avededo M., *Inculturation and the Challenges of Modernity*, Pontifical Gregorian University, Rome, 1982, p. 4. Cf., also, Robertson R., *Meaning and Change: Explorations in the Cultural Sociology of Modern Societies*, University Press, N.Y, 1978.
[708] Carrier H., *Evangelizing the Culture of Modernity,* Orbis Books, N.Y, 1993, p. 30.
[709] Ibid., p. 312.
[710] Wilfred F., *"Emerging Trends Challenge the Churches of Asia",* in Jenkinson W., and O'sullivan H., eds; *Trends in Mission Toward the 3rd Millennium,* Orbis Books, New York, p. 5.

Carrier's statement which says that "from the outset, modernity is seen as a state of mind, a mentality or a culture..."[711]

5.3. MODERNITY AND POST-MODERNITY

We stated earlier that modernization is a process. But it is not just an ordinary process; it is an irreversible one, a kind of permanent revolution, without any final goal. Hence, Baudelaire, calls it "the transient, the fleeting, the contingent".[712]

As a result of this, some scholars distinguish "old modern", "transitional", and "new modern" while the contemporary scene is termed "postmodern".[713] It is to be remarked, however, that scholars, are divided on how far post-modernity represents a decisive new stage in the development of modern culture. In other words, when ends and when begins modernity and postmodernity respectively? I would not like us to go into this area; we would rather leave this problem of periodization for historians and sociologists.

Although there have been anti-modern movements before, beginning perhaps near the outset of the nineteenth century with the Romanticists and Luddites, the rapidity with which the term post-modern has become wide-spread in our time suggests that the anti-modern sentiment is more extensive and intense than before, and also that it includes the sense that modernity can be successfully overcome only by going beyond it, not by attempting to return to a premier form of existence. Insofar as a common element is found in the various ways in which the term is used, post-modernism refers to a diffused sentiment rather than to any common set of doctrines – the sentiment that humanity can and must go beyond the modern.[714] So, in simple language, Post-modern means beyond the modern. "The concept of Post-modern" Alan would say "emerges when modernism seems exhausted and no longer capable of dealing with the "newness" of modern mass society."[715]

From our explanation of modernity above, especially from its general sense of the present – "newness" – as opposed to the past, "the old", we can say that every epoch has the experience of modernity, because man in his dynamism is ever changing and, of course, not without his environment, history and culture. However, the speed, profundity and character of the transformation that

---

711 Carrier H., *Evangelizating the Culture of Modernity,* op. cit., p. 30.
712 Quoted in Swingewood., *Cultural Theory and the Problem of Modernity,* op. cit., p. 141.
713 Cf., G. Ge/ P.M.H., *Modernization and Urbanization, Encyclopedia Britannica,* 1985, p. 255.
714 Griffin D., ed., *Spirituality and Society, Postmodern Vision.,* State University of New York Press, 1988, pp. ix - x.
715 Swingewood A., *Cultural Theory and the Problem of Modernity,* op. cit., p. 161.

has taken place in the past couple of decades have never been seen before in the history of humanity. Somehow, it is like saying that it is change that takes control of man and not man that controls change.

In our study, we shall lay emphasis on modernity, which has its root in the Western movement called Enlightenment. "The contemporary meaning of modernity is thus imbricated in enlightenment reason, the belief in progress, empirical science and positivism".[716] What makes this modernity "special" is not simply its culture of innovation, but its "rational ethos challenging traditional and rituals in the name of critical thought, empirical knowledge and humanism".[717]

Enlightenment emerged as an intellectual movement that describes as well as represents the extraordinary scientific, philosophical, religious and political development of that period in Europe. It showed first in England in theoretical writings on religion; in France it featured in philosophical books; and in the radical political changes of the American and French Revolutions. Thus, it inspires a big bulk of modern thought, spreading from England and France to North America, then from Portugal and Spain to South America, and like fluid, it has now reached all corners of the globe.

As an intellectual movement, Enlightenment places heavy emphasis on the intellectual powers of man. It holds that the intellect alone, the most valued faculty of man, is capable of liberating man from the dependence brought about by man's lack of courage to apply his intellect. In response to his own question, namely, "what is Enlightenment?" Immanuel Kant answered that it is "man's release from self-incurred tutelage".[718]

For Kant, the guiding principle of enlightenment was the use of individual critical reason without direction from any external authority and without reference to tradition. Thus, Kant put as the motto of Enlightenment this choice of admonition: "have courage to employ individual reason". According to him, culpability does not lie in lack of intelligence, but in lack of decision and courage to use intelligence without reliance to someone else. With this atmosphere charged with anthropocentrism, it is little wonder that the intellectuals of this period should see themselves as heralds of a modern age in which humanity would emerge from the bondage of immaturity and servility caused by spiritual and cultural inheritance.

---

[716] Ibid., p. 138.

[717] Ibid.

[718] Quoted in "Enlightenment" in Komonchak J.A., ed., *The New Dictionary of Theology,* Gill and Macmillan Ltd., Dublin, 1989, p. 323.

Since the new movement known as enlightenment was destined to penetrate all areas of human life, the thinkers who participated in it covered the whole field of knowledge that was then considered the exclusive province of the Church. Carrier is therefore correct to say that, "on the one hand, modern science had its origin in the Church".[719] Enlightenment offered a different view of the cosmos, the nature of man, of religion, of society, of history, and of morals. In a nutshell, "the world picture they created meant a loosing of the state and society from traditional and ecclesiastical controls and gave rise to a largely secular culture."[720]

European politics, philosophy, science and communications were radically reoriented during the course of the "long 18th century" (1685 – 1815) as part of a movement referred to by its participants as the Age of Reason, or simply the Enlightenment. Enlightenment thinkers in Britain, in France and throughout Europe questioned traditional authority and embraced the notion that humanity could be improved through rational change. The Enlightenment produced numerous books, essays, inventions, scientific discoveries, laws, wars and revolutions. The American and French Revolutions were directly inspired by Enlightenment ideals and respectively marked the peak of its influence and the beginning of its decline.[721]

It is pertinent to note that Enlightenment as a movement covers all human endeavours. For example, Locke argued that "human nature was mutable and that knowledge was gained through accumulated experience rather than by accessing some sort of outside truth. Newton's Calculus and optical theories provided the powerful Enlightenment metaphors for precisely measured change and illumination."[722]

There was no single, unified, Enlightenment. Instead, it is possible to speak of French Enlightenment, the Scottish Enlightenment and the English, German, Swiss or American Enlightenment. Individual Enlightenment thinkers often had very different approaches. Locke differed from Hume, Rousseau from Voltaire and Thomas Jefferson from Frederick the Great. Their differences and disagreements, though, emerged out of the common Enlightenment themes of rational questioning and belief in progress through dialogue.

Enlightenment period was a time of religious (and anti-religious) innovation, as Christians sought to reposition their faith along rational lines, and deists and

---

[719] Cf. Carrier H., *Evangelization and Culture of Modernity,* op. cit., p. 31.
[720] Bokenkotter T. A., *A Concise History of the Church;* Image Books, New York, 1996, p. 28.
[721] Cf., history.com/topics/enlightenment, accessed 6.12.2017.
[722] Ibid.

materialists argued that the universe seemed to determine its own course without God's intervention.[723] Modernism – all owe a heavy debt to the thinkers of Enlightenment.

5.4. SOME OF THE DEFINING CHARACTERISTICS OF MODERNITY

Here, we have to point out certain factors considered by some scholars as catalysts of the modernization process.

5.4.1. RATIONALIZATION

In philosophy, rationalism is the epistemological view that regards reason as the chief source and test of knowledge or any view appealing to reason as a source of knowledge or justification. More formally, rationalism is defined as a methodology or a theory in which the criterion of truth is not sensory but intellectual and deductive.[724]

In an old controversy, rationalism was opposed to empiricism, where the rationalists believed that reality has an intrinsically logical structure. Because of this, the rationalists argued that certain truths exist and that the intellect can directly grasp these truths. That is to say, rationalists asserted that certain rational principles exist in logic, mathematics, ethics and metaphysics that are so fundamentally true that denying them causes one to fall into contradiction. The rationalists had such a high confidence in reason that empirical proof and physical evidence were regarded as unnecessary to ascertain certain truth. In other words, there are significant ways in which knowledge are gained independently of sense experience.

Different degrees of emphasis on this method or theory lead to a range of rationalist standpoints, from the moderate position that reason has precedence over other ways of acquiring knowledge to the more extreme position that reason is the unique path to knowledge. Since the Enlightenment, rationalism is usually associated with the introduction of mathematical methods into philosophy as seen in the works of Descartes, Leibniz and Spinoza. This is commonly called continental rationalism, because it was predominant in the continental schools of Europe, whereas in Britain empiricism dominated.

The Frenchman, Rene' Descartes, has been identified as founder of rationalism. He applied to philosophy the mathematical method already proven so effective in science. He also based his whole enterprise on a radical methodical doubt, thereby laying the foundation of modern epistemology. This principle of

---

[723] Ibid.
[724] https: en.wikipedia.org/wik/rationalism, accessed 7.12.2017.

doubting everything eventually extended to all aspects of Christian tradition and even to the very idea of tradition itself. Hence, tradition was regarded as the epitome of inherited prejudices, and critical historical science was to take the place of tradition. Simply put, rationalization is "a mental attitude, which grew out of the conviction that things are knowable, not by relying on the benign intervention of some supernatural power, but the calculation based on their intrinsic laws."[725]

Rationalization is the awareness that not all aspects of human life and society are to be approached with religious sentiments; reality is susceptible to being subjected to man's cold-blooded investigation and manipulation. In the past, people evolved two complementary ways of arriving at truth. Scholars called these "mythos" and "logos".

5.4.1.1. "MYTHOS" AND "LOGOS"

"Mythos" and "logos" describe the transition in ancient Greek thought from the stories of goddesses and heroes (mythos) to the gradual development of rational philosophy and logic (logos). The former is represented by the earliest Greek thinkers such as Hesiod and Homer; the latter is represented by later thinkers called the "Pre-Socratic philosophers" and then Socrates, Plato, and Aristotle.[726]

In the earliest "mythos" stage of development, the Greeks saw events of the world as being caused by a multitude of clashing personalities – the "gods". There were gods of natural phenomena such as the sun, the sea, thunder and gods for human activities such as winemaking, war, and love. The primary mode of explanation of reality consisted of highly imaginative stories about these personalities. However, as time went on, Greek thinkers became critical of the old myths and proposed alternative explanations of natural phenomena based on observation and logical deduction. Under "logos", the highly personalized world-view of the Greeks became transformed into one in which natural phenomena were explained not by invisible superhuman persons, but by impersonal natural causes.

However, many would argue that there was no such a sharp distinction between mythos and logos historically, that logos grew out of mythos, and elements of mythos remain with us today. For example, ancient myths provided

---

725 Cf., Agu C.C., *Secularization in Igboland: Socio-Religious Change and Its Challenges to the Church Among the Igbo,* Frankfurt am Main, 1989, p. 40.
726 Cf., https://mythoslogos.org/2014/12/21what-is-mythos-and-logs/comment-page-1/, accessed 12.12.2017.

the first basic concept used subsequently to develop theories of the origins of the universe. We take for granted the words that we use every day, but the vast majority of human beings never invented a single word or original concept in their lives. They learn these things from their culture, which is the endproduct of thousands of years of speaking and writing by millions of people long dead. The very first concepts of "cosmos", "beginning", "nothingness", and differentiation from a single substance were not present in human culture for all time but originated in ancient myths. Subsequent philosophers borrowed these concepts from myths, while discarding extremely personal interpretations of the origins of the universe. In that sense, mythos provided the scaffolding for the growth of philosophy and modern science.[727]

An additional issue is the fact that not all myths are wholly false. Many myths are stories that communicate truths even if the characters and events in the story are fictional. Socrates and Plato denounced many of the early myths of the Greeks, but they also illustrated philosophical points with stories that were meant to serve as analogies or metaphors. Plato's allegory of the cave, for example, is meant to illustrate the ability of the educated human to perceive the true reality behind surface impressions. Could Plato have made the same philosophical point in a literal language, without using any stories or analogies? Possibly, but the impact would be less, and it is possible that the point would not be effectively communicated at all.

Some of the truths that myths communicate are about human values, and these values can be true even if the stories in which the values are embedded are false. Ancient Greek religion contained many preposterous stories, and the notion of personal divine beings directing natural phenomena and intervening in human affairs was false. But when the Greek built temples and offered sacrifices, they were not just worshiping personalities; they were worshipping the values that the gods represented.

Apollo was the god of light, knowledge, and healing; Hera was the goddess of marriage and family; Aphrodite was the goddess of love; Athena was the goddess of wisdom; and Zeus, the king of the gods, upheld order and justice. There is no evidence at all that these personalities existed or that sacrifices to these personalities would advance the values they represented. But a basic respect for and worshipful disposition toward the values the gods represented was part of the foundation of ancient Greek civilization.

---

[727] Cf., https://mythoslogos.org/2014/12/21/what-is-mythos-and-logs/comment-page-1/, accessed 12.12.2017.

It is also worth pointing out that worship of the gods, for all of its superstitious aspects, was not incompatible with even the growth of scientific knowledge. Modern Western medicine originated in the healing temples devoted to the god Asclepius, the son of Apollo, and the god of medicine. Both of the great ancient physicians, Hippocrates and Galen, are reported to have begun their careers as physicians in the temples of Asclepius, the first hospitals. Hippocrates is widely regarded as the father of western medicine and Galen is considered the most accomplished medical researcher of the ancient world. As love of wisdom was the prerequisite for philosophy, reverence for healing was the prerequisite for the development of medicine.

Karen Armstrong has written that ancient myths were never meant to be taken literally but were "metaphorical attempts to describe a reality that was too complex and elusive to express in any other way."[728] But some would argue that this use of metaphors to describe reality is deceptive and unnecessary. Yet a literal understanding of reality is not always possible, and metaphors are widely used even by scientists.

The transition of a mythos-dominated world-view to a logos-dominated world-view was a stupendous achievement of the ancient Greeks, and modern philosophy, science, and civilization would not be possible without it. But the transition did not involve a complete replacement of one world-view with another, but rather the building of additional useful structures on top of a simple foundation. Logos grew out of its origins in mythos and retains elements of mythos to this day. "We have seen that both "mythos" and "logos" were important. Each had its special area of competence. Mythos provided people with a context that made sense of their day-to-day lives; it directed their attention to the external and universal. "Logos" occupied the rational, pragmatic and scientific sphere. Unlike mythos, Logos must relate exactly to facts and correspond to external realities in order to be effective."[729]

Rationalism eliminates "mythos". There are no more attributing phenomena of the natural and social world to the superhuman and supernatural forces, the gods and spirits. In their place, it substitutes as the sole cosmology the modern scientific interpretation of nature.[730] Only the laws and regularities discovered by the scientific method are admitted as valid explanations of phenomena. Therefore, if it rains or does not rain for a very long time, it is not because the

---

[728] Cf., https://mythoslogos.org/2014/12/21what-is-mythos-and-logs/comment-pages-1/, accessed 12.12.2017.
[729] Cf., Karen A., *The Battle for God: Fundamentalism in Judaism, Christianity and Islam,* Harper Collins Publishers, London, 2000, pp. xiii - xiv.
[730] Kumark K., *"Modernization and Industrialization"* in Encyclopedia Britannica, op. cit., p. 286.

gods are angry but because of atmospheric conditions, as measured by the barometer and photographed by satellites. So, in modern terminology it is called "climate change". From this perceptive, we see Igbo Traditional Religion as involved in this process of modernization which the ancient religions of the world have undergone and the modern ones are still undergoing. With rationalization, science moves to scientism and beliefs based on superstition and mythology is elbowed out of the ring.

5.4.2. SCIENCE AND TECHNOLOGY

Science and technology can be used interchangeably. But the goal of science is the pursuit of knowledge for its own sake, while the goal of technology is to create products that solve problems and improve human life. Simply put, technology is the practical application of science.[731] Etymologically, the word "science" comes through the old French and is derived from the Latin word "Scientia" - knowledge, which in turn comes from "Scio" – "I know". From the Middle-Ages to the Enlightenment, science or Scientia meant any systematic recorded knowledge. Science therefore had the same sort of very broad meaning that "philosophy" had at that time.

In other languages, including French, Spanish, Portuguese, and Italian, the word corresponding to science also carries this meaning. Today, the primary meaning of "science" is generally limited to empirical study involving the use of the scientific method.[732] Science from the Latin word "Scientia" (knowledge) is a system of acquired knowledge based on the scientific method, as well as the organized body of knowledge gained through research. Science as defined here is sometimes termed pure science to differentiate it from applied science, which is the application of scientific research to specific human needs.

Technology is a term with origins in Greek, "technologies" ("techne" which means "craft" and "logia", which means saying, or knowledge). However, a strict definition is elusive. "Technology" can refer to material objects of use to humanity, such as machines, hardware or utensils, but can also encompass broader themes, including systems, methods or organization, and techniques. The term can either be applied generally or to specific areas: example, construction technology, medical technology or state-of-the art technology. [733]

Technology is a broad concept that deals with species' usage and knowledge of tools and crafts, and how it affects a species' ability to control and adapt to its

---

[731] Cf., https://www.diffen.com/difference/science-vs-technology, accessed 8.12.2017.
[732] https://www.diffen.com/difference/science-vs-technology, accessed 8.12.2017.
[733] Ibid.

environment. In human society, it is a consequence of science and engineering, although several technological advances predate the two concepts. Through technology, we have today some "telemetering" instruments, for example, monitor production systems and accurate control mechanism that regulate performances according to built-in criteria. These machines automatically perform functions of inspecting, checking, adjusting, and otherwise regulating the processing of materials and data.

In transportation, jet aircraft has made coast-to-coast travel a matter of hours and has made overnight freight service available between many national and international centers. A growing number of innovations that include palletization, container units, pipeline, super-tankers, and conveyor systems changing the character of bulk-freight shipping. Outer space experiments have opened the way for new communications, weather forecasting, and geographical surveying. The bathyscaphe[734]has made undersea exploration possible at great depths, and the submarine has made it possible in formerly in-accessible areas, such as under the polar-icecap.

Achievements in physics and chemistry are creating a new world of materials. Soil analysis, the use of hybrid seeds, chemical fertilizers, herbicides and pesticides, and the selective breeding and scientific feeding of animals have vastly increased the productivity of agriculture and are changing the nature of agricultural production. Developments in packaging, refrigeration, dehydration, and irradiation have increased the ability to store, preserve and distribute foods.

We cannot forget the cutting edge of science and technology into the Red Planet-Mars. Such an inhospitable zone as the Red Planet gradually is being drifted into alignment with the Earth, thanks to scientists. Already some people are dreaming of taking a vacation in space. It is being envisioned that "By 2020 - about the time that children born this year approach voting age, mankind's first tiny settlement on another world may be taking hold."[735]This means that: "...we could be a two-world species within a generation"[736] This gives us the impression that science has exhausted the content of the earth and now has faced the galaxies.

---

[734] Bathyscaphe is a manned vessel for deep-sea diving. It is a word derived from the Greek word 'bathus' meaning 'deep' and 'skaphos' meaning "ship". Cf., Oxford Reference Dictionary.
[735] Time Magazine, April 10, 2000, p. 36.
[736] Ibid.

5.4.3. BIOTECHNOLOGY

Biotechnology is the use of biological processes, organism or systems to manufacture products intended to improve the quality of human life. The earliest biotechnologists were farmers who developed improved species of plants and animals by cross pollination or cross breeding. In recent years, biotechnology has expanded in sophistication, scope, and applicability.[737]

The science of biotechnology can be broken down into sub-disciplines called red, white green, and blue. Red biotechnology involves medical processes such as getting organisms to produce new drugs or using stem cells to regenerate damaged human tissues and perhaps regrow entire organs. Biotechnology or reproductive technology employs a myriad of methodologies including the use of donor sperm, donor eggs, fertilization outside of the human body (in vitro fertilization), analysis and manipulation of genetic components, zygote transfers, and ultimately introduction of the embryo back into the womb.

Biotechnology works towards controlling and planning the human situation at the psychosomatic level of the individual and of all humanity. Today, the issues of genetic engineering or human experimentation, or organ transplantation, DNA and contraceptive pill and other forms of biotechnology dealing directly with the human person have become as normal as any other common issue. This manipulation of the genetic components, zygote transfer, including the contract or surrogate motherhood system uncover a radical shift in human relations. In this aspect of biotechnology, human being is the object of technology.

White (also called gray) biotechnology involves industrial processes such as the production of new chemicals or the development of new fuels for vehicles. This also involves the manipulation (as through genetic engineering) of living organism or their components to produce useful commercial products (such as pest resistant crops, new bacterial strains, or novel pharmaceuticals). It includes also any of various applications of biological science used in such manipulation.[738] Green biotechnology applies to agriculture and involves such processes as the development of pest-resistant grains or the accelerated evolution of disease-resistant animals.

Blue biotechnology, rarely mentioned, encompasses processes in marine and aquatic environments, such as controlling the proliferation of noxious water-borne organisms. "Biotechnology, like other advanced technologies, has the

---

[737] Cf., whatis.techtarget.com/definition/biotechnology, accessed 17.12.2017.
[738] Cf., https://en.wikipedia.or/wik/Biotechnology , accessed 17.12.2017.

potential for misuse. Concern about this led to efforts by some groups to enact legislation restricting or banning certain processes or programmes, such as human cloning and embryonic stem-cell research. There is also concern that if biotechnological processes are used by groups with nefarious intent, the end result could be biological warfare."[739]

5.4.4. INFORMATION TECHNOLOGY: WORLD WITHOUT BORDERS

Information technology involves the development, maintenances, and use of computer systems, software, and networks for the processing and distribution of data.[740] The term information technology is commonly used as a synonym for computers and computer networks, but it also encompasses other information distribution technologies such as television and telephones. Several industries are associated with information technology, including computer hard-ware, soft-ware, electronics, semi-conductors, internets, telecommunication equipment, and e-commerce.[741]

Developments in electronics and communication are an added ingenuity of man to overcome some formidable deficiencies of man in nature. We cannot but wonder at the latest development of what one may call "thinking machine", that is, the digital computational mechanism which give an added dimension to automatic control. Because computers can store information in the form of detailed instructions, they have opened the way for control systems that analyze complication data and make choices of control. They can perform countless business operations, such as customer billing, preparation of payrolls, and the calculation of dividends. Computer, so to speak, is a piece of technology without end.

The light-speed of advancement of information technology in the areas of satellite, television, internet, telephone, fax, newspaper together with transportation, just to mention but a few, has shrunk the dimension of the earth. Today, one can confidently talk of "a world without borders", or as some may prefer to call it "the global culture". Plathottam is therefore correct when he points out that "mass media is currently playing an irreversible role as great leveler of cultures".[742] Today all nations are aware of how other nations live. The flood in Africa for example, is also a headline in American dailies. The street protests

---

[739] https://en.wikipedia.org/wiki/information-technology, accessed 12.12.2017.

[740] Cf., https.www.merriam-webster.com/dictionary/information%20technology, accessed 12.12.2017.

[741] Cf., https://en.wikipedia.org/wiki/information-technology, accessed 12.12.2017.

[742] Plathottam G., *"Christian Mission in the Third Millennium and Information Superhighway: Challenges for Evangelization"*, in *Indian Missiological Review*, 20th December 1998, 4, 12-20, quotation, p. 14.

taking place in Europe are watched on television and internet in other countries, and most often large numbers as a result take to the streets themselves. Baum points out that "mass media do much more than mediate information ... they create the categories in which we perceive the world."[743]

Put in another way, information technology sells lifestyle and set of values and worldviews as well. It is only in our age that physical encounter is not so necessary for human relationship. Taking the internet as an example, we observe a faceless market known as e-commerce (electronic commerce) where pay cards (American Express card, Visa card etc.) act as "middleman" between buyers and sellers. This is unlike the traditional market system, which among other things, is a major point of meeting and interaction. Without doubt, this new market system, in all its efficiency, not only imposes consumerism by its avalanche supply of material options, but it also creates new and consolidates existing individualism through its non-physical contact-policy.

The hard fact remains that the allurement from communication media has become so irresistible that, in most cases, "Not to follow suit," to use the words of George Plathottam, "would imply that you are going to be left behind if not totally left out".[744] One therefore, can say without mincing words that this sweeping irreversible move towards homogeneous culture, makes the mass media a new form of colonialism. In actual fact, no one would claim being untouched in any degree by this colonialism of the mass media.

5.4.5. URBANIZATION AND INDUSTRIALIZATION

The world has developed a lot since the ages of industrialization in the 20th century. Industrialization seasons were marked by a change in the social and economic phenomena. The transformation involved a paradigm shift from an agricultural society to an industrial society.

The term "urbanization" can be defined in different ways to broaden the meaning thereof. It could refer to the increase in the number of people who dwell in urban areas. It can as well be defined as the process by which major towns and trading centers are formed to become larger, due to people moving into these towns for work and living.[745] Urbanization is predominantly a cause of the physical growth of a town or any urban area. Aspects that contribute to urbanization are mainly industrialization, modernization, and rationalization

---

[743] Baum G., *"The Church and the Mass Media"*, in *Concilium* 65 (1994) 2 46-47.
[744] Plathottam G., *Christian Mission in the Third Millennium and the Information Superhighway: Challenges for Evangelization,* op. cit., p. 14.
[745] Cf., www.differencebetween.net/miscellaneous/geography-miscellaneous/difference-industrialization-and-urabanization/, accessed 15.12.2017.

that results from social processes. It is a historical transformation on a global scale. It majorly involves the replacement of old cultural ways to a dominating urban culture.

Modernity does not only increase numbers by its improved life style; it distributes them in particular ways, concentrating mass populations in cities. Modern life is unquestionably urban life. In the traditional society of the past, people and fortunes used to move slowly, since economic life was to a large extent bound up with the earth. However, everything changed with industrialization. Today, people flock toward manufacturing centers, drawn by the lure of earnings. Little wonder why most sociologists link industrialization and urbanization. This goes in line with the words of the great sociologist, Emile Durkheim, who says that:

> Great cities are the uncontested homes of progress; it is in them that ideas, fashions, customs, new needs are elaborated and then spread over the rest of the country…. Minds naturally are there oriented to the future.[746]

At the same time, cities are destabilizing elements for traditional communities, particularly the family. Moreover, immigrants in industrial towns lose the life-style they were accustomed to in the villages. They lose their vital link with nature, its rhythms and its regulating symbolism, which are organizing elements of every religiously based traditional culture. The individual, so to speak, is forced into attitude of reserve and isolation. Community oneness is somehow lost, the traditional customs, practices and religion are almost no longer practised. Simmer laments that "one nowhere feels as lonely and lost as in the metropolitan crowd."[747] Shiner draws us to religious angle when he says:

> Sensitivity to cosmic sacredness tended to be lost when industrialization siphoned men off the land into this man-made domain where the rationalization of production and distribution took the place of providential rain and growth.[748]

5.4.5.1. THE INVENTIONS OF URBANIZATION AND INDUSTRIALIZATION

The industrial revolution was one of the most successful periods of inventions in the late 16th century and early 19th century. The era was paving way for lesser philosophical intrigues and more scientific discoveries. Carriages came into being. Coal was then discovered to be an energy source. This led to the discovery of engines, engines and machinery that relied on fuel to run. The discovery

---

[746] Quoted in Kumark K., *Modernization and Industrialization*, op. cit., p. 285.
[747] Ibid, p. 287.
[748] Quoted in Agu C.C., *Secularization in Igboland,* op. cit., p. 45.

of machinery increased the efficiency of production in the industries. Railways were constructed to ease the work of transportation.[749]

The process of urbanization had its own inventions as well. People invented new ways to build better houses. Construction became sophisticated. Architectural and civil engineers found out better ways to make long lasting roads. Better means of transporting people were being discovered. Carriages continue to be refined for use by people. Walking became less stylish than using carriage. City guards evolved to become administrative authorities who started to concern themselves over city planning and public health. Health centers came into the picture and the nursing profession was born. Orthodox medicine began to replace traditional medicine. As the invention in industrialization led to better ways of manufacturing and transporting, urbanization led to inventions that aimed at a much cozier life for the developing working class. Urbanization and industrialization have good as well as adverse effects. We shall explain this more when we discuss some encouraging qualities and alarming shortcomings of modernity. But suffice it to say that:

> Both industrialization and urbanization affected the people differently. Due to industrialization, the lifestyle that people lived was harsh. There were long hours to work in a day, the pay was meager and the working conditions were deplorable. For urbanization, the lifestyle of the people changed too. Selfish tendencies such as corruption emerged. People disregarded the need for family and society as well.[750]

5.4.6. GLOBALIZATION

Globalization is the increasing interaction of people, state or countries through the growth of the international flow of money, ideas, and culture. Globalization is primarily an economic process of integration that has social and cultural aspects. It involves goods and services, and the economic resources of capital, technology, and data. The steam locomotive, steamship, jet engine, and container ships are some of the advances in the means of transport while the rise of the telegraph and its modern offspring, the internet and mobile phones show development in telecommunications infrastructure. All of these improvements we enjoy in the modern era have been major factors in globaliza-

---

[749] Cf., www.differencebetween.net/miscellaneous/geography-miscellaneous/difference-between-industrialization-and-urbanization, accessed 10.12.2017.

[750] www.differencebetween.net/miscellaneous/geography-miscellaneous/difference-between-industrialization-and-urbanizastion, accessed 10.12.2017.

tion and have generated further interdependence of economic and cultural activities.[751]

In other words, Globalization can be said to be a process of interaction and integration among people, companies, and governments of different nations, a process driven by international trade and investment and aided by information technology. "This process has effects on the environment, on culture, on political systems, on economic development and prosperity, and on human physical well-being in societies around the world. Globalization unites the world for the common good of all."[752]Based on this definition, globalization is desirable and can lead to the greater happiness and fuller humanity of all people. Modernity from this angle, contrasts the attitude of self-centeredness of the past with the virtue or power of self-transcendence, the ability to transcend one's narrow interests in the dimension of both space and time. With particular reference to space, today, the joys and sorrows of those who live at a great distance have been enlarged to a global awareness and as such can attract a global responsibility.

Globalization is new, because for many years, people, countries and corporations have been buying from and selling to one another in lands at great distances. But policy and technological development of the past few decades have spurred increases in cross-border trade, investment, and migration so large that many observers believe the world has entered a qualitatively new phase in its economic development.

This current wave of globalization has been driven by policies that have opened economies domestically and internationally. In the years since Second World War, and especially during the past two decades, many governments have adopted free-market economic systems, vastly increasing their own productive potential and creating myriad new opportunities for international trade and investment. Governments also have negotiated dramatic reductions in barriers to commerce and have established international agreements to promote trade in goods, services, and investment. Taking advantage of new opportunities in foreign markets, corporations have built foreign factories and established production and marketing arrangements with foreign partners. A defining feature of globalization, therefore, is an international industrial and financial business structure.[753]

---

[751] Cf., https://en.wikipedia.org/wiki/Globalization, accessed 17.12.2017.

[752] Balasuriya T., *"Globalisation"*, in Febella V., and Sugirtharajah R.S., eds., *Dictionary of Third World Theologies*, Orbis Books, 200, pp. 91 - 94.

[753] Cf., www.globalization101.org/what-is-globalization/, accessed 12.12.2017.

Technology has been the other principal driver of globalization. Advances in information technology, in particular, have dramatically transformed economic life. Information technology has given all sorts of individual economic actors, consumers, investors and business valuable new tools for identifying and pursuing economic opportunities, including faster and more informed analyses of economic trends around the world, easy transfers of asserts, and collaboration with far-flung partners.

Globalization is somehow controversial. Proponents of globalization argue that it allows poor countries and their citizens to develop economically and raise their standards of living, while opponents of globalization claim that the creation of an unfettered international free market has benefited multi-national corporations in the western world at the expense of local enterprises, local cultures, and common people. Resistance to globalization has therefore taken shape both at a popular and at a government level as people and governments try to manage the flow of capital, goods, labour and ideas that constitute the current wave of globalization.[754] It is pertinent to emphasize that the real movers and beneficiaries of the process of the globalization are in fact the global transnational corporations, which control the greater share of the production, trade, finance, transportation, insurance, and communications media in the world.

In dire need of foreign investments, the local governments of debtor countries are constrained to offer incentives to the transnational corporations (TNCs) which may include guarantees for foreign capital, cheap labour, adequate infrastructure, and flexible labour and environmental laws, often at great social cost to the debtor country. In many Third World countries, national planning has been replaced by corporate strategic planning under the aegis of the transnational corporations (TNCs), aided by the Washington – based World Bank and International Monetary Fund (IMF).[755]

The argument for globalization is that the productivity of the world increases; marvelous technological advances that include long-distance instantaneous communication are available to all; the world's resources are used more efficiently; and thus, human needs are more readily satisfied. But poorer people may experience many drawbacks from such globalization. For example, cheaper food imports discourage local agriculture and make the poor countries dependent on the advanced countries for food; local industries are forced to

---

[754] Ibid.
[755] Balasuriya T., *"Globalisation"*, in Fabella V., and Sugirtharajah R.S., eds., *Dictionary of the Third World Theologies,* op. cit., p. 91.

close down or be integrated within the dominant trans-national corporations (TNCs); unemployment escalates when TNCs decide to relocate to another country where labour is cheaper. Poor countries thus compete with other poor countries, while competition between TNCs is reduced by mergers, takeover, monopolies and oligopolies.

5.4.7. SECULARIZATION

Secularization is the transformation of a society from close identification with religious values and institutions towards non-religious values and secular institutions. The secularization thesis refers to the belief that as society progresses, particularly through modernization and rationalization, religion loses its authority in all aspects of social life and governance.[756] Modernity, in a special way, involves the process of secularization. Secularization is usually defined as "the experienced, gradual disintegration of all mythical and religious legitimations of society".[757]

From the above definitions, one understands that "secularization manifests itself when explanation of reality previously attributed to mythical or religious sources is shown to have rational ones. It is also manifest when the scientist takes over from the witch doctor, when the psychologist assumes some previously priestly functions, or a technological discovery disintegrates a traditional explanation."[758] Where this is the case, as it is actually the case in our contemporary time, some people think that there is less need to look outside and above for God to give meaning to life. Secularization is seen also as a historical process in which religion loses social cultural significance. As a result of secularization, the role of religion in the modern societies becomes restricted. In secularized societies, faith lacks cultural authority, and religious organizations have little social power.

As secularization strictly pairs with rationalization, reason and science take over the stage. God and religion are not only confined to private sphere, but also secularization goes to the extreme of what is known as secularism whereby there is no need of the ultimate meanings. It denies transcendence. It affirms the absolute autonomy of the "secular" society. Secularism is very aggressive, Joinet takes us to some few examples:

---

[756] Cf., htts://www.bring.com, accessed 18.12.2017.

[757] O'Donnell D., *"Evangelization: The Challenge of Modernity"*, in Jenkinson W., and O'Sullivan H., ed., *Trends in Mission Towards the 3rd Millennium*, Orbis Books, New York 1991.

[758] O'Donnell D., *"Evangelization: The Challenge of Modernity"* in Jenkinson W., and O'Sullivan H., *Trends in Mission Towards the 3rd Millennium*, Orbis Books, New York, p. 121.

In 1792 in France, Churches were destroyed and priests put to death by secular governments. In Mexico in 1920, and in Spain in 1936 we have similar stories. Prayer in schools was banned in USA; Bavaria (Germany) tried to remove crucifixes from classrooms; God's name was never mentioned in the speeches of French politicians. It was strictly forbidden to wear signs of religious affiliation in French schools.[759]

Against this background, one can rightly say that secularization or its aberration secularism, begets agnosticism. By finding rational sources to realities previously attributed to mythical or religious sources, secularism:

creates an inquiring and inventive attitude of mind that disrupts cultural and religious unity and accepted "certitudes" and helps to produce a person who is either fragmented religiously, in which case there is a disregard or a tendency to reduce to irrelevance the high values or manifestations of human life – religion, philosophy, art, and so forth – or much still a person who claims not to believe at all –agnosticism.[760]

The above points, without doubt, leave secularization totally in a bad light. And for a long time only this negativity shrouded opinions, especially in the Church circle, about secularization. However, some bright sides stand out. Here, we remember that where secularization holds sways, no one religion has the monopoly of the state. Positively seen, the State is given to all religions; in other words, there is religious freedom for all. It promotes tolerance which allows all citizens, in the words of Joinet "to say I have my own ideas and stick to them; but I recognize that you have different ideas and convictions, and I respect your right to have them."[761]

In the 1960s, there was a dramatic shift toward secularization in Western Europe, North America (especially Quebec), Australia, and New Zealand. This transformation was intertwined with major social factors: economic prosperity, youth rebelling against the rules and conventions of society, women's liberation, radical theology, and radical politics.[762]

---

[759] Joined B., *The Challenges of Modernity in Africa,* Pauline Publications, Africa, Nairobi, Kenya, 2000, p. 41.

[760] Cf., O' Donnell D., *"Evangelization: The Challenge of Modernity",* in Jenkingson W., and O'Sullivan H., ed., *Trends in Mission Toward the 3rd Millennium,* op. cit., pp. 123 - 124.

[761] Joinet B., *The Challenges of Modernity in Africa,* op. cit., p. 22.

[762] Cf., https: en.wikipedia.org/wiki/secularization, accessed 7.1.2018.

5.4.8. CULTURAL PLURALISM

Cultural Pluralism is a condition in which minority groups participate fully in the dominant society yet maintain their cultural differences.[763]As a sociological term, the definition and description of cultural pluralism has evolved over time. It has been described as not only a fact but a societal goal.

> Cultural pluralism is distinct from (though often confused with) multiculturalism. Multiculturalism lacks the requirement of a dominant culture. If the dominant culture is weakened, societies can easily pass from cultural pluralism into multiculturalism without any intentional steps being taken by the society. If communities function separately from each other, or compete with one another, they are not considered culturally pluralistic.[764]

We can say that pluralism[765] flows strictly from secularization, though it cannot be divorced from other traits of modernization. Because of modernity, the individual has discovered himself or herself with a new degree of self-consciousness. At the same time, this new person is being bombarded with an unprecedented flow of information and options. This is a very volatile combination of high self-awareness and an almost unlimited supply of information.

Since cultural pluralism is rooted in a multiplicity of meanings as a result of and leading to various cognitive and normative options and choices, modern pluralism undermines traditional certitude and weakens the awareness of society. Azevedo asserts that "pluralism weakened the hold of religion on the society and on the individual".[766]

The watch-word of cultural pluralism is freedom and relativity. Under modernity, every doctrine, knowledge, truth, morality, etc. is relative and not absolute. What counts is the immediate cost of things, especially according as they are verifiable and realizable in a given situation. Modern world is a world where opinion reigns supreme. According to Guerra, our world is an epoch in which "the truth which thus rules is completely a new type – a social truth with its specific and at times apparently contradictory characteristics."[767]

---

[763] Cf., www.dictionary.com/brows/cultural-pluralism, accessed 19.12.2017.

[764] Cf., https://en.wikipedia.org/wiki/cultural-pluralism , accessed 18.12.2017.

[765] There are general basic types of pluralism: structural pluralism, religious pluralism and in political science the word pluralism comes into play. Here our main interest is on cultural pluralism, which borders on the religions, beliefs, customs and general lifestyle of a people. Cf., pluralism, race and ethnicity in selected African countries, in Smith M.G., *Theories of Race and Ethnic Relations,* Cambridge University Press, 1986.

[766] Azevedo M., *Inculturation and the Challenges of Modernity,* op. cit., p. 46.

[767] Guerra F., *"The paradox of Modernity",* in Mcinerny R., ed., *Modernity and Religion,* University of Notre Dame Press, Indiana, 1994, p. 25.

5.4.9. THE EMERGENCE OF MODERN SOCIO-POLITICAL STATE

Another remarkable feature of modernization is the emergence of centralized bureaucratic, representative state. The state came to undertake the function necessary for regulating the economic and social activities of groups with divergent interests. In doing so, the state tends to become an abstract power placing itself artificially above the real society, at the same time creating the illusion that the affairs of the state belong to the people. The state is meant to rank highest among social institutions and is to be viewed as the sum of rational individual beings and their rights, and consequently as the totality and actuality of all reason and all laws, as the highest and the only positive authority. The will of the state is the united will of all individuals and is absolute.

Based on secularized liberty and equality, modernity tends to severe the general acceptance of hereditary monarchical rule, the long-standing political tradition. Against this background, democracy for all emerged as a dominant political system first in United States and then all over Europe with the French Revolution in 1789. Today, for any political system to suit the time, it has to be democratic. While in the traditional society one of the most central functions of the state was to remove the burden of choice from individuals, in the modern democratic society, this process has been reversed. People are trained to ask leaders questions, to question their decisions, and reach a consensus after discussing the issue.

This democratic spirit stretches even to the family. Nowadays, parents, even in countries without democratic traditions, have to talk with their children, explain, argue and convince them. Parents have the obligation to help their children develop a personal conscience of their own not by using folklore, mythological tales but with facts. This cannot but be the case, because "the individual, as well as the group, is constantly faced with alternatives and pressed to make choices."[768]

It is pertinent to remark that in modern political society, the Constitution is drafted (in democratic system of government) with a desire to respect all religions as another way of defending the fundamental human right and freedom of worship. In this way it promotes pluralism. Again, as the state claims the sole authority with right to regulate all aspects of the lives of the citizens, and by removing certain aspects of life from religion's control and subjecting them to the control of the state, the Constitution imposes a process of secularization.

---

[768] Azevedo M., *Inculturation and the Challenges of Modernity*, op. cit., p. 38.

5.5. THE DUALITY OF MODERNITY: MODERNITY AS HOPE AND MODERNITY AS DOOM

One experiences in modernity a duality, a paradox, because of its ambivalent nature. On the one side, it admittedly holds some encouraging qualities and on the other side, it reveals some glaring shortcomings and crisis. Modernity serves comfort and rootlessness on the same platter. It presents a lot of optimism and at the same time a biting despair unknown to any age before. The very machine that eases workload also creates us into automatons. Excellent roads for cars and rails for trains and trams that facilitate journeys also claim a lot of fertile land for food production. The very credit card that lifts the risks of carrying heavy amount of money around, also records and publishes data about our public and private lives – our favorites, how often we eat at Chinese restaurant, how frequent we travel either by flight/train/bus; from buying tickets or through fueling of our cars, etc. Carrier is clear on this paradox when he writes:

> Modern humanity is confronted with a curious paradox on the one hand, it has managed to create technological marvels unknown to any previous civilization. On the other hand, it feels threatened as never before by the products of its mind and spirit.[769]

Modernization brought a series of seemingly indisputable benefits to people. Lower infant mortality rate, decreased death from starvation, eradication of some of the fatal diseases, more equal treatment of people with different backgrounds and incomes, and so on. To some, this is an indication of the potential of modernity, perhaps yet to be fully realized. In general, rational scientific approach to problems and the pursuit of economic wealth are seen by many as a reasonable way of understanding good social development.

At the same time, there are black spots of modernity pointed out by sociologists and others. Technological development occurred not only in the medical and agricultural fields, but also in the military. The atomic bombs dropped on Hiroshima and Nagasaki during World War II, and the following nuclear arms race in the post-war era, are considered by some as symbols of the danger of technologies that humans may or may not be able to handle wisely. Stalin's Great Purges and the Holocaust (or Shoah) are considered by some as indica-

---

[769] Carrier H., *Gospel Message and Human Cultures*, Dunquesne University Press, Pennsylvania, 1989, p. 29.

tions that rational thinking and rational organization of a society might involve exclusion, or extermination, of non-standard elements.[770]

Environmental problems comprise another category in the dark side of modernity. Pollution is perhaps the least controversial of these, but one may include decreasing biodiversity and climate change as results of development. The development of biotechnology and genetic engineering are creating what some consider sources of unknown risks. Beside these obvious incidents, many critics point out psychological and moral hazards of modern life – alienation, feeling of rootlessness, loss of strong bonds and common values, hedonism, disenchantment of the world, and so on.

Likewise, the loss of a generally agreed upon definitions of human dignity, human nature, and the resulting loss of value in human life have all been cited as the impact of a social process/civilization that reaps the fruits of growing privatization, subjectivism, reductionism, as well as a loss of traditional values and worldviews. Some have suggested that the end result of modernity is the loss of a stable conception of human and/or the human being.[771] O'Donnel must be referring to the same paradox when he comments:

> Each new piece of technology affects or will affect the human family: ecologically: controlling pests and damaging the ozone layer; economically: encouraging trade and causing unemployment, - politically: centralizing power and diffusing information – culturally: challenging traditions and undermining symbol systems - religiously: answering questions scientifically and purifying faith – humanly: developing genetic engineering. [772]

5.5.1. SOME OF THE GOOD QUALITIES OF MODERNITY

We cannot deny that modern culture has provided humanity with advantages that no previous period had even dared hope for. Our age feels a very special pride and legitimate satisfaction over the leap in quality discoveries brought about by modern research. Our contemporaries are literally fascinated by the advances in technology, electronics, and discoveries that have vastly improved the living conditions especially of so-called affluent societies or still some affluent individuals in non-affluent societies. The advances of this epoch seem to cover all spheres of existence which include the spheres of nutrition, health, education, communications, transport, just to mention but a few.

---

[770] Cf., http://en.wikipedia.org/wiki/modernity, accessed 24.12.2017, Cf., also www.3.dbu.edu/mitchell/modernit.htm, accessed 24.12.2017.

[771] www.3dbu.edu/mitchell/modernit.htm, accessed 24.12.2017.

[772] O' Donnell D., *"Evangelization: The Challenges of Modernity"*, in Jenkinson W., and O' Sullivan H., eds., *Trends in Mission Towards the 3rd Millennium*, Orbis Books, New York 1991, p. 119.

These discoveries and developments undoubtedly have some identifiable bright sides. Here, we shall sum up the encouraging qualities of modernity under the following heads:

1. Better discovery of the individual
2. Equal dignity of all persons
3. Amelioration of difficulties encountered in life style
4. Demythologization of Authority.

5.5.1.1. BETTER DISCOVERY OF THE INDIVIDUAL

It is a major credit of modernity that it has enabled the individual to gain an identity independently of the group. The individual has discovered himself or herself with a new degree of self-consciousness and self-reliance or autonomy.

In chapter two of this work, we said that the community gives meaning to the individual. According to Igbo traditional setting, the life of the individual has meaning only when it is lived in the community; outside the community, the individual has no identity. We recall that in the traditional society with its subsistence economy, a person can survive only in the family which is the basic unit of food production. We may remember that during the said traditional period someone (particularly women) who is ostracized from his or her village community for one taboo or another had greater chances of dying or even committing suicide. On the contrary, in the modern society, one can comfortably survive outside his or her traditional set-up. Some people even do their job from home with little or no contact to anybody. With credit cards and online shopping, people get practically all they want served at home without much human contact. Although not good news, here one is inclined to say that the time may come when only matters of sickness and funeral or special feasts would call for the others' help and presence.

5.5.1.2. EQUAL DIGNITY OF ALL PERSONS

In Greek philosophy, the concept of natural law recognized only the dignity of the Greek man, free and masculine. Today, there is in the world a great aspiration that equal dignity of all persons be recognized. People today are not satisfied with abstract principles; they want the dignity of all men and women to be recognized by all institutions, by all structures, and above all, by the concrete possibility that each person can express individual responsibility and co-responsibility in personal and social relations.[773]

---

[773] Häring B., *Evangelization Today, St. Paul's Publications, England, 1990, p. 14.*

Connected to dignity of persons is a new consciousness of liberty and liberation. Most of the things and situations, which the man of yesterday accepted as divinely willed in Igbo Traditional Religion and inevitable, have turned out malleable to the man of today. He becomes conscious that he can and must free himself from many encrustations and many conditionings. Modern mankind begins to feel with an ever-greater clarity that there are no immanent laws that will automatically guarantee human development. An authentic development is possible only in courageous and serene confrontation of the situation of conflict. The key word can no longer be 'development' alone, but 'liberation'[774] and development together.

5.5.1.3. AMELIORATION OF DIFFICULTIES ENCOUNTERED IN LIFE STYLE

Through constant research, the amount, depth, and a considerable accuracy in the findings or developments of technology, roughly in all fields of life – health, transport, agriculture, recreation, communication, just to mention but a few seem lightened from encumbrances. From the perspective of the history of technology, throughout the history of all the civilizations on earth existing before the present century, the technological activities that were carried on relied primarily upon a single source of power to perform most of the work that they required and, on the scale, they required, and this principal source of power lay in the muscles of humans and domestic animals. Wind and power, though known, were severely limited in their use, or rather, never employed on the scale needed to accomplish the productive operations being carried on in both ancient, medieval, and early modern times. Similar limitations in scale apply to all the other forms of power available, except muscle power.[775]

Today, on the contrary, what would have cost great deal of time and risk to achieve can only cost a dial of phone from the bedroom. With the Internet and E-mail, one can tour round the globe in minutes looking at the screen. Cars and computers, hair dryers and dish washers, and space travel, telephones and televisions, electricity, amplifiers, weather prediction, nuclear weapons, radio and video, genetic engineering, just to mention but a few, come from the intelligence of man to lessen the fatigue of the confrontation with nature. This is not only a dominion over the harshness of nature, but over and above all, a participation in God's act of creation.

---

[774] Synod of Bishops, 1971, Document on Justice in the World, nos. 6, 37.
[775] Price, D. De S., *Science since Babylon, Yale University, New Haven, 1962, p. 107.*

5.5.1.4. DEMYTHOLOGIZATION OF AUTHORITY

The process of modernization allows also the demythologization of authority. This does not mean that there is no more need for authority. Authority will, however, be conceived as service rendered to the community, so that all can grow in the knowledge of participation and co-responsibility. The awe surrounding authority is on the fast track of disappearance. People do respect rather than fear a constituted authority. The same justice, in the perspective of humanist and still more in that of the biblical 'new justice', demands that all search for good together in the articulation of co-responsibility.[776]

5.5.2. SOME OF THE SHORTCOMINGS OF MODERNITY

Another side of modernity presents us with some alarming shortcomings, what Zuern calls "vices". And by vices Zuern means "the attitude of thinking and living that are prevalent in modernized society but which are ultimately destructive and unsustainable in the light of a vision of humanity as God's people."[777]

Here, Zuern sees vices not only as they apply to individual morality, but more as characteristics of social system. We must admit, however, that the shortcomings, as we shall explain here, have been present throughout human history, but they receive special form today, arising from and feeding into the destructive aspects of modernization. Carrier rightly pointed out that "many times, in history uncontrolled change had threatened traditional communities, but never had the crisis been so deep and far-reaching in its cultural and spiritual consequences."[778]

5.5.2.1. CONSUMERISM

Consumerism is a social and economic order and ideology that encourages the acquisition of goods and services in ever-increasing amounts. With the industrial revolution, but particularly in the 20th century, mass production led to an economic crisis: there was overproduction – the supply of goods grows beyond consumer demand, and so manufacturers turned and planned obsolescence and advertised more to increase consumer spending.[779]

Consumerism is a very conspicuous effect of modernization that is worth remarking. Consumerism should be understood as "the modern equivalent to

---

[776] Häring B., *Evangelization Today*, op. cit., p 15.

[777] Zuern T.F., et al., *On Being Church in a Modern Society*, Pontifical Gregorian University, Rome, 1983, p. 74.

[778] Carrier H., *Evangelization and Culture of Modernity*, op. cit., p. 37.

[779] hattps://en.wikipedia.org/wiki/Consumerism, accessed 13.1.2018.

what Augustine called vane curiosity, an insatiable fascination or itch for spectacles that parades as a desire for knowledge."[780]Ours is a high-consumption society in which there is "the desire to draw the whole of the world into one-self, the desire to reach unlimited abundance".[781]There is the ceaseless desire and addiction for material wealth and sensual pleasure or concupiscence of the flesh. This greed is never satisfied; instead the drive to possess and devour more and more objects increases. This is because modernity maximizes the power to choose and increase the need for well-discerned decisions.

Consumerism as a disgusting shortcoming of modernity is seen in the following evil fruits it begets, namely, aggression, hatred, robbery, kidnapping, continuous growth of class consciousness, the big gap between the rich and the poor, structural injustice etc. Schineller sums up consumerism and its evils thus:

> Consumerism stands for the attitude of aggressive grasping for more and more, the measuring of success and happiness through one's possessions. The consumption and accumulation of goods and services become the central purpose of life, a meaning and end, rather than a means. Luxuries become necessities, while much of the world goes without basic needs. Every item becomes a fashion; the latest is the best, the pace-setter becomes the ideal; we live in the throw-away society, blind to the exploiting of earth and its limited resources.[782]

This inordinate desire for material things, the unending desire to have more, this attitude of consumerism, is fostered "through the advertising media, which fuels the imagination towards curiosity and concupiscence. The capitalism economy runs on this psychology of moreness, where the acquisitive is recklessly indulged."[783]

5.5.2.2. THE INDIVIDUATION OF PERSON AND DUPLICATION OF SELF-IDENTITY

Fragmentation or individuation of persons is another accompanying element of modernization. The increased mobility of people and the promiscuity of

---

[780] Zuern T. F., et al., *On Being Church in a Modern Society*, op. cit., p. 75.

[781] Ibid.

[782] Schineller P., *Ten Summary Statements on the Meaning, Challenge and Significance of Inculturation as Applied to the Church and Society of Jesus in the United States, in Light of the Global Processes of Modernization,* in Schineller P., et al., *On Being Church in a Modern Society*, op. cit., p. 76.

[783] Schineller P., *Ten Summary Statements on the Meaning, Challenge and* Significance *of Inculturation as Applied to the Church and Society of Jesus in the United States; in Light of the Global Processes of Modernization*, in Schineller P. et al; *On Being Church in a Modern Society*, op. cit., P., 76.

urban collectives cut individuals off from the communities to which they traditionally belong: the family, the village, and the parish or the religious group. The desire for autonomy exalted individuals, who henceforth tried freely to choose their roles in society, whereas previously these roles were assigned by their milieu, age-grade, family, and social condition. In chapter two of this work, we stated categorically that in Igbo traditional society, the individual loses his self-identity when he excommunicates himself from his community.

Today through the process of modernization, the individual acquired a new status and freedom within society. This phenomenon was brought about not only by the effects of the industrial and urban revolution that progressively took over in Europe, but also by the currents of thought springing from romanticism, the enlightenment, and the various philosophies that preached the ideal of a deeper awareness of freedom and a vigorous proclamation of individual rights.

Another great cultural consequence of modernization is the eventual collapse of the sense of value or worth of the individual. It is an irony seeing many philosophies in our time preaching the ideal of individual liberty, while the philosophy of technology places exaggerated emphasis on economic productivity. Consequently, workers are hired as economic objects rather than subjects; they only form a part of a large organization just like a chug in the wheel. Some of the concomitants of technological production at the level of consciousness are the segregation of work from private life, the separation of means and ends, anonymous social relations, a componential self (the self being in a partial and segmented way) that is, the same man in the office turns a different person at home.

The modernization process creates an impersonal idiom. This involves the dichotomization between public and private life. Hiebert distinguishes between "multiplex" and "simplex" roles.[784] In multiplex relationships, one meets the same person in many different social situations and so has a better chance of knowing the "whole" person. Modernization leads to simplex role relationship where one sees certain people only at work, others only at Church, others only in the stores, and others only in the neighbourhood. This causes stress, loneliness and suspicion. In search for identity and companionship, some people (mainly in the Northern hemisphere) now find solace in some domestic animals rather than in fellow human beings. This fits properly to what Berger and Kellner refer to as the "homeless mind" in their discussion of the effect of modernization on the consciousness. They assert:

---

[784] Hiebert P. G., *Cultural Anthropology, Baker Book, Michigan,* 1983, p. 90.

The reciprocity between individual and society, between subjective identity and objective identification through role, now come to be experienced as a sort of struggle. Institutions cease to be the 'home' of the self, instead they become oppressive realities that distort and estrange the self. Roles no longer actualize the self but serve as a 'veil of maya' hiding the self not only from others but from the individual's own consciousness.[785]

When life becomes fragmented in role relationships, no one knows the whole person. We know only a part of a person according to what the particular role relationship is. It becomes difficult to find security in the person one knows. Impersonalness is also found on the job, where only one's services are needed, not the whole person. Being paid in cash or with a cheque and on a regulated time brings little true affirmation for the actual work done. The employer's concern and evaluation are only in terms of the quality and quantity of work being accomplished.

As life becomes fragmented, it becomes difficult, if not impossible, to focus on the whole. If involved in production, one is likely doing just a part of the process. If one works as a labourer, the clock likely determines how much one has accomplished not the finishing of the project. Private life often becomes regimented around activities requiring one to be away from home. One experiences the transformation of time with endless striving and restlessness.

5.5.2.3. ECOLOGICAL TENSION

Ecological problems do not occur in a vacuum. There are no ecological problems in the world without a cause. For example, no ecological problems occur on the moon because there is no existence of life there. There were no ecological problems on the earth before the existence of life. There are no ecological problems in the world with an ecosphere but without human activity.

There are actual ecological activities only in the world with an ecosphere, human activities and human consciousness. Ecological problems are problems peculiar to today's human beings. Today, we hear of climate change. Climate change is an off-shoot of ecological tension. Ecological problems are witnessed today because of the destruction of ecosystems by human beings themselves.

Ecological disaster is another expression of mindlessness of modernity. Nature is torn apart by technological and industrial revolution. The environment is exploited by big money and power. And humankind, as it were, has alienated itself from nature by excessive domination of nature such as the clear-cutting

---

[785] Berger P. L. and Kellener H., *The Homeless Mind: Modernization and Consciousness,* Random House, New York, 1973, p. 93.

of the rain forest, the over-fishing of the world's oceans and the dumping of atomic and chemical waste into the oceans. In fact, there seems to be a concerted effort towards environmental degradation. The irony of the entire situation is clear from the fact that, while industrial societies are largely insulated by their sophisticated technologies and knowledge, they remain dependent on nature for the basic resources to support life and industry. Factories cannot replace photosynthesis, at least, not yet. However, no one knows, as Hiebert would say "the next level of subsistence adaptation may well be synthetic foods production from inorganic materials."[786]

Today, there is great tension as to what awaits humankind as a result of pollution of the environment and wearing out of the ozone layer. Hiebert expresses his fear in the following words:

> The introduction of new technology over the past century has initiated a revolution, with consequences that cannot be fully predicted. The old balances between people and nature are gone, and no new stable balance relationship has developed, so far. The vast scope of the imbalance and the tension rising from it are only now becoming apparent.[787]

The situation that gave room to ecological tension is that human needs are infinite, while utilizable resources are finite. Such a contradiction cannot be solved. Human beings exist by means of changing the world. By contrast, animals live in a way that complies with the order of nature. For example, in the grasslands of Africa, the desertification caused by herbivorous animals has a negative impact on the subsistence of these animals in reverse. It seems to be an ecological problem but actually is not, because the ecological destruction caused by animals will be adjusted by natural causation rather than the animals themselves.[788]

It is through so-called modernization that human beings created a comprehensive objectified relationship with nature through scientific knowledge, technology and engineering. "Modernization allows for human income to accumulate systematically, but at the same time, accumulates destruction in the ecological system. In the pre-modern age, the accumulation of income was achieved by individuals, and the impact of accumulation of destruction was communal. Both kinds of accumulations are discontinuous. Both in the modern age, the accumulation of income is achieved by a given society, while the accumulation

---

[786] Hiebert P. G., *Cultural Anthropology,* op. cit., p. 91.
[787] Ibid., p. 101.
[788] http://scholarworks.sjsu.edu/cgi/viewcontent.cg:?article, accessed 30.12.2017.

of destruction becomes overall. Today, the accumulation of income and destruction are both global and irreversible."[789]

5.5.3. THE TENSION THAT EXISTS BETWEEN MODERNIZATION AND IGBO TRADITION

The coming of the Europeans and their introduction of "modernization" to Igboland and to the Igbo people created a tension between Igbo tradition and the western civilization. This tension persists somehow up till today. In line with this is the Chinua Achebe's famous work entitled "Things Fall Apart." In this novel, Achebe demonstrates the tension between Igbo tradition and western civilization (modernization).[790] From the point of view of Achebe, modernization has a great effect on the traditional Igbo culture. So, to speak, it led to the loss of the traditions that the Igbo have so much held to. Modernization brought about language change in the sense that the people changed their official language and adopted the language of the Europeans.

In the same line of thought, modernization brought about an introduction of a new religion – Christianity. It was not only religion that the missionaries brought to Igboland. They also introduced western education. The Igbo system of government that formerly consisted of the male council of elders was replaced by the British system of government. The traditional practices held by the Igbo people were made of no good value in the light of Christianity. Having been faced by modernization, the Igbo traditional culture was almost totally destroyed. This can well be understood by studying the stability of the society. The cohesion and the solidarity of the Igbo community would be seen to be weakened by modernization. The western life-style was introduced into the Igbo community in which individualism instead of communalism sometimes takes upper hand.

---

[789] Cf., ibid., accessed 30.12.2017.

[790] In "Things Fall Apart", Chinua Achebe tries to present a raw and primitive early Igbo traditional society. The said society "Umuofia" had its own set up including its own traditional religion; they had their dos and don'ts. They also had their taboos and that was why the principal character Okonkwo was seriously reprimanded by the priest of "Ani" when he desecrated the week of peace by beating one of his wives, "we live in peace with our fellows to honor our great goddess of the earth without whose blessing our crop will not grow... you have committed a great evil". Injustice was condoned hence the torture of a lad, "Ikemefuna" who was killed because the oracle had decreed. No one dared question the decision of the oracle or gets equally killed. However, all these practices stopped when the Umuofia community encountered another form of religion, Christianity. For some "the society changed for the better" and for others Igbo culture has been destroyed. Cf., ibid.

In Igbo life-setting, an individual draws strength from the community that he belongs to and vice versa. Another thing we should note is that whenever different cultures come into contact there is always struggle for dominance. In the course of the struggle, one culture has to be superior to the other. According to Chinua Achebe, the Igbo traditional culture was overtaken by the western culture:

> Retrieving of the native land, tradition and religion become impossible. In this regard, with Igbo people, it was almost impossible to recover their culture and religion instead, Christianity swept the traditional Igbo culture.[791]

The repression of Igbo language reveals that modernization brought about cultural changes even in terms of language. Cultures have proved to be limited or rather partially limited in accommodating other cultures. Therefore, modernization implies a kind of reconstruction in terms of culture. Although modernization is a good thing, it should not be forced on a people. Nonetheless, modernization has effects on Igbo traditional cultures ranging from positive to negative ones. It is pertinent to note that religion, Christianity, is seen as the main agent of change in Igboland. We must quickly add that colonization also played its own part in terms of introducing new system of governance to the Igbo.

5.5.4. THE CHURCH AS A VEHICLE OF CIVILIZATION

5.5.4.1. THE SCHOOLS AS BAROMETER OF DEVELOPMENT

Since man is mortal, every society must perpetuate itself physically by procreation and socially by process of education. Through education, the customs, values, beliefs, skills and so forth are passed on from generation to generation. Without this, the society would disintegrate. This generation must be taught the ways of thinking and behaving which have preserved the society in the past and believed to keep it in the future. The function of education is to mold individuals to abide by the social norm.

Education goes on in various forms in virtually every human society. Today, formal education is the dominant form of education in Igboland. Introduction of formal education in Igboland is one of the legacies of colonialism, especially the Christian Missionary bodies, who were the pace-setters in this venture. Nduka observed that "as subsequent events were to prove, hardly any other

---

[791] Cf., https://supremeessayas.com/samples/art/modernization-and-traditional-africian-culture, accessed 30.12.2017.

people in Nigeria took more readily to the Whitman's religion and education than did the Ibos."[792]

It may be difficult to change ideologies of a people by the use of force. But ideologies and cultures can easily be changed by enlightenment and education. The missionaries applied the use of enlightenment and education in order to change Igbo traditional ideologies that were inimical to the Gospel of Christ and replaced them with Christian ideologies. Some Igbo ideological thinking, customs and traditions were eradicated, such as the killing of twins, "Osu", slavery, and human sacrifice, just to mention but a few.

The colonial master applied the use of force in some areas of Nigeria in order to change the people's ideologies and cultures; and this was strongly opposed by the people. But the missionaries never used force; rather they showed love and used education as a tool for changing the Igbo ideologies and customs, which they found to be inimical to the teachings of Christianity. Education, whether formal or informal, is the recognized means whereby a person acquires most of his ideas, beliefs and attitudes. In short, a person's knowledge, skill and manners are necessary, not only to combat the hazards and problems of life (physically, theoretically and psychologically), and to secure the needs of life (biological, social and economic), but also fit into the company of fellow human beings.

Right from the home to the wider social groups, from his parents, nurses, elders and mates, the child is constantly acquiring knowledge, skills and manners. In traditional societies, there was little or no formal education although people spent years learning certain crafts and skills for example weaving, carving, sculpture. People also received vocational training from grandmasters (in priesthood, native medicine, divination), trading, etc. They also received training in farming, fishing, hunting, agricultural activities, building houses, citizenship, moral and religious knowledge. Education in these areas go on informally through culturally determined modes of learning. Through folk stories, music, songs, festivals, precepts and proverbs, through subtle remarks aimed at encouraging or discouraging some behaviours, the child receives his education as a means of equipping him for his individual life and life in the society. It is one or a combination of talents, interest, disposition, parental wishes, vocation and the general cultural setting that determines a child's eventual career. Informal education in the traditional society assumes that the child is ignorant (amagh ihe), because he just does not know, and so he must be taught. And he is

---

[792] Nduka O., *Western Education and the Nigerian Cultural Background,* London, Oxford University Press, 1964 in Nwala T.U., *Igbo Philosophy,* op. cit., p. 324.

taught not only skills but also manners, in the form of religious and moral knowledge in order to fit into the highly ritualized life of the society.

It is the duty of the child's parents and elders to teach him, and he is guided in the course of his life and education in such a way that some measure of critical attitude is development. The values and philosophy of his community equip him with the basic premises for his judgments. But he is not trained to challenge those basic norms and religious principles of the society. Social values and norms are transmitted, hedged with taboos and sanctions, over which the child has no choice. The stock of wisdom of the society that is transmitted is, therefore, unquestioned. Hence, traditional education tends to breed conformists. This is necessary in the interest of order and harmony as well as of the health and welfare of the group to which he belongs. However, when the child grows into maturity and displays some level of intellectual sagacity, he becomes an authority to whom the society may turn to for guidance in interpreting traditional values, norms and religious beliefs.[793]

In the recent past, when people spoke of mission, they usually had in mind the mission schools. Equally for many, perhaps for many missionaries, the schools were the most important institutions. "For the historian, schools could well be used as the barometer of Africa's development."[794] Therefore, from this view, the time up to the World War 1 (1900 - 1920) could be called the age of the bush school in Africa; the time between the wars (1920 – 1940) the age of the primary school, the time after world war II (1945 – 1960) the age of the secondary school; and with independence there came the age of the university. Parallel to this development, there went a growing missionary involvement in education.[795]

Europe or the Christian missionaries did not bring the concept and practice of education to Igboland. The Igbo had their traditional system of education. What the Europeans brought was the Western type of education. Long before 1858, education had been practised largely informally in that it had neither fixed venues (schools) for its practice nor professional teachers or graded durations (classes 1, 2, 3, etc., years 1, 2, 3 or intervals of rest 7 holidays. It was also non-literate in that it did not utilize reading of books or writing. Knowledge

---

[793] Cf., Nwala T.U., *Igbo Philosophy, op. cit.,* pp. 324 - 325.
[794] Baur J., *2000 Years of Christianity in Africa: An African Church History, 2nd revised edition,* Paulines Publications Africa, Nairobi, Kenya, 1998, p. 412.
[795] Ibid.

and skills were transmitted orally through parents, relations and acquaintances to the young adolescents and adults.[796]

The Igbo in pre-independence era of Nigeria were mostly farmers. In the past, many Igbo carried out their farm work outside the living zones of their communities. Some stayed in their farms for months with their children and wives. Normally, they had huts built in their farms which served as shelters. When the missionaries came to Igboland and noticed this system of farm work practised by some Igbo, they introduced what is called "bush schools" which in today's terminology is called "nomadic schools". These schools were run where the farmers had their farmlands.

Nevertheless, almost every mission station had also a central school. In a sense, traditional education, whether formal or informal, is a means of transmitting the civilization of the people from one generation to the other. By its nature, education can transform a person's habit of thought, his attitudes and his emotions. Traditional Igbo society did not have the advantage of developed writing and documentation.

In actual fact, British colonial education was designed to 'civilize' the Igbo (like other Africans) by making them forget some of their culture in order to embrace British culture. It was again aimed at producing the necessary manpower for the administrative and economic needs of the colonies. The missionaries aimed at converting them into the Christian fold and destroying the native (rather 'pagan') religion. In the course of this, both harm and good were done. Not only did some Igbo acquire this noble European culture and civilization, they learnt to despise all that is noble and ignoble in their traditional culture and civilization.

The major objective of the missionaries for building schools and instituting formal education was to enable the Igbo develop their own Church. The Lutherans insisted that the converts should be able to read the Bible; the Anglicans wanted a self-reliant Church as soon as possible; the Presbyterians and specially the Catholics aimed at spreading Christian civilization. So, they all built schools; yet for them all the immediate purpose of the school was to convert as many as possible.[797] Schools were then seen as barometer of development and at same time instrument of evangelization. Baur would say that:

---

796 Cf., Ozigbo I.R.A., *A History of Igboland in the 20th Century,* op. cit., p. 119.
797 Baur J., *2000 Years of Christianity in Africa: An African Church History, 2nd revised edition,* op. cit., p. 413.

> All investments in schools seemed to be well justified; for it looked as if Africa became Christian to the extent that its children went to school. Concretely speaking, 80 to 90% of all Christians may have been converted in schools.[798]

A good number of Igbo went – or were sent – to schools in order to acquire the "white man's" knowledge, the secret of his power and mostly, to learn in order to get a job. Yet once in school, their hearts opened themselves quite naturally to the message of Christ, making true what Tertullian had said of the early converts in North Africa: *anima naturaliter Christiana* – the human soul is by its very nature Christian. The parents knew that their Children would learn the white man's religion and did not object.[799]

Whatever the motive of the colonial master and the missionaries in particular may have been for the introduction of schools in Igboland, in the sociological perspective, the mission schools were the greatest service done to the development of Igboland. It is in this respect that Dr. Kwame Nkrumah of Ghana, a former student of a Catholic mission school, said at a students' seminar shortly after Ghana got her Independence: "the rise of our country is properly due to the missionaries. To their work and their assistance, I and others owe what we now are."[800]

The school was also a stepping-stone in the emancipation of women, "the greatest single achievement of the missions besides general education."[801] The school gave to the girls a new self-consciousness and prepared them to earn their own living as teachers and nurses. This made them independent in choosing their husbands and in running their family affairs. However, the education of the girls was a very slow process, as parents, caught in their traditional views of the female role in society, would tenaciously oppose their girls' European education.

Nigerian communities, prior to their increasing contact with the Christian missionaries in the 19th century and their forcible subjugation to British political control in the opening years of the 20th century, had evolved over some time, techniques of dealing with different kinds of human diseases. In many pre-colonial Nigerian communities, medical and health care was a more or less specialized occupation practised by specially trained people who combined

---

[798] Ibid., p. 414.

[799] Welbourn *in Colonialism II.,352, in* Baur J., *2000 Years of Christianity in Africa: An African Church History, op.* cit., p. 414.

[800] Cf., *Pax Romana Seminar,* Accra 1957, in Baur J., *2000 Years of Christianity in Africa: An African Church History, op.* cit., p. 415.

[801] Welbourn *in Colonialism II, 352, in* Baur J., *2000 Years of Christianity in Africa: An African Church History, op.* cit., p. 414.

knowledge of herbal cure with powers of divination and mediation between the patient and supernatural forces (like one's ancestors or malevolent gods, witches and wizards) believed to be capable of afflicting people with ill health or even death.[802]

5.5.4.2. RELIGION (CHRISTIANITY) AS A SCHOOL FOR SOCIAL AND ETHICAL DEVELOPMENT IN IGBOLAND

Society has been defined in various ways by various people. Etymologically, the word "society" comes from the Latin word *socius* which means association or companionship. Oxford English Living Dictionary defines society as "the aggregate of people living together in a more or less ordered community."[803] It is the community of people living in a particular country or region and having shared customs, laws, and organizations.[804] Society is also defined as a larger group of individuals, who are associated with each other. Wright defines it as a system of relationships that exists among individuals of a group.[805]

All the definitions made so far take account of three key concepts, namely, people, institutions, and relationships. This implies that a society comprises the above three concepts. To this end, a society is simply a group of people sharing distinct institutions and culture, which are passed on from one generation to another. The society is a number of individuals connected by interaction; it is any group of people who have lived and worked together long enough to get themselves organized and to think of themselves as a social unit.

The word "Ethics" etymologically comes from the Greek word *ethos* meaning "custom or a habitual code of conduct."[806] Ethics or moral philosophy is the study of human actions in respect to their being right or wrong, the actions of individuals and social groups are the subject matter of ethics. Ethics is concerned with voluntary actions carried out with sufficient knowledge. Ethics considers social forms and institutions from the point of view of their completeness and coherence as expressions of human nature. It asks whether the social life is best or the only life for human soul.

---

[802] Ikime O., ed., *Groundwork of Nigeria History,* Heinemann Educational Books, Ibadan, Nigeria, 1980, p., 594.

[803] Oxford English Living Dictionary.

[804] Cf., https://www.bing.com/search?qathe , accessed 31.12.2017.

[805] Cf., www.studylecturenotes.com/social-sciences/sociology/133-what-is-society, accessed 31.12.2017.

[806] Okwueze M.I., ed., *Religion and Societal Development: Contemporary Nigerian Perspectives,* op. cit., p. 85.

In Igbo traditional society, morality is divided into major and minor. The major ones are stealing of yams, homicide, incest, sexual relationship between an *osu* and freeman, suicide, poisoning, theft of domestic fowl or sheep, theft of any kind by an *ozo* titled man, etc. The minor ones are wife throwing her husband on the ground during a fight, killing and eating of totem animals, deliberate cutting of yam tendrils, burning of a person's house etc. All these moral codes as identified are attached with the dictum "thou shall not". They all have some moral guilt attached to them. In some places in Igbo traditional society, there is what is called "week of peace" during which people are supposed to maintain absolute peace. There should be no fighting or exchange of hot words. People who run fowl of this all-important laws go against the moral tenets of their society. Unmasking of masquerade is also a crime in Igboland.[807]

It is important to say that some of these major and minor crimes in Igboland as enumerated above with the corresponding consequences attached to them, may have undergone some modifications or may not be as effective as they were before the advent of Christianity to Igboland.

Every society possesses a way of life, a way of doing their own things. This way of life is called culture.[808]This was exactly what Chinua Achebe highlighted in "Things Fall Apart". This was depicted in the town of "Umuofia" and its nine villages where every aspect of culture in its primitive and crude form was found. It has to be noted that the changes in the society are brought about by various factors such as cultural diffusion, discoveries and inventions, wars and colonization, etc. Following the introduction of Christianity (1841)[809], Western education (1858)[810], Western culture and British colonialism (1902)[811] into Igboland, a new Igbo society eventually emerged. As Chinua Achebe aptly observed, "Igboland, became ill at ease and, with time, her traditional institution, norms, traditions and practices were rudely shaken and drastically modified."[812] What has happened to Igbo society in barely ten decades can be seen as a veritable revolution. A visiting century-old Igbo ancestor can scarcely rec-

---

[807] Ibid.

[808] Ibid., pp. 83-84.

[809] Christianity was first preached in Igboland in 1841 but was established in 1857. Cf., Kalu O. U., *The Embattled gods: Christianization of Igboland, 1841 -1991 (Lagos 1996).* in Ozigbo I. R. A., *A History of Igboland in the 20th Century,* op. cit., p. 115.

[810] The first primary school in Igboland was opened at Onitsha on 15th November, 1858. Cf., Ekechi F.K., Missionary *Enterprise and Rivalry in Igboland 1857 - 1914* (London 1972) p. 24, in Ozigbo I.R.A., op. cit., p. 115.

[811] The Aro Expedition (Nov. 1901 - May 1902) marked the formal commencement of British colonization of Igboland. The Royal Niger Company rule (1886 - 1899) was largely informal. Cf., Ozigbo I.R.A., *A History of Igboland in the 20th Century,* op. cit., p. 115.

[812] Cf., Achebe C., *Things Fall Apart,* London, 1958; No longer at Ease, London, 1960.

ognize the Igbo society any longer. Its traditional communities with their housing patterns and furniture, their physical structures, their people and clothing, their religious beliefs and practices, their traditional education and values, their ideas, attitudes and aspirations must certainly appear totally strange and incredibly bizarre to the ancestor visitor.[813]

---

[813] Ozigbo I.R.A., *A History of Igboland in the 20th Century*, op. cit., p. 115.

CHAPTER SIX

6. BRIDGING THE GAP BETWEEN CHRISTIANITY AND IGBO TRADITIONAL RELIGION

6.1. INTRODUCTION

What we need today in the world is the establishment of a common ground, where all the religions of the world can have a more frequent dialogue. With this in place, the religious violence and terrorism we are experiencing today around the world may be prevented. When the adherents of the religions of the world understand that many are worshipping the one true God but differently, there would be better understanding of one another and the respect for one another. It is an obvious fact that Christianity has come to Igboland and has come to stay. It is also pertinent that the Igbo traditional religionists have to accept this fact. We should note that:

> Religion and culture are so intimately related and connected that in reality it is impossible for a society to have a culture without religion or religion without culture. In a sense, a living religion is as inseparable from culture – and culture as inseparable from religion – as a living fish from its water. Though religion and culture are not identically one and the same thing, as fish and water are not the same thing.[814]

If the above assertions are correct, then one can equally say that the only way possible to replace Igbo Traditional Religion with Christianity is to destroy Igbo culture which is not possible. Christian missionaries in their invincible anthropological ignorance of the Africans, conceived or seemed to have conceived their mission as that of imparting not only the Christian religion but also culture and civilization – and the western civilization precisely. The missionaries were convinced of the immense superiority of the western culture which Africa (Igbo), as cultural "tabula rasa", must wholly absorb if it is to be rescued from the claws of paganism, savagery, barbarism and superstition. Such was the mentality of the early missionaries in Africa who did not penetrate the mind and culture of the Africans. This cultural arrogance and superiority complex were definitely responsible for the strife between African (Igbo) culture and westernized Christian institutions and values.

In this chapter, we have to investigate the avenues and ways through which these two religions, Christianity and Igbo Traditional Religion, can co-exist for

---

[814] Iwe S.S.N., *Christianity and Culture in Africa,* Varsity Industrial Press, Onitsha, Nigeria, 1987, p. 19.

the benefits of the Igbo people. We have to show what the two religions have in common and where they differ. This may act as a substratum for better dialogue between them.

6.2. THE AREAS OF AGREEMENT AND DISAGREEMENT BETWEEN CHRISTIAN THEOLOGY AND THE IDEOLOGIES OF IGBO TRADITIONAL RELIGION

It is obvious that there are some areas of agreement and also disagreement between Christian thoughts and Igbo traditional ideology. To portray this fact, let us recall a debate or better put, a dialogue, which Chinua Achebe narrates in "Things Fall Apart", between a Christian Missionary and an Igbo traditional priest. The dialogue runs thus:

Whenever Mr. Brown went to that village, he spent long hours with Akunna in his "Obi" (living room) talking through an interpreter about religion. Neither of them succeeded in converting the other but they learnt more about their different beliefs.

'You say that there is one Supreme Being who made heaven and earth', said Akunna on one of Mr. Brown's visits. "We also believe in him and call him, 'Chukwu'. He made all the world and the other gods".

To this Mr. Brown retorted that there are no other gods and that what Akunna and his men call gods are pieces of carved wood. But Mr. Akunna said that both the wood and the gods are made by God as his messengers and through whom he could be approached. As to whether Akunna's men give all the worship to false gods which they 'have created', Mr. Akunna said: 'That is not so. We make sacrifices to the little gods, but when they fail and there is no one else to turn to we go to Chukwu (the Supreme Being). It is right to do so. We approach a great man through his servants. But when his servants fail to help us, then we go to the last source of hope'.

Explaining why they appear to pay more attention to the smaller gods, Mr. Akunna said: 'We worry them more because we are afraid of their master. Our fathers knew that Chukwu was the overlord and that is why many of them gave their children the name 'Chukwuka' – (God is supreme).

When Mr. Brown told Akunna that in his religion ... Chukwu is a loving Father and not to be feared by those who do His will; Mr. Akunna replied: 'But we must fear Him when we are not doing His will – and who is to tell His will. It is too great to be known.'[815]

The above citation is a good comparative analysis of the theology of the two religions – Christianity and Igbo Traditional Religion. "Today, there is no longer any doubt as to whether the traditional Igbo possesses a religion or not. His religion is no longer seen as that of paganism and devil-worship, nor is his culture any longer seen as the devil's work, nor even are his ancestors any longer held to dwell in hell, as was hitherto the fashionable view among some Christians." [816]

From what we have discovered so far, there are some similar elements in Christianity and Igbo Traditional Religion. But the problem one may encounter in harmonizing Christianity and Igbo Traditional Religion is that ever since the introduction of Christianity in Igboland, the carriers of this good message (the missionaries) "have retained a medieval outlook. It has not been easy for most Christians to think differently from the logic of the world-view inherited from medieval Christianity. It was possible but not easy to transfer the allegiance and reverence held for traditional deities and ancestors to the Christian God, Christ, the Angels and the Saints."[817] We can quickly also add that:

Basically, the entities found in both Igbo Traditional Religion and Christianity are similar in the sense that both are transcendental, mystical and held sacred. Both systems are built on an act of faith and rationalization, taboos and sanctions. They are authoritarian and unquestionable, ritualistic and full of myths and festivals. Above all, each system has a theoretical answer for all human problems, from the problem of health, poverty, death, to the problems of social injustice. It is in their practical solution to these problems that they reveal what they are.[818]

Another similarity which we may find in both religions is in the area of conversion of the unbeliever. Christianity never uses force in her mission of evangelization. Igbo Traditional Religion also does not apply the use of force in her message of conversion. We said earlier in this work that Igbo Traditional Religion does not have missionaries and does not intend to have any in future; conversion in Igbo Traditional Religion and Christianity is left to one's conscience. When we look at these two religions in their method of conversion,

---

[815] Achebe C., *Things Fall Apart,* with introduction and notes by Aigboje Higo, London, Heineman, 1970, pp. 62 -63, in Nwala T.U., *Igbo Philosophy, second edition, op.* cit., p. 309.
[816] Cf., ibid., p. 309.
[817] Ibid., p., 310.
[818] Ibid.

we notice that they act alike, unlike some religions of the world who have shown in recent times that the use of force is applied in their method of conversion and not a matter of one's conscience.

As pointed out by Akunna, the priest in Achebe's Things Fall Apart, the Christian world-view and attitude to life are logically similar to that of the Igbo Traditional Religion. Both of them, as we have already pointed out, are religious and metaphysical; both refer to entities which human beings do not see. Events are explained in both systems in non-empirical terms embodying ideas that people have to accept on faith. The impact of such ideas depends on the way they are rationally and analogically linked to human experiences. For example, in Christian thought, if one meets with misfortune, the explanation is that it is the work of the devil. "If the person prays to God to let him out of the misfortune and nothing happens, and he asks why the good God does not answer his prayers, then he is told that God has not answered him because He has allowed the devil to tempt the man in order to test the man's faith, to prove whether the man, so tempted, deserves to be a child of God. That gives the man the heart and strength to undergo his misfortune less painfully or even painlessly depending on how religious he is. It enables him to keep going no matter the odds."[819]

But in summary, Christians accept suffering and cross as part of life. For the Christians, when one's prayer is not answered, one should continue to pray and not lose faith in God. This is because God does not exist in space and time. Two million years are like one day in the eyes of God and one day is equally like two million years before God. This means that what comes out of one's situation, whether one's prayer is answered or not, God loves him and one should not lose faith in God.

But in Igbo Traditional Religion, suffering and cross are not acceptable. They always have a negative connotation and always have a cause. For the Igbo traditionalist who is faced with a misfortune – for example a terrible illness - this person ultimately visits a diviner in order to discover the cause of his illness. Sometimes, the diviner tells him that one deity or an ancestor is responsible for his misfortune and why it happened – (maybe the sufferer sinned or his relation sinned). There is always an explanation – a cause. The will of God is never considered in this case. The diviner normally tells the sick man what he should do to atone for the sin and appease the deity. He also tells him what type of "dibia," (medicine man) to consult for the cure. When these attempts fail, he goes to consult another diviner and so on.

---

[819] Nwala T.U., *Igbo Philosophy,* op. cit., p. 312.

So, the sick man does not see the devil, or God or even temptation itself, which this manner of speaking may personalize. But the fact of misfortune (like the attack of a terrible disease) is so real to him that he needs either cure or the mind to accommodate it. What the Christian explanation offers him is the mind to accommodate and bear it when all has failed, and see it as a cross. This methodology is somewhat different from the methodology of Igbo Traditional Religion. This explains why the Igbo traditionalists refused to bury or perform burial ceremonies for people who died of terrible diseases like leprosy, small pox, other noxious diseases and those whose death could not be accounted for satisfactorily. Their corpses were thrown out unburied into "ajo ofia" (evil forest). But this practice has stopped. This is one of the changes Christianity brought to Igbo Traditional Religion.

It is certainly clear that there are similarities and differences that exist between Christianity and Igbo Traditional Religion. This is the issue we are emphasizing here. Thus, Nwala asserts:

> The closeness between the Christian ideas and traditional Igbo (nay African) ideas, as systems of rationalization exists. However, they differ in terms of the overall picture of their worldviews; the basic conceptual entities posited as well as in their methodology. There is, the Christian notion of the Trinity of Father, Son and Holy Ghost as components of the Godhead. For the Igbo, they have the duality of Chi (the Supreme Being, Chukwu) and *Eke* (God the creator otherwise called Chineke). Virgin Mary, the Angels and the saints are part of the institutional Christian God-head, and they may be compared to the local deities (Agbara) and the venerable ancestors -*Ndichie* in Igbo conceptual system that are part of the traditional God-head and as such worshipful.[820]

Similar to the Christian prophets, the Igbo traditionalists have diviners. Both Christianity and Igbo Traditional Religion have priests. "The Christian ideas of heaven and hell are fused in traditional notion about the spirit world, where a man's spirit enjoyed an everlasting bliss if the man lived a morally and religious upright life in the visible world or doomed if otherwise"[821] Both religions hold that heaven is a state devoid of sadness, worries and sufferings. It is a state of everlasting bliss.

The principle of good (as personalized by the person of God) and the principle of evil (in the person of the devil) are not as differentiated in traditional Igbo thought, as we find them in Christian thought. The Supreme Being (*Chi-ukwu* or *Chineke*) is thoroughly a principle of good in Igbo traditional thought; the

---

[820] Nwala T.U., *Igbo Philosophy,* op. cit., p. 313.
[821] Ibid.

people do not associate Him with any bad event or unhappy experiences of theirs. The deities or local gods, on the other hand, are both malevolent and benevolent. They bless and curse, reward and reproach as the case may be.

"Ekwensu", the deity of war and victory in Igbo Traditional Religion has been wrongly translated and equated with the devil in Christian thought. This translation and interpretation were done most probably by the missionaries. In terms of rituals and their objects, both religions have something in common. Ordination of priests and initiation are vital elements in both religions – Christianity and Igbo Traditional Religion. Harvest and thanksgiving ceremonies, the celebrations of feasts like Christmas, Easter of the Christians could be compared with similar harvest (*Ifejioku*) and thanksgiving occasions in addition to ceremonies marking the days associated with certain deities like "Emume Ala", that is, "Ala day" (in honour of the Earth Deity). Prayers and sacrifices are common to both. [822]

Other similarities that can be found in both religions are the use of fire, water, oil, bells, incense, priestly robes, altars and temples (shrines), invocation and incantations, gestures, just to mention but a few. These are used in the process of rituals which are common to both religions. There are also similarities in their institutional codes of morality. The prescribed priestly sanctity and unquestionable authority of the priest, primacy of prayer, worship and confession are enjoined by each system. Instead of the Roman Catholic requirement for absolute priestly celibacy, the traditional Igbo system demands limited and seasonal celibacy. For instance, the traditional Igbo priest does not sleep with his wife nor eat her food during certain holy periods, or during her menstrual periods. Confession is a common religious attitude. The traditional Igbo confesses at critical moments in his life. Women confess infidelity or any other moral lapses during childbirth. Men confess on their deathbed before their first son so that adequate reparations may be made to the gods to enable him live peacefully in the spirit world.

Any world-view which is centered on the belief in God and the supernatural forces is bound to share in certain broad characteristics such as myths, dogmas and sanctions. The Christian religion shares these in common with Igbo traditional religious system and thought.

Both religions share the same intellectual background with all belief systems based mainly on authority. For the Christians, this authority is the Bible and

---

822 Nwala T.U., *Igbo Philosophy*, op. cit., p. 313.

tradition of the Church as laid down and interpreted by the "Magisterium"[823] – the teaching authority of the Church. For the adherents of Igbo Traditional Religion, the authority is "Omenala" (customs or conventions) with elders and priests as custodians and interpreters. Religious beliefs are dogmatic, and not open to question or personal interpretations. They deal with beings and realities that we do not encounter in ordinary experiences, but which are explained in terms of happenings in natural life. For example, the birth of a child shows how creative God is or how benevolent "Ala" (Earth Deity) or any other deity is.

Both systems are very comprehensive and claim to have answers to almost all questions about reality and every human experience including every practical human problem. Each has answers to such puzzles like what is the nature and origin of the universe? What is the meaning and end of life and existence; as well as the question: Why has my child got measles and how do I cure the measles?[824]

6.3. THE POSSIBILITY OF HARMONIZING THE IDEOLOGIES OF IGBO TRADITIONAL RELIGION AND CHRISTIAN THOUGHTS

Considering the problems confronting the educated Igbo Christians who are equally faced with the stronghold (both conscious and unconscious) of traditional thoughts and who are confronted with the religious moral, social and pragmatic decision of what to do in the face of Christian hostility to traditional values, one begins to ask for the possibility of harmonizing the ideologies of Igbo Traditional Religion and Christian thoughts. This will also help for the co-existence of the two religions in Igboland. In line with this, Ilogu calls for an

---

[823] The magisterium of the Catholic Church is the Church's authority or office to establish teachings. That authority is vested uniquely in the Pope and the Bishops, under the premise that they are in communion with the correct and true teachings of the faith which is shown in the catechism of the Catholic Church. Sacred Scripture and sacred tradition make up a single sacred deposit of the word of God, which is entrusted to the Church and the magisterium is not independent of this, since all that it proposes for beliefs as being divinely revealed is derived from this single deposit of faith. Cf., Thomas Stork, "What is the Magisterium"? Quoted in https://en.wikipedia.org/wiki/Magisterium , accessed 17.1.2018. The task of interpreting the Word of God authentically has been entrusted solely to the magisterium of the Church, that is, to the Pope and to the college of bishops in communion with Him. Cf., Catechism of the Catholic Church, 100, and Dogmatic Constitution on Divine Revelation Dei Verbum, 10, quoted in https://en.wikipedia.org/wiki/Magisterium , accessed 17.1.2018.

[824] Nwala T. U., *Igbo Philosophy*, op. cit., p. 314.

integration, which he refers to as "revealed ethics of Christianity with evolutionary ethics of traditional society."[825]

It is pertinent to say that the denial of a place for Igbo culture and ideas in the Christian scheme of things stems from the old prejudice that they are thoroughly superstitious, primitive and pagan. Today, this attitude against the Igbo, nay, African culture and ideas has changed. Vatican II Council, for example, advocated for "norms and rules for adapting the liturgy to the genius and tradition of the people."[826]Nwala agrees to this idea of harmonization of Igbo traditional ideology and Christian theology. He states that:

> This means that the idea of religious conformism is called for. And indeed, this intolerant attitude is responsible for much of the rebellion and other radical changes currently taking place in the religious practices of today. People are made to become strangers in their own environment by being forced to embrace, in a somewhat dogmatic manner, the Hebrew Greco-Roman-Cum-European ways of life in utter neglect of the positive elements of their traditional culture as well as contemporary realities.[827]

Anyone who wishes to become a man in Christ must become a new creature, in his environment, in his social and cultural life. But Ilogu would argue that this "does not mean becoming a stranger in one's environment, in one's social and cultural milieu which in fact is the reality in which one can love his neighbour as himself."[828]

In Igboland, Christianity has, for long, unsuccessfully battled to eradicate such social and cultural practices as polygamy, title taking, age grades and secret societies, ancestor veneration, divination, oath-taking on traditional shrines and spirit-forces and traditional medicine, just to mention but a few, (which are deeply embedded in the philosophy of the people). The fact that after nearly a century of Christian influence in Igboland, these practices and beliefs still persisted, show how basic and fundamental these beliefs are to the peo-

---

[825] Cf., Ilogu E.C., *The Problem of Christian Ethics among the Igbo of Nigeria. Ikenga, Journal of African Studies.* Institute of African Studies: University of Nigeria, Nsukka, vol. 3, Nos. 1-2-1-9, 1975, pp. 38 - 52, in Nwala T.U., *Igbo Philosophy,* op. cit., p. 315.

[826] The Second Vatican Council summoned by Pope John XXIII in 1962, which advocates aggiornamento in the mission of the Church; which Bishop Butler B.C., refers to as the process of 'bringing up to date'. Butler explains that any institution that lives and means to play an active, not to say aggressive part in the mainstream of human history must from time to time, and even continuously be making minor adaptations to its ever-changing environment. According to Butler, such change was already in progress long before the Second Vatican Council opened. Cf., vatican2voice.org/3buttlerwrites/aggioma.htm, accessed 5.1.2018.

[827] Nwala T.U., *Igbo Philosophy,* op. cit., p. 316.

[828] Ilogu E.C., op. cit., in Nwala T.U., *Igbo Philosophy,* op. cit., p. 317.

ple's philosophical consciousness and notions about life and the world around them.

It is an obvious fact that Christianity cannot completely eradicate Igbo Traditional Religion. It can only transform some of the traditional religious elements into its own image, that is, appropriate them and fashion them as its own elements. It has done this in the use of music, art and other cultural elements. In Latin America, it has even transformed native shrines into Christian shrines.[829] In modern terminology, this is what we may call inculturation.[830]

As we have explained earlier, the missionaries in Igboland were not able to remove all the social and cultural practices which in their thinking were inimical to the gospel of Christ. Nwala, therefore explains and suggests:

> Total cultural annihilation of some Igbo culture and tradition is not possible. It can only be possible if the entire population of the people is completely wiped out and their socio-cultural environment equally erased from the earth. What is possible is cultural integration, assimilation or partial transformation.[831]

Nwala further explains that "both Christianity and traditional religion, as we have maintained, are religions sharing common theological and ritual elements. They are essentially transcendental and idealist, being religions of control. Traditional religions, as we have shown, does not exist as a separate element from the rest of traditional peasant society. It is dominated by elders who are the heads of the families (the units of social and economic organization), and who control its political, social and religious ideas and practices. Traditional religious ideas and ethical codes are not only expressions of traditional understanding of nature and human society; they are instruments of social control."[832]

Both Christianity and Igbo Traditional Religion have similar philosophical and intellectual characteristics, though they emerged in somewhat different socio-economic environments. Igbo Traditional Religion emerged from a culture with low-level scientific character. Therefore, the harmonization of the elements of the two religions – Christianity and Igbo Traditional Religion - is possible and practicable. But one would ask how? We have to quickly emphasize that Igbo

---

[829] Nwala T.U., *Igbo Philosophy,* op. cit., p. 317.
[830] Inculturation is the adaptation of the way Church teachings are presented to non-Christian cultures and, in turn, the influence of those cultures on the evolution of these teachings. This is a term that is generally used by Roman Catholics, whereas Protestants tend to use the term "contextual theology." Cf., hattps://en.wikipedia.org/wiki/ inculturation, accessed 17.1.2018.
[831] Nwala T.U., Igbo Philosophy, op. cit., 317.
[832] Ibid.

Traditional Religion cannot be revived in its pre-colonial form. It can only be transformed to suit the sensibilities and realities of the present capitalist industrial society.

One of the possible ways of harmonizing Igbo traditional ideologies and Christian thoughts, as suggested by Ilogu is: "enlarging the theological concept of the saints to include the good ones among the Igbo ancestors. Anticipating critics usually men, who for ignorant or selfish reasons hold onto orthodox views."[833] Inculturation is another possible way of harmonizing the Christian theology and Igbo traditional thoughts.

6.3.1. INCULTURATION THEOLOGY

The term "inculturation", as applied to Christianity, denotes the presentation and re-expression of the Gospel in form and terms proper to a culture.[834]Inculturation theology concerns itself fundamentally "with the relationship of Christian theology to African culture. It evinces a particular concern to relate this to the Bible and Christian tradition."[835]

The use of the term 'inculturation' in African theology can be traced back to the Pan-African Conference of the Third World Theologians held two months after the synod on Catechesis in Accra, Ghana in December 1979. This Pan-African Conference brought together for the first-time theologians, Catholics and Protestants of the Francophone and Anglophone Africa. At the end of the meeting, the Conference's new concept of theological unity came to be expressed with the term 'inculturation'.[836] From some African theologians' voice, inculturation can be described as:

> The continuous movement which aims at making Christianity permanent in Africa by making it a people's religion and a way of life which no enemy or hostility can ever succeed in supplanting or weakening. It is the endeavor to make Christianity truly 'feel at home' in the cultures of the African people.[837]

Inculturation however, is not an African affair alone. It is the concern of the universal Church in her evangelizing mission. The use of African inculturation

---

[833] Ilogu E.C., op. cit., in Nwala T.U., *Igbo Philosophy*, op. cit., pp. 318 - 319.

[834] Cf., www.encyclopedia.com/religion/encyclopedias-almanacs-transcripts-and-maps/ inculturation-theology, accessed 10.1.2018.

[835] Parrat J., *Re-inventing Christianity: African Theology Today,* Wm. B. Eerdmans Publishing Co., Grand Rapids, Michigan and Africa World Press Inc., Trenton, New Jersey, 1995, p. 25.

[836] Cf., Martey E., African *Theology: Inculturation and Liberation,* Orbis Books, Mary-knoll, New York, 1993, p. 67.

[837] Waliggo J.M., *"Making a Church that is truly African",* in A.A. V.V., *Inculturation: Its Meaning and Urgency*, St. Paul Publication – Africa, Nairobi, 1986, p. 12 - 13.

theology as an expression simply explains Africans' particular share of the universal mission of the Church, just like any other people. With particular reference to Africa, Martey noted that in order to express the Christian message with the African idioms and conceptual tools, expressions such as 'indigenization', "localization", "africanization" and so forth have been employed.[838]

The special position which inculturation enjoys as against other terms mentioned above stems from its being able to express the mutual and reciprocal penetration between the Gospel and culture just like Christ's taking human flesh and humans receiving the divine redemption. Hence, inculturation finds its model in the incarnation. Fabella lucidly explains it thus:

> Just as the word became incarnate to reveal God's Message of Salvation to humankind … so God's Good News should also be 'incarnated' in every culture, purifying and ennobling it. At the same time, the gospel read (and lived out) through different cultural lenses is broadened and enriched. This reciprocal process not only allows for pluralism but actually encourages it.[839]

African inculturation theology concerns itself with expressing Christianity in African religio-cultural terms creating a synthesis between African culture and Christianity. African theology "engages itself with the interpretation of essential Christian faith in authentic African language in the flux and turmoil of our time, so that there may be genuine dialogue between the Christian faith and African cultures."[840]

In as much as "I am first African and second a Christian",[841] it follows that, the aim of African inculturation theology is africanization of Christianity[842]rather than Christianization of Africa. A look at the following areas for inculturation, identified by the African Synod, shows the vastness of the field of inculturation.[843] It is the entire Christian life that needs to be inculturated.[844] Let us outline some of the areas inculturation concerns itself with.

---

[838] Cf., Martey E., *African Theology: Inculturation and Liberation*, Orbis Books, Maryknoll, New York, 1993, p. 65. See also Oborji F.A., *Trends in African Theology since Vatican II,* Tipografica Leberit, Roma, 1998, p. 92.

[839] Fabella V., *"Inculturation" in* Fabella V., *and* Sugirtharajah R. S., eds., *Dictionary of Third World Theologies*, Orbis Books, Maryknoll, New York, 2000, p. 105.

[840] Cf., Pobee J.S., *Toward African Thelogy*, Abingdon press, Nashville, 1979, p. 22.

[841] Pobee J.S., *"I am first African and second a Christian"*, in Indian Missiological Review 10 (1985)3 208 - 277.

[842] Cf. Ukpong J.S., *"African Theologies Now: A Profile"*, Gaba, Publications (spearhead), Eldoret, Kenya 1984, p. 22.

[843] Cf., Synod of Bishops Special Assembly for Africa, Message of the Synod, 6 May 1994, 18.

[844] Ibid.

1. Faith formation in a serious and authentic African Christian theology.

2. Ecclesial structures, embodying the Church as family and community, with appropriate new ministries.

3. Religious and monastic life and their expression.

4. Moral life: Individual and social, in the light and context of modern challenges. Liturgical/sacramental life and practices: Eucharistic celebration, the possibility and desirability of African Rite or Rites. This also includes: music, songs, dances and use of instruments like shakers, drums, and horns. Oral tradition – poetry, myths, proverbs to enrich prayer etc.[845]

5. Initiation rites of the Church and of different cultures. Baptism; using indigenous names, incorporation of initiation rites with communitarian and individual touch.

6. Marriage: A radical reassessment of our pastoral and canonical attitude to some African marriage practices like the role of the extended family in marriage by stages, and the practice of Levirate marriage or inheritance of widows. Other marriage-related areas of concern include: family based, customary nuptial rituals to be incorporated, family planning and traditional methods, ethical norms and purity, polygamy and Eucharistic famine, religious profession envisaged as marriage ritual to be incorporated into actual rites.

7. Healing: Sickness, anointing, care, solidarity and respect for elders.

8. Celebration of life and death: Liturgy based on birth, death events, anniversaries or remembrance of the dead, the ancestors and their veneration.

9. Holy Orders: Objects symbolizing services, protection, authority, spears, stools, special cloaks, anointing. There is also concern for traditional formation in the seminary and novitiate formation.

10. African Code of Canon Law.

11. African art: Statues in Churches with an African touch. African setting in sitting, for example, African architecture.

12. African spirituality.

---

[845] Synod of Bishops Special Assembly for Africa, Message of the Synod, 6 May 1994,18.

13. African language: Thought form and patterns.

14. Promotion of African forms of organizations: Patriarchal and matri-archal setting in hierarchical form, respecting authority and elders' opinions.

15. The current socio-cultural problems: underdevelopment, dehuman-ization and marginalization: inculturation is linked with liberation. It takes into account the anti-life components in both the local culture and the Gospel (its patriarchal orientation, for example), which must be critiqued and transformed.[846]

6.3.2. SOME OF THE ACHIEVEMENTS MADE SO FAR IN INCULTURATION

The Fathers of the African Synod have the following as some tangible achieve-ments made so far in inculturation theology.

1. Eucharistic celebrations with music, dance, songs and traditional gestures. Greater participation in liturgy.

2. The phenomenon of Small Christian Communities and their effect on the Church structures. The ministries within Small Christian Communities.

3. Translation of the Bible, liturgical books and catechism brought some rea-sonable clarity and understanding.

4. New Catholic University, Institutes and Major Seminaries with an empha-sis on study and research of African religious values and cultures.[847]

6.3.3. METHODS OF AFRICAN INCULTURATION THEOLOGY

It is pertinent to say that renowned African theologians seem to agree on two methods namely "Adaptation" or "Stepping-Stones" method and Critical or Radical method.[848]

6.3.3.1. ADAPTATION METHOD

In the early period of African theology, the focus was on adaptation. From the name, the approach seeks to "adapt the practices of the western Church as

---

[846] Fabella V., *"Inculturation"*, op. cit., p. 105 in Obasi S.O., *Evangelization and Modernity, Cul-tural Issues as Missiological Imperative in Ecclesia in Africa*, op. cit., pp 291 - 292.

[847] *AA. VV., African Synod a Step Forward, Pauline Publications Africa,* Nairobi, 1995, p. 43. This publication followed the Post-Synodal Special Assembly of African Bishops held in the Carmelite center in Nairobi, on 8, July 1994.

[848] Cf., Mushete N.A., *"The History of Theology in African: From Polemics to Critical Theology"* in Gibellini S., ed., Paths *of African Theology*, SCM Press Ltd., London, 1994, pp. 16 - 17.

much as possible to the socio-cultural life of African peoples."[849] Adaptation method (also called moderate method) is used to represent or incorporate "every inculturation tentative that has its roots in a theology that merely tries to replace cultural values with what the missionary calls Christian values".[850] Here, terms such as Christianization, accommodation, indigenization, and localization, were applied.

The outstanding characteristic of this method, as Ukpong pointed out, is that in doing African theology, the theologian seems to feel obliged to follow more or less strictly the format and procedure of Western theology, that is, a systematic application of philosophy in the explanation of doctrines. In doing this, the themes chosen for discussion and the way the themes are organized and presented are all influenced by Western theology and reflect with modifications the way traditional western theology manuals are organized.

In effect, the theologian of this camp has just two tasks, namely, identification of themes in African cultures that are appropriate for transmitting the Christian message and then identification of the kernel message embedded in the Western cultural pattern. Thus, the theologian sees his work as that of "translating the Christian message from its Western cultural setting into African cultural setting."[851]

Some may criticize adaptation method for falling into what is called "concordance" – a fitting into Western straight jacket. For Mulago, adaptation theology is "merely a matter of presenting dogma in such a way that it will be accessible to the People".[852]Ukpong believes that, with adaptation method, "the assumed attitude to African traditional religion and culture is that of mistrust, hence the need for a "rigorous criticism" of elements and themes taken from these for the transmission of the Christian message."[853] Other scholars like Boka, would simply see adaptation theology as:

---

[849] Mushete N.A., *"The History of Theology in African: From Polemics to Critical Irenis"*, in Appiah-Kubi, K., and Torres S., eds., *African Theology en Route,* Orbis Books, Mary-knoll, New York, 1979, p. 27. The publication were papers from the Pan-African Conference of Third World Theologians, December, 17 - 23, 1977, Accra, Ghana.

[850] Njoku F.O.C., *"Some Indigenous Models in African Theology and An Ethic of Inculturation"*, in Bulletin of Ecumenical Theology (Published by the Ecumenical Association of Nigeria Theologians), 8 (1996)24 - 32. Quotation p. 6.

[851] Ukpong J.S., *"African Theologies Now: A Profile,"* op. cit., p. 28.

[852] Mulago V., *Un Visage Africain du Christianisme*, Presence Africaine, Paris,1965, p. 24.

[853] Upon J.S., *"African Theology Now: A Profile"*, op. cit., p. 29.

A missionary theory that was employed to transplant a Christianity developed elsewhere into Africa, as if Africans have no culture of their own on which the Christian faith could anchor.[854]

6.3.3.2. RADICAL METHOD (CRITICAL APPROACH)

This is a dynamic as well as critical African theology free from the garbage in garbage out of adaptation methodology just discussed. For the radical method, it is enough to search in African Traditional Religion and culture the "positive values that cry for baptism".[855] In the words of Mushete, it is a method that rather takes up "theological problems anew, from the ground up, and to manifest their presence in the field of serious scholarly theological research."[856] It is a method that acknowledges the systematic use of philosophy, but at the same time, emphasizes less of systematization.[857] The radical method is expressed by the term *inculturation, interculturation, incarnation* and *africanization.*[858] It emerges from a sustained critical relationship between Christianity and cultures. The two major concerns that dominate these methods are:

1. The desire for closer contact with the primary sources of revelation (the Bible and tradition).

2. The determination to be completely open to the African world and its problems as opposed to mere selection and fitting of themes from them.[859]

The former "affords theologians of this approach the chance to recapture the spirit and the faith of early Christianity and to see how these guided the development of Christian reflection down the ages."[860] The latter looks to African Traditional Religion for insights as to the sense of direction and pattern in theologizing.[861]

Viewed globally, inculturation theology in its radical dimension is a theology of life, penetrating the very existence and day-to-day life of the African people. Referring to this point Ukpong explains:

---

[854] Cf., cited in Oborji F.A., Trends *in African Theology since Vatican II*, op. cit., p. 68.

[855] Cited in Oborji F.A., *Trends in African Theology since Vatican II*, op. cit., p. 18.

[856] Ibid.

[857] Cf., Ukpong J. S., *"African Theologies Now: A Profile"*, op. cit., p. 29.

[858] Cf., ibid, p. 27ff.

[859] Mushete N. A., *"An Overview of African Theology"*, op. cit., p. 18.

[860] Ukpong J. S., *"African Theologies Now: A Profile"*, op. cit., p. 29.

[861] Ibid.

Since African traditional religion is a way of life and not a collection of doctrines, African theology in this approach therefore becomes life-oriented as opposed to knowledge-oriented theology.[862]

Being life-oriented, it is correct to say therefore that African theology in this approach does not look outwards for a pattern but inwards into African culture. Against this background, Ukpong calls this approach a "grassroots method". He says:

The problem it raises, however, is how to help the people at the grassroots to give expression to their experience of faith; how to help them attain the freedom necessary for this self-expression. For if they do not possess such freedom, they cannot live out the faith in terms of their cultural milieu.[863]

In this radical method, the theologian's task consists in re-thinking and re-expressing the original Christian message in an African cultural milieu. It is the task of confronting the Christian faith and African culture. In the process, there is inter-penetration of both. Christian faith enlightens African culture and the basic data of revelation as contained in Scriptures and tradition are critically re-examined for the purpose of giving them African cultural expression.[864] Hence, there is integration of faith and culture, and from it is born a new theological reflection that is African and Christian.[865]

The response to the call for a critical theology capable of giving an authentic African face to Christianity has given birth to various inculturation models. They are ancestral model (Charles Nyamiti), the staurological (Fortunatus Nwachukwu), proverbial (John Egbulefu), hospitality (Elochukwu Uzukwu and Greg Olikenyi) and convenant (Francis O.C. Njoku)[866] and finally "the Church-as-a-family" (rooted in the 1994 Africa Synod)[867] models of inculturation. We shall not delve into the treatment of these models since that is not relevant here.

It is pertinent to point out that although differences exist between both methodologies, they both combined to give a new and dynamic understanding of the local Church in Africa. Both methods balance each other; therefore, they

---

[862] Ibid.

[863] Ukong J.S., *"African Theologies Now: A Profile"* op. cit., 30.

[864] Cf., Vatican Council II, *Decree on the Church's Missionary Activity Ad Gentes Divinitus*, 7 December 1965, 22: AAS 58 (1966) 947-990.

[865] Cf., Ukpong J.S., *"African Theologies Now a Profile"*, op. cit., p. 30.

[866] For in-depth study of these models Cf., Njoku F.O.C., "Some Indigenous Models in African Theology and an Ethic of Inculturation", in Bulletin of Ecumenical Theology, op. cit., 8 (1996)2 4-32.

[867] For a detailed study on the Church-as-family model, cf., Oborji F.A., *Trends in African Theology since* Vatican II, op. cit., chapter 7.

need one another for effective incarnation theology. While the adaptation method, "translates" Christianity, looking for the kernel or essence of pure Christianity, the radical method gives birth or sows seeds, re-examines the data of Christian revelations and reinterprets them in the light of the African cultural milieu without which the people cannot internalize it. Over and above all, we shall not neglect the fact that whatever argument in favour or against one method or another, shows the all-round liveliness of the Church in modern Africa.

6.3.4. THE AVOIDANCE OF RELIGIOUS SYNCRETISM

What we should avoid in the harmonization of the ideologies and tenets of these two religions – Christianity and Igbo traditional religion is: "half convert-ed Christians and half Igbo religion traditionalists." By this we mean when a person practises the two religions – Christianity and Igbo Traditional Religion simultaneously. We have to state categorically that the aim of our proposal for this harmonization is not for conversion from one religion to another neither is it for the practice of syncretism. This proposal is for the peaceful co-existence of the two religions in Igboland. But the danger we have today is that some Igbo practise the two religions simultaneously. Some have become "half Christians" and "half Igbo traditional religionists". They are neither "hot nor cold"; this is a dangerous position to take. Nwala captures well what we are trying to explain here when he says that:

> The introduction of Christianity has merely increased the range of alternative values and attitude which the modern Igbo man could turn to. And as a matter of fact, science and secular thought haven added more alternative methods, values and attitudes. If an educated Igbo falls sick today, he prays on his bed (if he is a Christian), then he goes to the hospital for (scientific) medical care. If after several attempts of combining prayers and scientific medical care, he fails to get cured, then he turns to a traditional diviner and a native doctor. He would offer sacrifices to his ancestors and local deities, when these become necessary. All the while, he continues to pray. He continues doing these until he recovers or dies. For the protection of his job, he would work hard and try to win the favor of his seniors. He would equally be prayerful, but very often he carries charms hidden in one place or the other for both productive and protective effects. (That is to ward off the evil manipulations of his jealous neighbors and fellow workers).[868]

Therefore, one concludes that some modern Igbo belong to various strands of thought and practice, secular, traditional and Christian. Sometimes, they try to live out these thought and practice together, which we would not like to advo-

---

[868] Nwala T.U., *Igbo Philosophy,* op. cit., p. 315.

cate for. When we search for the reasons for this double practice by some Igbo, one can say that it is traced to the structure of the mind of the Igbo man, who looks for causes in things and tries to harmonize lots of contradictions experienced in life.

As we mentioned earlier in this work, "suffering" and "cross" have no place in Igbo Traditional Religion. The Igbo traditionalist's conception of "suffering" and "cross" is totally different from the Christian notion of them. For the Igbo traditionalists, the end product of suffering can never be positive. "Suffering" comes as a punishment for evil deeds. Therefore, every misfortune is traceable to one's misconduct or crime. When we trace this further, we find out that this is one of the reasons for upsurge and proliferation of Pentecostal churches and prayer houses in Africa. Some people move from one prayer house to another and from one native doctor to another seeking for solutions to their problems. The reason why these prayer houses continue to multiply is that they are being patronized. Ndiokwere would say that:

> The rate at which the independent church movements in Africa have continued to multiply and expand has been described in many Church circles as alarming and at present it shows no signs of abating. Any attempt at compiling up-to-date statistics has proved impossible.[869]

Like a bush-fire, prayer houses have multiplied and are now uncountable in Nigeria and Igboland and are commonly referred to as the spiral phenomenon of the proliferation of churches. For quite some time now, this phenomenon has continued to gain an unprecedented momentum so much so that it has become a palpable reality. In his book, "The Divine Deceit: Business in Religion," Obiora, enumerates at least 831 churches in Nigeria today, and thus concludes: "Up till now, I have not known of anybody who has drawn up a complete list of the churches. Any effort would be futile, because there are many borderline cases."[870]

6.3.4.1. THE POLYGAMOUS NATURE OF IGBO TRADITIONAL SOCIETY AND THE MALE CHILD SYNDROME

The process of evangelization and Christianization in Igboland brought Igbo and European cultures into contact. Both cultures experienced reciprocal

---

[869] Ndiokwere N.I., *Prophecy and Revolution: The Role of Prophets in the Independent African Churches and in Biblical Tradition*, the Camelot Press Ltd., Southampton, Great Britain, 1981, p. 15.

[870] Obiora F.K., *The Divine Deceit (Business in Religion): On the phenomenon of the Upsurge and Proliferation of Pentecostal and Mushroom Churches in the World Today*, Optimal Publishers, Enugu, Nigeria, 1998, p. 33.

shocks. However, the Igbo culture has suffered greater disadvantages from this shock. The waves of missionary activities and westernization have cast a stifling shadow over some of the cultural values of the Igbo. Some of these Igbo cultural values have refused to be suppressed by Christianity and the waves of westernization.

The Igbo traditional society allows the practice of polygamy. Christianity rejects polygamy and insists on monogamy. In Igbo society, male children are valued more than the female ones. This may have its root from the patriarchal nature of the Igbo society. Children are so valued to the extent that childless couples suffer a lot of pressures from their parents and relations. Pressures are often more on the man, advising him to get another wife in order to beget children. Some Christians who found themselves in this problem have succumbed to the pressure of getting another wife which Christianity does not accept. "The Igbo have great love for children. In some areas of Igboland, the traditional number which will make a couple contented is nine (ten, for some people) children."[871] Presently, things have changed a little. Many couples would like to have children but not up to nine or ten. Family planning has changed this traditional inclination of having many children.

Therefore, from the Igbo traditional background, "a family without children has little or no meaning for the Igbo."[872] Some Igbo have found themselves in the situation of practising two religions concurrently, that is, Christianity and Igbo Traditional Religion. As we have said earlier in this work, the Igbo cultural values cannot be totally separated from the Igbo Traditional Religion. This is why some Igbo practise Christianity in the morning and in the evening Igbo Traditional Religion, especially when they are confronted with some problems that deal with cultural values which for them Christianity cannot give immediate solution to.

In the past, the traditional Igbo society were mainly made up of farmers. Even today, those who trade in the big towns do not forget the farm. The chief crop is the yam, a large root tuber (*dioscorea*) which is planted when the rains begin. Yam demands constant attention and manpower. But where the soil is good it can give a rewarding harvest. Apart from the love for children and big family which the Igbo have, the traditional Igbo families need enough manpower in their farms; therefore, more children are needed in the family. In addition to this, children in Igbo traditional setting are life assurance to their

---

[871] Jones puts it rather crudely: "The main energies of the Ibo were devoted to raising as many children and yams as possible". Cf., Jones and Mulhall, art. cit. in *Journal of the Royal Anthropological Institute*, 79 (1949), 11 in Arinze F., *Sacrifice in Igbo Traditional Religion*, op. cit., p. 4.
[872] Arinze F., *Sacrifice in Igbo Traditional Religion*, op. cit., p. 4.

parents. The Igbo do say: "Nne na nna zucha nwa, nwa tolite ozuba nne na nna" (when parents complete training their child, the child grows up and he or she takes up the responsibilities of looking after the parents).

CHAPTER SEVEN

7. GENERAL CONCLUSION

The major religions of the world have their founders. For example, Christianity was founded by Jesus Christ; Islam by Prophet Mohammed and Buddhism by Buddha. But Igbo Traditional Religion was not founded by a single person. The Igbo came to know about the Supreme Being and the deities through their reflections on nature and on the forces of nature. Their knowledge of God is intuitive and intrinsic; they did not acquire it from any nation or persons. Igbo Traditional Religion has no written down generally and official accepted tenets, neither does it have those who propagate the religion (Evangelizers or missionaries) as some other major religions of the world have.

Polytheism and Monotheism are two known classical theories about the nature of God in Western thought. The two positions have been classified as stages or phases of the religious development of mankind. Polytheism is often seen as the early stage in the process of modernization of some religions of the world, while monotheism is often believed to represent an advanced stage in the evolutionary history of this modernization.

From our investigation and examination of modernization of Igbo Spirituality, it is clear that the use of polytheism alone or monotheism does not qualify to describe the practice obtainable in Igbo Traditional Religion. The mistake some writers and commentators dabble into is using Christianity as a yardstick in measuring some of the practices found in Igbo Traditional Religion. Unfortunately, many practices found in Igbo Traditional Religion may not fit into the straight-jacket of Christianity. Moreover, many practices which were previously obtainable in Igbo Traditional Religion are no longer there today. A lot has changed in it which we have already discussed. Arazu warns that:

> The issue of polytheism in Igbo traditional religion is very often swept under the carpet of missionary propaganda and catechesis by the theologians who claim without objective proof that the Igbo people were monotheists i.e. worshipped only one Supreme Being or God before the missionaries came. A careful study of the "Memorandum on Ozo Title-Taking in Ihilala Clan" ... reveals that so much evidence of Igbo polytheism is contained in the document. It is this polytheism that prevents Christians from embracing the Ozo institution for fear of syncretism in their religious practice.[873]

Our investigation into the nature of worship obtainable in Igbo Traditional Religion reveals a unique view, which we call in this work "mono-polytheism".

---

[873] Arazu R.C. *Our Religion – Past,* Martin-King Press, Nigeria, 2000, p. 197.

When we try to judge the practice of these two positions, "monotheism" and "polytheism" together which we call "mono-polytheism" in the light of Christianity, it will never pass that judgment. This is because in the light of Christianity, and in the judgment of many Christians, the practice of Polytheism is categorized as "ife-Alusi" (idolatry). When we measure this with Christian barometer, one may question seriously how possible it is to practice the two extreme positions – "monotheism" and "polytheism" simultaneously. The Holy Scripture says in the Book of Exodus 20: 3 – 5; God says:

> You shall have no other gods to rival me. You shall not make yourself a carved image or any likeness of anything in heaven above or on earth beneath or in the waters under the earth. You shall not bow down to them.[874]

We should avoid using one religion to judge another. This is because every religion is unique and must be conceived that way. The false theory of a withdrawn High God of the Igbo, born out of ignorance coupled with the unlimited number of indirect approaches to God through these gods are no reasons at all for denying the Igbo this unique and intrinsic belief in one Supreme Being. Neither is anyone justified to use the influence of any of the religions of the world which are late-comers and strangers in Igboland and Igbo world-view to cancel out the Igbo man's magnificent conceptions of God both at the ontological and epistemological levels.

Monotheism forms part of the essential metaphysical beliefs of the pre-modern Igbo man. Consequently, it cannot be taken singularly as the best appropriate term to describe the nature of Igbo ontology. Polytheism equally needs to be qualified; although the Igbo believe in the existence and worship of a unifying and Transcendental Ultimate Being. This is characterized in their belief system. The gods are conceived by the Igbo traditional religionists as creatures of "Chukwu" (God) and are subordinate to Him. But God's domain is radically differentiated from that of the gods.

The Igbo belief in the existence of many gods (deities) indicates that these gods receive prayers, petitions and sacrifices either in themselves or on behalf of the Supreme Being. There is no way Igbo traditional ontology can fit into anyone of the two positions of worship held by Western thoughts, except by combining both terms to embrace the one unifying and transcendental Ultimate Being – *Chukwu* and the many mediator (gods) to whom designated various areas of influences and authority. These gods according to the Igbo traditionalists do not constitute a hindrance to the Supreme Being's absolute power and authority.

---

[874] Cf., Exodus 20: 3-5, The New Jerusalem Bible, Standard Edition.

As we have earlier said, the objects of Igbo religious belief and worship are three, namely, God, non-human spirits, and the Ancestors. It is obvious that the Igbo worship God. But do they really worship the non-human spirits, the deities and the Ancestors? Some writers and commentators have argued that the deities are not worshipped by the Igbo traditionalists but rather they are the mediators between the Supreme Being "Chukwu" and man. If they are not worshipped, how can we then explain the human sacrifice offered to them in the past?

Human sacrifice practised in the past in Igbo Traditional Religion was a community affair. Often, ordinary animals were used as victims of sacrifice to carry the sins of the community in the sacrifice termed "scape goats" which we have earlier explained. But in exceptional circumstances it was thought necessary to have a human victim. The person chosen was good-looking, often a strong young man or girl. From every indication, the "human sacrifice" was not offered to the Supreme Being – God, but rather to the deities (alusi). This portrays that in Igbo Traditional Religion, the deities (alusi) are worshipped.

When we want to harmonize the above thought with the Christian thought, we can make references to the scriptures. In the Book of Hebrews, the offering of animals to God could not remove the sins of mankind; so, God sent His only son, Jesus Christ to the world to offer Himself as a sacrifice in order that the sins of the world might be taken away and human beings freed from the bondage and slavery of sin. The Book of Hebrews 10:3 – 7 says:

> But in fact, the sins are recalled year after year in the sacrifices. Bulls' blood and goats' blood are incapable of taking away sins, and that is why he said, on coming into the world: You wanted no sacrifice or cereal offering, but you gave me a body. You took no pleasure in burnt offering or sacrifice for sin; then I said: 'here I am, I am coming, in the scroll of the book it is written of me, to do your will God.'[875]

The same idea that the sins of many – the sins of the whole community - may be removed was behind the ritual performance of the sacrifice of "scape goat" in Igbo Traditional Religion in which on many occasions human beings were used as victims of sacrifice. Today human sacrifice is no longer performed in Igbo Traditional Religion.

Some writers and commentators fall into error in saying that the ancestors are worshipped in Igbo Traditional Religion. Some even refer to the entire Igbo Traditional Religion as ancestor worship. The ancestors are not worshipped but

---

[875] Cf., Hebrews 10: 3-7, The New Jerusalem Bible, Standard Edition.

are revered and honoured. Analogically, they are like the saints in Christianity. The saints are not worshipped but rather they are revered and honoured; petitions can be directed to them so that they can present them to God because they are before God. The saints are like a channel through which the prayers of those in the world reach the throne of God faster; likewise, the ancestors are seen in the same light.

It is pertinent to say that we cannot explain everything practised in Igbo Traditional Religion empirically or logically. We have to accept certain things at the level of faith. The practice of "mono-polytheism" cannot be explained but ought to be accepted at the level of faith. It can be seen as a mystery. In some religions we have mysteries. For example, in Christianity we have the mystery of the Blessed Trinity – the mystery of the Three Persons in One God. But it is accepted by the Christians as truth revealed by God Himself. We cannot say therefore, that these mysteries are not truth because they cannot be proved empirically or logically.

One element which we may find very conflicting and at the same time may sound paradoxical is the issue of the origin of gods (deities) in Igbo Traditional Religion. The gods in Igbo ontology evoke emotional intensity. Some hold that they are "man-made" and should be differentiated from each other by their various characteristics or kinds. Others hold that the gods exist, contrary to the belief in Christian theology which denies them real existence. Many others hold that the gods relate to God as creator is related to creature, father to son and master to servant. They may receive sacrifice on their own as token and remuneration to inspire them in their role as "mediators" between God and man. They occupy strategic position in the hierarchy of beings such that all interactions and inter-communications between the visible created order and the invisible world of God, spirits and gods are possible through them.

The problem in Igbo Traditional Religion is that it does not have tenets or dogmas like we have in the Catholic Church and in some other religions. Sometimes one finds it very difficult to articulate what is obtainable in Igbo Traditional Religion. Some Igbo traditionalists make the matter worse by holding opposing views as we noticed for example in our study of "Chi" in Igbo Traditional Religion. It is very difficult to find a yardstick to analyze the views and positions of some. But in the Catholic Church, for example, we do have dogmas which act always like a "police man," safe-guarding the authentic and revealed truth of the teachings of the Church, which makes it difficult for anyone to dilute or mitigate these teachings of the Church.

Igbo Traditional Religion is still in the process of modernization. Modernization is an ongoing process. Igbo Traditional Religion within its process of modernization has acquired a lot of knowledge from Christianity which has great influence on it. Christianity and other foreign cultures have taught the pre-modern Igbo the best concepts of God. Similarly, Igbo Traditional Religion prepared the soil for effective evangelization by Christianity in Igboland.

The thrust of our effort in this work is to show that the idea of the Supreme Being in Igbo Traditional Religion is not a borrowed one; that Igbo Traditional Religion originated in Igboland. The most appropriate term to use in describing what is being practised in Igbo Traditional Religion is "mono-polytheism".

A lot has been modernized in Igbo Traditional Religion. But it is pertinent to say that there are cultural traits which have persisted among the Igbo in spite of changing circumstances. A well-directed Christian ministry should not shy away from identifying these traits, with a view to mellowing them down with prudence where they contradict the Gospel and encouraging them if they do not. This is what we mean by the peaceful co-existence of Christianity and Igbo Traditional Religion. This was captured in the writings of Pope Pius XII many years ago, when he wrote:

> Everything in the customs of people that is not inextricably bound up with superstition or error should be examined favorably and, if possible, preserved intact.[876]

It is unfortunate that in some places in Africa the Christian pastoral ministry has not heeded to this advice. But when it is heeded, we will get much nearer to genuine inculturation of the Christian message.

Wars affect not only physical structures but also all aspects of human life. Therefore, the Nigeria-Biafra war affected not only the physical structures in Igboland but also the spirituality of the Igbo as well as their relationship with other tribes of Nigeria. The civil war in Nigeria was really a period of test for the Igbo Traditional Religion. After the war, the number of adherents of Igbo Traditional Religion decreased. During the war, many Igbo traditional religionists were killed and some of the shrines dedicated to some deities were destroyed and were not rebuilt and rededicated when the war was over. As already said, Igbo Traditional Religion does not have missionaries or what we may call, in modern terminology, evangelizers. This makes the spread of this religion to be difficult. Modernization and civilization are other factors that seriously affected the growth and spread of Igbo Traditional Religion.

---

[876] Cf., *Pope Pius XII, Summi Pontificatus, 1939*, in Oguejiofor J., *The Influence of Igbo Traditional Religion on the Scio-Political Character of the Igbo*, op. cit., p. *97*.

BIBLIOGRAPHY

Abiola E.O., *A Textbook of West African History (A.D. 1000 to the Present Day), revised and enlarged*, Molayo Standard Press and Bookshops Ltd., Nigeria, 1984.

Abraham K. C., ed., *Third World Theologies: Commonalities and Divergence* Orbis Books, Mary-Knoll, New York, 1990.

Achebe C., *Things Fall Apart,* Heinemann, England and Wales, 1958.

----------------, *There was a Country: A Personal History of Biafra*, Penguin Books, England, 2012.

----------------, *The Trouble with Nigeria*, Heinemann, England and Wales, 1983.

----------------, *Arrow of God*, Heinemann, England and Wales, 1974.

----------------, *No Longer at Ease:* Heinemann, London, 1964.

----------------, *The World of the Ogbanje*, Fourth Dimension Publishers, Enugu, Nigeria, 1986.

----------------, youngafrikanpioneers.wordpress.com/2014/03/20chi-in-Igbo-cosmology.

Achunike H.C., *Catholic Charismatic Movement in Igboland 1970-1995*, Rex Charles and Patrick Ltd, Nimo, Nigeria, 2009.

Achuzie J.O.G., *Requiem Biafra*, Fourth Dimension Publishers, Enugu, Nigeria, 1986.

Ade Ajayi, J.F., ed., *General History of Africa: Africa in the Nineteenth Century until the 1880s, Vol. VI, abridged edition*, University of California Press, California, 1998.

Adedeji A., ed., *Africa within the World: Beyond dispossession and dependence,* Zed, London, 1993.

Adegbola E.A.A., *Traditional Religion in West Africa,* Day Star Press, Ibadan, Nigeria, 1983.

Ademoyega A., *Why We Struck, the story of the first Nigerian coup,* Evans Brothers, 1981.

Adesogan K., *Friendship, Courtship and Christian Marriage,* Scripture Union Press and Bookshop Ltd., Ibadan, Nigeria, 1984.

Adesu M.O.,   *Understanding African Traditional Religion, Part one*, Dorset Publishing Company, London, 1985.

Adibe G.,   *Igbo Issues: Values, Chi, Akala Aka, Ikenga, Magic, Agwu and Manipulation of Divinities,* Mid-Field Pub., Ltd., Onitsha, Nigeria, 2009.

----------------,   *Igbo Mysticism: Power of Igbo Traditional Religion and Society,* Mid-field Publishers Ltd., Onitsha, Nigeria, 2008.

Adigwe F.,   *Essentials of Government for West Africa,* University Press PLC, Ibadan, Nigeria, 2011.

Afigbo A. E.,   *Ropes of Sand: Studies in Igbo History and Culture,* Press, Nsukka, Nigeria, 1981.

----------------,   *The Igbo and their Neighbors*, University Press, Ibadan, Nigeria, 1987.

Agostini T.,   *Every Citizen's Handbook*, Pauline's Publications, Africa, Nairobi, 1994.

Agu C.C.,   *Secularization in Igboland: Socio-Religious Change and its Challenges to the Church among the Igbo,* Frankfurt am Main, 1989.

Agunna J.,   *The Agwu Deity in Igbo Religion*, Fourth Dimension Publishers Ltd., 1995.

Ajaji A.,   *50 Q/A on West African Traditional Religion,* Omolayo Standard Press & Bookshops co., Nig. Ltd., 1981.

Allan D.J.,   *The Philosophy of Aristotle, (2nd Edition),* Oxford University Press New York, 1970.

Aligwekwe P. E., *The Continuity of Traditional Values in the African Society*: The Igbo of Nigeria, Totan Publishers Ltd., Owerri, Nigeria, 1991.

Amadi E.,   *Sunset in Biafra,* Cox and Wywan Ltd., Britain, 1973.

Anowai E. (ed.), *Corruption: The Bane of Nigeria's Development*, Demercury Bright Printing Publishing Co., 2011.

Anozie I.P.,   *The Religious Import of Igbo Names,* unpublished doctoral thesis, Urbaniana Rome, 1968.

Anyanwu H.O., *Religion and Societal Development: Contemporary Nigeria perspectives*, International Publications, Lagos, Nigeria, 2004.

Arazu R.C., Our Religion – Past and Present, Martin-King Press, Awka, Nigeria, 2005.

------------------, *Covenant Broken and Reconciliation* (Sin in Salvation History), Liz Press Services Ltd., Enugu, Nigeria, 1994.

Arene E.O., *The 'Biafran' Scientists: The Development of an African Indigenous Technology*, Arnet Ventures, Lagos, Nigeria, 1997.

Arinze F., *The Baton of Faith, Personal Recollections,* Interviewed by Isizoh D.C., Rex Charles and Patrick Ltd., Nimo, Nigeria, 2008.

------------------, *Church in Dialogue: Walking with other Believers,* Chuka Printing Company Ltd., Enugu, Nigeria, 1990.

------------------, *Sacrifice in Igbo Traditional Religion,* St. Stephen's Press, Inc., Onitsha, Nigeria, 2008.

Avededo M., *Inculturation and the Challenges of Modernity,* Pontifical Gregorian University, Rome, 1982.

Awolalu J.O. & Dopemu P.A., *West African Traditional Religion*, Oniboje Press, Ibadan, Nigeria, 1989.

Azikiwe N., *My Odyssey,* Spectrum Books, Ibadan, Nigeria, 1970.

Barratt B.M., & Tiffin P., *Short Changed: Africa and world Trade*, Pluto, London, 1992.

Barrett L., *Danjuma: The making of the General*, Fourth Dimension Publishing Co. Ltd., Nigeria, 1979.

Basden G.T., *Among the Ibos of Nigeria*, Academy Press Ltd., Lagos, Nigeria, 1921.

------------------, *Niger Ibos*: Seeley Service, London, 1938.

Baur J., *2000 Years of Christianity in Africa: An African Church History,* 2nd *revised edition,* Pauline's Publications, Africa, Nairobi, Kenya, 1998.

Beatie J., *Other Cultures,* Routledge and Kegan, London, 1972.

Beier U., *The Origin of Life and Death,* Heinemann, London, 1966.

Beidelman T. O., *Colonial Evangelism: a socio-historical study of an Eastern African Mission at the Grassroots,* Indiana University Press, Bloomington, 1982.

Bell D., *Cultural Contradictions of Capitalism*, Heinemann, London, 1979.

Berger P., *Facing up to Modernity*, Basic Books, New York, 1977.

-----------------, *The Homeless: Modernization and Consciousness*, Random House, New York, 1973.

Black C., *The Dynamics of Modernization, A Study in Comparative History,* New York, Harper and Row, 1966.

Birch C., et al., *Liberating Life: Contemporary Approaches to Ecological Theology,* Orbis Books, New York, 1990.

Boahen Adu, A., ed., *General History of Africa, vol. 7,* Heinemann, London, 1985.

Bokenkotter T.A., *A Concise History of the Church, Image Books, N.Y.,* 1996.

Bosch D. J., *Believing in Future: Towards a Missiological of Western Culture,* Trinity Press International, Harrisburg,   Pennsylvania, 1995.

Bradshaw J., *Healing the Shame that Binds You,* Health Communications Inc., California, 1988.

Bujo B., *African Theology in its Social context,* St. Paul Publications, Nairobi, 1992.

Burke R., & Prunty P. eds., *Pope John Paul II in Nigeria, Feb., 12th – 17th 1982, Homilies and Addresses*, Port Harcourt, Nigeria, Marian Books Centre Publications, 1982.

Burns E.M., Ideas in Conflict: London, Methuen & Co. Ltd., 1963.

Campbell J., *The Power of Myth,* Doubleday, New York, 1988.

Carrier H., *Evangelizing the Culture of Modernity*, Orbis Books, Mary-Knoll, New York, 1993.

-----------------, *Gospel Message and Human Cultures: from Leo XIII to John Paul II*, Duquesne University Press, Pittsburg, 1989.

Chieka I.,   *Traditional Human Living among the Igbo: A Historical Perspective*, Fourth Dimension Publishers, Enugu, Nigeria, 1977.

Claridge G.C.,   *Wild bush tribes of tropical African*, London, 1922.

Conyers A.J.,   *Eclipse of Heaven: The Loss of Transcendence and its effect on modern life*, Carthage reprint, St. Augustine's Press, Indiana, U.S.A., 1999.

Chukwuemeka N., *"Pragmatism and traditionalism in Concept of God in African Culture"*, Journal of Department of Philosophy of Nigeria, Nsukka, Nigeria, 1981.

Crowder S., & Taylor J.C., *The Gospel on the Bank of the Niger (1857 – 1859),* Dowson, London, 1968.

Crowder M.,   *West Africa under Colonial Rule,* Ethiopia Publishing Corporation, Benin City, Nigeria, 1976.

Curtin P., et al., *African History*, Longman Group Limited, London, 1981.

-----------------, *African Slave Trade: A Census,* University of Wisconsin Press, Madison, 1969.

Davidson B., & Buah F.K., *The Growth of African Civilization: History of West Africa, 1000 – 1800*, Longmans, London, 1965.

David-West, Tam S., *Philosophical Essays*, Ibadan University Press, Nigeria, 1980.

De Gruchy J. W., *Christianity and Democracy,* Cambridge University Press, Cambridge, 1995.

Denquah J.B.,   *The Akan Doctrine of God,* Lutier Work Press, London, 1967.

Donovan V.J.,   *Christianity Rediscovered*, Orbis Books, New York, 1982.

Doro M.E. & Stultz N. M., eds., *Governing in Black Africa: Perspectives on New States,* Englewood Cliffs, New Jersey, 1970.

Dupre W.,   *Religion in Primitive Cultures*: *A Study in Ethnophilosophy,* Mouton, The Hague and Paris, 1976.

Durkheim E.,   *The Elementary Forms of Religious Life*, George Allen and Unwin Ltd., 1915.

Echeruo M.J.C., *A Matter of Identity*, Ministry of Information, Owerri, Nigeria, 1979.

Echiegu A.O., *Sacral Igbo and its Rhetoric, vol. 3,* K. Rave, Ottmarsbocholt, Germany, 1984.

Ebiem O., Nigeria, Biafra and Boko Haram, Ending the Genocide through Multi-State, Gen Computers, Nigeria, 20124.

Edeh E.M.P., *Towards an Igbo Metaphysics,* Chicago: Loyola Press, 1985.

Edwards P., *Equiano's Travels, the Interesting Narrative of the Life of Olaudah Equiano of Gustavus Vassa the African*, Edinburgh, Heinemann, 1996.

Effiong P., *Nigeria and Biafra, My Story*, Songai Corp, Nigeria, 2003.

Ejizu C.I., *Ofo, Igbo Ritual Symbol*, Fourth Dimension, Publishers, Enugu, Nigeria, 1986.

Ekechi F. K., *Missionary Rivalry and Enterprise in Igboland,* London, 1972.

Ekejiuba F. I., 'The Aro System of Trade in the Nineteenth century' Ikenga, Journal of the Institute of Africa Studies Nsukka, Vol.　No.　1, 1972.

Ekwemmuor E. I., *Israel, the Progenitor of World Igbo Race, Social Leadership and Cultural Civilization*, Albany State University Press, U.S.A., 2010.

Ekwunife A.N.O, *Consecration in Igbo Traditional Religion*, Jet Publishers, Enugu, Nigeria, 1990.

----------------, *Meaning and functions of "Ilo Uwa" (Reincarnation) in* Igbo Traditional Religious Culture, Snaap Press, Enugu, Nigeria, 1999.

Ezeabasili N., *African Science: Myth or Reality?* Vantage Press, New York, 1977.

Eze C.E., ed., *Race and the Enlightenment,* Blackwell Publishers Ltd., Oxford, 1997.

Ezeani E., *In Biafra Africa Died. The Diplomatic Plot, 3rd edition*, Veritas Lumen Publishers, England, 2014.

Ezeanya S.N., *"Spirit, God and Spirit World"*, Biblical Revelation and African Beliefs, ed., Kwesi Dickson and Paul Ellingweorth, New York, Mary-Knoll, Orbis Book, 1969.

Ezekwugo C.U.M., *Chi the true God in Igbo Religion*, India, Mar Mathews Press Muvattupuzha, 1987.

Eze-Uzomaka P., *Nigerian Peoples and Cultures (ed.),* Parakletos, Immunnis Drive, Nigeria, 2008.

Fade J. D., *A History of Africa,* Routledge, London, 1995.

Fage J.D., ed., *The Cambridge History of Africa (vol. 2),* Cambridge University Press, New York, 1979.

Ferkiss V.C., *Africa's Search for Identity,* George Brazicler, New York, 1966.

Forde C.D., & Jones G.E., *The Ibo-speaking Peoples of the Southeastern Nigeria:* I.A.I., London, 1950.

Forsyth F., *The making of an African Legend: The Biafra Story*, Penguin Books, Ltd., England, 1969.

-----------------, *Emeka,* Spectrum Books Ibadan, Nigeria, 1982.

Garba J., *Diplomatic Soldering*, Spectrum Books, Ibadan, Nigeria, 1987.

Gay P., *The Enlightenment,* Alfred A. Knopf, New York, 1967.

Geertz C., *The Interpretation of Cultures,* Princeton University Press, London, 1975.

Getui M., & Kanyandago P., eds., *From Violence to Peace: A Challenge to African Christianity*, Action Publishers, Nairobi, 1999.

Gibellini S., ed., *Paths of African Theology*, SCM Press Ltd., London, 1994.

Gifford P., *African Christianity Its Public Role*, C. Hurst & Co. Publishers Ltd., 1998.

Gray R., *Black Christians and White Missionaries*, Yale University Press, London, 1990.

Griffin D., ed., *Spirituality and Society, Post Modern Vision*, State University of New York Press, 1988.

Gutkind P.C.W., & Wallerstein I., eds., *Political Economy of Contemporary Africa,* Cage, Beverly Hills, 1985.

Harden B., *Africa Dispatches from a Fragile Continent*, Harper Collins, London, 1991.

Häring B., *Evangelization Today*, St. Paul's Publications, England, 1990.

Harris J., *Africans and their History*, New American Library, New York, 1972.

Hastings A., *The Church in Africa*: 1450-1950, Oxford University, Press, Oxford, 1994.

------------------, *A History of African Christianity 1950-1975*, Cambridge University Press, Cambridge, 1979.

------------------, *African Catholicism*: *Essays in Interpretation*, Geoffrey Chapman, London, 1976.

Hartle D.D., "*Archaeology in Eastern Nigeria*", *Magazine 93*, Nigeria, 1967.

Herskovits M.J., *Man and his Works: The Science of Cultural Anthropology*, Alfred A. Knopf, New York, 1950.

Hesselgrave D.J., *Communicating Christ Cross-Culturally*, St. Paul Publications, India, 1978.

------------------, et al, *Contextualization: Meanings, Method, and Models*, Baker Book House, Grand Rapids, Michigan, 1989.

Hewett J.F., *European Settlements on the West Coast of Africa*, London, 1862.

Hick J., *The Existence of God*, Macmillan, Company, New York, 1962.

Hiebert P.G., *Cultural Anthropology*, Baker Book, Grand Rapids, Michigan, 1983.

Hospers J., *An Introduction to Philosophical Analysis,* Prentice-Hall, Inc., Englewood Cliffs, New York, 1953.

Huntington S.P., *The Clash of Civilizations: Remaking of World Order*, Touchstone Book, New York, 1996.

Huyssen A., *After the Great Divide: Modernism, Mass Culture, Postmodernism,* University press, Indiana, 1986.

Idowu B.E., *African Traditional Religion: A definition*, SCM Press Ltd., London, 1973.

----------------, *Olodumare: God in Yoruba Belief*, Longman, London, 1962.

----------------, *Biblical Revelation and African Beliefs*, ed., Mary-knoll, New York, 1969.

Ifesie E.I., *Religion at the Grass Roots: Studies in Igbo Religion*, Snaap Press, Enugu, Nigeria, 1989.

Igbo P.C., *Elements of Igbo Culture and tradition*, Good Mark Prints Inc., Onitsha, Nigeria, 2012.

Ike O.F. ed., *Catholic Social Teaching En-Route in Africa*, Snaap Press Ltd., Enugu, Nigeria, 1991.

Ikime O., ed., *Groundwork of Nigerian History,* Heinemann Educational Books (Nig.) PLC, Ibadan, Nigeria, 1980.

Ikoku S.G., *Nigerian Fourth Coup d'etat options for Modern Statehood,* Fourth Dimension Publishing Co. Ltd., Enugu Nigeria, 1985.

Ilogu E., *Christianity and the Igbo Culture*, University Publishing Company, Onitsha, Nigeria, 1985.

----------------, *Igbo Life and Thought*, University Publishing Co., Onitsha, 1985.

----------------, *The Problem of Christian Ethics among the Igbo of Nigeria,* Ikenga, *Journal of African Studies,* Institute of African Studies, University of Nigeria, Nsukka, Nigeria, vol.3, Nos. 1-2 1-9 1975, pp. 38 – 52.

Iroegbu P., *Metaphysics the Kpim of Philosophy,* International University Press, Ltd., Owerri, Nigeria, 1995.

Isichei E., *The Ibo People and the Europeans*, Faber & Faber Ltd., 1971.

----------------, *The History of Igbo People*, Macmillan Press Ltd., London, 1976.

----------------, *The Igbo Worlds: An Anthology of Oral Histories and Historical Descriptions*, Macmillan, London, 1977.

----------------, *History of West Africa since 1800*, Macmillan Education Limited, London and Basingstoke, 1978.

Iwe N.S.S., *Igbo Deities*, in the 1988 Ahiajoku Lectures available on www.igbonet.com.

----------------, *Christianity and Culture in Africa*, Varsity Industrial Press, Onitsha, Nigeria, 1987.

Jackson J.G., *Introduction of African Civilization*, the Citadel Press, Secaucus, 1970.

Jackson M., *The Kuranko: Dimensions of Social Reality in a West African Society*, C. Hurst and Company, London, 1977.

Jedin H., & Dolan J., eds., *History of the Church, vol. II*, Burns & Oates, London, 1980.

Jenkinson W., & O'sullian H., eds., *Trends in Mission: Towards the 3rd Millennium,* Orbis/Sedos, Mary-knoll, 1991.

Joinet B., *The Challenges of Modernity in Africa,* Pauline Publications Africa, Nairobi, Kenya, 2000.

Jones G.P., The Ibo and Ibibio Speaking People of South Eastern Nigeria, International Institute, London, 1967.

Jordan J., *Bishop Shanahan of Nigeria,* Dublin, 1948.

Kalu O.U., ed., *The History of Christianity in West Africa*, Longman Group Limited, London and New York, 1980.

Kanu *asks Federal Government of Nigeria to absorb Biafran scientists:* http:www.vanguardngr.com/2011/03/kanu-ask-fg-to-absorb-biafran-scientists.

Kaplan R.D., *The Ends of the Earth: A Journey at the 21st Century*, Random House, New York, 1996.

Karen A., *The Battle for God: Fundamentalism in Judaism, Christianity and Islam*, Harper Collins Publishers, London, 2000.

Martemper S., et al eds., *Following Christ in Mission: A Foundational Course in Missiology*, Pauline Books & Media, Boston, 1996.

Kant E., *Critique of Pure Reason*, Anchor Books, New York, 1966.

Kirk J.A., *Mission under Scrutiny: Confronting Contemporary Challenges,* First Fortress Press edition, 2006.

Ki-zerbo J., ed., *General History of Africa: Methodology and African Pre-history, vol. 1, abridged edition*, University of California Press, California, 1989.

Knitter P.F.,   *One Earth many religions: Multi-faith Dialogue and Global Responsibility*, Orbis Books, Mary-knoll, N. Y., 1995.

Kore D.,   *Culture and Christian home*, Baraka Press and Publishers Ltd., Kaduna, Nigeria, 1989.

Koren H.J.,   *To the Ends of the Earth: A General History of the Congregation of the Holy Ghost*, Duchesne University Press, Pittsburg, 1983.

Kraft M.G.,   *Understanding Spiritual Power: A forgotten Dimension of Cross-Cultural Mission and Ministry*, Orbis Books, New York, 1995.

Kuehn H.R.,   *The Essential: An Anthology of the Writings of Romano Gaurdini*, Liturgy Training Publications, Chicago, 1997.

Kwesi D., & Ellingworth P., eds., *Biblical Revelation and Africa Beliefs,* Orbis, Mary-knoll, 1969.

Lampe S.,   *The Christian and Reincarnation,* Millennium Press, Ltd., 1987.

Laye C.,   *The African Child,* Fontana/Collins, Great Britain, 1981.

Leonard M. A.G., *The Lower Niger and its Tribes,* Frank Cass, London, 1968.

Leith R.S.,   *African Women: A Study of the Ibo of Nigeria*, Routledge & Kengan Paul, 1965.

Locke J.,   *Essay Concerning Human Understanding,* Dover Publication, New York, 1959.

Lucien R.,   *Vatican II: The Unfinished Agenda*, Paulist, New York, 1987.

Luzbetak L.J.,   *The Church and Culture: New Perspectives in Missiological Anthropology*, Orbis Books, Mary-knoll, New York, 1995.

Madiebo A.A., *The Nigerian Revolution and the Biafran War*, Fourth Dimension Publishing co., Ltd., Enugu, Nigeria, 1980.

Magesa L.,   *African Religion: The Moral Traditions of Abundant Life,* Mary-knoll, New York, 1997.

-----------------,   *The Church and Liberation in Africa*, Gaba Publications, Eldoret, Kenya, 1976.

Mainasasa A.M., *The Five Majors – Why They Struck*, Hudahuda Publishing Com., Zaria, Nigeria, 1982.

Martin P.M., *Nigeria: Current Issues and Historical Background,* Science Publishers, New York, 2002.

Martey E., *African Theology: Inculturation and Liberation,* Orbis Books, Mary-knoll, New York, 1993.

Mbaegbu C., *Hermeneutics of God in Igbo Ontology,* Fab Education Books, Awka, Nigeria, 2012.

Mbiti J.S., *African Religions and Philosophy (2nd ed.),* Heinemann Educational Publishers, Oxford, 1997.

------------------, *New Testament Eschatology in an African Background,* Oxford University Press, 1971.

------------------, *The Prayers of African Religion,* Orbis Books, Mary-knoll, 1975.

------------------, *Introduction to African Religion,* Heinemann, London, 1975.

McCallum D., ed., *The Death of Truth,* Bethany House Publishers Minneapolis, 1996.

McCarthy S., *Africa: The Challenges of Transformation,* I.B. Tauris & Co Pub., New York, 1994.

McEwan A.C., *International Boundaries of East Africa,* Clarendon Press, Oxford, 1971.

McInerny R., ed., *Modernity and Religion,* University of Notre Dame Press, Notre Dame, 1994.

Meek C.K., *Law and Authority in a Nigeria Tribe,* Oxford University Press, London, 1937.

Metuth-Ikenga E., ed., *Nigeria Cultural Heritage,* IMICO Pub. Comp., Onitsha, Nigeria, 1990.

------------------, *Comparative Studies of African Traditional Religion,* IMICO Publishers, Onitsha, Nigeria, 1987.

------------------, *The Nature of African Theism in Uzukwu E., (ed.), Religion and African Culture,* Spiritan Publications, 1988.

------------------, *African Religions in Western Conceptual Schemes: The Problem of Interpretation, (studies in Igbo religion),* IMICO Press, Onitsha, Nigeria, 1991.

----------------, *God and Man in African Religion,* Geoffrey Chapman, London, 1981.

Mgbobukwa J., *Alusi, Osu and Ohu in Igbo Religion and Social Life*, Fulladu Publishing Company, Nsukka, Nigeria, 1996.

Mihevc J., *The Market Tells Them So: The World Bank and Economic Fundamentalism in Africa,* Zed Books, London, 1996.

Minoni A.J. jr., ed., *The Popes Against Modern Errors: 16 Papal Documents,* TAN Books and Publishers, Rockford, 1999.

Moghalu K.C., *Emancipation as a Paradigm*, Fourth Dimension Publishers, Enugu, Nigeria, 1996.

Motlhabi M., *Essays on Black Theology*, University Christian Movement Pub., Johannesburg, 1972.

Muffet D.J.M., *Let Truth be Told: The Coup d'etat of 1966*, Hudahuda Publishing Company Ltd., Nigeria, 1982.

Mugambi J.N.K., et al., eds., *Moral and Ethical Issues in African Christianity*, Initiatives Publishers, Nairobi, 1992.

----------------, *From Liberation to Reconstruction*, East-African Educational Publishers Ltd., Nairobi, 1995.

Murphy J.E., *History of African Civilization,* Dell, New York, 1972.

Muyebe S., & Muyebe A., *The African Bishops on Human Rights,* Pauline Publications, Africa, Nairobi, Kenya, 2001.

Mwoleka C., *Ujamaa and Christian Communities*, Gaba Publications, Eldoret, Kenya, 1976.

Naylor W.S., *Daybreak in the Dark Continent: Society of Christian Endeavour*, Chicago, U.S.A., 1905.

Ndiokwere N.I., *Prophecy and Revolution: The Role of Prophets in the Independent African Churches and in Biblical Tradition*, the Camelot Press Ltd., Southampton, Great Britain, 1981.

New World, 2011, *Igbo People,* available at: www.newworldencyclopedia.org/entry/Igbopeople.

Neill S., *Christian Faith and Other Faith,* Oxford University Press, Oxford, 1970.

Neuner J., & Dupuis J., eds., *The Christian Faith, rev. ed.,* Alba House, New York, 1982.

Newbigin L., *Honest Religion for Secular Man*, Philadelphia, 1966.

Nickerson B. ed., *Chi-letters from Biafra*, Toronto, 1970.

Njaka E.N., *Igbo Political Culture,* Evanston, University Press, 1974.

------------------, *A History of the Christian Missions,* Penguin Books, London, 1990.

Nkafu N.M., *African Vitalogy*, Pauline's Publications Africa, Nairobi, 1999.

Nkeonye O., "Pragmatism and Traditionalism in the Concept of God in *African Culture", a reply to Dr. Nze, Journal of the Department of Philosophy*, University of Nigeria Nussuka, Nigeria, 1982

Nkrumah K., *Neo-colonialism: The Last Stage of Imperialism*, Panaf, London, 1965.

Nkwo M., *Igbo Cultural Heritage,* University Publishing Company, Onitsha, Nigeria, 1984.

Nnamani A.G., *The Paradox of a Suffering God*, Peter Lang, Germany, 1995.

------------------, *Consciencism: Philosophical and Ideology of Decolonization and Development with particular reference to the African Revolution,* rev. ed., Heinemann, London, 1964.

Nwabueze B., *The Igbo in the Context of Modern Government and Politics in Nigeria,* Owerri, Ministry of Information, 1985.

Nwala T.U., *Igbo Philosophy*, Triatlantic Books Ltd., Nigeria, 2010.

Nwankwo A.A., *Nigeria: The Challenge of Biafra*, Rex Collings, Ltd., Nigeria, 1972.

------------------, *Emancipation as a Paradigm,* Fourth Dimension Publishers, Enugu, Nigeria, 1996.

Nwoga D.I., *The Supreme God as Stranger in Igbo Religious Thought*, Hawk Press Ekwereazu, Nigeria, 1984.

------------------, *"Nka na Nzere: The Focus of Igbo World View" in* Ahiajoku Lectures, Ministry of Information, Culture, Youth and Sports, Owerri, Nigeria, 1984.

Nwosu V.A., ed., *The Catholic Church in Onitsha: People, Places and Events,* 1885 – 1985, Etukokwu Press Ltd., Onitsha, Nigeria, 1985.

Nyamiti C., *Christ as our Ancestor,* Mambo Press, Zimbabwe, 1984.

Nzimiro I., *Studies in Ibo Political Systems,* London, 1972.

Obasanjo O., *Not My Will,* University Press, Ltd., Ibadan, 1990.

Obasi S.O., *Evangelization and Modernity: Cultural issues as Missiological Imperative in Ecclesia in Africa,* Hamburg, 2008.

Obi C.A., ed., *A Hundred Years of the Catholic Church in Eastern Nigeria* 1885 – 1985, Africana – FEP Publishers Ltd., 1985.

Obiechina E., *Literature for the Masses. An Analytical Study of Popular Pamphleteering in Nigeria,* Nwamife Books, Enugu, 1971.

Obiezuofu-Ezeigbo C.E., The *Biafran War and the Igbo in Contemporary Nigeria Politics,* Pan Negro Continental Ltd., Lagos, Nigeria, 2007.

Obinwa I.M.C., (ed.), *Collaboration Ministry in the Context of Inculturation,* Africana First Publishers Ltd., Nigeria, 2006.

Obiora F.K., *The Divine Deceit: Business in Religion,* Optimal Publishers, Enugu, Nigeria, 1998.

Oborji A.F., *Trends in African Theology Since Vatican II:* A Missiological Orientation, Tipografica Leberit, Roma, 1998.

Odoemene N.A., *The Fundamentals of African Traditional Religion (A Key to African Development)* Snaap Press, Enugu, Nigeria, 1988.

Odogwu B., *No Place to Hide (Crisis and Conflicts inside Biafra),* Fourth Dimension Publishers 1985.

Odumegwu-Ojukwu, E., *"Because I am Involved,"* Spectrum Books, Ibadan, Nigeria, 1989.

Offodile C., *The Politics of Biafra and the Future of Nigeria,* Safari Books Ltd., Ibadan, Nigeria, 2016.

------------------, *Dr. M.I. Okpara: A Biography,* Fourth Dimension, Nigeria, 1980.

Ofomata G.E.K., ed*., A Survey of the Igbo Nation,* Africana First Publishers Ltd., Onitsha, Nigeria, 2002.

Ogbalu F.C.,   *Omenala Igbo: The Book of Igbo Custom,* University Publishing Company Ltd., Onitsha, Nigeria, 1979.

Ogbukagu I.N.T., *Traditional Igbo Beliefs and practices, (A study on the Culture and people of Adazi-Nnukwu),* Novelty Industrial Enterprises Ltd., Owerri, Nigeria, 1997.

Ogot B.A.,   *Africa from the sixteenth to the eighteenth century; General History of Africa,* vol. V, UNESCO, Paris, 1992.

Oguejiofor J.O., *The Influence of Igbo Traditional Religion on the Socio-Political Character of the Igbo*, Fulladu Publishing Company, Nsukka, 1996.

-----------------,   *"The Spirit of the Igbo of Nigeria"* Pietes Africaines, 1989.

Ojike M.,   *My Africa*: Blandford, London, 1955.

Ojo O.,   *Olusegun Obasanjo, in the Eyes of Time*, A Biography of the African Statesman, Pine Hill Press Inc., U.S.A., 1997.

-----------------,   *I have two Countries: John* Day, New York, 1947.

Okafor F.U.,   *Igbo Philosophy of Law,* Fourth Dimension Publisher, Enugu, Nigeria, 1992.

Okafor O.D.,   *A Nigerian Village in Two Worlds,* Faber Limited, London, 1965.

Okafor S.A.,   *Death, Burial, Funeral and Widowhood in the Catholic Diocese* of Awka, Fides Publications Awka, Nigeria, 1996.

Okeke I.R.,   *The "Osu" Concept in Igbo Land,* Access Publishers, Enugu, Nigeria, 1986.

Okeke V.M., (ed.), *Christian Witness: Essays in Memory of Archbishop Stephen Nweke Ezeanya,* Delta Publications, Ltd., Enugu, Nigeria, 2003.

Okere T.,   *African Philosophy: Historical Hermeneutical Investigation of the Conditions of its Possibility*, University Press of America, Lanham, 1983.

Okigbo P.,   *Reconstruction of Political Economy of Igbo Civilization*, Owerri Ministry of Information, 1989.

Okolo B.C.,   *From Cross to Crucifix, (what Christianity adds to suffering),* Snaap Press, Ltd., Enugu, Nigeria, 1992.

Okolo C.B., *Problems of African Philosophy and other Essays,* Cecta, Nig. Ltd., Enugu, Nigeria, 1993.

--------------, *African Philosophy: A Short Introduction,* Cecta Nig., Ltd., 1993.

--------------, *African Social and Political Philosophy, Selected Essays,* Fulladu Publishing Company, Nsukka, Nigeria, 1993.

--------------, *What is to be African,* Cetca Nig. Ltd., Enugu, Nigeria, 1993.

--------------, *African Traditional Religion and Christianity:* The Neglected Dimension, Fulladu Publishing Company, Nsukka, Nigeria, 1995.

Okonkwo M.N., *In the Bowels of Biafra,* Vougasen Ltd., Enugu, Nigeria, 2003.

Okonkwo R., *"National Integration in Nigeria" in Anichebe (ed.), Issues in Nigeria Peoples and Culture,* Afro-Obis Publication Ltd., Nsukka, Nigeria, 2009.

Okoye M., *A Letter to Dr. Nnamdi Azikiwe,* Fourth Dimension, Nigeria, 1979.

Okwudibia N., *Ethnic Politics in Nigeria,* Fourth Dimension Publishing Co., Ltd., Enugu, Nigeria, 1978.

Okwueze M.I., ed., *Religion and Social Development: Contemporary Nigerian Perspective,* Merit International Publications, Lagos, Nigeria, 2004.

Olaniyan R., ed., *African History and Culture,* Longman, Nigeria, 1996.

Olikenyi G.I., *African Hospitality: A Model for Communication of the Gospel in the African Cultural Context,* Steyler Verlag, Nettetal, 2001.

Omosade J., & Adelumo P., *West African Traditional Religion,* Onibonoje Press and Books Industries, Ibadan, Nigeria, 1979.

Omotoson K., *Just before Dawn,* Spectrum Books Ltd., 1988.

Onunwa U., *Studies in Igbo traditional Religion,* Pacific publishers, Nigeria, 1990.

Onuoha B., *'Schools must be free from Religious Dogmatism',* the Renaissance, Enugu, Nigeria, 1972.

Onuoha E., *Four Contrasting World-Views,* Empress Publication Ltd., Enugu, Nigeria, 1987.

Onwubiko K.B.C., *School Certificate History of West Africa, BK. Two, 1800 - Present Day*, Africana Educational Publishers, Nigeria, 1973.

Onwubiko O.A., *Echoes from the African Synod*, SNAAP Press Ltd., Enugu, 1994.

----------------, *African Thought, Religion and Culture*, vol. I, Snaap Press, Enugu, Nigeria, 1991.

----------------, *Facing the Osu issue in the African Synod (A personal Response),* Snaap Press Ltd., Enugu, Nigeria, 1993.

----------------, *Wisdom Lectures on African Thought and Culture*, Totan Publishers, Owerri, Nigeria, 1988.

Onwuejeogwu M.A., *'A short history of the Odinani Museum'*, *The Journal of Odinani Museum,* Nri, Vol. 1, No.1, 1972.

Opata D., *Essays on Igbo Worldview,* AP Express Publishers, 1998.

Opoku K.A., *West African traditional Religion,* FEP International Private Limited, Accra, 1978.

Oreilly M., *The Challenge of Being a Religious in Africa Today,* AMECEA Gaba Publications, Eldoret, 1996.

Osaghae E.E., *Nigeria since Independence, Crippled Giant*, Hurt and Company, London, 1998.

Osuagwu C.G., *Truth and Chaos: Dynamics of Truth within Igbo Cosmology,* African World Communications, Owerri, Nigeria.

Otagburuagu E. J., ed., *New Brides, More Hopes: Igbo Women in Socio-Economic Change,* Institute of African Studies, University of Nigeria, Nsukka, Nigeria, 2008.

Ottenberg S. & Phoebe., *Cultures and Societies in Africa*, Random House 1960.

Oyebola A., *Black Man's Dilemma,* Board Publications Ltd., Lagos, Nigeria, 1976.

Oyewole F., *Reluctant Rebel,* Rex Collings Ltd., London, 1975.

Ozigbo I.R.A., *A History of Igboland in the 20th Century,* Snaap Press, Enugu, Nigeria, 1999.

Pagels E., *The Gnostic Gospels,* Random House, New York, 12979.

Parrat J., *Reinventing Christianity: African Theology Today*, Wm. B. Eerdmans Publishing Co., Grand Rapids, Michigan and Africa World Press Inc., Trenton, New Jersey, 1995.

Parrinder E.G., *West African Religion: A Study of the Beliefs and Practices of Akan, Ewe, Yoruba, Ibo, and Kindred Peoples, The* Epworth Press London, 1961.

-----------------, *African Traditional Religion,* Sheldon, Press, 1974.

Pobee J.S., *Religion in a Pluralistic Society,* ed., E.J. Brill, Leiden, 1976.

-----------------, *Towards African Theology,* Abingdon Press, Nashville, 1979.

Pocock M., et al., *The Changing Face of World Missions: Engaging Contemporary Issues and Trends,* Baker Academic Grand Rapids, MI, 2005.

Poking R.H. and Stroll, *A Philosophy Made Simple*, London, W.H., Allen, 1956.

Popper K., *The Open Society and its Enemies, 2 Vols.* Rutledge & Kegan Paul Ltd., London, 1957.

Price D. De S., *Science since Babylon,* Yale University, New Haven, 1962.

Quarcoopome T.N.O., *West African Traditional Religion,* African University Press, Ibadan, Nigeria, 1987.

Ranger T.O., ed., *Aspects of Central African History,* Heinemann, London, 1968.

Reader J., *A Biography of the Continent Africa,* Vintage Books, New York, 1999.

Robertson R., *Meaning and Change: Explorations in the Cultural Sociology of Modern Societies,* University Press, New York, 1978.

Rodney W., *How Europe Underdeveloped Africa,* Howard University Press, Washington D.C., 1982.

Rogers E., *Modernization among Peasants: The Impact of Communication,* Holt, Rinehart and Winton, New York, 1969.

Royce, *Man and his Nature,* McGraw Hill Book Company, New York, 1961.

Russell B. *Outline of Philosophy*, George Allen & Unwin, London, 1979.

----------------,   *Skeptical Essays:* G. Allen & Unwin, Ltd., London, 1960.

----------------,   *History of Western Philosophy*, George Allen and Unwin Ltd., 1962.

Saacman A.,   *Anti-Colonial Activity in the Zambesi Valley 1850-1921*, University of California Press, Berkeley, 1976.

Saldanha J.,   *Inculturation, St. Paul Publications*, Bandra-Bombay, 1987.

Sanneh L., and Carpenter J.A., ed., *The Changing Face of Christianity: Africa, the West and the World*, Oxford University Press, New York, 2005.

Schillebeeckx E., *God the Future of Man*, sheed and Ward, London and Sydney, 1969.

----------------,   *The Understanding of Faith: Interpretation and Criticism*, Sheed and Ward, London, 1974.

Schineller P.,   *A Handbook on Inculturation*, Paulist Press, New York, 1990.

Schmidt,   *African Ideas of God,* Edinburgh, 1966.

Smith M.G.,   *Theories of Race and Ethnic Relations*, Cambridge University Press, 1986.

Schreiter R.J., ed., *Faces of Jesus in Africa*, SCM Press, London, 1991.

Senghor L.S.,   *On African Socialism (trans. Mercer Cook), American Society for African Culture, New York, 1959.*

Setiloane G.,   *The Image of God Among the Satha-Tswana, Balkema*, Rotterdam, 1976.

Shaw T.,   *Igbo Ukwu: An Accout of Archeological discoveries in Eastern Nigeria (2 Vols.)* Faber & Faber, 1970.

Sawyeer H.E.,   *God, Ancestor or Creator? Aspects of Traditional Belief* in *Ghana, Nigeria and Sierra Leone*, Longman, London, 1970.

Sheen F.J.,   *Theology for Beginners*, Sheed & Ward, London, 1976.

Shorter A.,   *Evangelization and Culture*, Geoffrey Chapman, New York, 1976.

----------------,   *Toward a Theology of Inculturation*, Orbis Books, Mary-knoll, New York, 1997.

----------------,   *Christianity and the African Imagination,* Paulines Publications Africa, Nairobi, Kenya, 1996.

----------------,   *Evangelization and Culture,* Geoffrey Chapman, London, 1994.

----------------,   *African Christian Theology: Adaptation or Incarnation?* Geoffrey Chapman, London, 1975.

Sim S.,   *Fundamentalist World: The New Dark Age of Dogma,* Icon Books UK, Cambridge, 2005.

Sindima H.J.,   *Africa's Agenda: The Legacy of Liberalism and colonialism in the Crisis of African Values,* Greenwood Press, Westport, 1995.

----------------, & **Williams E.,** Capitalism *and Slavery,* University of North Carolina Press, Chapel Hill, 1944.

Singer P.,   *Hegel,* Oxford University Press, New York, 1983.

Singh Y.,   *Social stratification and Change in India,* Manohar, Delhi, 1989.

Smart N.,   *The World's Religions: Old Traditions and Modern Transformation,* Cambridge University Press, Melbourne, 1995.

Smith H.,   *Beyond the Post-modern Mind,* Quest Books, Wheaton, 1996.

Sofola J.A.,   *African Culture and the African Personality,* Ibadan, 1982.

Stace W.T.,   *The philosophy of Hegel,* Dover & Publications, Inc., 1955.

Stumpf S.E.,   *Philosophy: History and Problems, (2nd ed.),* McGraw-Hill Book Company, 1977.

Southern R.W., *Western Society and the Church in the Middle Ages,* Penguin Books, England, 1970.

Swingewood A., *Cultural Theory and the Problem of Modernity,* St. Martin's Press, New York, 1998.

Talbot P.A.,   *Tribes on the Niger Delta,* Sheldon Press, 1937.

Taylor C.,   *Hegel,* Cambridge University Press, London, 1975.

Taylor J.V.,   *The Coming of Post-Industrial Society,* Basic Books, New York, 1973.

----------------, *The Primary Vision,* S.C.M, Press Ltd., London, 1963.

Temples P., *Bantu Philosophy, Presence Africaine,* Paris, 1959.

Thomas S., *"The Global Resurgence of Religion and the Changing Character of International Politics"*, in **Stackhouse M.L.,** eds., *Christ and the Dominions of Civilization*, Trinity Press International, Harrisburg, 2002.

Thomas N.W., *An Anthropological Report on the Igbo-Speaking People of Nigeria, Part IV, Law and Custom of the Ibo of Asaba District, Southern Nigeria*, Harrison & Sons London, 1914.

Torres S., & Fabella V., The *Emergent Gospel, Theology form the Underside of* History Orbis Books, Mary-knoll, 1978.

Tosolini T., *To Speak of God in the Twilight*, Fowler Wright Books, England, 1997.

Trimingham S., *The Christian Church and Islam in West Africa*, SCM Press, London, 1955.

Ubahakwe E., *Igbo Names*, Daystar Press, Ibadan, Nigeria, 1978.

Ubesie T., *Odinala Ndi Igbo,* Daystar Press, Ibadan, Nigeria, 1978.

Uchechukwu Dine, G.G., *Traditional Leadership as Sample of African Democracy Among the Igbo of Nigeria: Christian Evaluation*, Snaap Press, Nig. Ltd., Enugu, Nigeria, 2007.

Uchendu V.C., *The Igbo of Southeastern Nigeria,* Holt, Rinehart and Winston, Inc. New York, 1965.

Udobata O., *Studies in Igbo Traditional Religion*, Pacific Publishers, Obosi, Nigeria, 1990.

Ugboaja P., *"Culture Conflict, Urbanism and Delinquency: A case study of Colonial Lagos"* in **Babawale T., and Ogen O.,** ed., *Culture, Language and Intergroup Relations*, Concept Publications, Nigeria, 2015.

Ugwu C.O.T., ed., *Corruption in Nigeria: Critical Perspective, A book of Readings,* Chuka Educational Publishers, Nsukka, Nigeria, 2002.

Umeh C., *The Human Suffering: Concept, Nature and Cause: Any Way Out?* Rex Charles and Patrick Ltd., Nimo, Nigeria, 2006.

Ukpong J.S.,   *African Theologies Now a Profile*, Gaba Publications, Eldoret, Kenya, 1984.

Uwalaka J.,   *The Struggle for An Inclusive Nigeria: Igbos to be or not to be? A Treatise on Igbo Political Personality and Survival in Nigeria*, Snaap Press Ltd., Enugu, Nigeria, 2003.

Uwechue R.,   *Reflections on the Nigerian Civil War: Facing the Future*, Africana Publishing Corporation, Nigeria, 1971.

Uzukwu E.E.,   *A listening Church: Autonomy and Communion in African Churches,* Orbis Books, Mary-knoll, New York, 1996.

------------------, ed., *Religion and African Culture*, Spiritan Publications, Enugu, 1988.

Van Gorder A.C., *Violence in God's Name, Christian and Muslim Relations in Nigeria,* African Diaspora Press, Houston, USA, 2012.

Vattimo G.,   *The End of Modernity*, Polity Press, Cambridge, 1991.

Verkuyl J.,   *Contemporary Missiology: An Introduction*, Wm. B. Eerdmans Publishing Co. Grand Rapids, Michigan, 1978.

Wallace A.F.C., *Culture and Personality,* Random, New York, 1961.

Wand J.W.C.,   *A History of the Modern Church from 1500 A.D.*, London, 1952.

Waugh P. *ed.,*   *Postmodernism: A Reader*, Edward Arnold, London, 1992.

Webster H.,   *Taboo: A Sociological Study*, Octagon Books, New York, 1973.

Wedgewood C., *The Nature and Function of Secret Societies*, Occeania, Vol. 1, 1930.

Westermann D., *Africa and Christianity*, Oxford University Press, 1937.

Whitehead A.N., *Process and Reality*, Macmillan, New York, 1978.

Wilks I.G.,   *Asante in the Nineteenth Century*, Cambridge University Press, Cambridge, 1975.

Witte Jr., J. ed*., Christianity and Democracy in Global Context,* Westview Press, Boulder, Co. 1993.

Zuern T.F., et al., *On Being Church in a Modern Society,* Pontifical Gregorian University, Rome, 1983.

2. DICTIONARIES AND ENCYCLOPAEDIAS

The Christian Faith (**Neuer J. & Dupuis J.,** eds.), Alba House, 1982.

Harper's Bible Dictionary (**Achtemeier P. J.,** ed.), Harper and Row Pub., New York 1971.

A New Dictionary of Christian Theology, (**Richardson, A. and Bowden J**.), SCM Press, London, 1983.

A Dictionary of Cultural and Critical Theory, (**Payne M.,** et al.), Blackwell Publishers, Oxford, 1997.

The Twentieth Century Encyclopedia of Catholicism, Hawthorn Books, New York, 1962.

Oxford English Reference Dictionary (**Pearsall, J. and Trumble B.),** eds. Oxford University Press, Oxford, 1996.

Dictionary of Black African Civilization, (**Balandier G., and Maquaet J.),** Leon Amiel Publisher, New York, 1974.

The Oxford Dictionary of World Religions (**Bowker J.,** ed.), Oxford University Press, Oxford, 1997.

International Encyclopedia of Social Sciences, (**Sills L.D.,** ed), The Macmillan Company and Free Press New York, vol. 5 and 6, 1972.

The New Bible Dictionary, (**Douglas J.D**.), William B. Erdmanns Publishing Co., Grand Rapids, 1975.

Dictionary of Race and Ethnic Relations, (Cashmore E.), Routledge Books, London, 1996.

Dictionary of Third World Theologies, (**Favella V., and Sugirtharajah R.S.,** eds.), Orbis Books, Mary-knoll, New York, 2000.

The New Encyclopedia Britannica, Encyclopedia Britannica Inc., 15 Edition, Chicago, London, et al., 1980.

New Catholic Encylopedia, vols., 1,3,5 & 13, McGraw-Hill Books Co.,

*Encyclopedia of African History and Culture, (**Page W.F.),** vols. 1 – 3,* The Learning Source Ltd., New York, 2001.

SELECTED ARTICLES AND JOURNALS

Akpan M. B.,   *"Ethiopia and Liberia"*, in: **Boahen Adu A.,** ed., *General History of Africa*, vol. 7, Heinemann, London, 1985.

Alexander A.S., jr., *"The Ivory Coast Constitution: As Accelerator, Not a Brake"* in **Doro, M.E.,** and **Stultz, N.M.** eds. *Governing in Black Africa: Perspectives on New States*, Englewood Cliffs, New Jersey, 1970.

Amaladoss M., *"A Christian Vision of a New Society"*, SEDOS 31 (1999) 11 288 - 294.

-----------------,   *"Secularization and India: Modernization and Religion in an Eastern Country"*, in SEDOS 24 (15 September, 1992) 11 233-240.

Anyika F.,   *"The Supreme God in Igbo Traditional Religious Thought and Worship,"* Communio Viatorum, Antheological Quarterly XXXII (1989), pp. 5 – 20.

Arinze F.,   *"Evangelization in Nigeria,"* in **Ejiofor**, ed., *Africans and Christianity* (vol. IV), Optimal Computer Solutions Ltd., Nsukka/ Enugu, 1990, pp. 103 – 120.

Arinze F., & **Fitzgerald M. L.,** *"Pastoral attention to African Traditional Religion (ATR)"* in AFER, 30 (June, 1988) 3 131 – 134.

Armstrong R.G., *"Is Earth Senior to God? An Old West African Theological Controversy"*, African Notes, 1 (1982), pp. 7 – 14.

Athyal L.,   Mythg/Folktale" in **Favella, V.,** and **Sugirtharajah, R.S.** eds., *Dictionary of Third World Theologies,* Orbis Books, Mary-Knoll, New York, 2000, pp. 151 – 152.

Baladier G., and Maquaet J., *"Africa"*, *in Dictionary of Black African Civilization,* Leon Amiel Publishers, New York, 1974.

Balasuriya T.,   *"Globalization"*, in **Fabella V., & Sugirtharajah R.S.,** eds., *Dictionary of Third World Theologies*, Orbis Books, 2000, pp. 91 94.

Banton M.,   *"Race as Classification"*, in **Cashmore E.,** et al., *Dictionary of Race and Ethnic Relations,* 4th ed., Routledge Books, London, 1996, pp. 294 – 296.

Barber W.J., *"The Movement into World Economy"*, in **Herskovits,** M.J. and Harwitz M., eds., *Economic Transition in Africa,* Norther-west University Press, Evanston, 1964.

Boesak A., *"A Prophetic Call to Faithfulness",* in Wilson, F.R., ed., *The San Antonio Report: Your Will be Done Mission in Christ's Way*, WCC Publications, Geneva, 1990, pp. 156 – 161.

---------------, *"Liberation Theology in South Africa"*, in **Appiah-Kubi,** K & **Torres S.,** eds., African Theology en Route, Orbis Books, Mary-Knoll, New York, 1979, pp. 169 – 175.

Bosch J.D., *"Evangelism, Evangelization"*, **Müller Karl, Sundermeier Theo.,** eds., *Dictionary of Mission*, Orbis Books New York, 1997, pp. 151 - 154.

Brungs R.J., *"Contemporary Technology and the Church,"* in *COMMUNIO 2* (1978) 135 – 157.

Buthelezi M., *"An African or a Black Theology?"* in **Motlhabi M.,** ed., *Essays on Black Theology,* University Christian Movement pub. Johannesburg, 1972.

Cashmore E., et al*., "Colonialism", in Dictionary of Race and Ethnic Relations,* 4th ed., Routledge Books, London, 1996, pp. 79 – 84.

Chia E., *"A New Way of Being Church"*, in SEDOS 30(April 1998)4 106 – 112.

Creed-Page, Kethleen, *"Reproductive Technologies"*, in **Payne M.**, et al., *A Dictionary of Cultural and Critical Theory*, Blackwell Publishers, Oxford, 1997, pp. 463 – 466.

Crossette B., *"A Continent is Seething: No Remedy for Africa"*, in *Herald* International Tribune, May 12, 2000.

Chukwukere B.I., *"Chi in Igbo Religion and Thought: The God in Every man"*, *Anthropos*, 78 (1983), pp. 519 -534.

Davey A.P., "Globalization as Challenge and Opportunity in Urban Mission: An Outlook from London", in SEDOS 32 (March 2000) 79 – 83.

Dwyer J.A., "Peace", in **Komonchak J.A.,** et al. eds., The New Dictionary of Theology, Gill and Macmillan Ltd., Dublin, 1990, pp. 748-753.

Ekechukwu A., "The Problem of Suffering in Igbo Traditional Religion", in **Afer**, 24 (April 1982) 81 – 89.

Ekejiuba F., *"Aro World-View: An Analysis of the Cosmological Ideas of Aro Chukwu People of Eastern Nigeria"*, West African Religion, 8 (1970).

Ervwo S.U., *"The Concept of God Among the Urhobo of the Niger Delta"*, Ikenga 2(1973), pp. 83 – 89.

Etchegaray R., *"A Jubilee on Poverty"*, In SEDOS 30(March)3 67 – 69.

Ezeanya S.N., *"The Place of the Supreme Being in Traditional Religion of the Igbo"*, West African Religion, Department of Religion, U.N.N., 1 (1963), pp. 1 – 4.

----------------, *"God, Spirit, and Spirit World"*, In **Kw. Dickson and P. Illingworth** eds., *Biblical Revelation and African Beliefs*, Mary-Knoll, Orbis (12969), pp.30 – 46.

Ezeanya S., & Maduka M., *"From Igbo Sacrifice to the Mass"*, in LUX 2 (1952-1953), pp. 43 – 44.

Ezeogu E., *"Bible and Culture in African Christianity* in IRM, LXXXVII (January, 1998) 344 26 (25 – 39).

Faniran J.O., *"Evangelizing the Media: A Challenge to the Church in Africa"*, AFER 40 (April 1998)2 111 – 127.

Ferrao S., *Transformation of Hearts and Minds: Major Task for the Church in Africa*, in AFER 38 (1996)3 188 – 189.

Germani G., & Hauser P.M., *"Modernization and Urbanization"*, Encyclopedia Britannica, vol. 24, 1985.

Geertz C., *"Ethos, World-View and the Analysis of Sacred Symbols"* in **Dundes** A., *Every Man His Way: Readings in Cultural Anthropology*, Prentice Hall New Jersey, 1968.

George S., *"Uses and abuses of African debt"*, in **Adedeji A.,** ed., *Africa within the World: Beyond Dispossession and Dependence*, Zed., London, 1993.

Giglioni P., *"Evangelization Process: Kerygma to Local Church"* in Karotemprel S., et al ends., *Following Christ in Mission:*

a foundational course in Missiology, Pauline Books and Media, Boston, 1996, pp. 203 212.

Gueera F., *"The Paradox of Modernity"* in **McInerny R.** ed., Modernity and Religion, University of Notre Dame Press, Notre Dame, 1994, pp. 19 – 29.

Hanratty G., *"Enlightenment"*, in **Komonchak J.A.** ed., *The New Dictionary of Theology*, Gill and Macmillan, Dublin, 1987, pp. 323 – 324.

Hanson J.H., *"Islam and African Societies"*, in **Martin P. M** and **O'mera P.,** eds., Africa, Indiana University Press, Indiana, 1995, pp. 97 – 114.

Hefner P.J., *"Science, Technology and Christian Faith:* The Warp and Weft of Mission", in Mission Studies; XV-2 (1998) 30 51 – 65.

Henige D., *"Measuring the Immeasurable: The Atlantic Slave Trade, West African Population and Pyrrhonian Critic"*, in JAH (1986) 2 295 - 313.

Hickey R., *"Authentic African Religion"* in: AFER, 27 (August, 1985) 4.

Horton R., *"God, Man and the Land in a Northern Ibo Village – Group"*, *Africa,* 26 (1956), pp. 17 – 28.

----------------, *"The High God"*, A Comment on Father O'Connell's Paper, Man 42-219 (1975), pp. 137 – 140.

----------------, *"On the Rationality of Conversion"*, *Africa*, 3 (1975), pp. 219 – 235.

Howe I., *"Mass Society and Post-modern Fiction"*, **In Waugh, P.,** ed., *Postmodernism:* A Reader, **Edward Arnold**, London, 1992.

Inikori J.E., *"Africa in World History; The Export Slave Trade from Africa and the Emergence of the Atlantic Economic Order"*, in **Ogot, B.A.,** *Africa from the sixteenth to the eighteenth century; General History of Africa vol. V.* UNESO, Paris, 1992, pp. 80 83.

Iwuagu A.O., *"Chukwu: Towards a Definition of Igbo Traditional Religion"* (1975), pp. 26 – 34.

Johnson M., *"The cowrie currencies of West Africa"*, in JAH 112 (1979)17.

Joseph R., *"The Christian Churches and Democracy in Contemporary Africa"*, in **Witte Jr., J.,** ed., *Christianity and Democracy in*

Global Context, Westview Press, Boulder, Co. 1993, pp. 231 - 247.

Kalilombe P.A., *"Salvific Value of African Religions"*, in **Anderson G.H.,** & **Stransky T.F.** eds., *Mission Trends No. 5*, Paulist Fathers & Wm. B. Eerdmans Publishing Co., Grand Rapids, Michigan, 1981, pp. 50 – 68.

------------------, *"Self-Reliance of the African Church: A Catholic Perspective"*, in **Appiah Kubi K & Torres S.** eds., African Theology en Route, Orbis Books Mary-knoll, New York, 1979, pp. 36 – 58.

Kanyandago P., *"Violence in Africa: Search for Causes and Remedies"*, in **Getui M., & Kanyandago P.** ed., *From Violence to Peace: A Challenge to African Christianity*, Action Publishers, Nairobi, 1999, pp. 7 – 40.

Kanyoro M.R.A., *"Ecumenism",* in **Fabella V., & Sugirtharajah R.S.,** eds., *Dictionary of Third World Theologies*, Orbis Books, Mary-Knoll, New York, 2000, pp. 82 – 83.

Karp I., *"African Systems of Thought"* in: **Martin P. & O'meara P.,** eds., Africa, Indiana University Press, Indiana, 1995, pp. 211 – 222.

Keim C.A., *"Africa and Europe before 1900",* in: **Martin P. & O'meara P.,** eds., Africa, Indiana University Press, Indiana, 1995, pp. 115-134.

Kenny M., *"TV's Hidden Program".* Tablet 14 November, 1987.

Kozhamthadam J., *"The Cloning of Dolly: Some Reflections"*, in VJTR 62 (February 1998)2 844 – 856.

Krieg R.A., *"Romano Guardini's Theology of the Human Person"*, in *THEOLOGICAL STUDIES 59* (September 1998) 3, 457 – 474.

Lamb M.L., *"Modernism and Americanism",* in COMMUNIO, XXI (1994) 4 631 – 662.

Lampe A., *"The Globalization of Poverty"*, In SEDOS 32 (May 2000) 5 130 - 135.

Law B.F., *"To Evangelize a Global Culture",* in CULTURES AND FAITH, V (1997)2 120 – 121.

391

Lebulu L.J.,   *"The Church's Social Teaching on Development"* in AFER 37 (October/December 1995) 5 & 6 316 – 327.

Leffel J. and McCallum D., *"The Postmodern Religious Shift: Five Case Studies"*, in: McCallum D., ed., *The Death of Truth,* Bethany House Publishers, Minneapolis, 1996, pp. 215 – 234.

----------------,   *"The Church-As-Family: Its Implications for the Formation* of *Agents",* in AFER 41 (August/October/December 199) 4, 5 & 6 180 – 193.

Long C.H.,   *"The West African High God: History and Religious Experience"*, History of Religion, 2 (1964), pp. 323 – 342.

Magesa L.,   *"Africa's Struggle for Self-Definition during a Time of Globalization",* in SEDOS 31 (August – September 1999) 8/9, pp. 235.

----------------,   *"Aids and Survival in Africa: A Tentative Reflection"*, in **Mugambi J.N.K.,** et., eds., *Moral and Ethical Issues in African Christianity,* Initiatives Publishers, Nairobi, 1992, pp. 197 – 216.

----------------, *"Christ the Liberator and Africa Today, "*in **Schriter R.J.,** ed., *The Faces of Jesus in Africa,* SCM Press, London, 1991, pp. 151 - 163.

----------------,   "Instruction on the Theology of Liberation: A Comment", AFER 27 (1985)1.

Mahir S.,   *"Economic Life in Africa Villages and Towns"*, in **Martin P.,** & **O'meara, P.,** eds., Africa, Indiana University Press, Indiana, pp. 190 – 210.

Majawa C.,   *"The Church's Role in Defining Genuine Democracy in Africa"*, in AFER 42 (February – April, 2000) 1 & 2 52 – 80.

Masson M.A.,   *"Missionary Activity, Response to Today's World,* in LV (1967) 9 – 28.

Mauny R.,   *"Trans-Sahara contacts and the Iron Age in West Africa"* in FAGE J.D., ed., The Cambridge History of Africa (Vol. 2), Cambridge University Press, New York, 1978, pp. 272 – 341.

Mbiti J.S.,   *"Cattle Are Born with Ears, Their Horns Grow later"*, ATJ 8 (1979) 1 15 – 25.

392

McNulty M.L., *"The Contemporary Map of Africa"*, in M.P., et al eds., Africa, Indiana University Press, Indiana, 1995, pp. 10 – 45.

Metuh E.I., *"Igbo World-View: Premise for Christian Traditional Religious Dialogue"*, West African Religion, 13 & 14, (1972), pp. 51 – 58.

----------------, *"The Nature of African Theism: Analysis of Two Nigerian Models,"* in **Metuh-Ikenga E.,** ed., *Nigeria Cultural Heritage*, IMICO Pub. Comp., Onitsha, 1990.

Moltmann J., *"The Theology of Liberation"*, TD 45 (Spring 1998) 1 3 – 6.

Mondin B., *"Cultura"* in Dizionario Di Missiologia, EDB, Bologna, 1993, 167 – 175.

Mulyungi J.M., *"A Call to the Church to Empower People Through Development"*, AFER 37 (October/December 12995) 5 & 6 328 – 341.

Munono B., *"Synthesis of National Reports on Social Thought and Action of the Church in English and Portuguese-Speaking Africa"*, in **Munono B.,** ed., *The Challenge of Justice and Peace: The Response of the Church in Africa Today*, Liberia Editrice Vaticana, Vatican, 1998.

Mushete N.A., *"An Overview of African Theology,* in **Gibellini S.,** ed., Paths of African Theology, SCM Press Ltd., London, 1994, pp. 9 – 26.

----------------, *"Modernity in Africa"*, in **Jenkinson, W., and O'sullivan H.,** eds., Trends in Mission: Towards the 3rd Millennium, Orbis/Sedos, Mary-Knoll, 1991, pp. 143 – 154.

Newbigin L., *"Culture of Modernity"*, in Müller K., Sundermeier T., eds., Dictionary of Mission Dictionary of Mission, Orbis Books, New York, 1997, pp. 98 – 101.

Nicol D.S.H.W., *"Africa"*, in the New Encyclopedia Britannica, (Macropaedia) vol., 1, Encyclopedia Britannica Inc., 15th Edition, Chicago, London, et al, 1980, p. 177.

Njoku F.O.C., *"Some Indigenous Models in African Theology and an Ethic of Inculturation"*, in BULLETIN OF ECUMENICAL THEOLOGY (Published by The Ecumenical Association of Nigeria Theologians), 8 (1996) 2 4 – 32.

Nunnenmacher E., *"Culture,"* in **Müller K, Sundermeier T.,** eds., Dictionary of Mission Dictionary of mission, Orbis Books, New York, 1997, pp. 94 – 98.

Nwala T.U.*,* *"Oracles: Their Place in the Traditional Cosmological Order of the Igbo, A Research Description"*, Ikorok, 2 (1971), pp. 1 – 2.

Nwatu F., *"The Church's Prophetic Role in Africa's Search for Selfhood"*, SEDOS 29 (April 12997) 4 115 – 121.

Nyamiti C., *"Approach to African Theology"*, in **Torres S.** & **Fabella V.,** *The Emergent Gospel, Theology from the Underside of History,* Orbis Books, Mary-knoll, 1978, pp. 31 – 36.

---------------, *"Contemporary African Christologies"*, in Gibellini S., ed., Paths of African Theology, SCM, Press, London, 1994, pp. 62 – 77.

Nyerere J., *"The Church's Role in Society*, in Parratt J., ed., *A Reader in African Christian Theology,* SPCK; London, 1987, pp. 117 – 130.

Nze C., *"The Concept of God in African Culture"*, Uche, Journal of the Department of Philosophy, U.N.N. 5 (1981), pp. 33 – 51.

---------------, *Pragmatism and Traditionalism in the Concept of God in Africa*, Uche, Journal of the Department of Philosophy U.N.N.5 (1981), pp. 20 – 26.

---------------, *"Sacrifice as a Restitution of Vital Force among the Igbo"*, Africana Marburgensia, XIX (1986), pp. 29 – 38.

Obiego C.O., *"Igbo Ideas of God"*, (1978), pp. 26 – 42.

---------------, *"An Attempt at Reconciling the Double Role of Chi"*, The Torch, 66 (1980), pp. 6 – 14.

---------------, *"The Igbo, Death and Immortality: Towards Igbo Theology of Death"*, The Torch, 67(1980), pp. 6 – 12.

O'Connell J., *"The Withdrawal of the High God in West African Religion: An Essay in Interpretation"*, Man, 109 (1962), pp. 67 – 69.

O'Donnell D., *"Evangelization: The Challenge of Modernity"*, in **Jenkinson W.,** ed., Trends in Mission: Towards the 3rd Millennium, Orbis Books, New York, 1991.

Okolo C.B., *"The African Person: A Cultural Definition"*, Indian Philosophical Quarterly, 1 (1988), pp. 99 – 107.

----------------, *"The Ontological Status of African Folk Philosophy"*, Quest Philosophical Discussions, An International African Journal of Philosophy, (1995), pp. 107 – 115.

Okongwu S.P.C., *"Africa and the Emerging World Order in the 21th Century: Challenges and Prospects"*, in SEDOS 31 (May 1999), pp. 147 – 153.

Onyewuenyi I., *"A Philosophical Reappraisal of African Belief in Reincarnation"*, International Philosophy Quarterly, 22 (1982), pp. 157 – 168.

Otakpor N., *"Pragmatism and Traditionalism in the Concept of God in African Culture"*, A Reply to **C. Nze,** Uche, Journal of the Department of Philosophy, 6 (1982), pp. 64 – 68.

Ottenberg S., *"Ibo Oracles and Inter Group Relations"*, South-Western Journal of Anthropological 14 (1958), pp. 295 – 317.

Payne M., *"Culture"* in **Payne, M.,** ed., *A Dictionary of Cultural and Critical Theory,* Blackwell Publishers Ltd., Oxford, 1996, pp. 128 – 129.

Plathottam G., *"Christian Mission in the Third Millennium and the Information superhighway: Challenges for Evangelization,"* in Indian MISSIOLOGICAL REVIEW 20 (December, 12998) 4 12 – 20.

Raiser K., *"Opening Space for a Culture of Dialogue-the missionary objectives of the WCC in an age of Globalization and Religious Plurality,* in SEDOS 31 (June and July 1999) 6 172 – 177.

Retif L., et al., *"The Church's Mission in the World",* in the Twentieth Century Encyclopedia of Catholicism, Hawthorn Books, New York, 1962, pp. 89 – 90.

Rutz, S., *"Popular Religiosity and Evangelization in Latin America,"* in Jenkinson W., ed., *Trends in Mission: Towards the 3rd Millennium,* Orbis Books New York 1991, pp. 107 – 117.

Sanneh L., *"Christian Mission in the Pluralist Milieu: The African Experience",* MISSIOLOGY; XII (1984) 4 422.

Schick K.D., *"Prehistoric Africa"*, in Martin M. P., et al (ed.), Africa, Indiana University Press, Indiana, 1995, pp. 49 – 72.

Schineller P., *"Ten Summary Statements on the Meaning, Challenge and Significance of Inculturation as applied to the Church and Society of Jesus in the United States, in Light of the Global*

Process of Modernization", in **Zuern T.F., *On Being Church in a Modern Society***, Pontifical Gregorian University, Rome, 1983, pp. 51-83.

Schoen U., *"Dialogue"*, in Müller K., et al, eds., Dictionary of Mission, Orbis Books, Mary-Knoll, New York, 1997, pp. 109 – 113.

Seigel M., *"Beyond Mere Cancellation of Debt: The Moral Imperative of a Just Society"*, in SEDOS 32 (April 2000) 4 117 – 124.

Shehu S., *"Between Deregulation and Human Face"*, Vanguard (Nigerian), April 23 2001.

Shelton A.J., *"The Presence of the Withdrawn High God in North Ibo Religious Belief and Worship"*, Man 4 (1964), pp. 15 – 18.

Stanislaus L., *"Ecology: An Awareness for Mission",* in SEDOS 31 (December 1999) 12 320 – 327.

Stenger J., *"The Congo Free State and the Belgian Congo Before 1914"*, in Gann L.H., & Duigan P., eds. *Colonization in Africa 1870 – 1960,* Cambridge University Press, Cambridge, 1969.

Stransky T.F., *"The Mission of the Church: Post-Vatican II Development* in 'Official' *Roman Catholic theology"*, in ONE IN CHRIST XXXV (1999)1 51 – 68.

Synod of Bishops Special Assembly for Africa, *Message of the Synod,* 1994.

Synod of Bishops, 1971, Document on Justice in the World, nos. 6, 37.

Turner F., *"The Future of the gods: Note Toward a post-modern Religion"*, in rebirth of value, State University Press, Albany, 1991, p. 70-86.

Ubah C.N., *The Supreme Being, Divinities and Ancestors in Igbo Traditional Religion. Evidence from Otanchara and Otanzu"*, Africa, 2 (1982), pp. 90 – 105.

Ukpong S.J., *"Contemporary Theological Models of Mission: Analysis and Critique"*, in AFER, 27 (1985) 162 – 171.

Van Den Berghe L.P., *"Race as Synonym"*, in CASHMORE, E., et al., *Dictionary of Race and Ethnic Relations, 4th ed.*, Routledge Books London, 1996, pp. 296 – 298.

Vargas L., *"Human Rights"*, in **Fabella V.,** and **Sugirtharajah R.S**. eds., *Dictionary of Third World Theologies*, Orbis Books, Mary-Knoll, New York, 2000, pp. 101 – 102.

Vatican Council II, *Decree on the Church's Missionary Activity, Ad Gentes Divintus,* 1965.

Waligo J.M., *"Making a Church that is Truly African"*, in A.A. V.V., *Inculturation: Its Meaning and Urgency*, St. Paul Publication - Africa, Nairobi, 1986, 11 – 30.

------------------, *"Corruption and Bribery: An African Problem"*, in **Lejeune M.,** et al., eds., *Business Ethics in the African Context Today*, Nkozi: Uganda Martyrs University press 1996, pp. 115 – 139.

Walls A., *"Towards an Understanding of Africa's Place in Christianity History"*, **Pobee, J.S.,** Religion in a Pluralistic Society, ed., E.J. Brill, Leiden, 1976.

Wells A.T., *"Gnosticism", in Douglas, The New Bible Dictionary,* William B., Erdmanns Publishing Co., Grand Rapids, 1975.

Wilfred F., *"Emerging Trends Challenge; the Churches of Asia,"* in **Jenkinson W., & O'sullivan H.,** ed., *Trends in Mission Toward the 3rd Millennium*, Orbis Books, New York, 1991, pp. 3 – 22.

Wieschoff H.A., *"The Social Significance of Names among the Ibo of Nigeria"*, American Anthropologist, 2 (1941), pp. 211 – 222.

THE MAP OF NIGERIA

The Map of Nigeria showing the 6 Geo-Political Zones in Nigeria.[877]

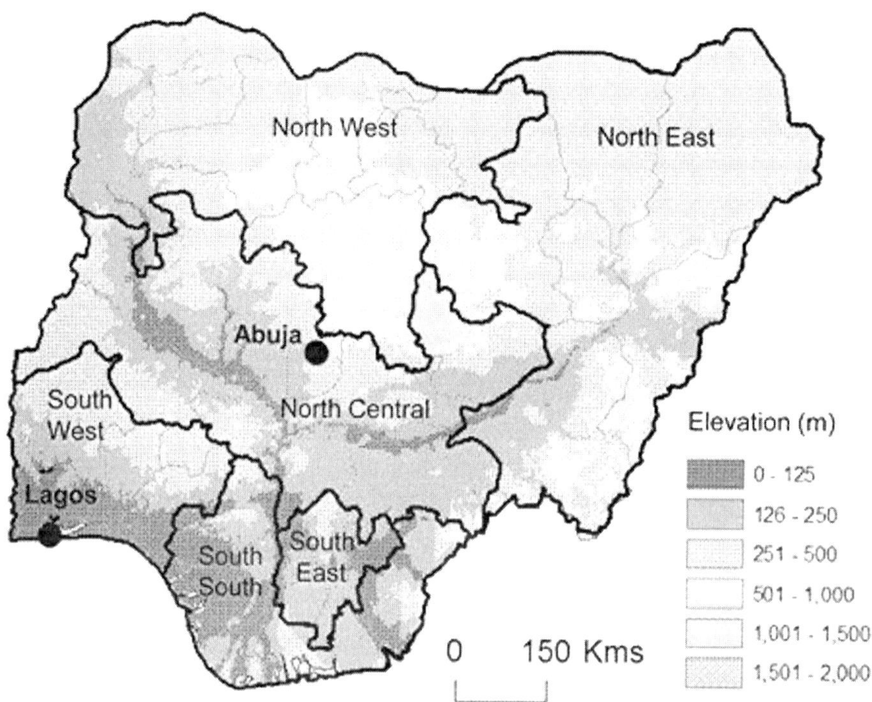

---

[877] https://s3-eu-west-1.amazonaws.com.

THE MAP OF NIGERIA SHOWING THE PRINCIPAL LINGUISTIC GROUPS IN NIGERIA.[878]

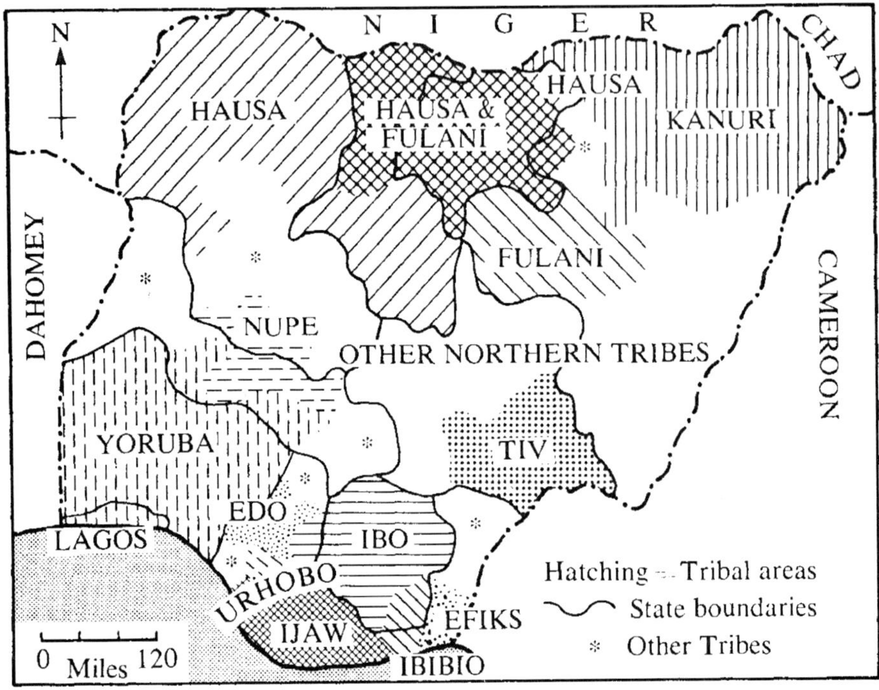

---

[878] https://www.nairaland.com

Chibueze C. Udeani; Klaus Zapotoczky (Hg.)
Die Rede von Gott – Discourse on God
Interdisziplinäre und interkulturelle Zugänge – Interdisciplinary and intercultural Approaches
Gegenwärtig sind die Gottesfrage und ihre zuweilen zerstörerischen Folgen so konflikthaft geworden, dass bisweilen die Abschaffung Gottes zugunsten eines friedlicheren Zusammenlebens gefordert wird. So ist die „Rede von Gott" ein Themenfeld, das die *Internationale Gesellschaft für interkulturelle Theologie und Studium der Religionen (ISRIT)* diskutiert und dabei Expertinnen und Experten aus diversen Fachgebieten (Theologie, Psychologie, Physik etc.) mit historischen wie aktuellen Implikationen der Gottesproblematik aus interdisziplinären und interkulturellen Perspektiven zu Wort kommen lässt.
In our present time, talking about God with reference to its at times destructive consequences has become so much conflictive that sometimes even the abolition of God to the advantage of a more peaceful mutual co-existence is demanded. Hence the "Discourse on God" is another theme, upon which the *International Society for Intercultural Theology and Study of Religions (ISRIT)* deliberates involving experts from diverse fields of science – Theology, Psychology, Physics etc. – hereby focussing on the historical as well as the current implications of the God-problematic from interdisciplinary and intercultural perspectives.
Bd. 6, 2018, 318 S., 34,90 €, br., ISBN 978-3-643-90989-3

L IT Verlag Berlin – Münster – Wien – Zürich – London

Auslieferung Deutschland / Österreich / Schweiz: siehe Impressumsseite